More Praise for *Documentary Storytelling*

"Bernard demonstrates to documentarians how story can be more effectively incorporated into every level of nonfiction filmmaking from conception to development and pre-production, in the field and in the editing room. Her discussions incorporate many examples from contemporary documentaries to illustrate a variety of salient points."

—*Documentary* (International Documentary Association)

"Sheila Curran Bernard's *Documentary Storytelling* is an essential, pragmatic, common-sense approach to making nonfiction films for the student and/or first-time filmmaker, based on the author's deep awareness of documentary film history and theory, and her intimate knowledge of how today's most important documentarians formulate their works."

—Gerald Peary, film critic, *The Boston Phoenix*

"Invaluable for documentary filmmakers as well as anyone who uses information and evidence to portray real events. But the value of this book goes beyond its service to storytellers; the consumers of documentary films and all journalism can benefit by more fully understanding the narrative structures that we all use to construct order and meaning in the world."

—Pennee Bender, Media Director, Center for Media and Learning, City University of New York, The Graduate Center

"While documentaries are nonfiction, they are certainly not objective, and even the smallest choices in writing, filming, interviewing, narrating, or scoring can drastically alter the perspective of the film, and in turn, the audience. Bernard is keenly aware of the power of persuasive images, and her insistence on complexity and integrity is a consistent theme throughout the book."

—Alyssa Worsham, *The Independent*

"If you fancy yourself as a documentary film-maker, or simply want to improve your understanding of observational storytelling, buy this book, read it, and apply the ideas contained within."

—Quentin Budworth, *Focus Magazine*

"Documentary *Storytelling*. That's what this book is about. It's about the story, how to convey that story eloquently, effectively, and ethically. . . . This book is absolutely brilliant . . . packed full of interviews with award-winning documentary filmmakers offering up information, advice, and wisdom you'll find interesting and useful."

—Krista Galyen, *AAUG Reviews*

Praise for *Archival Storytelling* (with Kenn Rabin)

"I am often asked how to work with archival materials. Now I have an easy answer: Get a copy of *Archival Storytelling* and read it. Everything's there—how to use archival materials, acquire them, and most of all, how to think about them. *Archival Storytelling* is indispensable."
—David Grubin, Filmmaker, *LBJ, FDR, Napoleon,*
and *The Jewish Americans*

"This is it, the book that will save you thousands of dollars and untold hours of frustration. It will be the single best purchase your production company will make. *Archival Storytelling* clearly explains the entire process of researching, acquiring and licensing archival footage and music. Included are time-tested tips and techniques for efficiently managing the work flow and negotiating rights."
—Ann Petrone, Archival Supervisor, *The Fog of War*

"One of the best—and most needed—texts I have seen in a while. The challenge is to keep what is a fairly technical aspect of filmmaking interesting without compromising the quality and depth of information. The authors have done an exceptional job in this regard by the careful interweaving of interviews with researchers, filmmakers and legal experts through the factual material. There is the strong sense of being in the presence of experienced filmmakers and researchers who accept that while there are standard practices, archival use and intellectual property laws, etc. are contingent fields in which each case must be assessed and dealt with on its merits."
—Bruce Sheridan, Chair, Film & Video Department, Columbia College

"I've been making historical documentaries for many years, yet I learned new things from this book. This is the definitive guide for archival research for documentary filmmakers. An invaluable resource."
—Mark Jonathan Harris, Distinguished Professor,
School of Cinematic Arts, University of Southern California,
and writer/director, *The Long Way Home* and *Into the Arms of Strangers*

Documentary Storytelling

Third Edition

Documentary
Storytelling

Creative Nonfiction on Screen

Third Edition

Sheila Curran Bernard

AMSTERDAM • BOSTON • HEIDELBERG • LONDON
NEW YORK • OXFORD • PARIS • SAN DIEGO
SAN FRANCISCO • SINGAPORE • SYDNEY • TOKYO

Focal Press is an imprint of Elsevier

ELSEVIER

Focal Press

Focal Press is an imprint of Elsevier

30 Corporate Drive, Suite 400, Burlington, MA 01803, USA
The Boulevard, Langford Lane, Kidlington, Oxford, OX5 1GB, UK

Notices
Knowledge and best practice in this field are constantly changing. As new research and experience broaden our understanding, changes in research methods, professional practices, or medical treatment may become necessary.

Practitioners and researchers must always rely on their own experience and knowledge in evaluating and using any information, methods, compounds, or experiments described herein. In using such information or methods they should be mindful of their own safety and the safety of others, including parties for whom they have a professional responsibility.

To the fullest extent of the law, neither the Publisher nor the authors, contributors, or editors, assume any liability for any injury and/or damage to persons or property as a matter of products liability, negligence or otherwise, or from any use or operation of any methods, products, instructions, or ideas contained in the material herein.

Library of Congress Cataloging-in-Publication Data
Bernard, Sheila Curran.
    Documentary storytelling : creative nonfiction on screen / Sheila Curran Bernard. – 3rd ed.
    p. cm.
    Includes bibliographical references and index.
    ISBN 978-0-240-81241-0 (pbk. : alk. paper) 1. Documentary films–Production and direction. 2. Documentary films–Authorship. I. Title.
    PN1995.9.D6B394 2010
    070.1'8–dc22
                                                                    2010017155

British Library Cataloguing-in-Publication Data
A catalogue record for this book is available from the British Library.

ISBN: 978-0-240-81241-0

For information on all Focal Press publications
visit our website at www.elsevierdirect.com

11   12   13   5   4   3   2
Printed in the United States of America.

In memory of Henry Hampton

Table of Contents

Preface to the Third Edition

The phrase *documentary storytelling* has become commonplace since this book was first published in 2003; it describes the powerful merging of visual and literary narrative devices to enable media makers to reach and engage audiences with nonfiction content. But the need for "storytelling" is also sometimes used to justify nonfiction work that is overly sentimental or sensational, poorly researched, and poorly crafted. That's not what this book is about, and it's not what the filmmakers featured in these pages do.

Instead, it's about an organic and often time-consuming process in which a filmmaker approaches a subject, *finds* (as opposed to imposes) a story within that subject, and then uses a wealth of narrative devices—structure, character, questions, point of view, tone, stakes, and more—to tell that story truthfully and artfully, so as to attract and actively engage an audience. In this way, the documentary filmmaker joins the ranks of other master storytellers, whether they work in fiction or nonfiction. The astonishing work of directors like Alex Gibney, Ari Folman, James Marsh, Deborah Scranton, and many others continues to set a high bar for those seeking to work in nonfiction media. *Documentary Storytelling*, in this and previous editions, puts the tools used by these filmmakers into the hands of anyone seeking to tell nonfiction stories, whether for broadcast or theatrical release or use in educational and community settings.

With this new edition, I hope to challenge the use of the term "documentary" to describe any and all forms of nonfiction audio-visual programming. For an analogy, consider the nonfiction section of a bookstore or library. There are books with advice on cooking and gardening and pet care; graphic novels and how-to manuals and celebrity tell-alls; histories that are scrupulously researched and histories that appeal primarily through images and sentiment; rigorous science alongside pseudoscience. Go a step farther, and include in this list the glossy brochure that advertises your dentist's practice, the report published by a particular charity to attract supporters, or the incendiary flier put out on behalf of a controversial cause.

We would never lump all of this nonfiction material—as different as it is in quality, purpose, audience, format, and form—together as one thing (*docubooks*, perhaps). Instead, we've learned, as readers, to recognize these differences. Similarly, we need to learn, as viewers, to better recognize the range of media presented as nonfiction. And so for this edition, I've chosen a subtitle that sets documentary films alongside a particular form of nonfiction prose, "creative nonfiction." The intent is to start with the *best* in documentary and explore it as the model for any kind of production, even those that more accurately would be billed as the audiovisual equivalent of *tabloid, magazine,* or *vanity* pieces, and perhaps *advocacy, public relations,* and even *advertising.*

This new edition has been restructured and contains more than 20 percent new material, including an examination of new films, new conversations with award-winning filmmakers (Brett Culp, Alex Gibney, Susan Kim, James Marsh, and Deborah Scranton), and a closer look at the use of story as a tool for *analysis* (not prescription) at every step of production, from research through editing. Unfortunately, this meant that some material from the previous edition had to be dropped, including the interview with archivist, filmmaker, and writer Kenn Rabin, with whom I worked in 2007 and 2008 to jointly author *Archival Storytelling: A Filmmakers Guide to Finding, Using, and Licensing Third-Party Visuals and Music* (Focal Press, 2008).

With only a few exceptions, works discussed in this edition are easily bought or rented through major vendors. Some films that are aired on television series, such as BBC's *Storyville* and PBS's *Frontline* and *American Experience,* may also be available for online viewing.

Acknowledgments

My thanks to Focal Press for shepherding not only three editions of this book into print but also overseeing its publication in Portuguese (2008) and Chinese (2010). Elinor Actipis, Michele Cronin, Dawnmarie Simpson, Laura Aberle, and their colleagues are the kind of publishing team any author would want. My thanks also to Cathy Gleason and Deborah Schneider for their ongoing counsel; to proposal reviewers for this edition; and to transcribers Amanda Burr and (especially) Johanna Kovitz for amazingly fast and accurate turnaround. Thank you to friends and colleagues at Princeton University, the University at Albany, and Goddard College, and to a community of nonfiction film-makers worldwide for work that challenges, inspires, and informs.

I owe a special thanks to the many filmmakers interviewed for this and previous editions; a list can be found in Part IV. For everything else, as always, I thank my parents, David and Kathleen Bernard; my friends and family; and, of course, Joel and Lucky.

Sheila Curran Bernard
September 2010

About the Author

Sheila Curran Bernard is an Emmy and Peabody Award–winning media maker and consultant whose credits include projects for prime-time national broadcast, theatrical release, and community and class-room use. She has taught at Princeton University, Westbrook College, and the University at Albany (SUNY), and lectured on documentary storytelling at the Niemann Conference on Narrative Journalism, Christopher Newport University, the Pennsylvania College of Technology, and elsewhere. With Kenn Rabin, Bernard is also the author of *Archival Storytelling: A Filmmaker's Guide to Finding, Using, and Licensing Third-Party Visuals and Music* (Focal Press, 2008).

Please visit the book's website, **www.documentarystorytelling.com**.

CHAPTER 1

Introduction

A surprisingly large number of people, including documentary filmmakers, will strive to differentiate the nonfiction films they enjoy (and make) from something they've stereotyped as "documentaries." Documentaries, from the reputation they seem to hold, are the films some of us had to watch during fifth grade history or eighth grade science. Sometimes derided as "chalk and talk," they tended to be dry, heavily narrated, filled with facts, and painful to sit through. So ingrained is this model, it seems, that inexperienced or polemical filmmakers still imitate it, creating films that are little more than illustrated research papers created to "show" or "prove" something through a steady recitation of data. And so nonfiction films that *work*—that grab and hold audiences through creative, innovative methods—are set apart by their makers and audiences as being some-how *more* than documentaries: they're *movies*. Like Hollywood fiction, these films may emphasize character, conflict, rising stakes, a dramatic arc, resolution. They bring viewers on a journey, immerse them in new worlds, explore universal themes. They compel viewers to consider and even care about topics and subjects they might previously have overlooked. And yet, unlike Hollywood fiction, they are based on a single and powerful premise: These stories, and the elements with which they are told, are true.

In other words, they're documentaries—and this book shows you how they're made.

DEFINING DOCUMENTARY

Documentaries bring viewers into new worlds and experiences through the presentation of factual information about real people, places, and events, generally—but not always—portrayed through the use of actual images and artifacts. A presidential candidate in Colombia is kidnapped (*The Kidnapping of Ingrid Betancourt*); children in Calcutta are given cameras and inspired to move beyond their limited circumstances (*Born into Brothels*); executives and traders at Enron play fast and loose with ethics and the law (*Enron: The Smartest Guys in the Room*). But factuality alone does not define documentary films; it's what the filmmaker does with those factual elements, weaving them into an overall narrative that strives to be as compelling as it is truthful and is often greater than the sum of its parts. "The documentarist has a passion for what he finds in images and sounds—which always seem to him more meaningful than anything he can invent," wrote Erik Barnouw in his 1974 book, *Documentary*. "Unlike the fiction artist, he is dedicated to *not* inventing. It is in selecting and arranging his findings that he expresses himself."

Story is the device that describes this arrangement. A story may begin as an idea, hypothesis, or series of questions. It becomes more focused throughout the filmmaking process, until the finished film has a compelling beginning, an unexpected middle, and a satisfying end. Along the way, the better you understand your story, even as it's evolving, the more prepared you'll be to tell it creatively and well. You're likely to identify characters and scout locations more carefully, and the visuals you shoot will be stronger. Perhaps surprisingly, you'll be better prepared to follow the unexpected—to take advantage of the twists and turns that are an inevitable part of documentary production, and recognize those elements that will make your film even stronger.

Puja running, from *Born into Brothels*. Photo by Gour, courtesy of Kids with Cameras.

DOCUMENTARY AS A SUBSET OF NONFICTION FILM AND VIDEO

As discussed in the preface, the range of film and video categorized loosely as "documentary" is extremely broad and varies widely in quality, in terms of both content and craft. At their best, documentaries should do more than help viewers pass the time; they should demand their active engagement, challenging them to think about what they know, how they know it, and what more they might want to learn. When the audience is caught up in a life-and-death struggle for a union (*Harlan County, U.S.A.*), in Mick Jagger's futile efforts to calm the crowd at a free Rolling Stones concert (*Gimme Shelter*), or in the story of a family's rift over whether or not a deaf child should be given a chance to hear (*Sound and Fury*), there is nothing as powerful as a documentary.

Some documentaries have surprising impact. Jeanne Jordan and Steven Ascher learned that their Academy Award–nominated film, *Troublesome Creek: A Midwestern*, about the efforts of Jordan's parents to save their Iowa farm from foreclosure, had influenced farming policy in Australia; Jon Else's *Cadillac Desert*, the story of water and the transformation of nature in the American West, was screened to inform policy makers on Capitol Hill. Alex Gibney learned that *Taxi to the Dark Side*, his Academy Award–winning look at the U.S. military's treatment of detainees in Iraq and Iran, was viewed by individuals campaigning for the U.S. presidency in 2008 and by the U.S. Army in its training of the Judge Advocate General (JAG) Corps. To achieve this level of impact, films must not only reach audiences through compelling, nuanced storytelling, but they must also earn their audiences' trust through reliable, honest content.

Although the storytelling tools explored in this book can be applied to any kind of nonfiction media production, with projects of any length and subject, the examples are drawn primarily from longer-form work, including broadcast hours and theatrical-length features. As discussed in the preface, these films and their creators have their counterparts in the world of creative nonfiction prose, where authors use the the tools of the novelist and dramatist to present factual, journalistic content.

CREATIVE NONFICTION ON SCREEN

Consider this list of the "five characteristics" that make nonfiction writing *creative*, as described by author Philip Gerard in his book, *Creative Nonfiction: Researching and Crafting Stories of Real Life*:

- "First, it has an apparent subject and a deeper subject. . . .
- Second, and partly because of the duality of subject, such nonfiction is released from the usual journalistic requirement of *timeliness*. . . .
- Third, creative nonfiction is narrative, it always tells a good story [Gerard cites another writer, Lee Gutkind, in explaining that to do this, the nonfiction writer "takes advantage of such fictional devices as character, plot, and dialogue. . . . It is action-oriented. Most good creative nonfiction is constructed in scenes."]. . . .
- Fourth, creative nonfiction contains a sense of *reflection* on the part of the author. . . . It is a *finished* thought. . . .
- Fifth, such nonfiction shows serious attention to the craft of writing."

How does this evaluation apply to documentary films?

An Apparent Subject and a Deeper Subject

There may be a deceptively simple story that *organizes* the film, but the story is being told because it reveals something more. *Sound and Fury*, on the surface, is a documentary about a little girl who wants a cochlear implant, an operation that may enable her to hear. But in telling that story, the filmmakers explore the world of Deaf culture, what it means to belong to a family and a community, how language is acquired, and more. *The Donner Party*, at its most basic level, tells the story of pioneers who took an ill-fated shortcut across the Sierra Nevada, became trapped by winter snowfall, and in desperation resorted to cannibalism. But filmmaker Ric Burns chose that story not for its shock value, but because it revealed something about the American character.

Released from the Journalistic Requirement of Timeliness

Even when documentaries are derived from news reports, they are not bound to tell the story while it's still "news." Instead, they take the time to consider events and put them in more detailed and often layered context. The financial meltdown of Enron; the abuse of prisoners at Bagram, Abu Ghraib, and Guantánamo; the suicide of writer Hunter S. Thompson—all, at one time, were news stories, for example, and all have been used as fodder for enduring, thought-provoking documentaries by director Alex Gibney.

Tells a Good Story

This means that a filmmaker uses the tools of creative writing to *identify* and *shape* a good story, one that accurately represents the truth. It does not mean inventing or distorting characters or plots or conflicts for the purpose of enhancing a documentary's appeal.

Contains a Sense of Reflection on the Part of the Author

A documentary is not a news report. It is a thoughtful presentation of a subject that has been explored, researched, weighed, considered, and shaped by the filmmaker over a period of time, and then communicated outward in a voice and style that are unique. Who is a film's author? The conventional view is that it is the director, provided the director is principally responsible for the story that is told, from outlining it prior to shooting to overseeing how it's shaped and reshaped in the editing room. Many films, more accurately, have multiple authors, reflecting close relationships between a producer(s), a director, a writer, and an editor, or some combination within that group. But the author is the one whose vision, ultimately, is reflected on screen.

Shows Serious Attention to the Craft of Film Storytelling

A filmmaker's palette is different, in many ways, from that of a novelist or playwright, but the underlying considerations remain the same. Craft is about wielding the unique tools of a chosen medium to the full and best advantage, without going too far. Told well, a story will feel seamless and inevitable, fully and actively engaging the viewer.

SUBJECTIVITY

The power of documentary films comes from the fact that they are grounded in fact, not fiction. This is not to say that they're "objective." Like any form of communication, whether spoken, written, painted, or photographed, documentary filmmaking involves the communicator in making choices. It's therefore unavoidably subjective, no matter how balanced or neutral the presentation seeks to be. Which stories are being told, why, and by whom? What information or material is included or excluded? What choices are made concerning style, tone, point of view, and format? "To be sure, some documentarists claim to be 'objective,'" noted Barnouw, "a term that seems to renounce an interpretive role. The claim may be strategic but is surely meaningless."

Within that subjectivity, however, there are some basic ethical guidelines for documentary filmmaking. Audiences trust documentaries, and that trust is key to the form's power and relevance. Betray that trust by implying that important events happened in a way that they did not, selecting only those facts that support your argument, or bending the facts in service of a more "dramatic" story, and you've undermined the form and your film. This doesn't mean that you can't have and present a very strong and overt point of view, or, for that matter, that you can't create work that is determinedly neutral. It does mean that your argument or neutrality needs to be grounded in accuracy. How to do this is discussed at length throughout this book.

HOW IMPORTANT IS STORY?

In today's documentary marketplace, story is what commissioning editors are looking for and training in storytelling is deemed necessary for filmmakers. A small sampling:

- From the website of the Sundance Institute Documentary Film Program: "The program encourages the exploration of innovative nonfiction storytelling, and promotes the exhibition of documentary films to a broader audience." The week-long, invitation-only Documentary Edit and Story Lab provides filmmakers "the opportunity to focus on story, character development and dramatic structure while working intensively with accomplished editors and directors on selected scenes from their work-in-progress." (www.Sundance.org)
- At the BBC, *Storyville* remains the preeminent strand for one-off, international documentary films. "The strand looks for ambitious, narrative, contemporary films from all over the world to commission in co-production with other funders...." (www.bbc.co.uk/commissioning/tv/network/genres/docs_strands.shtml#storyville)
- The Australian Broadcasting Corporation "commissions its documentaries from Australia's highly competitive independent documentary industry," according to its website (www.abc.net.au/tv/documentaries/about/). "We seek a broad slate of quality documentaries which will tell strong stories, which are well researched, which are well made, and which will entertain and

inform our audience. They can be single subject series or one off specials."

- From ZDF Enterprises (a private subsidiary of ZDF): "A trademark of many years' standing is the Sunday evening ZDF Expedition series from the History and Science department.... Every documentary requires a well-structured dramatic format and a clear storyline; at the beginning the questions that will be handled during the course of the documentary should be clearly and explicitly stated. At the same time, complex issues can be conveyed in an accessible and comprehensible manner." (www.zdf-enterprises.de/en/documentaries.672.htm)
- The Independent Television Service's "International Call" (www.itvs.org/producers/international_guidelines.html):   "Through the ITVS International Call, storytellers from other countries introduce U.S. audiences to their global neighbors, opening a window onto unfamiliar lives, experiences and perspectives." The program is looking for "Single, story-driven documentaries with broadcast hour versions." Note that this is not a grant, but a licensing agreement.

WHO TELLS DOCUMENTARY STORIES?

The range and breadth of documentary filmmaking worldwide is actually quite astonishing. Some documentary filmmakers work within production houses or stations; many more work independently, with varying degrees of financial and technical support from national or local governments, commissioning stations or broadcast venues, and/or foundations and corporations. Some filmmakers work to reach regional or local audiences, including community groups; others strive for national theatrical or broadcast release and acclaim at prestigious film festivals; a growing number put their work online, reaching virtual communities.

STORYTELLING, NOT WRITING

Documentary storytelling does not refer specifically or even primarily to writing, nor is it strictly the province of someone identified as a writer. The tools described in this book are employed by almost anyone involved in documentary production, including producers, directors, editors, cinematographers, sound recordists, and researchers. Storytelling describes the conceptual process that begins at the moment an idea is raised and continues to be applied and reapplied as a project is shot and edited, conceived and reconceived, structured and restructured. Before they shoot, while they shoot, and throughout the process of editing, filmmakers routinely address story issues: "Who are the central characters? What do they want? What are the stakes if they don't get it? Where is the tension? Where is the story going? Why does it matter?" Even if the film is structured as an essay, there should be an escalating sense of urgency, discovery, and relevance as the answers and subsequent questions are revealed.

Only rarely is a documentary scripted prior to production (there is no counterpart to the "spec screenplay" market of Hollywood), and that is generally because it involves extensive dramatization. Otherwise, a "script" evolves organically through the entire process, and is the term used to encompass the storytelling conveyed by the finished film.

In recognition of the importance of story to documentary, the Writers Guild of America, West and the Writers Guild of America, East (writers' labor unions) in 2005 began to offer an annual "Documentary Screenplay Award." The script must be for a film that's at least 40 minutes in length, and the film as exhibited "must have had an on-screen writing credit (i.e., a 'written by,' 'story by,' 'screenplay by,' 'documentary script by,' or 'narration written by' credit, as appropriate) related to the writing of the film." Winners to date include *Super Size Me* (Morgan Spurlock), *Enron: The Smartest Guys in the Room* (Alex Gibney), *Deliver Us From Evil* (Amy Berg), *Taxi to the Dark Side* (Alex Gibney), *Waltz with Bashir* (Ari Folman), and *The Cove* (Mark Monroe). Monroe is the only writer who did not also direct the nominated film; notably, only some of these films are narrated.

ABOUT THE BOOK

The idea for this book emerged from my experiences as a documentary filmmaker, writer, and consultant on a range of projects, large and small. I've worked with established as well as emerging filmmakers on productions intended not only for broadcast and theatrical release but also for museum and classroom use. It became clear to me that underlying issues of story and structure can generally be applied regardless of a project's style or length. It also became clear that despite the growing popularity of documentary films and filmmaking, discussion of the form was still too often clouded by misinformation and misconceptions. In particular, this book is written to counter two prevailing and equally false notions: One, that it's better and more "real" to shoot a documentary first and find the story later, and two, that the need for "story" permits a filmmaker to impose a shallow and external framework on a subject.

INTENDED READERSHIP

Documentary Storytelling is intended for those who have an interest in understanding how story and structure work, and in particular, why some nonfiction films seem to have so much more power than others and whether that power is built on credible content. It's my hope that by understanding the storytelling choices filmmakers make, viewers will become better and more critical consumers of nonfiction programming in general. They'll have a clearer understanding of why something does or does not "ring true," why some films seem to carry greater emotional or intellectual weight, why some programs leave them feeling manipulated or bored, and how shifts in point of view or tone can change the nature of the presentation. In today's media-saturated world, such media literacy is more important than ever.

For filmmakers, this book focuses primarily on longer-form work, but the principles of documentary storytelling can and do apply in a range of forms and formats. I have applied the story and structure tools contained in this book to six-minute historical documentaries, eight-minute natural history films, and even 90-second audio presentations. Brett Culp, interviewed in Chapter 18, applies these tools as an event filmmaker, crafting stories from key moments in his clients' lives.

FORMAT AND METHODOLOGY

The sections of this book are primarily organizational; the strategies in Part I apply to work under way in Part II, and the concepts discussed in the first two parts are explored at greater length in the interviews of Part III. Additional material from these interviews and from conversations with several other filmmakers is interspersed throughout the book.

The stages of filmmaking generally described in this book are research and development, preproduction, production, and editing (assembly, rough cut, fine cut, lock). In most cases, there is not a clear division between steps: filmmakers may be fundraising well into editing, for example. Discussions of story and structure, likewise, will continue throughout this process. It's very common for a team in the editing room to revise a preliminary outline (on paper), and even a pitch, to be sure that they can articulate the story as it's evolved during research and production. Surrounded by hours of material—still and motion images, audio interviews, music, archival materials—filmmakers often find that stripping a project back to its bare bones, its narrative structure, is the best and most effective way to begin a project's final and best construction.

Examples in this book that are drawn from actual films are identified as such. Otherwise, the examples were created by me for illustration purposes, and any resemblance to actual films, whether produced or proposed, is purely coincidental. At the back of the book, I've included some information on films cited, many of which are now available for purchase or rental through online vendors.

CRAFT, NOT FORMULA

Documentary storytelling describes an *organic* editorial approach to making choices about a film's structure, point of view, balance, style, casting, and more, at every stage of a film's creation. It uses language familiar to anyone who has worked on a creative endeavor, but because it uses the palette of filmmaking, it is in some ways most akin to dramatic screen storytelling. The difference is that documentarians are not free to invent plot points or character arcs and instead must find them in the raw material of real life. Our stories depend not on creative invention but on creative arrangement, and our storytelling must be done without sacrificing journalistic integrity. It's a tall order, which is why this book—the first to comprehensively apply the rules of Hollywood screenwriting to documentary filmmaking—was written. It's not about formula. Understanding what story is and how it works to your advantage is a step toward finding your own creative and ethical voice as a filmmaker.

OBSERVATIONS

In preparing all editions of this book, I screened a wide variety of films and spoke with a range of filmmakers, many of whom raised the same basic points:

- It's not about the technology. Too often, filmmakers get caught up in the *tools* of storytelling. The best equipment in the world, even the best *shots* in the world, won't save a film from a lack of focus.

- Time is an increasingly rare commodity for filmmakers, especially during preproduction and editing. Yet time is often what enables a film to have depth, in terms of research, themes, and layers of storytelling; it can enhance creativity. As a group, we need to resist the pressure to turn out documentary products, rather than documentary films.
- Story does not have to mean three-act drama, and it definitely does not mean artificial tension that is imposed from without. Story comes organically from within the material and the ways in which you, the filmmaker, structure it.
- Documentary filmmakers, increasingly, offer a powerful addition to or contradiction of information presented by mainstream media. It is critical that our work be ethical and truthful, even as it is also creative and innovative.
- Share the humor. No matter how grim the situation or subject, audiences cannot take a program that is unrelieved misery. Watch any of the top documentaries of the past few years, and notice not only how often you're on the verge of tears, but also, even within the same film, how often you're laughing.
- Think easier. Some of the best documentaries made recently are built on a narrative train that is very basic; that's often what allows for their overall complexity.

There are many ways to tell a quality documentary story, many stories to be told, an increasing number of filmmakers to tell them, and more affordable tools with which to tell them. So tell an honest story and a good one. Contribute to our understanding of who we are, where we've been, and what we might become. Take the viewer into a new world. Be open-minded. Be rigorous. Have fun. And stand proud. Make a wonderful, truthful, brilliantly creative and exciting nonfiction movie, and then call it what it is: a *documentary*.

PART I

Understanding Story

CHAPTER 2

Story Basics

A story is the narrative, or telling, of an event or series of events, crafted in a way to interest the audience members, whether they are readers, listeners, or viewers. At its most basic, a story has a beginning, middle, and end. It has compelling characters (or questions), rising tension, and conflict that reaches some sort of resolution. It engages the audience on an emotional and intellectual level, motivating viewers to want to know what happens next.

Don't be confused by the fact that festivals and film schools commonly use the term *narrative* to describe only works of dramatic fiction. Most documentaries are also narrative, which simply means that they tell stories (whether or not those stories are also narrated is an entirely different issue). How they tell those stories, and which stories they tell, are part of what separates the films into subcategories of genre or style, from cinéma vérité to film noir.

Efforts to articulate the basics of good storytelling are not new. The Greek philosopher Aristotle first set out guidelines for what he called a "well-constructed plot" in 350 BCE, and these have been applied to storytelling—onstage, on the page, and on screen—ever since. Expectations about how storytelling works seem hardwired in audiences, and meeting, confounding, and challenging those expectations is no less important to the documentarian than it is to the dramatist.

SOME STORYTELLING TERMS

Exposition

Exposition is the information that grounds you in a story: who, what, where, when, and why. It gives audience members the tools they need to follow the story that's unfolding and, more importantly, it allows them inside the story. The trick to exposition is not to give too much away too soon, and not to withhold information that's necessary. Watch films that you enjoy and pay attention not only to what you know, but also when you learn it.

DOI: 10.1016/B978-0-240-81241-0.00002-2

Exposition in theater used to be handled by the maid who bustled onstage at the start of a play and said (to no one in particular, or perhaps to a nearby butler), "Oh, me, I'm so very worried about the mistress, now that the master has gone off hunting with that ne'er-do-well brother of his, and without even telling her that his father, the Lord of Pembrokeshire, has arranged to sell this very house and all of its belongings before a fortnight is up!" In documentary films, the corollary might be those programs that are entirely front-loaded with narration that tells you information you don't yet need to know—and when you do need the information later, you generally can't remember it. Front-loading also frequently occurs when film-makers decide to put the entire backstory—all the history leading up to the point of their story's attack—at the beginning of the film.

Exposition can be woven into a film in many ways. Sometimes expository information comes out when the people you're filming argue: "Yeah? Well, we wouldn't even be in this mess if you hadn't decided to take your paycheck to Vegas!" Sometimes it's revealed through headlines or other printed material, a device used quite often in films, including *The Thin Blue Line*. Good narration can deftly weave exposition into a story, offering viewers just enough information to know where they are. (Voice-over material drawn from interviews can sometimes do the same thing.) Exposition can also be handled through visuals: an establishing shot of a place or sign; footage of a sheriff nailing an eviction notice on a door (*Roger & Me*); the opening moments of an auction (*Troublesome Creek*). Toys littered on a suburban lawn say "Children live here." Black bunting and a homemade shrine of flowers and cards outside a fire station say "Tragedy has occurred." A long shot of an elegantly dressed woman in a large, spare office high up in a modern building says "This woman is powerful." A man on a subway car reading an issue of *The Boston Globe* tells us where we are, as would a highway sign or a famous landmark—the Eiffel Tower, for example. Time-lapse photography, title cards, and animation can all be used to convey exposition, sometimes with the added element of humor or surprise—think of the cartoons in *Super Size Me*.

There's an art to giving out key information at the right moment. Too soon, and it will not seem relevant and will be quickly forgotten. Too late, and the audience will either have figured it out for themselves or grown frustrated with the filmmaker for withholding facts they feel the need to know. Offered at the right time, exposition enriches our understanding of characters and raises the stakes in their stories. Watch *Daughter from Danang* and pay attention to when we learn that Heidi's father was an American soldier, for example; that her mother's husband was fighting for the Viet Cong; and that Heidi's adoptive mother has stopped communicating with her. Watch *The Way We Get By* and notice how and where in the film details are added to the stories of the three elderly people who spend their days (and often nights) at the airport in Bangor, Maine, greeting returning soldiers. When do we learn that Bill is in debt and fighting prostate cancer? That Jerry lost a son to a childhood illness? That Joan is about to watch two grandchildren head to Iraq? These details add to our understanding of who these characters are and why they do what they do, and the information is effective because of the careful way it's seeded throughout the film.

Theme

In literary terms, theme is the general underlying subject of a specific story, a recurring idea that often illuminates an aspect of the human condition. *Eyes on the Prize*, in 14 hours, tells an overarching story of America's civil rights struggle. The underlying themes include race, poverty, and the power of ordinary people to accomplish extraordinary change. Themes in *The Day after Trinity*, the story of J. Robert Oppenheimer's development of the atomic bomb, include scientific ambition, the quest for power, and efforts to ensure peace and disarmament when it may be too late.

"Theme is the most basic lifeblood of a film," says filmmaker Ric Burns (see also Chapter 17). "Theme tells you the tenor of your story. This is what this thing is about." As mentioned, Burns chose to tell the story of the ill-fated Donner Party and their attempt to take a shortcut to California in 1846 not because the cannibalism they resorted to would appeal to prurient viewers but because their story illuminated themes and vulnerabilities in the American character. These themes are foreshadowed in the film's opening quote from Alexis de Tocqueville, a French author who toured the United States in 1831. He wrote of the "feverish ardor" with which Americans pursue prosperity, the "shadowy suspicion that they may not have chosen the shortest route to get it," and the way in which they "cleave to the things of this world," even though death steps in, in the end. These words presage the fate of the Donner Party, whose ambitious pursuit of a new life in California will have tragic consequences.

Themes may emerge from the questions that initially drove the filmmaking. On one level, *My Architect* is about a middle-aged filmmaker's quest to know the father he lost at the age of 11, some 30 years before. But among the film's themes are impermanence and legacy. "You sort of wonder, 'After we're gone, what's left?'" Kahn says in bonus material on the film's DVD. "How much would I really find of my father out there? . . . I know there are buildings. But how much emotion, how much is really left? And I think what really kind of shocked me is how many people are still actively engaged in a relationship with him. They talk to him as if he's still here. They think of him every day. In a way I find that very heartening."

Understanding your theme can help you determine both what and how you shoot. Renowned cinematographer Jon Else explains this as he discusses planning for a scene that follows workers building a trail at Yosemite National Park, for his film, *Yosemite: The Fate of Heaven*. "What is this shot or sequence telling us within the developing narrative of this film, and what is this shot or sequence telling us about the world?" Else says. "Are we there with the trail crew and the dynamite because it's dangerous? Are we there because all the dynamite in the world is not going to make a bit of difference in this giant range of mountains, where people are really insignificant? Are we there because these people are underpaid and they're trying to unionize?" Alternatively, Else says, "If the scene was about the camaraderie between the members of the trail crew, all of whom had lived in these mountains together, in camp, for many months by that time, you try to do a lot of shots in which the physical relationship between people shows." In this case, the workers were not trying to unionize, he says, "But if in fact we had been doing a sequence about the labor conditions for trail workers in Yosemite, we probably would have made it a point to shoot over the course of a long day, to show how long the day was, show them eating three meals on the trail, walking home really bone-tired in the dark. Basically, the more you're aware of what you want these images to convey, the richer the images are going to be."

Arc

The arc refers to the way or ways in which the events of the story transform your characters. An overworked executive learns that his family should come first; a mousy secretary stands up for himself and takes over the company; a rag-tag group of kids that nobody ever notices wins the national chess tournament. In pursuing a goal, the protagonists learn something about themselves and their place in the world, and those lessons change them—and may, in fact, change their desire for the goal.

In documentary films, story arcs can be hard to find. Never, simply in the interest of a good story, presume to know what a character is thinking or feeling, or present a transformation that hasn't occurred. If there is change, you will discover it through solid research and multiple strands of verifiable evidence. For example, in *The Day after Trinity*, physicist J. Robert Oppenheimer, a left-leaning intellectual, successfully develops the world's first nuclear weapons and is then horrified by the destructive powers he's helped to unleash. He spends the rest of his life trying to stop the spread of nuclear weapons and in the process falls victim to the Cold War he helped to launch; once hailed as an American hero, he is accused of being a Soviet spy.

In *The Thin Blue Line*, we hear and see multiple versions of a story that begins when Randall Adams's car breaks down on a Saturday night and a teenager named David Harris offers him a ride. Later that night, a police officer is shot and killed by someone driving Harris's car, and Adams is charged with the murder. The deeper we become immersed in the case, the more clearly we see that Adams's imprisonment and subsequent conviction are about politics, not justice. He is transformed from a free man to a convicted felon, and that transformation challenges the viewer's assumptions about justice and the basic notion that individuals are innocent until proven guilty.

In *Murderball*, a documentary about quadriplegic athletes who compete internationally in wheelchair rugby, a few characters undergo transformations that together complement the overall film. There's Joe Soares, a hard-driving American champion now coaching for Canada, whose relationship with his son changes noticeably after he suffers a heart attack. Player Mark Zupan comes to terms with the friend who was at the wheel during the accident in which he was injured. And Keith Cavill, recently injured, adjusts to his new life and even explores wheelchair rugby. All of these transformations occurred over the course of filming, and the filmmakers made sure they had the visual material they needed to show them in a way that felt organic and unforced.

Plot and Character

Films are often described as either plot or character driven. A character-driven film is one in which the action of the film emerges from the wants and needs of the characters. In a plot-driven film, the characters are secondary to the events that make up the plot. (Many thrillers and action movies are plot driven.) In documentary, both types of films exist, and there is a lot of gray area between them. Errol Morris's *The Thin Blue Line* imitates a plot-driven noir thriller in its exploration of the casual encounter that leaves Randall Adams facing the death penalty. Circumstances act upon Adams; he doesn't set the plot in motion except inadvertently, when his car breaks down and he accepts a ride from David Harris. In fact, part of the film's power comes from Adams's inability to alter events, even as it becomes apparent that Harris, not Adams, is likely to be the killer.

Some films are clearly character driven. *Daughter from Danang*, for example, is driven by the wants of its main character, Heidi Bub, who was born in Vietnam and given up for adoption. Raised in Tennessee and taught to deny her Asian heritage, Bub is now estranged from her adoptive mother. She sets the events of the film in motion when she decides to reunite with her birth mother. Similarly, in *Waltz with Bashir*, Israeli filmmaker Ari Folman sets events in motion when he decides to look back at a past he cannot remember.

From *Waltz with Bashir*. Photo courtesy Bridget Folman Film Gang.

As mentioned, the difference between plot- and character-driven films can be subtle, and one often has strong elements of the other. The characters in *The Thin Blue Line* are distinct and memorable; the plot in both *Daughter from Danang* and *Waltz with Bashir* is strong and takes unexpected turns. It's also true that plenty of memorable documentaries are not "driven" at all in the Hollywood sense. *When the*

Levees Broke, a four-hour documentary about New Orleans during and after Hurricane Katrina, generally follows the chronology of events that devastated a city and its people. As described by supervising editor and co-producer Sam Pollard in Chapter 23, there is a narrative arc to each hour and to the series. But the complexity of the four-hour film and its interweaving of dozens of individual stories, rather than a select few, differentiate it from a more traditional form of narrative.

Some shorter films present a "slice of life" portrait of people or places. With longer films, however, there generally needs to be some overarching structure. Frederick Wiseman's documentaries are elegantly structured but not "plotted" in the sense that each sequence makes the next one inevitable, but there is usually an organizing principle behind his work, such as a "year in the life" of an institution. Still other films are driven not by characters or plot but by questions, following an essay-like structure; examples include Michael Moore's *Fahrenheit 9/11* and Daniel Anker's *Imaginary Witness: Hollywood and the Holocaust* (Chapter 21). Some films merge styles: *Super Size Me* is built around the filmmaker's 30-day McDonald's diet, but to a large extent the film is actually driven by a series of questions, making it an essay. This combination of journey and essay can also be found in Nathaniel Kahn's *My Architect*.

Point of View

Point of view describes the perspective, or position, from which a story is told. This can be interpreted in a range of ways. For example, point of view may describe the character through whom you're telling a story. Imagine telling the story of Goldilocks and the three bears from the point of view of Goldilocks, and then retelling it from the point of view of Papa Bear. Goldilocks might tell you the story of a perfectly innocent child wandering through the woods who grew hungry and went into an apparently abandoned house, only to find herself under attack by bears. In contrast, Papa Bear might tell you the story of an unwanted intruder.

By offering an unexpected point of view, filmmakers can sometimes force viewers to take a new look at a familiar subject. Jon Else's *Sing Faster: The Stagehands' Ring Cycle* documents a performance by the San Francisco Opera of Richard Wagner's *Ring Cycle* from the point of view of the union stagehands behind the scenes. *The Way We Get By*, directed by Aron Gaudet, looks at the wars in Iraq and Afghanistan through the stories of three elderly "troop greeters" in Maine.

Point of view can also be used to describe the perspective of the camera, including who's operating it and from what vantage point. Much of Deborah Scranton's *The War Tapes*, for example, was filmed by the soldiers themselves, rather than by camera crews *filming* the soldiers. Point of view can also refer to the perspective of time and the lens through which an event is viewed. As one example, *The War Tapes* looks at the aftermath of a car bombing outside Al Taji through footage of the event as it unfolds (from the camera operated by Sgt. Steve Pink, who was there); an interview with Pink conducted within 24 hours of the event by Spc. Mike Moriarty; audio from an interview Scranton conducted with Pink in the months after he returned to the United States; and Pink in voice-over, reading (after he had returned home) from a journal he kept while he was in Iraq. "So it's all layered in there, this multi-faceted perception of that event," Scranton explains in Chapter 24.

There is also, of course, "point of view" of the filmmaker and/or filmmaking team.

Detail

Detail encompasses a range of things that all have to do with specificity. First, there is what's known as the "telling detail." A full ashtray next to a bedridden man would indicate that either the man or a caregiver is a heavy smoker. The choice of what to smoke, what to drink, when to drink it (whisky for breakfast?), what to wear, how to decorate a home or an office or a car, all provide clues about people. They may be misleading clues: That African artwork may have been left behind by an old boyfriend, rather than chosen by the apartment renter; the expensive suit may have been borrowed for the purpose of the interview. But as storytellers, our ears and eyes should be open to details, the specifics that add layers of texture and meaning. We also need to focus on detail if we write narration. "The organization grew like wildfire" is clichéd and meaningless; better to provide evidence: "Within 10 years, an organization that began in Paris with 20 members had chapters in 12 nations, with more than 2,500 members worldwide."

A "GOOD STORY WELL TOLD"

In their book, *The Tools of Screenwriting*, authors David Howard and Edward Mabley stress that a story is not simply about somebody experiencing difficulty meeting a goal; it's also "the way in which the audience experiences the story." The elements of a "good story well told," they write, are:

1. This story is about *somebody* with whom we have some empathy.
2. This somebody wants *something* very badly.
3. This something is *difficult*, but possible, to do, get, or achieve.
4. The story is told for maximum *emotional* impact and *audience participation* in the proceedings.
5. The story must come to a *satisfactory ending* (which does not necessarily mean a happy ending).

Although Howard and Mabley's book is directed at dramatic screen-writers, who are free to invent not only characters but also the things that they want and the things that are getting in the way, this list is useful for documentary storytellers. Your particular film subject or situation might not fit neatly within these parameters, however, so further explanation follows.

Who (or What) the Story Is About

The *somebody* is your protagonist, your hero, the entity whose story is being told. Note that your hero can, in fact, be very "unheroic," and the audience might struggle to empathize with him or her. But the character and/or character's mission should be compelling enough that the audience cares about the outcome. In *The Execution of Wanda Jean*, for example, Liz Garbus offers a sympathetic but unsparing por-trait of a woman on death row for murder. You also may have multi-ple protagonists, as was the case in *Spellbound*.

The central character doesn't necessarily need to be a person. In Ric Burns's *New York*, a seven-episode history, the city itself is the protagonist, whose fortunes rise and fall and rise over the course of the series. (Throughout that series, however, individual characters and stories come to the fore.) But often, finding a central character through whom to tell your story can make an otherwise complex topic more manageable and accessible to viewers. For *I'll Make Me a World*, a six-hour history of African-American arts that's no longer being distributed, producer Denise Green explored the Black Arts Movement of the 1960s by viewing it through the eyes and experi-ence of Pulitzer Prize–winning poet Gwendolyn Brooks, an estab-lished, middle-aged author whose life and work were transformed by her interactions with younger artists responding to the political call for Black Power.

What the Protagonist Wants

The *something* that somebody wants is also referred to as a goal or an objective. In *Blue Vinyl*, filmmaker Judith Helfand sets out, on camera, to convince her parents to remove the new siding from their home. Note that a filmmaker's on-screen presence doesn't necessarily make him or her the protagonist. In Steven Ascher and Jeanne Jordan's *Troublesome Creek: A Midwestern*, the filmmakers travel to Iowa, where Jeanne's family is working to save their farm from foreclosure. Jeanne is the film's narrator, but the protagonists are her parents, Russel and Mary Jane Jordan. It's their goal—to pay off their debt by auctioning off their belongings—that drives the film's story.

Active versus Passive

Storytellers speak of active versus passive goals and active versus passive heroes. In general, you want a story's goals and heroes to be active, which means that you want your story's protagonist to be in charge of his or her own life: To set a goal and then to go about doing what needs to be done to achieve it. A passive goal is something like this: A secretary wants a raise in order to pay for breast enhancement surgery. She is passively waiting for the raise, hoping someone will notice that her work merits reward. To be active, she would have to do something to ensure that she gets that raise, or she would have to wage a campaign to raise the extra money she needs for the surgery, such as taking a second job.

An exception is when the passivity *is* the story. In *The Thin Blue Line*, for example, Randall Adams, locked up on death row, is a passive protagonist because he can't do anything to free himself, as no one believes him when he claims to be innocent. In general, though, you want your protagonist to be active, and you want him or her to have a goal that's worthy. In the example of the secretary, will an audience really care whether or not she gets larger breasts? Probably not. If we had a reason to be sympathetic—she had been disfigured in an accident, for example—maybe we would care, but it's not a very strong goal. Worthy does not mean a goal has to be noble—it doesn't all have to be about ending world hunger or ensuring world peace. It does have to matter enough to be worth committing significant time and resources to. If you only care a little about your protagonists and what they want, your financiers and audience are likely to care not at all.

Difficulty and Tangibility

The something that is wanted—the goal—must be *difficult* to do or achieve. If something is easy, there's no tension, and without tension, there's little incentive for an audience to keep watching. Tension is the feeling we get when issues or events are unresolved, especially when we want them to be resolved. It's what motivates us to demand, "And then what happens? And what happens after *that*?" We need to know, because it makes us uncomfortable *not* to know. Think of a movie thriller in which you're aware, but the heroine is not, that danger lurks in the cellar. As she heads toward the steps, you feel escalating tension because she is walking *toward* danger. If you didn't know that the bad guy was in the basement, she would just be a girl heading down some stairs. Without tension, a story feels flat; you don't care one way or the other about the outcome.

So where do you find the tension? Sometimes, it's inescapable, as is the case with the National Guardsmen enduring a year-long tour of duty in Iraq, in Deborah Scranton's *The War Tapes*. Sometimes, tension comes from conflict between your protagonist and an opposing force, whether another person (often referred to as the *antagonist* or *opponent*), a force of nature, society, or the individual (i.e., internal conflict). In Barbara Kopple's *Harlan County, U.S.A.*, for example, striking miners are in conflict with mine owners. In Heidi Ewing and Rachel Grady's *The Boys of Baraka*, the tension comes from knowing that the odds of an education, or even a future that doesn't involve prison or death, are stacked against a group of African-American boys from inner-city Baltimore. When a small group of boys is given an opportunity to attend school in Kenya as a means of getting fast-tracked to better high schools in Baltimore, we want them to succeed and are devastated when things seem to fall apart. In *Born into Brothels*, similarly, efforts to save a handful of children are threatened by societal pressures (including not only economic hardship but also the wishes of family members who don't share the filmmakers' commitment to removing children from their unstable homes), and by the fact that the ultimate decision makers, in a few cases, are the children themselves. The audience experiences frustration—and perhaps recognition—as some of these children make choices that in the long run are likely to have significant consequences.

Note that conflict can mean a direct argument between two sides, pro and con (or "he said, she said"). But such an argument sometimes weakens tension, especially if each side is talking past the other or if individuals in conflict have not been properly established to viewers.

If we don't know who's fighting or what's at stake for the various sides, we won't care about the outcome. On the other hand, if the audience goes into an argument caring about the individuals involved, especially if they care about *all* the individuals involved, it can lead to powerful emotional storytelling. Near the end of *Daughter from Danang*, for example, the joyful reunion between the American adoptee and her Vietnamese family gives way to feelings of anger and betrayal brought on by the family's request for money. The palpable tension the audience feels stems not from taking one side or another in the argument, but from empathy for all sides.

Weather, illness, war, self-doubt, inexperience, hubris—all of these can pose obstacles as your protagonist strives to achieve his or her goal. And just as it can be useful to find an individual (or individuals) through whom to tell a complex story, it can be useful to personify the opposition. Television viewers in the 1960s, for example, at times seemed better able to understand the injustices of southern segregation when reporters focused on the actions of individuals like Birmingham (Alabama) Police Chief Bull Connor, who turned police dogs and fire hoses on young African Americans as they engaged in peaceful protest.

Worthy Opponent

Just as you want your protagonist to have a worthy goal, you want him or her to have a worthy opponent. A common problem for many filmmakers is that they portray opponents as one-dimensional; if their hero is good, the opponent must be bad. In fact, the most memorable opponent is often not the opposite of the hero, but a complement to him or her. In the film *Sound and Fury*, young Heather's parents oppose her wishes for a cochlear implant not out of malice but out of their deep love for her and their strong commitment to the Deaf culture into which they and their daughter were born. Chicago Mayor Richard Daley was a challenging opponent for Dr. Martin Luther King, Jr., in *Eyes on the Prize* specifically because he wasn't Bull Connor; Daley was a savvy northern politician with close ties to the national Democratic Party and a supporter of the southern-based civil rights movement. The story of his efforts to impede Dr. King's campaign for open housing in Chicago in 1966 proved effective at underscoring the significant differences between using nonviolence as a strategy against *de jure* segregation in the South and using it against *de facto* segregation in the North.

As stated earlier, it's important to understand that you should not in any way be fictionalizing characters who are real human beings.

You are evaluating a situation from the perspective of a storyteller, and working with what is there. If there is no opponent, you can't manufacture one. Mayor Daley, historically speaking, was an effective opponent. Had he welcomed King with open arms and been little more than an inconvenience to the movement, it would have been dishonest to portray him as a significant obstacle.

Tangible Goal

Although difficult, the goal should be possible to do or achieve, which means that it's best if it's both concrete and realistic. "Fighting racism" or "curing cancer" or "saving the rainforest" may all be worthwhile, but none is specific enough to serve as a story objective. In exploring your ideas for a film, follow your interests, but then seek out a specific story to illuminate them. *The Boys of Baraka* is clearly an indictment of racism and inequality, but it is more specifically the story of a handful of boys and their enrollment in a two-year program at a tiny school in Kenya. *Born into Brothels* illuminates the difficult circumstances facing the children of impoverished sex workers in Calcutta, but the story's goals are more tangible. Initially, we learn that filmmaker Zana Briski, in Calcutta to photograph sex workers, has been drawn to their children. "They wanted to learn how to use the camera," she says in voice over. "That's when I thought it would be really great to teach them, and to see this world through their eyes." Several minutes later, a larger but still tangible goal emerges: "They have absolutely no opportunity without education," she says. "The question is, can I find a school—a good school—that will take kids that are children of prostitutes?" This, then, becomes the real goal of the film, one enriched by the children's photography and exposure to broader horizons.

Note also that the goal is not necessarily the most "dramatic" or obvious one. In Kate Davis's *Southern Comfort*, a film about a transgendered male dying of ovarian cancer, Robert Eads's goal is not to find a cure; it's to survive long enough to attend the Southern Comfort Conference in Atlanta, a national gathering of transgendered people, with his girlfriend, Lola, who is also transgendered.

Emotional Impact and Audience Participation

The concept of telling a story for greatest emotional impact and audience participation is perhaps the most difficult. It's often described as "show, don't tell," which means that you want to present the evidence or information that allows viewers to experience the story for themselves, anticipating twists and turns and following the story line in a way that's active rather than passive. Too often, films tell us what we're supposed to think through the use of heavy-handed narration, loaded graphics, or a stacked deck of interviews.

Think about the experience of being completely held by a film. You aren't watching characters on screen; you're right there with them, bringing the clues you've seen so far to the story as it unfolds. You lose track of time as you try to anticipate what happens next, who will do what, and what will be learned. It's human nature to try to make sense of the events we're confronted with, and it's human nature to enjoy being stumped or surprised. In *Enron: The Smartest Guys in the Room*, you think Enron's hit bottom, that all the price manipulation has finally caught up with them and they'll be buried in debt—until someone at Enron realizes that there's gold in California's power grid.

Telling a story for emotional impact means that the filmmaker is structuring the story so that the moments of conflict, climax, and resolution—moments of achievement, loss, reversal, etc.—adhere as well as possible to the internal rhythms of storytelling. Audiences expect that the tension in a story will escalate as the story moves toward its conclusion; scenes tend to get shorter, action tighter, the stakes higher. As we get to know the characters and understand their wants and needs, we care more about what happens to them; we become invested in their stories. Much of this structuring takes place in the editing room. But to some extent, it also takes place as you film, and planning for it can make a difference. Knowing that as Heidi Bub got off the airplane in Danang she'd be greeted by a birth mother she hadn't seen in 20 years, what preparations did the filmmakers need to make to be sure they got that moment on film? What might they shoot if they wanted to build up to that moment, either before or after it actually occurred? (They shot an interview with Heidi and filmed her, a "fish out of water," as she spent a bit of time in Vietnam before meeting with her mother.) In the edited film, by the time Heidi sees her mother, we realize (before she does) how fully Americanized she's become and how foreign her family will seem. We also know that the expectations both she and her birth mother have for this meeting are very high.

You want to avoid creating unnecessary drama—turning a perfectly good story into a soap opera. There's no reason to pull in additional details, however sad or frightening, when they aren't relevant. If you're telling the story of a scientist unlocking the genetic code to a certain mental illness, for example, it's not necessarily relevant that she's also engaged in a custody battle with her former husband, even if this detail seems to spice up the drama or, you hope, make the character more "sympathetic." If the custody battle is influenced by her husband's mental illness and her concerns that the children may have inherited the disease, there is a link that could serve the film well. Otherwise, you risk adding a layer of detail that detracts, rather than adds.

False emotion—hyped-up music and sound effects and narration that warns of danger around every corner—is a common problem, especially on television. As in the story of the boy who cried wolf, at some point it all washes over the viewer like so much noise. If the danger is real, it will have the greatest storytelling impact if it emerges organically from the material.

Raising the Stakes

Another tool of emotional storytelling is to have something at stake and to raise the stakes until the very end. Look at the beginning of *Control Room*. The film intercuts story cards (text on screen) with images of everyday life. The cards read: *March 2003 / The United States and Iraq are on the brink of war. / Al Jazeera Satellite Channel will broadcast the war ... / to forty million Arab viewers. / The Arab world watches ... / and waits. / CONTROL ROOM.* Clearly, these stakes are high.

In the hands of a good storyteller, even small or very personal stakes can be made large when their importance to those in the story is conveyed. For example, how many people in the United States—or beyond, for that matter—really care who wins or loses the National Spelling Bee, held each year in Washington, D.C.? But to the handful of children competing in *Spellbound*, and to their families and communities, the contest is all-important. Through skillful storytelling, the filmmakers make us care not only about these kids but about the competition, and as the field narrows, we can't turn away.

Stakes may rise because (genuine) danger is increasing or time is running out. In *Sound and Fury*, for example, the stakes rise as time passes, because for a child born deaf, a cochlear implant is most effective if implanted while language skills are being developed. How do the filmmakers convey this? We see Heather's much younger cousin get the implant and begin to acquire spoken language skills; we also learn that Heather's mother, born deaf, would now get little benefit from the device. As Heather enrolls in a school for the deaf without getting an implant, we understand that the decision has lifelong implications.

In terms of your role as the storyteller, stakes also rise because of the way you structure and organize your film: What people know, and when they know it, what the stakes of a story mean *to your characters* and how well you convey that—all of these play a role in how invested the audience becomes in wanting or even needing to know the outcome of your film.

A Satisfactory Ending

A *satisfactory ending*, or resolution, is often one that feels both unexpected and inevitable. It must resolve the one story you set out to tell. Say you start the film with a problem: A little girl has a life-threatening heart condition for which there is no known surgical treatment. Your film then goes into the world of experimental surgery, where you find a charismatic doctor whose efforts to solve a very different medical problem have led him to create a surgical solution that might work in the little girl's situation. To end on this surgical breakthrough, however, won't be satisfactory. Audiences were drawn into the story of the little girl, and this surgeon's work must ultimately be related to that story. Can his work make a difference in her case? You need to complete the story with which the film began. With that said, there is never just one correct ending.

Suppose, for example, that your film is due to be aired months before the approval is granted that will allow doctors to try the experimental surgery on the girl. Make that your ending, and leave the audience with the knowledge that everyone is praying and hoping that she will survive until then. Or perhaps the surgery is possible, but at the last minute the parents decide it's too risky. Or they take that risk, and the outcome is positive. Or negative. Or perhaps the doctor's breakthrough simply comes too late for this one child but may make a difference for hundreds of others. Any of these would be a satisfactory ending, provided it is factual. It would be unethical to manipulate the facts to imply a "stronger" or more emotional ending that misrepresents what you know the outcome to be. Suppose, for example, that the parents have already decided that no matter how much success the experimental work is having, they will not allow their daughter to undergo any further operations. You cannot imply that this remains an open question (e.g., with a teaser such as "Whether the operation will save the life of little Candy is yet to be seen.").

Ending a film in a way that's satisfying does not necessitate wrapping up all loose ends or resolving things in a way that's upbeat.

The end of *Daughter from Danang* is powerful precisely because things remain unsettled; Heidi Bub has achieved the goal of meeting her birth mother, but even two years after her visit, she remains deeply ambivalent about continued contact. At the end of *The Thin Blue Line*, Randall Adams remains a convicted murderer on death row, even as filmmaker Errol Morris erases any lingering doubts the audience might have as to his innocence.

CHAPTER 3

Finding the Story

Armed with an understanding of story, how do you find one within a chosen *subject* for a documentary? Suppose, for example, that you're thinking of doing a film about Elvis Presley, a diner in your home town, or images of Islam in American popular culture. Something about the topic has caught your interest, and you think you want to take it to the next level.

First, ask yourself what it is about the topic that grabs you. As the initial audience for your film, your gut reaction to the subject is important. Chances are it wasn't a sweeping notion of Elvis Presley that caught your attention, but an account, perhaps, of his time in the military. It's not the fact that there's a diner in your home town, but that rising taxes and a dwindling customer base have left the owners open to offers from developers looking to build a mall despite significant local opposition. You hadn't thought much about images of Islam in America until you watched a couple of newly arrived students from Iraq and the Sudan trying to make their way through a pep rally at your son's school, and you found yourself seeing American culture—high school culture—through their eyes.

We're surrounded by subjects that offer potential for documentary storytelling. Current events may trigger ideas, or an afternoon spent browsing the shelves at a local library or bookstore. Some filmmakers find stories within their own families. Alan Berliner made *Nobody's Business* about his father, Oscar; Deborah Hoffman made *Confessions of a Dutiful Daughter* about her mother's battle with Alzheimer's. Even when you're very close to a subject, however, you'll need to take an impartial view as you determine whether or not it would make a film that audiences will want to see. This is also true when you adapt documentaries from printed sources; a story may read well on paper, but not play as well on screen. In making the series *Cadillac Desert*, drawn from Marc Reisner's book of the same name, producer Jon Else chose three of the roughly 40 stories in Reisner's book; Else and his team then conducted their own research and determined the best way to tell those stories on film.

DOI: 10.1016/B978-0-240-81241-0.00003-4

STORY RIGHTS

In general, if you're using a range of books and magazines solely for research purposes, you don't need to obtain any of the underlying rights. When the film is indelibly linked to a book, however, as was the case with *Enron, A Brief History of Time* (Errol Morris's film built on Stephen Hawking's book), or *A Midwife's Tale* (Laurie Kahn's film built on Laurel Ulrich's book), you will need to come to a legal arrangement with the author or copyright holder. (Don't confuse this with companion books that are written during or after production. Like *Eyes on the Prize*, authored by the Blackside publishing staff and journalist Juan Williams during postproduction, these draw on the production teams' research and interviews. The books are based on the documentaries, rather than vice versa.)

Note that when you are negotiating for the rights to a story, you will want to retain creative control over your film. The author may be an expert on the subject, but you are an expert on translating it on film to a general audience. You don't need a degree in science to make an extraordinary science documentary or a degree in social work to create a compelling portrait of runaway teens. What you need are intelligence, curiosity, an ability to learn fast, and a readiness to consult with people who *are* experts in those fields. Ideally, there is a positive collaboration between expert and filmmaker that serves to enrich the film.

"FINDING" THE STORY DURING PRODUCTION

One of the biggest misconceptions about documentary filmmaking is that it happens spontaneously. In fact, it's fairly common to hear filmmakers talk about the story revealing itself over the course of the production or even in the editing room. With experienced filmmakers, however, this tends to mean *not* that a filmmaker has simply shot material without any story in mind, but that he or she alters the story's focus or, more likely, its *structure* during production and postproduction. Even vérité projects—which are significantly crafted in the editing room—are generally not shot until filmmakers have some confidence that a story will unfold. You can't know where real life will take you, but you can anticipate a range of outcomes and determine whether or not a subject holds sufficient promise.

Sometimes an opportunity comes along that precludes extensive planning. Filmmakers Gail Dolgin and Vicente Franco had just days to decide whether or not to travel to Vietnam after they learned about an upcoming reunion between Heidi Bub and the birth mother who'd given her up during "Operation Babylift" in 1975. "We all really believed that we were going into a happy reunion, and we had no idea whether we would come back with anything more than that," Dolgin says. "It just grabbed us with the possibilities of raw emotion and passion, and those are great elements for a documentary. And we're also drawn to films where we don't know what's going to happen—we have a concept and we go with it." At a minimum, the filmmakers had a basic, straightforward narrative of an adoptee returning to her homeland, although whether or not that could be turned into a documentary remained to be seen. "Maybe there would be a film that would explore what happens when you lose your birthplace identity," Dolgin says. "Heidi grew up in southern Tennessee, and we imagined going back with her and having her rediscover her roots in some way. But we had no idea, truly. We just went. And of course as soon as we got there it became clear that what we had anticipated was going to go in a different direction." In Vietnam, the filmmakers found themselves immersed in the complex story they told in *Daughter from Danang.*

Frederick Wiseman, renowned for his exploration of American institutions (*Hospital, Basic Training, Welfare, Public Housing, Domestic Violence*), has told interviewers that once he is given permission to film, he moves quickly, spending weeks shooting and then finding his themes and point of view over the course of several months of editing. But note that there is an inherent structure to Wiseman's work—the rhythms of daily life and of the individual stories he picks up over the course of filming—and a distinctive style that he brings to his films. For an interview (published in *The Boston Phoenix*) about the film *Public Housing*, writer and filmmaker Gerald Peary asked Wiseman if he looked for "drama" while shooting. "The first thought: I'm trying to make a movie," Wiseman responded. "A movie has to have dramatic sequences and structure. . . . So yes, I am looking for drama, though I'm not necessarily looking for people beating each other up, shooting each other. There's a lot of drama in ordinary experiences." It's also worth noting that Wiseman's style of shooting almost invariably necessitates a high shooting ratio (footage filmed versus footage that ends up on screen) and a lengthy editing period.

SERENDIPITY

It's not unusual for filmmakers to begin one project, only to be drawn by the characters and situations they encounter toward a film that is both different and stronger than they anticipated. In publicity material for the film *Sound and Fury*, director Josh Aronson says that he initially intended to film five deaf individuals whose experience covered a range of viewpoints on deafness. But in his research, he discovered the Artinians, a family in which two brothers—one hearing, one not—each had a deaf child. This created an opportunity to explore conflict within an extended family over how to raise deaf children. In another example, filmmaker Andrew Jarecki was making a film about birthday party clowns when he discovered, through one of his characters, the story that he eventually told in his documentary, *Capturing the Friedmans*—that of a family caught up in a devastating child abuse case.

Knowing that this may happen, or is even *likely* to happen, doesn't mean that you shouldn't approach a general idea by looking first for the best story you can, given the subject as you then understand it. Knowing at least your baseline story helps you to anticipate, at minimum, what you'll need to make the film, including characters and location setups. In his work with emerging filmmakers at the University of California, Berkeley, Jon Else requires that they head out "with some bomb-proof fallback plan," so that even if everything on the shoot goes wrong, they still come back with something.

EVALUATING STORY IDEAS

Beyond the conviction that a story you're developing will work well on film, the following important practical considerations may be helpful to consider.

Access and Feasibility

Does your film provide entré into new or interesting worlds, and can you obtain access to those worlds? Whether it's the worlds of Cuban immigrants, both before and after they arrive in the United States (*Balseros*) or the lives of would-be basketball stars (*Hoop Dreams*), a film that takes viewers inside experiences beyond their own is often well received. Aside from exclusive or extraordinary access, any film, even one shot in your grandmother's kitchen, depends on some kind of access being granted, whether it be personal (your grandmother), location (permission to bring your equipment into her home), or archival (access to her photo album or those poems she's been writing all these years). Sometimes, *lack* of access may become part of the story, as with Michael Moore's pursuit of General Motors chairman Roger Smith, in *Roger & Me*.

As you develop your idea, you need to determine whether the elements needed for production are really available to you. Can you get inside a cyclotron to film? Will that Pulitzer Prize–winning author grant you an interview? Will you be allowed to follow a third-grade student during that spelling bee? Several years ago, I worked on a science documentary for which we wanted to film cyclists in the Tour de France to illustrate the conservation of mass and energy. The success of a good portion of that film depended on access to the Tour and to exclusive CBS Sports coverage of it. Had we not been able to arrange these, we would have had to find a different illustration.

As an additional note, gaining access usually means establishing a relationship and building trust with the people who can grant it. This is a professional relationship, although filmmakers often grow very close to their subjects. It's important to respect that trust, so be truthful about yourself and your project from the start. You can generally get people to talk to you even if they know that you don't agree with their position, as long as you make it very clear that they will be given a fair hearing and that you value their point of view. (Again, there are exceptions. Filmmakers such as Nick Broomfield [*Kurt & Courtney*] and Michael Moore may push the boundaries of access as a matter of style; they may show up with the cameras rolling deliberately to put their subjects on edge.)

Affordability

In terms of budget and schedule, is it realistic to think that you can afford to tell the story you want to tell, in the way you want to tell it? Even if digital technology can put a relatively inexpensive camera in your hands, getting your film shot, edited, and technically ready for broadcast or theatrical release will still be very expensive. Even celebrated filmmakers have trouble raising money these days. Have you set your sights too high? Don't think small, just realistically. Know that some types of documentaries are costlier to produce than others, and that "extras," such as the rights to use a clip of archival film from a private collection or a short piece of music from your favorite album, could set you back thousands of dollars.

Passion and Curiosity

Do you care deeply about the subject? Passion is going to be your best weapon against discouragement, boredom, frustration, and confusion. Passion is not the unwavering conviction that you are right and the whole world must be made to agree with you. Instead, it is the commitment to the notion that this idea is exciting, relevant, and meaningful, and perhaps more importantly, that it's something you can look forward to exploring in the months or even years to come.

Passion is also an ingredient that commissioning editors and funders want to see when filmmakers approach them for support. Filmmaker Hans Otto Nicolayssen, currently Senior Advisor at the Norwegian Film Institute, used to review proposals for short and documentary films on behalf of Filmkontakt Nord (FkN), which he helped to found. His first criteria for making a grant? "Passion," he says. "I always start with the question, 'Why are you telling me this story now?'" Nicolayssen says a proposal should convey not only the filmmaker's skill but also his or her connection to the material.

Audience

Who is your intended audience? Many documentaries, whether produced independently or in-house, are created with an audience in mind. It's always possible that the film you thought would only reach your immediate geographic region will be a break-out hit, but in general, you should have some idea of whom you *want* it to reach: age, geographic area, educational level, etc. This doesn't mean that you shouldn't try to also reach a wider audience, just that you're likely to approach MTV's audience differently, for example, than Discovery's, or that you'll plan differently if you're trying to reach a local public television audience rather than an international one. Is your film not intended for broadcast, but for use by community or educational groups? Do you want to try to release your film theatrically? Does it have the potential to be the next *Super Size Me* or *March of the Penguins*? These questions are worth thinking about early on.

On the other hand, plenty of filmmakers simply begin to develop their films without worrying, at first, about audiences or even funding, as was the case with *The Kidnapping of Ingrid Betancourt* (Chapter 16). Sometimes, events necessitate working quickly—an opportunity will pass if no action is taken. The subject may seem too obscure or too personal to seek sponsorship early on, and a more convincing case for the film's appeal may be made when there is footage to show. In some cases, filmmakers nearly complete their films before submitting them to "open calls" for program slots or festival competition, and in that way they gradually find an audience and possibly funds for completion.

Relevance

Will anybody care about your film, or can you make them care? This can be a tough one. You may be passionate about 14th-century Chinese art or the use of mushrooms in gourmet cuisine, but can you find a compelling story that will be worth others not only funding but watching? It's possible to make people care about all sorts of things, but it usually takes the right approach.

Timeliness

One aspect of relevance, though not always the most important one, is timeliness, which is not to be confused with the timeline of news reporting. In this context, it means that television executives, for example, may hope to plan documentary programming to coincide with an event, such as a historical anniversary or a high-profile motion picture release on a related topic. The fact that a subject is or may become topical, however, is not by itself a reason to pursue it, because by the time you finish the film, interest in that issue may have passed. In fact, the quality of being "evergreen," meaning the film will have a shelf-life of many years as opposed to many months, can be a positive selling point. A film on elephant behavior or the American electoral process in general may be evergreen, whereas a film that specifically explores a particular environmental campaign or issues in the American presidential campaign of 2004 probably will not be.

Visualization

Is the story visual, and if not, can you make it visual? This is an important question whether you're telling a modern-day story that involves a lot of technology or bureaucracy, or you're drawn to a historical story that predates the invention of still or motion picture photography. A film subject that doesn't have obvious visuals requires additional foresight on the part of the filmmaker; you'll need to anticipate exactly *how* you plan to tell the story on film. The opposite may also be true: a subject can be inherently visual—it takes place in a spectacular location or involves state-of-the-art microscopic photography, for example—without containing an obvious narrative thread.

Hook

Another question to ask as you evaluate the story is, does it have a hook? In its simplest form, the hook is what got you interested in the subject in the first place. It's that bit of information that reveals the essence of the story and its characters, encapsulating the drama that's about to unfold. *Sound and Fury*, for example, is the story of the little girl who wants a cochlear implant. The hook is not that she wants this operation, nor that the implant is a major feat of medical technology. The hook is that the little girl's parents, contrary to what many in the audience might expect, aren't sure they want her to have the operation. It's the part of the story that makes people want to know more.

Existing Projects

What else has been done on the topic? It's useful, before you get too far, to explore what other films have been made on a subject and when. In part, this may simply inform your own storytelling. What worked or didn't work about what a previous filmmaker did? How will your project be different and/or add to the subject? It's not that you can't tackle a subject that's been covered; look at the range of projects on the American civil rights movement, the threat of nuclear war, or dinosaurs. Just because HBO broadcast a film on the 1963 church bombing in Birmingham (*4 Little Girls*) doesn't mean there isn't a different angle you could take in telling the story for the History Channel or for theatrical release. But knowing as much as you can about your subject also means knowing how else it's been treated on film.

Is This a Film You'd Want to See?

Given the freedom to do a short documentary on a subject of their choosing, students often seem to go first to "important" topics and the kinds of films that mimic the stereotype of what documentaries are. In fact, as discussed at greater length in Part II, they really should think backward, not only in terms of what's possible on a very tight schedule and budget, but what they would *enjoy* making a film about—and perhaps more importantly, what kind of film they'd want to see. Not every film has to expose cruelty or raise profound issues; some of the most profound films are the simplest.

DEVELOPING THE STORY

Once you've decided that your idea is worth pursuing, you'll need to start refining the story and planning how you'll tell it. There's no single way to do this, and furthermore, it's a process that tends to continue from the moment an idea strikes you until the final moments of postproduction. In general, though, depending on the needs of the project, the budget, and the schedule, you are likely to at least write some form of outline or treatment, so that you know—before you spend a lot of time and money shooting—that you have a story that works, and can plan not only what you need to shoot but also why.

IF YOU ALREADY KNOW YOUR STORY, WON'T YOUR PRESENTATION BE BIASED?

Knowing your story (or at least the germ of it) at the start of a project is not the same thing as knowing exactly what you want to say and how. It simply means having an idea of the narrative spine on which you could hang your subject and having at least some idea of themes you want to explore. From there, you need to research, develop, and shoot your story with questions and an open mind. Building on an earlier example, as sympathetic to the diner owners as you may feel at the start of your project, you might come to find yourself sympathizing with the developers, or discovering that a third solution, while meaning the end of the diner, is best for the town.

Suppose you've decided to explore the story of Thomas Jefferson and his relationship with a slave, Sally Hemings. That's a complex story that can be tackled from many points of view, past and present. If you start that project having already decided to paint Jefferson solely as exploiter and Hemings as victim, you probably shouldn't make the film, because it will likely be a one-sided rant that is neither engaging nor informative. Besides, if there's nothing in it for you as the filmmaker—nothing to learn, to discover, to be surprised or confused or challenged by—why expend the energy?

Films that end up advocating a position or idea—that these chemicals shouldn't have been dumped, that law enforcement used too much force, that laws are being broken—can be as hard-hitting or irreverent or personal as you want. But as you make them, you want to remain open to new and even conflicting information, whether or not it ends up on screen. The more effectively you can present your case, the better the film will stand up to scrutiny.

TELLING AN ACTIVE STORY

A significant percentage of the documentaries on television these days are about events that are over and done with. You still need a narrative to unfold over the course of the film; one solution is to keep the storytelling (and interviews) in the moment. You build the story and tell it in ways that leave the outcome uncertain. Witnesses, for example, do not say: "I found out later he was fine, but at this point I got a call from somebody, Andy I think it was, he later became mayor, and Andy told me that my boy Jimmy was down the well." Instead, ask your storytellers to stick to what is known at this point in your narrative, such as, "I got a call that Jimmy was in the well. I ran screaming for help." By doing this, you build tension. Starting with, "I found out later he was fine," lets all of the suspense out of your story. Surprisingly, this is a common mistake, not only in interviews but in scripted narration, such as, "Although he wasn't badly hurt, Jimmy had fallen down a deep well." Your adherence to present tense does not mean that you can't offer interpretations of the past. For example, an expert witness might be interviewed saying, "People complain about overregulation, that there's too much of it. But there are laws that should have made the contractors responsible for sealing that well up. Instead, they left it open, and a little boy fell in." The expert hasn't yet said when or how the boy got out.

When considering a topic or story that's in the past, whether recent or distant, you'll also need to consider how you're going to bring that story to life on screen. For example, suppose that members of the local historical society want you to make a film about their town's founding in 1727, and they want to fold in some material about the origins of some of the wonderful old architecture that still survives. They're excited by the fact that many of the local families are descended from early residents, so they have access to a decent collection of old oil portraits as well as photographs and even some letters. What does it add up to? Not much that will interest anyone who's not a direct relative of the folks on camera because there's no story being told on screen—yet. When Ken Burns, Ric Burns, and Geoffrey Ward used artifacts and images from the 19th century in *The Civil War*, they used them in the service of a powerful story—the North against the South. What's the *story* of this town's history?

In the search for narrative, some filmmakers find a "guide" to the past—for example, the town's mayor says, "Let's set out to see where this great city came from," and off he or she goes. But there are often more creative devices, and it can be useful to find a present-day story that would motivate a look back. For example, what if students from the local middle school are researching the town's history in order to write a play that they will perform later that year? That's a possible framework. What if a local builder is trying to restore the town's oldest house, which has been renovated repeatedly over the years? In order to do so he's got to peel back the layers one by one, offering a reason to explore the town's architectural history while also giving us a chance to follow the kind of home building renovation that audiences enjoy. These aren't earth-shattering ideas, but they demonstrate ways to consider a subject that might not seem, at first glance, to have much potential as a film.

"When approaching a film, I always try to find at least two stories that unfold simultaneously," says filmmaker Jon Else. "One of them almost always is a very simple, straight-ahead, forward motion through time. For instance, in *Sing Faster*, the forward motion is just the simple story that is told in Wagner's *Ring Cycle*, in the operas. It's this crazy soap opera about the gods fighting, a giant Aristotelian drama with characters and rising conflict and resolution and all that. And then parallel to that is the much less linear story of the stage-hands preparing this production for opening night."

Ken "Spike" Kirkland, in *Sing Faster: The Stagehands' Ring Cycle.*
Photo courtesy of Jon Else.

WORK BACKWARD

This one piece of advice touches on everything else in this chapter, but goes a step farther. First, understand that limitations can be enormously helpful in sparking creativity, while too much freedom can have the opposite effect. Second, be honest about what your limitations are, in terms of experience, access to equipment or personnel, and the level of resources available to you (including not only money but also time). Without substantial resources, you cannot create a comprehensive film history of World War II. Instead, play to your strengths. Find one local World War II veteran, or a group of them who meet weekly to play darts, that sort of thing. If one of those veterans happens to be your grandfather or great-grandfather, even better: less time gaining their trust.

Think about what your end product is going to be and what it will take to get there in terms of your schedule and budget. Be sure to factor in all the costs of finishing the film, especially if you'll need to produce masters and clear rights. Especially, consider your time frame. If you don't have a lot of time to edit, you don't want to go overboard in shooting—you want to shoot less and shoot smarter. Part of working backward is considering the overall length of the finished film, notes Boston-based filmmaker Tracy Heather Strain, whose credits include commissioned films for the PBS series *American Masters* and *Race: The Power of an Illusion*. Earlier in her career, she was talking to a series producer about everything she wanted to include in an hour-long film she was making and where she wanted the story to go. The series producer reminded her that with credits, her film would only run about 55 minutes. "It hit me to think about it," Strain says. "All the things I want to say are not going to fit in a 55-minute film. And so one of the first things I do now is look at how long I have [on screen] and I sketch out a little three-act, minute breakdown." With classic three-act structure (see Chapter 4), for example, the first and third acts are roughly a quarter of the film, with the second act roughly half. A 20-minute film, therefore, needs to get a story going within five or six minutes, with the tension ratcheting up through the second and third acts—a total of maybe 10 to 12 minutes—before reaching a quick resolution. The more focused the story, the better the chances of accomplishing this.

Shooting with the story in mind, even knowing that the focus might shift later, is generally far more effective than just heading out to cover a vaguely defined subject. "Films don't go over budget because you paid a sound guy too much and put the crew in a hotel for an extra day," says Jon Else, who heads the graduate program in documentary at the University of California, Berkeley. "They go over budget because people waste two months of editorial time figuring out what the story is. If you're talking about doing inexpensive work, that's the single most important thing, finding a story that comes with a ready-made through line. It's much more cost-efficient to figure out the story beforehand."

The downside, Else notes, is that "it's very, very tough to do any kind of cinema vérité film—which involves really discovering the story—inexpensively." Even when filmmakers carefully select a subject for the strength of its characters and the potential of a strong narrative line, the films, such as *Salesman* or *Control Room*, are built on an observational approach that takes considerable time to shape in an editing room.

CHAPTER 4

Story Structure

One of the best ways to gauge the status of a film in progress is to ask the filmmaker to tell you what it's about. If he or she immediately launches into a lengthy description of the opening shot or an amazing scene—and this happens all the time—the film is probably in trouble. Visuals *serve* a story; they are not the story. As filmmaker Ronald Blumer has said, "Film is not a visual medium, it's a story medium."

In previous chapters, we've looked at what a story is. In this chapter, we'll explore ways to see the story at its most basic level, its structure. One good way to do this is through pitching—not just at the start of a project, but throughout shooting and especially editing. Pitching forces you to take everything you know about your subject and focus it. As director and screenwriter David Mamet has noted, citing another director, Georgi Tovstonogov, "a director may fall into one of the deepest pits by rushing immediately to visual or pictorial solutions." Mamet explains: "A good writer gets better only by learning to *cut*, to remove the ornamental, the descriptive, the narrative, and *especially* the deeply felt and meaningful. What remains? The story remains."

Simplicity of structure allows for complexity in the overall film. If you have a strong narrative spine, you can hang a tremendous amount of content onto it and audiences will stay with you. This strategy is a big part of what distinguishes and defines the best of creative nonfiction film: It not only tells a story, it tells a rigorous, detailed, and even authoritative story—and yet it can be described in simple and compelling terms.

THE NARRATIVE SPINE, OR TRAIN

Films move forward in time, taking audiences with them. You want the storytelling to move forward, too, and to motivate the presentation of exposition. This means that you want the audience to be curious about the information you're giving them. When exposition involves backstory—how we got to where we are now—it's often a

DOI: 10.1016/B978-0-240-81241-0.00004-6

good idea to get a present-day story moving forward (even if the story happened in the past) before looking back. This overall story—your film's narrative spine—is also sometimes referred to as the film's *train*.

The train is the single thread, the plot, that drives your film forward, from the beginning to the end. Get a good train going, and you can make detours as needed for exposition, complex theory, additional characters—whatever you need. Sometimes, these detours let you seed in information that will pay off later in the film. Sometimes, the detours are motivated by the train, and the audience wants to take a side track to learn more. A train is your story boiled down to its simplest form. The train for *Super Size Me* might be stated as: *To test whether or not fast food is really as bad for your health as people claim it is, a filmmaker sets out to eat only what is offered at McDonald's for 30 days, measuring his health with the aid of doctors*. The train in *Daughter from Danang* might be stated as: *A young Amerasian woman returns to Vietnam to meet the birthmother who gave her up for adoption 22 years earlier, in 1975, as Saigon was evacuated*. The train sets out a story that has a clear beginning and an outcome that can, to some extent, be anticipated: Either the McDiet will harm the filmmaker or it won't. Either the reunion will go well or it won't.

An interesting example of a film with a less apparent train is *An Inconvenient Truth*. The film is built around a PowerPoint presentation developed by former Vice President Al Gore and presented by him to a range of audiences. We see him on a lecture tour, and these speeches (and voice overs) are intercut with sync and voice over from a conversation Gore had with filmmaker Davis Guggenheim about his life, career, and family. The train of this film doesn't come from the subject of global climate change, nor did the filmmakers build a train around any particular lecture tour itinerary. The train builds from Gore's interview and his first words, "I used to be the next president of the United States." The personal, introspective essay about Gore drives this film, although in terms of screen time and import, it takes a backseat to the warnings about global warming.

Your Train May Change

It is possible, over the course of production and especially editing, that the train you thought would work will not, or that it needs some adjustment. These are not written in stone; they are *tools* for diagnosis and understanding. If you find your film pulling in another direction or simply not working, imagine what other possible trains might exist. It would also be a useful exercise to watch a number of successful documentaries that are very different in subject and style and see if you can identify the train. You should be able to articulate it in a sentence or two.

Sometimes, you can confirm your hunch about a train by looking at the DVD box: *Waltz with Bashir*, for example, "chronicles one man's descent into his own half-forgotten past." (If you are stating it as a train, you'll want to add specifics: an *Israeli* man's descent; half-forgotten past *as a soldier in Lebanon*.) *Alexander Hamilton* is "a gifted statesman brought down by the fatal flaws of stubbornness, extreme candor, and arrogance." (This film sets this train in motion clearly in its opening moments: Hamilton is fatally wounded in a duel, and as he lays dying, friends and colleagues struggle to find the proper words to eulogize him.) *Man on Wire* shows how Philippe Petit "overcame seemingly insurmountable challenges to achieve the artistic crime of the century."

Remember, though, that the train may not be neatly articulated on the box, and that in fact there may not be a clear-cut train. Eugene Jarecki's *Why We Fight* is a well-structured and complex film, but the description on the box ("an unflinching look at the anatomy of American war-making") doesn't describe the train. The film uses the arc of a grieving father, retired police officer Wilton Sekzer, as a narrative *frame* for this film. Having lost his son in the 9/11 attack on the World Trade Center, Sekzer wants revenge and believes the government's argument that the target should be Iraq. By the end of the film, his views have changed. This is not a train, but a human element that helps to organize this film's overall essay. Somewhat similarly, Alex Gibney uses Dilawar, the taxi driver in *Taxi to the Dark Side*, as a narrative frame—the organizing principle—for his film. Like Sekzer, Dilawar and his family form a sort of bookend to the overall film, put a human face to policy, and serve as individuals with whom the audience can identify: These are innocent people victimized by forces and policies set into motion by others.

A Train Is Both Universal and Specific

Films generally appeal to our emotions before they appeal to our heads. In fact, the reason to tell a story for maximum (genuine) emotional impact is so that you *can* appeal to people's heads. Think about the documentaries and even the fictional dramas that appeal to you. At their most basic level, the questions they raise are: Will the guy get the girl? Will the outbreak be stopped? Will the town/puppy/hostage be saved? Will the team/first grader/unemployed father win the competition?

The train is the device that gets to the heart of your film, whether it's a story of competition or a question that demands an answer. It's how you create a film that will attract and engage viewers even when they think, at the outset, that they have absolutely no interest in your topic.

Here's an example. I am not naturally drawn to space exploration. I appreciate it, and I understand that it's complex and important and all the rest of it, but when people start going into details about lunar modules and orbits and heat shields, my eyes glaze over. There are, of course, people who will buy any book or video that comes out about the space program, people who know everything there is to know about Sputnik and Goddard and the Sea of Tranquillity. So the question is, how do you make a film that will appeal to both groups? You don't want to make it so superficial that you bore the aficionados, or so dry that you will never attract audiences like me. (Note that I did not say "so technical," because if you get a good train going, you can be surprisingly technical and people will *get it*.) A student of mine came up with a solution that I thought worked well.

The assignment was to write a treatment for a historical documentary on any U.S. subject. He chose the tragic Apollo 1 mission. (In 1967, a month before they were to become the first men to land on the moon, three U.S. astronauts died in a fire during a routine test.) One possible train that he considered was the government investigation that followed the fire, but it quickly became apparent that this would mire the film in bureaucracy—committees and reports and testimony—and lose anyone not interested in the details. Instead, he used the day of the fire as his train, moving the events forward in a way that motivated a look into the history and politics of space research and the lives of the astronauts involved. Since he presented the story from the point of view of those with something at stake in its outcome, he was able to bring the "initially disinterested" audience members along, giving us a reason to care and want to learn more.

Be Specific

Being specific means being clear on what your train really is. For example, it might seem accurate to say that Stanley Nelson's film, *The Murder of Emmett Till*, is about the brutal, racially motivated murder of a Chicago teenager while he was visiting relatives in Mississippi in 1955. But that doesn't encompass the film's full train, which is made clear in the opening minutes. Till's murder and the rapid acquittal of the men responsible was the case that "held the whole system [of racial segregation and oppression] up for inspection by the rest of the country and the rest of the world," as Mississippi's former governor William Winter says in the film's open. Journalist Rose Jourdain builds on this: This was the spark that launched "the mass civil rights movement.... Everybody knew we were under attack and that attack was symbolized by the attack on a 14-year-old boy." And so the train of this film is not only the story of a teenager's murder; it is also the story of what happened afterward. The midpoint of this film comes when Till's mother, seeing her son's damaged body, insists that the casket remain open for the world to see, and the modern U.S. civil rights movement is launched. The train of this film might be stated as: *When an African-American teenager from Chicago is tortured and murdered in Mississippi, his family fights back, drawing the world's attention to a corrupt system of justice—and igniting the U.S. civil rights movement.*

ELEMENTS OF STRUCTURE

The train summarizes the film's structure at its most succinct. Carrying that structure out over the course of the entire film, whether 20 minutes or 120, is the next challenge. We've all sat through documentaries that seemed pointless and meandering. Maybe they had great beginnings, but then they seemed to start again, and again, and again. The film seemed to be about one thing, but the rousing conclusion was about something altogether different. The story started in the present, and then quickly plunged into background and never resurfaced. Or the situation and characters were so weakly developed that we found ourselves caring little about the outcome. These are often problems of structure.

Structure works in response to the audience's built-in expectations. It's human nature to try to make sense of patterns and arrangements, to work at filling in the blanks and guessing what happens next. Filmmakers can heighten or confound those expectations, thereby increasing the viewer's involvement in a story and investment in its outcome. There's no such thing as a lack of structure; even in an experimental film, something's stringing those images together. That something, for better or worse, is structure.

The building blocks of a film's structure are shots, scenes, sequences, and, in some but not all cases, acts. Because these are commonly used words that at times have conflicting meanings, the following definitions clarify how they're being used here.

Shot

A shot is a single "take" on an image. There may be camera movement during the shot, or it may be static. It may be a close-up, a wide shot, a pan, or a tilt. But it begins and ends with the action of the cinematographer turning on and off the camera; later, the editor will further refine the shot by selecting from within it, giving it a new beginning and end point. Individual shots can convey a great deal of storytelling information: point of view, time of day, mood, emotion, character, rhythm, theme. A single shot may also include a "reversal," which is a twist in the plot, sometimes described as a change in values from one state to another. An example of a shot that contains a reversal can be found in *Yosemite: The Fate of Heaven*. We follow a cascading waterfall down through what appears to be pristine wilderness—until we land in a crowded tram full of noisy tourists. The reversal is from isolation to crowds, nature to humankind, pristine to polluted.

Scene

A scene is a consecutive group of shots within a single location. You might have a "scene at the courthouse" or a "scene on the boat." A scene is usually more than simply a snapshot of a location, however; it's a subset of the overall action. A scene is made up of a series of *beats*. In *Born into Brothels*, the scene "The children ride a bus to the beach" might be broken down like this:

- A few shots (interior, then exterior) show the children's excitement that a bus has arrived and is waiting;
- From inside the bus, we see a child ask if she can sit by a window, because she wants to take pictures. Everyone's on board; another quick shot, and then filmmaker Zana Briski makes sure the children all have their cameras;
- With a honk, we see the driver's point of view (POV) as the trip gets under way. From inside and outside the bus, we see a range of shots: children looking, taking pictures, their point of view as they look out; the bus moving forward;
- Inside the bus, the children eat and begin to sing (various shots);
- One child is sick;
- The music shifts as the bus gets into a more rural area (seen from various points of view);

- Inside the bus, several of the children have fallen asleep (various shots), intercut with more traveling shots, as the landscape becomes more rural;
- The bus has stopped; the children gather their things and look out at the ocean.

In other words, the scene started with the excited shout, "Hurry up, the bus is here," and ended with "Look at the water!" Like shots, sequences, and acts, scenes like this contain a beginning, middle, and end, and often, they culminate in a reversal, called a turning point, that motivates a shift in action of the overall story. Here, the reversal ties in with some of the film's themes. Boarding a bus in a congested, dirty city, the children arrive at the bright, open seaside. This reversal motivates the next scene—enjoying and photographing the beach.

To be satisfying, a scene should feel complete, which means that those filming the scene need to remain aware that events being witnessed will need to be condensed in the editing room, and shot accordingly. Filmmaker Steven Ascher (*So Much So Fast*) adds, "Filming real life is a constant struggle to distill reality into a meaningful subset of itself...the telling moments, the telling gestures, the lines of dialogue that will suggest the rest of the scene without actually having to see the rest of the scene."

Sequence

A sequence is a collection of shots and scenes that together tell a more or less continuous story of an event that is a piece of your bigger story. *Frankie goes to the prom*, for example, is a (hypothetical) sequence that might begin with Frankie rushing home from her job at the mall and continue with her emerging from her bedroom in a long white gown, dancing with her boyfriend, crying in the ladies' room because she's been dumped, and then arriving home, where she collapses into her mother's arms.

Sequences are different from scenes in that they may cover a series of locations, and the turning point at the end of a sequence will usually be bigger than one at the end of a scene or a shot. Story expert Robert McKee says that ideally, each scene creates a shift or reversal that is at least minor; each sequence, a change that is moderate; and each act, a change that is major.

Like a book's chapter, a sequence has a beginning, middle, and end. And, like a book's chapter, your sequences should be different from each other; each should have a unique job to do in the overall storytelling, while also moving the film's train—its underlying plot, or narrative—forward. If, for example, you're doing a film about Frankie working doggedly to earn a college scholarship, you might not have as much use for a sequence about Frankie going to the prom as you would for one such as *Frankie gets an internship* or *Frankie retakes her SATs*. (The latter might begin with Frankie hiring a private tutor and continue with a montage of her studying late at night and on Saturdays, getting ready to take the test, and entering the test room, and end with her nervously taking the envelope, with her results, out of the mailbox.) If Frankie going to the prom is just a pleasant distraction from her real task at hand—and your story—it's probably not worth the time and effort to film. And if two sequences are essentially about the same thing, one of them will have to go. (Scenes and sequences are a big part of how you establish and vary the rhythm of a film. If it all feels the same, and there's no change of tone, mood, pace, or even content throughout, the film is going to be very difficult to stay focused on.)

Going back to the example of *Born into Brothels*, we can see how the bus scene fits into a bigger sequence, which might be called "the day at the beach." The sequence begins with two quick exterior shots before the girl announces the bus's arrival, and continues through the bus ride and into a long scene of the children at the beach, discovering the ocean, playing in the waves, doing cartwheels, and taking pictures. And then it's night, and they're dancing on the bus as it heads back to Calcutta. It arrives, and we see the children make their way up the street, past "the line" of sex workers, and inside the narrow passages to their homes. (The entire sequence runs from a fade in at 36:48. Timed from the film's first frame of action, to a fade out at 43:53.)

This sequence achieves a number of things that serve the overall film. It shows the children interacting as a group and as independent, lively, spirited people. The pictures, especially Avijit's "Bucket," will be featured later in the film. Furthermore, the joy of the scene is immediately contrasted by the next scene, in which we see one of the children being beaten and his mother (and possibly grandmother) screaming obscenities at him and at neighbors. In the scene after that, we see some of the children in a car and hear Briski, voice over: "I'm not a social worker, I'm not a teacher, even. That's my fear, you know, that I really can't do anything and that even helping them to get an education's not going to do anything. But without help, they're doomed." Having seen them in a brief day's escape, we want more than ever for her to succeed.

Act

An act is a series of sequences that drives to a major turning point—a climactic moment that springs directly from the story and makes necessary the next series of sequences in the act that follows. Each act plays a role in the overall storytelling, and the tension and momentum within each should be increasing. In traditional three-act (also known as dramatic) structure, the first act covers the bulk of the story's exposition and, to paraphrase the late showman and writer George M. Cohan, gets your hero up a tree. In the second act, you throw rocks at him, forcing him higher up in the tree. In the third act, you force him to the edge of a branch that looks as if it might break at any moment ... and then you turn the corner to your story's resolution, and let your hero climb down.

There are three important things to know about acts. The first is that there is something about dramatic structure that seems built into the way we receive and enjoy stories. The second is that many documentaries do not fit neatly into this structure, but an approximation of it. Third, there are many ways to create a compelling structural throughline—what fiction writer Madison Smartt Bell describes as "narrative design"—in a documentary without going anywhere near dramatic three-act structure. The film still needs to have compelling characters and rising tension, each scene should move the narrative forward, and the film should satisfactorily conclude the story (or mission, essay, journey, etc.) with which it began. But it doesn't have to do it in three acts.

Before we move into some specifics of act structure, here are a few other useful terms.

Inciting Incident

The inciting incident is the event that sets the action of the story (the actions that relate to the train, not the subject) into motion. It may be something that's occurred before you start filming. In *Troublesome Creek*, for example (discussed in Chapter 15), it's the decision of the Jordan family, faced with debt, to farm one more year before auctioning off everything but their land. It's this decision that sets the story of the film in motion. In *Spellbound*, the inciting incident for each of the competitors we meet is that they are qualifying, or have qualified, to compete in the National Spelling Bee. In *Super Size Me*, the inciting incident, arguably, occurs when filmmaker Morgan Spurlock first learns of the lawsuit against McDonald's, and comes up with the notion of filming a 30-day McDiet.

Point of Attack

Not to be confused with the inciting incident, the point of attack is where you, as the filmmaker, enter the story. It's generally agreed that this is one of the hardest decisions to make over the course of production. In fact, it's often made and unmade many times before the right point of attack is found and you can't imagine why you ever tried anything else.

The point of attack ushers the viewer into the world of your film and its themes and characters. Discussing the opening visuals of his film *The City and the World*, episode seven of *New York* (1945– present), Ric Burns says, "It wasn't until fairly late in the editing process that we realized the beginning of the film was a moment in 1944 when Helen Leavitt borrows a 16mm movie camera and takes it up to the streets of East Harlem, and with a couple of friends, including James Agee, begins to shoot the footage that becomes her extraordinary film, *In the Streets*. That scene is absolutely, in my view, the best way to start that film, and it seems so completely inevitable— but it wasn't inevitable in the sense that we knew it from the beginning."

Where you begin your film is a critical decision, because it sets your train in motion and draws the audience into your story and its themes. As they discuss in Chapter 16, filmmakers Victoria Bruce and Karin Hayes attracted attention at the Slamdance Film Festival with their documentary, then called *Missing Peace*, about a Colombian presidential candidate who'd been kidnapped before the election and was still in captivity. But the film as shown had a soft start. "We had a slow build of getting to know this woman," Bruce says. When HBO Cinemax bought the film after the festival, HBO editor Geof Bartz moved the kidnapping up. The film now begins with images of a woman campaigning; a title card reads, *In January 2002, Ingrid Betancourt campaigned to become president of war-torn Colombia*. After a bit more campaign footage, the filmmakers cut to a view of mountains, as the credits and new title appear on screen: *The Kidnapping of Ingrid Betancourt*. The film then goes to previously filmed footage of Betancourt with her children, as the story (beginning well before the kidnapping) gets under way. "It's brilliant," Bruce says, crediting the move to HBO executive producer Sheila Nevins, who argued that audiences would care more about Betancourt's time with her kids if they knew she'd be gone soon. In other words, the point of attack is the kidnapping. The film then goes back in time, and as in the cut at Slamdance, the first act continues with exposition about who Betancourt is and how she came to be running for president. Your point of attack is very likely to change as you grow closer to your material and see which themes best serve the story you want to tell. You simply start with the best opening you have at that time and let it evolve from there.

Backstory

Backstory is a form of exposition, but the two terms are not always synonymous. The backstory includes the events that happened before (sometimes long before) the main story being told; it often includes material a filmmaker thinks is critical for the audiences to understand in order to "get" the story.

Backstory can be conveyed in a number of ways, including title cards (text on screen), interviews, narration, and conversation. To some extent, backstory involves the details of exposition that are revealed over the course of the film and add complexity to the story and its characters. Far along in *Grizzly Man*, for example, we learn that Timothy Treadwell very nearly won the role in the television series *Cheers* that went to actor Woody Harrelson. It is backstory—part of the complex journey that led Treadwell to live dangerously close to bears in the Alaskan wilderness. Placed where it is in the film, the detail adds a further layer of complexity to our understanding, and the filmmaker's, of the forces that led to Treadwell's death.

Often, and sometimes painfully, backstory gets dropped in the cutting room because the story itself has become so compelling and the themes so evident that the backstory is more of an interruption than a necessity. Backstory is most likely to stay in if it directly enhances and enriches the story unfolding on screen, adding depth to a character's motivation, illuminating themes and issues, or underscoring irony or historical continuity. A little goes a long way, however. If the backstory starts taking over your film, you might need to rethink which story, past or present, you really want to tell.

You may also need to look at where it's placed. In *The Kidnapping of Ingrid Betancourt*, the backstory (details about who the kidnapped candidate is, and how she came to be running for president) worked best after the train was under way: a candidate is kidnapped, and her family continues the campaign in her absence. In *When the Levees Broke*, a segment that presents the backstory of New Orleans's history doesn't appear until the third hour of the film. That hour "deals with the whole notion of coming back or staying— are people going to go back to New Orleans or stay where they are, are their lives better now in other places?" explains co-producer Sam Pollard. The notion of connection to the history and culture of the city motivates a look back at New Orleans in the years before the hurricane.

THREE-ACT DRAMATIC STRUCTURE

Three-act dramatic structure is a staple of the Hollywood system, but as noted elsewhere, it was first articulated by Aristotle. It describes the basic way that many humans tell and anticipate stories: a setup, complications, resolution. "I think that's just the way we as humans are neurologically and culturally structured," says writer Susan Kim (see Chapter 21), noting, for example, that the mind constructs narratives even as we sleep. "I think there is something inherent in the dramatic form that's really powerful. And I think that's why, as storytellers, as people who want to make documentary or write plays, it behooves us to understand the potential of that structure."

There are many books that describe three-act structure, but the best way to learn it is to take films apart and analyze them. Which story (or spine, or train) is *driving* the act structure? Where do the act breaks come, and how are they connected to the train? How do sequences fit into the acts, and how does each play a role in driving the overall story forward? You may not be able to really "see" the act structure until you're all the way through the film, but what you'll tend to find is that it roughly divides as follows.

Act One

The first act generally runs about one-quarter the length of the story. In this act, you introduce your characters and the problem or conflict (in other words, this act will contain most of your important exposition). Act One often contains the "inciting incident"—the event that gets everything rolling—although this event sometimes has already occurred when the story begins. There tends to be a "first turning point," which is somewhat smaller than the turning point that ends the act. By the end of Act One, the audience knows who and what your story is about and, at least initially, what's at stake. The first act drives to an emotional peak, the highest in the film so far, necessitating the action that launches the second act.

Act Two

The second act is the longest in the film, about one-half the length of the story. The stage has been set in Act One and the conflict introduced. In the second act, the story's pace increases as complications emerge, unexpected twists and reversals take place, and the stakes continue to rise. The second act can be difficult, because there is a risk that the story will bog down or become a succession of "and then this happened, and then this." You need your second act to continue to build as new information and new stakes are woven into your story. The second act drives to an emotional peak even greater than at the end of Act One, necessitating the action that launches the third act.

Act Three

The third act is usually slightly less than one-quarter the length of the overall film. As this act unfolds, the character is approaching defeat; he or she will reach the darkest moment just as the third act comes to a close. It's a common misperception that your third act resolves the story, but it doesn't. It intensifies it; the tension at the end of the third act should be even greater than the tension at the end of Act Two. That tension then pushes you into the resolution, those last moments where you resolve the story, tie up loose ends as necessary, and let your hero out of the tree.

Structuring Multiple Story Lines

Although you can tell only one primary story, it's possible to follow two or even three story lines within that story. In Hollywood terms, these are "A" stories, "B" stories, and possibly even "C" stories. The "A" story carries the primary weight and is the story around which the piece is structured, but the other stories should also have emotional peaks and valleys.

Most importantly, the stories should inform each other, meaning that at some point they should connect to form a coherent whole and advance a single overall story line. *Yosemite: The Fate of Heaven*, for example, contrasts the primeval Yosemite that survived until the 19th century with the national park that today accommodates several million visitors a year. The filmmakers interweave two stories, one more clearly narrative than the other. The first is built around an 1854 diary kept by Lafayette Bunnell, who was part of a battalion that entered Yosemite on an Indian raid. The second is a more impressionistic look at the ongoing, day-to-day struggle to balance use of the park by those who love it with the needs of those who maintain it and are working to preserve it for the future.

The use of multiple story lines often enables filmmakers to create films that are more complex than would be possible with a strictly linear approach. Rather than tell everything in the order in which it occurred, they select an event and use that to focus the primary film narrative, which frees them to look back into the past or even ahead into the future as needed. This can be seen in the *Daughter from Danang*, for example, as well as *Murderball* and, more recently, *The Way We Get By*.

What Three-Act Structure Is Not

Three-act structure does not mean taking a film and dividing it into three parts and calling each part an act. An act can only be considered as such if it advances the one overall story (or essay) that you set out to tell. For example, a film that looks at early settlements in the United States can't be structured, "Act One, Plymouth, Massachusetts; Act Two, Jamestown, Virginia; Act Three, New York, New York." There is no common story there; there may be common themes and this may work as an organizational construct for a film, but these aren't acts. On the other hand, you could tell three individual dramatic stories within that structure, one within each location that you then combine into a film.

Three Acts in Five or One or Two

Whether your film is described as having five acts or one, it can still follow dramatic (three-act) structure. There are many practical reasons to divide a story, including breaks for commercials (television) or audience intermission (theater). But "one-act" plays and "five-act" television specials can often still be divided into three acts. For example, even though David Auburn wrote *Proof* as a fictional, two-act stage play, the action can easily be broken into three-act dramatic structure. Auburn's "first act" contains all of his Act One and the first half of Act Two; his "second act" contains the balance of Act Two and all of Act Three. Where you break a story for reasons like commercials or intermissions is part of the structural discussion, but does not necessarily interfere with your use of dramatic storytelling.

Conversely, simply because a story is divided up for commercial breaks doesn't mean it's divided into acts. Many commercial documentaries are described as having four or five "acts," which may accomodate the points at which there is an interruption for advertising. These breaks come at dramatic moments, but that does not describe the overall structure. (For example, many commercial biographies present a fairly chronological portrayal of a person's life, driving to key moments, without being shaped by three-act structure.)

If you are working on a film that is not going to be interrupted with commercials, but your editor is insisting that your film requires four or even five acts or more, I would strongly suggest that you do a barebones outline of each of the acts. Where does it start, what does it drive to, and how does it relate to your underlying train? While it's possible to structure an interesting film in four or more parts, they may not be acts—or if they are acts, they are likely covering the same ground a few times too many.

APPLYING FILM STRUCTURE

Some documentary filmmakers think about structure over the course of production but don't focus on it until they're editing. Others play with structure from the start, sketching outlines that they return to during production and postproduction, revising them and reshaping them as needed.

In projects where an outline and/or treatment is needed prior to filming, whether to get a greenlight from commissioning editors or to get production funds from a public or private source, you may try to anticipate an act structure that you think will work. This is often the case, for example, with historical films, and can also work with films where the outcome is unknown but can generally be anticipated because of the train. In other words, by the time a filmmaker is seeking support for a film about something with an inherent arc—a competition (for example, an athletic event or a spelling bee), a time-limited event (a state fair, a school prom), a political campaign, even a day in the life—that filmmaker will also, in all likelihood, have a sense of the characters, issues, and themes that have drawn him or her to the story, and can *anticipate* an act structure, even if it ends up changing.

Finding an Act Structure in the Edit Room

In some cases, filmmakers will shoot a story that offers a basic narrative arc but wait until they're editing to specifically consider structure. This usually means a considerably longer editing period. For example, Susan Froemke describes working with editor Deborah Dickson on the Academy Award–nominated *Lalee's Kin: The Legacy of Cotton*, produced for HBO. Maysles Films had been commissioned by HBO to explore the subject of poverty at the end of the 20th century, and the company spent months researching the issue and seeking out stories that would illuminate it. They chose two related stories: that of Reggie Barnes, a superintendent of schools in the Mississippi Delta seeking to get an impoverished school system off of academic probation (one narrative arc), and Lalee Wallace, a matriarch struggling to educate the grandchildren and great-grandchildren left in her care (the arc of the school year).

The filmmakers were based in New York, and travelled to Mississippi periodically over a period of several months, shooting about 42 days in all. Their footage ratio was relatively conservative, about 70:1 (meaning that 70 hours of film were shot for each hour that ended up on screen; the film runs 90 minutes). They began to edit about a year and a half into the filming, before production was over. Froemke notes that it's better to have completed shooting before editing starts, because you can build to the end of the film, its climax. With *Lalee's Kin*, they instead began by editing scenes. "Let's say that there are 10 moments, or maybe 20, that we think really could make great scenes, so we cut those together," she says. "And then we do a very rough assembly, like four hours long. And you see how the scenes play against each other.... Right away you start to see which story lines are working and which ones are weak. And you keep editing down, you keep sculpting, down and down."

Part of that sculpting involves deciding which job a particular scene or sequence does in moving the story forward. Scenes that reveal character or backstory, for example, could be used in a variety of ways (provided that each use is truthful), or a scene may contain two or three key points, only one of which will be the focus for now. "Often you try to assign a value to the scene," Froemke says. "For example, 'This scene is going to tell Lalee's backstory, her family upbringing.' Or, 'This scene is going to explain what Reggie's dilemma is.' Or, 'This scene, you're going to understand Granny's despair.'"

Froemke says that act structure is part of how this work is organized. "We often call it Act One, Act Two, Act Three. We'll say, when we're screening, 'This is Act One information'—it's setting up the situation. We don't yet know where it's going to appear in Act One, but we put it in that section. And then Act Two and Act Three. Act Two is always the hardest in vérité, it's the hardest part of the film not to sag. You've got to get a few of your feisty scenes into Act Two." Another issue she notes is that special attention must be paid to those scenes that move the plot forward; with vérité, there often aren't many of them, so care must be taken in how they're placed.

Lalee's Kin ended up taking a bit less than two years to edit. An earlier Maysles production, *Grey Gardens*, took two and a half years, Froemke says. "It took a whole year just to figure out what you had in the footage and what story line you were going to go for. Nothing happens in that house in *Grey Gardens*. So how do you structure a film about it? It took a long time to figure out that there was a balance of power between Little and Big Edie [Edie Beale and her mother, Edith Bouvier Beale, reclusive relatives of Jacqueline Kennedy Onassis]."

Revising an Act Structure in the Edit Room

Rather than fully discover a film's structure in the editing room, it's more likely you'll be revising the structure that suggested itself to you over the course of research, development, and production. Be careful when making changes that you are not bending your footage to satisfy a story it doesn't represent. This is most likely to happen when filmmakers shoot one story (or no story, just a lot of footage) and then stumble on a story late in the process of editing that might actually work.

ANALYZING DOCUMENTARIES USING ACT STRUCTURE

Three-act structure can offer a grid that allows you to anticipate and critique the rhythms of your storytelling. You should map out your film at rough cut or fine cut and try to analyze it the same way you've been analyzing completed films (try to see your film as if for the first time). What story do you think is being told? Where are the turning points? Do the act breaks relate to the specific story (the train)? Does the film bring a satisfying end to the story with which it began?

What's interesting is how many successful documentaries, even those that seem vastly different in style and approach (including essay films), can be analyzed in terms of acts. But act structure or not, the important thing to keep in mind is that if your film is working—even if the charts and stopwatches say it shouldn't be—leave it alone. Storytelling is an art, not a science. Go with your gut. If the film's great, who cares what "rules" you broke?

Sulfur gatherers in East Java, Indonesia, from *Workingman's Death*.
Photo © M. Iqbal, courtesy of Michael Glawogger/Lotus Film.

OTHER STRUCTURES

There are plenty of examples of successful, interesting documentaries
that do not tell character-driven dramatic stories. Look, for example,
at Austrian filmmaker Michael Glawogger's *Workingman's Death*, a
two-hour film that *The New York Times* aptly described as having "the
structure and tone of an epic historical poem." It is nonfiction and it
is literary—in other words, creative nonfiction—but the filmmaker
has created a structure that is unique to this project. The film won the
British Film Institute's Grierson Award and the Jury Award at the Gijon
Film Festival, among many other honors. Glawogger set out to show
work: "I wanted to make a movie where you sit in the cinema and actually feel the weight on your back," he said in a 2005 interview. The film
offers five portraits of heavy manual labor that is all but invisible to
many people these days: *Heroes* visits coal miners of Krasni Lutsch,
Ukraine; *Ghosts* looks at men hauling tremendous loads of sulfur from
the top of a mountain in East Java, Indonesia, to the valley below; *Lions*
keeps up with the workers in Port Harcourt, Nigeria, as they process
live goats and bulls into meat for sale; *Brothers* stays with workers in
Gaddani, Pakistan, as they risk their lives to convert massive rusted tan-
kers into scrap metal; and *Future*, a much shorter segment, looks at steel
workers and industrial progress in the Chinese province of Liaoning.
In the film's epilogue, we visit the Duisburg-Nord Country Park in

Germany, a recreational facility in what was once the Duisburg-Meiderich Steelworks.

German director Eva Weber's *City of Cranes*, originally produced for Channel 4 and awarded Best Documentary Short at the Los Angeles Film Festival (among numerous honors), is another example of a chaptered approach to structure. Unlike the Glawogger film, all four chapters have the same subject: this 14-minute film brings viewers into the world of crane drivers, who climb up into tiny cages to spend their days working hundreds of feet above the ground. Each of the four chapters is thematically titled: *The City Above*, *The Last Topman*, *Ballet of Cranes*, and *Solitary*. The film has a sort of overarching structure as well—the first shot is of a man climbing up into a crane, at the start of the day; it ends on a contemplative note at dusk, from the vantage point of a driver high above the city.

U.S. filmmaker Liane Brandon's 1972 film, *Betty Tells Her Story*, consists of two 10-minute interviews, played in sequence. Brandon had met the film's subject when both were consulting for the Massachusetts Department of Education, and was drawn to a story Betty told about buying a dress and then losing it before she had a chance to wear it. "I borrowed Ricky Leacock's camera, and John Terry, who worked with Ricky at M.I.T., volunteered to do sound," Brandon says. At Betty's house, the crew loaded the first of three 10-minute black-and-white film magazines, and Brandon asked Betty simply to tell her story. "The first version that you see in the film is the first take that we did. I never told her how long a magazine was, but somehow she ended the story just before we ran out of film." It was basically the story as Betty had first told it to Brandon: a witty anecdote about a dress she'd found that was just perfect—and how she never got to wear it.

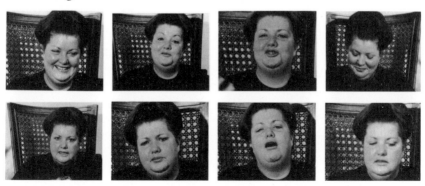

Betty, from *Betty Tells Her Story*. Photo courtesy of Liane Brandon.

A second take was interrupted by a truck. In the third take, Brandon asked Betty to try telling the story as she felt about it while it was happening, rather than as she remembered it. "Everything changed: body language, eye contact," Brandon says. "I don't think she'd ever told or even thought about the story that way." Told from within rather than without, the story is no longer a humorous anecdote; it's the painful memory of a plain, overweight woman who found a dress that made her feel beautiful, then lost it before she ever had a chance to wear it.

In the final film, the first and third takes are run consecutively, with some black leader in between that reads, *Later that day, the filmmaker asked Betty to tell her story again*. The contrast between the two takes is what gives this film its power.

CHAPTER 5

Time on Screen

In the previous chapters, we looked at the basics of storytelling and the importance of structure. A key element in structure is how the storyteller arranges the presentation of chronological time, without altering cause and effect. Most of us have grown up with storytelling that does this. A television show may start with strangers discovering a body, for example, move forward as detectives arrive on the scene, and then move back in time to the events leading up to the murder as the detectives piece it together. Some stories, for sure, are told entirely in chronological order. Others, more rarely, are told in *reverse* chronological order, from the end to the beginning. This is how playwright Harold Pinter structured *Betrayal*, for example, and screenwriter Christopher Nolan, working off a short story by Jonathan Nolan, structured the dramatic feature *Memento*.

The treatment of time on screen is important because of the way we experience movies: Film is a linear medium. People watch it from beginning to end, with one shot following another, one sequence following another, until the film is over. "I've never seen an even vaguely successful documentary film that does not move forward through time," says filmmaker Jon Else, citing a number of disparate examples. "*Night and Fog* has an absolutely traditional, very simple forward chronological motion through the late 1930s to the end of World War II. *Tongues Untied*, Marlon Riggs's film, appears to be a nonlinear rumination about what it means to be young and gay and black in America in the 1980s, but in fact it moves through his life. Even Chris Marker's *Sans Soleil*, which is often described as being nonlinear, moves forward through time. This whole business of a plot moving forward, I think, is just so inextricably embedded in our cultural DNA." Michael Glawogger's *Workingman's Death*, described in the previous chapter, has a forward moving structure within each of the stories as well as overall.

As is already probably clear by the discussion of structure, moving a story forward through time does not necessitate resorting to a plodding narrative that is strictly a chronological recitation of events in the order that they occurred. Instead, and often, it involves the inter-weaving of chronological and nonchronological elements in and out of order to form a cohesive and satisfying whole. *Daughter from Danang* selects an event within the chronology of Heidi Bub's life—her trip to Vietnam in 1997 to meet her birth mother—as the frame-work, or train, through which to explore issues and events that cover the entire span of her life, including her birth in 1968 and, especially, her mother's decision to give her up for adoption in 1975. *Jonestown: The Life and Death of Peoples Temple* begins on a specific day in 1978, continues through a scene that is not specifically grounded in time, and then moves back to the 1930s and generally follows chronological order back to that day in 1978.

There is one very important caveat. You may not *distort* or *falsify* chronology. What we are discussing is the order in which you tell the story, not the order in which you are saying the story occurred.

TELLING A CHRONOLOGICAL STORY, BUT NOT CHRONOLOGICALLY

As a documentary storyteller, you decide where to begin and end the story. You can begin in the middle, go back to the beginning, catch up with your story, and then move ahead to the end. You can start at the end before moving to the beginning to ask, "How did we get here?" You can flash forward or back. The only thing you can't do, in a documentary that's driven by a narrative sequence of events, is change the important facts of the main underlying chronology.

Suppose you've unearthed a story in the archives of your local his-torical society. The following are the events in chronological order:

- A young man becomes engaged;
- His older brother enlists to fight in World War II;
- The young man also enlists;
- Their father dies;
- The young man is shipped overseas;
- He learns that his brother has been killed;
- His fiancée sends a letter, breaking off their engagement.

These events haven't happened in an order that's particularly dra-matic, and there's no way to tell, on the surface, which events are linked by cause and effect. It may be that because his brother enlisted, the young man also felt obligated, but there could be other reasons.

If you can verify your characters' motivations, whether through records or eyewitnesses, you can state them; otherwise, present the facts and let the audience draw its own conclusions. By the same token, you may not rearrange the underlying chronology to imply a more interesting cause and effect. For example, based on the previous chronology, you might be tempted to:

- Show the two sons enlisting after their father's death, to create the impression that they enlisted in his honor;
- Film a recreation in which the young man, already in uniform, proposes marriage;
- Present the fiancée's letter in voice over as the young man enlists, implying that he's enlisting in reaction to the breakup.

Each of these might be dramatic, but they all lead the audience to a false understanding of cause and effect. But respecting cause and effect, there are still some more dramatic choices. Start with the young man's rejection by his fiancée, for example, and then reveal that this is another in a string of losses. Leave the father and fiancée out of the story and focus on the two brothers at war. Tell the story of the young man going to war, and then go back to follow the story of his engagement. There's plenty of room for creativity.

An example of a documentary that creates a false impression of chronology, to the detriment of an otherwise powerful argument and film, is Michael Moore's *Roger & Me*. Critic Harlan Jacobson published a detailed review of this film in *Film Comment*, outlining some of the problems. The film's present-day narrative begins in late 1986, when, according to Moore, General Motors chairman Roger Smith closed 11 plants in Flint, Michigan, leaving 30,000 people jobless and sending the city on a downward spiral.

Moore then presents a series of events, including these, in this order:

- Eleven GM plants are opened in Mexico, where, Moore says, workers can be paid 70 cents an hour;
- The last vehicle rolls off the assembly line in Flint;
- Ronald Reagan visits Flint; over archival news footage, Moore narrates, *Just when things were beginning to look bleak, Ronald Reagan arrived in Flint*. At the end of the scene, Moore says someone *borrowed the cash register on his way out the door*;
- A parade is held in Flint, and Moore interviews Miss Michigan shortly before she'll compete to be Miss America;
- Evangelist Robert Schuller comes to Flint to cheer people up;

- As Moore presents an abandoned and decaying Flint, he says, *The city had become the unemployment capitol of the country.* Just when it looked like all was lost, the city fathers came up with one last great idea. This plan includes the building of a Hyatt Regency hotel downtown; the Water Street Pavilion, a new shopping center; and the opening of Auto World.

Remember that the film began with the closing of 11 plants in Flint, late in 1986. From Harlan Jacobson's article, here is the actual chronology of the events:

- In 1980, Ronald Reagan arrives in town as a presidential candidate and buys folks pizza. Two days before his visit, the cash register was stolen;
- In 1982, Reverend Schuller comes to Flint and the Hyatt Regency is opened;
- Auto World opens in mid-1984 and closes in early 1985;
- In 1986, the Water Street Pavilion opens, the result of a plan that may have been under way since the early 1970s. Also in 1986, the number of layoffs at GM do not total 30,000 but about 10,000, according to Jacobson. The real "watershed" of layoffs had occurred much earlier, in 1974. The net loss of jobs since 1974 was about 32,000.
- In the fall of 1988, shortly after the parade, Miss Michigan is crowned Miss America.

In other words, many of the events presented by the filmmaker as the efforts of the powers-that-be to staunch the bleeding from the 1986 layoffs actually occurred, or were under way, long before those layoffs took place. Jacobson's article includes an interview with Moore, in which he asks the filmmaker about these issues. "The movie is about essentially what happened to this town during the 1980s," Moore responded. "As far as I'm concerned, a period of seven or eight years ... is pretty immediate and pretty devastating" [*ellipses in the original*]. Moore argued that he was trying to "tell a documentary in a way they don't usually get told. The reason why people don't watch documentaries is they are so bogged down with 'Now in 1980 ... then in '82 five thousand were called back ... in '84 ten thousand were laid off ... but then in '86 three thousand were called back but later in '86 ten thousand more were laid off.'"

In fact, telling an accurate story doesn't have to mean getting bogged down in detail or needing to tell the story sequentially. Arguably, you could leave the edit of *Roger & Me* exactly as it is and simply rewrite Moore's narration. For example, there's nothing to stop your use of footage of candidate Reagan stumping through Flint years before the plant closings; you simply write into it in a way that acknowledges the time shift. Here's Moore's narration, building on the aftermath of the 1986 layoff: *Just when things were beginning to look bleak, Ronald Reagan arrived in Flint and took a dozen unemployed workers out for a pizza. He told them he had come up with a great idea, and if they tried it they'd all be working again.* (In archival footage, a woman then explains that Reagan suggested they move to another state to find work.)

Alternative narration: *People had been trying to help the unemployed in Flint for years. As a candidate in 1980, future president Ronald Reagan took a dozen workers out for some pizza and inspiration.*

The narration needs to keep track of where you are in the film's present—in this case, somewhere between 1986 and 1988—while letting us know that what we're seeing is from the past, and how it informs the present. What to do about the cash register theft? This sounds like one of those facts that is "too good to check," but it must be done. If you know that the theft occurred two days before Reagan's visit, and you really want to use it, you have to be a bit creative.

Moore's words: *None of Reagan's luncheon guests got back into the factories in the ensuing years, and the only bright spot to come out of the whole affair was the individual who borrowed the cash register on his way out the door.*

It's unclear whether these luncheon guests were already laid off before Reagan arrived (and stayed that way) or if they were employed between Reagan's visit and the layoffs later in the 1980s. In any case (or if you can't find out the specifics about the individuals in this footage), you could say something more general, such as: *In the years to come, Reagan's luncheon guests may have wished that instead of listening to the candidate, they'd taken a cue from the guy who'd robbed the pizza parlor two days earlier and made off with the cash register.*

While mine is not brilliant voice over, it's a quick example of how you can tell a story out of order, with as much irreverence as you want, without building a case that has a weak or inaccurate foundation. To imply that the visits of Reverend Schuller and Ronald Reagan and the opening of the Hyatt Regency and Auto World occurred both after and because of a plant closing in 1986 is simply inaccurate. In his defense, Moore told Jacobson that *Roger & Me* isn't a documentary but "an entertaining movie that hopefully will get people to think a little bit about what is going on." (To be fair, it was his first major film, released in 1989; he has made several blockbuster documentaries since.) However, audiences and critics received the film as a documentary, and it's highly regarded as such. The power of documentaries comes from their veracity, and it's undermined if people discover that in the interest of a compelling argument, they've been misled.

Not all documentaries, or sequences within them, need to adhere to a strict chronology; filmmakers may rearrange filmed sequences if they are typical but not necessarily specific to a time line, such as routine events (skateboard practice, Sunday church, an annual holiday). Where you place this material in the film, regardless of when it was shot, is generally up to you. If you're following a group of people—residents in an assisted living center, for example—your choice of which scenes and stories to present and when may be driven by the emotional argument you're building, rather than any specific chronology or the order in which stories were filmed. (Within each story, however, rules of cause and effect still apply. If a woman suffers a heart attack, recovers, and then dances with her husband at a formal dinner, it would be dishonest to edit the sequence to imply that the dancing led to the heart attack.)

Material filmed for thematic reasons may also stand apart from the chronological sequence. An example of this can be found in *Troublesome Creek: A Midwestern*. The chronology is built on the Jordans's efforts to pay off a bank debt by auctioning off their belongings. For thematic reasons, the filmmakers asked the Jordans to return to a farm they'd rented for many years before moving to the farm they're now at risk of losing. The scene's exact placement in the film, other than sometime before the auction, isn't specific. Filmmaker Jeanne Jordan's voice over simply says, "Early one morning we took a trip to Rolfe to visit the farm I grew up on." Jordan's parents are upset to discover that the old place is abandoned, but their visit doesn't motivate any action. Instead, it serves a filmmaking purpose—shedding light on the historical context of the overall film and on themes of change and loss.

COLLAPSING AND EXPANDING TIME

Filmmaking, from shooting through editing, is a process of expanding and/or collapsing real time. The event needs to be covered with the editor in mind, so that there is enough variety of shots, cutaways, and transitional material to make a creative edit possible.

For the most part, simple editing can imply a passage of time. Your characters are at home, seated around the breakfast table, and then they're on the school basketball court; or your character is trying on a tux for the prom, and then he's at the prom. If the story has been taking place in the summertime, and you cut to children playing in the snow, the season has changed. Sometimes, filmmakers emphasize passage of time with dissolves, time-lapse photography, an interlude with music, or a montage. If the passage of time is part of the story, the filmmaker might comment on that visually. Errol Morris used a clock to mark the hours that passed while Randall Adams was being pressured to confess in *The Thin Blue Line*.

Some scenes may be granted more or less emotional weight than others through the length of time you devote to them. For example, you might spend two minutes of screen time bringing the audience up to date on 10 years of history prior to a candidate's decision to run for office, and then spend the next 45 minutes on an eight-month campaign; you've collapsed the first part of the chronological story in order to focus more time on the campaign itself. And sometimes you expand time because you've built to an emotional moment and you need to let it play, as was true at the end of *Bridge to Freedom*, in the last episode in the first season of the series *Eyes on the Prize*.

FILMING OVER TIME

In some cases, a documentary's complexity comes not only from its immediate story but from an opportunity to check in on characters months or even years later. An example of this is the Spanish film *Balseros*. The film begins in 1994 and follows a handful of determined emigrants from Cuba who risk their lives in order to reach the shores of the United States, traveling on dangerous, makeshift rafts. Some don't make it far offshore; others are picked up by the U.S. Coast Guard and held in detention at Guntánamo for many months. Eventually, though, each makes his or her way to the United States, and we see them settling down in small towns and big cities throughout the country. The filmmakers check in on them nine months later, to see how they're doing, and then they check in on them again five years later. The result is a look at immigration and the American dream, at opportunities seized and squandered, and at choices and mistakes that can have a lasting impact.

Another noted example is British filmmaker Michael Apted's *Up* series. In the 1960s, Apted worked on *Seven Up!*, a documentary in which 14 seven-year-olds of various economic backgrounds were interviewed about their lives and hopes for the future. Apted, who is also known as a feature film director (*Coal Miner's Daughter, The World Is Not Enough*), assumed direction of the project, returning in seven-year intervals to see how the children and their dreams were holding up at ages 14, 21, 28, 35, 42, and most recently, 49. A few of the original subjects dropped out of the project over the years, but most continue to participate, and in their achievements and frustrations audiences get a profound look at what it means to live ordinary, extraordinary lives.

COLLAPSING INTERVIEWS

There are two primary reasons to edit an interview: to focus information and to shorten the time it takes to convey that information. A person will talk to you for 10 minutes, an hour, maybe two or three hours, and you'll usually end up using only a few bites, unless the entire film is "a conversation with." You must condense the interview material in a way that does not alter its initial meaning and remains true to the intent of the speaker. For example, here's the (fictional) raw transcript of a witness describing your character, Sanders:

> CHARLIE: *Sanders wasn't a bad man, in fact I'd have to say he was a pretty good guy, overall, which is why nobody could figure out—at least I couldn't figure out—uh, what the, what he was doing even thinking about embezzlement. I don't know, but I think, I mean, who knows, but in my opinion, he was just panicked about money. I mean for crying out loud, this guy's got three, uh, three, uh, you know, he's got three kids and another one on the uh, on the way—maybe it got to him, I don't know, maybe he just couldn't figure out how he was going to support all these little ones or whatever, you know? He was selling auto parts, used auto parts. Besides, embezzlement's a white collar crime, he's a blue collar guy—well, not really, he's not working with the auto parts, he's more the manager of the store, driving to work in his, oh, what was it, Tercel, his blue Tercel, shirt and tie and all the while I guess he's thinking nobody above him would miss that thirty thou. Arrogance, I guess. Yeah. Arrogance.*

What can't you use? No matter how catchy it sounds, I wouldn't use, "embezzlement's a white collar crime, he's a blue collar guy" for two reasons. Sanders is not, in fact, blue collar, and furthermore, the witness himself corrects this statement.

In terms of editing for time, however, condensing the essence of this paragraph, you could do any number of cuts depending on the point you want Charlie to make and where it will be used in the film. What material is the interview bite following? What will it precede?

One of the ways to see this before trying it in the editing room is to make the cut on paper, which you can then give to the editor. Two things to remember. First, don't make the editor crazy by cutting out every third word and expecting him or her to construct a sentence or a paragraph out of the bits and pieces. This is very difficult and very time-consuming, and furthermore, any interview material that's hacked to bits will have to be used as a voice over. In any case, if you're hacking an interview to bits, chances are good that either you've interviewed the wrong person or you're asking this interview to do a job in the film that it wasn't meant to do, and you should probably look for other solutions.

The second thing to remember is that a cut on paper may not work on film. The way people speak often reads differently than it sounds. People end sentences with a question, or they run two sentences together, or they burp or sigh, or a plane flies overhead, or their energy level shifts so much that you can't cut between two bites. You do the best you can to note the big issues when you're watching rushes (the raw footage) with the transcripts in hand, but there will still be times when something that should work just doesn't.

With that said, there are a few tricks to increasing the odds that your paper cut will work. It's generally easier to cut into a hard consonant, such as b, t, or v. Words that begin with soft consonants, such as s or h, can be more difficult. Note that just because you cut the "Well" from "Well, I think it started" doesn't mean that the editor can make the excision. Usually, though, if one bite or cut doesn't work, there will be something else available that's close enough.

Whether or not you "cover" the edits with cutaways is a stylistic choice. When you cut from two different parts of an interview, especially when the focal length (e.g., close-up, medium shot) hasn't changed, the cut—known as a jump cut—can be jarring. Some film-makers find an elegance or at least an honesty in a jump cut; there is no disguising that the material has been edited. Others "cover" the edit with a cutaway, so that the soundtrack continues, apparently seamlessly. (For example, you're on someone's face as they talk; while they're still talking, the film cuts to the person's hands, fidgeting; then to a neighbor, listening from a nearby chair; then to a clock on the wall; and then back to the speaker's face.) How long you cut away from someone before you need to see them speaking again is a matter of taste, as is the decision about how long you can hear someone's voice "over" before you show who is speaking. Sometimes, you let an interview play simply because you don't want to interrupt the answer. And sometimes, the entire interview will be voice over (v/o), especially if the footage is all of one person and/or it's very obvious who is speaking. Effective portraits of people at work—a zookeeper, an underwater explorer—have been done this way.

Of course, editing within an interview is only one solution. You can also synthesize a story by using multiple storytellers and cutting between them, or using narration to reduce the amount of interview needed or to state concisely something with which the interviewee struggled. For this chapter, the focus is on reducing the length of the interview in a way that is consistent with generally-accepted principles of documentary ethics. For example, here are some ways to shorten the interview in which Charlie discusses his friend, Sanders:

> *CHARLIE: Sanders wasn't a bad man, in fact I'd have to say he was a pretty good guy, overall, which is why nobody could figure out—~~at least I couldn't figure out—uh, what the,~~ what he was doing even thinking about embezzlement. Arrogance, I guess. Yeah. Arrogance.*

> *CHARLIE: (beginning v/o) he was just panicked about money. ~~I mean for crying out loud, this guy's got three, uh, you know,~~ (now, possibly on camera) he's got three kids and another one on the uh, on the way—maybe it got to him, I don't know, maybe he just couldn't figure out how he was going to support all these little ones or whatever, you know?*

> *CHARLIE: (beginning v/o) He was selling auto parts, used auto parts. ~~Besides, embezzlement's a white collar crime, he's a blue collar guy—well, not really, he's not working with the auto parts, he's more the manager of the store,~~ driving to work in his, oh, what was it, Tercel, his blue Tercel, shirt and tie and all the while I guess he's thinking nobody above him would miss that thirty thou.*

Depending on what your story is and where you're going with it, each of these edits might work. The first gets to the root of why Sanders did it, at least in Charlie's opinion—arrogance. The second explores a more sympathetic reason behind the crime. And the third paints a picture and gives some specific information about Sanders and his job. If you already have Sanders's wife describing him staying up late at night panicked by bills, you might not want to use version #2. If in fact he was not at all arrogant, just blindly panicked, you might not use #1. And if you find out that he drove a used BMW, you can't use #3 because it's not accurate. Your talking heads must be fact checked, and errors can't be left in simply because you, the filmmaker, didn't say it. By leaving it in, you are saying it. Note that a significant exception is when the falsehood is part of the story, as was the case with the "eyewitnesses" rounded up by law enforcement personnel in *The Thin Blue Line*.

Another problem to watch out for when condensing interview material (or any sync material, which includes footage of people talking to others on camera) is that out of context, something may honestly seem to mean one thing, but those who were on the shoot know that it meant something else. This is why it's important that someone connected with the original shooting be involved in the edit, or at least given a chance to sign off on it. Usually, the director and/or producer maintain this oversight, but cost cutting has led some venues to farm out bits of production and effectively separate the editing and packaging of a documentary from the shooting of it. When that happens, all editorial decisions are made by people with no direct connection to those filmed, which can be risky. (For the same reason, a writer or consultant who begins work on a film late in the process of editing should refer back to original transcripts and unedited footage.)

Throughout the editing process, and perhaps especially when collapsing interviews, filmmakers need to be careful to maintain accuracy. Something as simple as taking a sentence from late in the interview and putting it at the beginning might make sense for the overall film argument, but if it distorts the meaning of the specific interview, you can't do it. "You've always got to try to know when to back away from that stuff," says filmmaker Sam Pollard (Chapter 23), "not to manipulate it to such a degree that it's like a lie."

CHAPTER 6

Creative Approach

Give any group of filmmakers the same general *subject*—even the same general *story*—and you'll still end up with films that are very different in style, tone, point of view, focus, and more. These differences describe the *approach*: how a story is presented on screen. Is it a half-hour special or a 10-hour series? Is the tone humorous? What production elements are used, such as live shooting, recreations, a narrator, time-lapse photography, or animation? Is the program produced quickly and inexpensively, or does it take a more considered approach to both content and the craft of storytelling?

Even within a subset of films, such as high-end features intended for theatrical release, the range of approaches is considerable. Consider, for example, the numerous, award-winning theatrical documentaries that explore the U.S. involvement in Iraq and Afghanistan since 2001. These include *Iraq for Sale* (Robert Greenwald), *Standard Operating Procedure* (Errol Morris), *Control Room* (Jehane Noujaim), *Taxi to the Dark Side* (Alex Gibney), *Why We Fight* (Eugene Jarecki), *The Way We Get By* (Aron Gaudet), and *The War Tapes* (Deborah Scranton).

Even when films have a similar focus (such as the Gibney and Morris films, which both look at the issue of detainee abuse), their approach may be completely different. Morris focuses on the story behind the infamous photographs at Abu Ghraib, while Gibney untangles policies and procedures that led to the death of an innocent taxi driver at Bagram. For *Control Room*, Jehane Noujaim embedded herself, essentially, inside the Al Jazeera satellite network to get a different perspective on the war than that offered by U.S. networks. For *The War Tapes*, Deborah Scranton "virtually embedded" herself in Iraq by putting cameras in the hands of National Guardsmen headed there and staying in touch through e-mails and instant messages. Jarecki and Greenwald both set out to look at the military-industrial complex and the dangers of war profiteering, but Greenwald's film is rapid-paced and filled with data that lacks context, resulting in an

DOI: 10.1016/B978-0-240-81241-0.00006-X

argument that is more emotional than substantive; Jarecki's, on the other hand, is more considered and balanced. And so on.

SGT Zack Bazzi on a radio in a Humvee, in *The War Tapes*. Photo credit: SenArt Films/Scranton/Lacy Films.

WHEN TO THINK ABOUT APPROACH

It's helpful to begin thinking about your approach almost as soon as you come up with a subject or story that interests you. If you've become passionately interested in an 18th-century battle, for example, you'll need to think about how to visualize a story that occurred before the invention of photography. (Peter Watkins's *Culloden*, for example, used the style of a 1950s black-and-white television documentary to recreate and report on the 1746 Battle of Culloden.) If you want to film residents of a local group home, it's important to know what it is about the residents that interests you: following them on a week-long trip to Jerusalem is very different than filming them at home, over the course of a year, as neighbors seek their eviction. Your approach will evolve as your knowledge of the material increases and you have a better sense of what's practical, but it's good to start off with some ideas.

One way to begin the process is to screen many films and talk with your collaborators about which elements you like or don't like, and which might best serve the project at hand. Do you want to create an intimate portrait or a stylized whodunit? A historical film that uses archival footage, or one that uses recreations (or both)? Watching several films by the same filmmaker can also help you to get a sense of how style and approach change depending on the project. Conversely, you'll notice how some filmmakers bring a fairly established style to subjects chosen, in part, because they are suited to that style.

Approach involves the essence of the film itself. Suppose, for example, that you're drawn to the issue of abused, abandoned, and stray pets and what happens to them in shelters. You might decide to:

- Create a journalistic piece on animal welfare that uses experts and news-style footage to explore controversial issues such as unethical breeding, the culture of "fight dogs," and the issue of euthanasia;
- Create a vérité portrait of one shelter and its staff for whom these issues are part of a day-to-day struggle, as Cynthia Wade and Heidi Reinberg did in the feature-length documentary, *Shelter Dogs*;
- Script and narrate a film that involves a family reenacting their search in local shelters for a dog to bring into their home, and then film the process by which experts can rebuild trust and calm aggression in dogs that have been abused; or
- Put yourself in the picture, with the "train" being your search in local shelters for the perfect dog, a journey that allows you to take side trips and find out more about how the dogs came to be there, how many are in shelters nationwide, and what fate they face if they aren't adopted. In the end, you either find or don't find the dog of your dreams.

As another example, suppose you know what elements you want to use for a historical film, but not how to use them. You have a collection of diaries, letters, and newspaper clips pertaining to your story, which is set in the past. You might do the following:

- Have actors read this material in voice over as you present archival stills or footage, perhaps complemented with evocative modern-day footage;
- Have actors in period costume embody the authors of this archival material, speaking the words on camera as if in an interview. This approach can be seen in the work of Middlemarch Films, such as their production of *Liberty! The American Revolution*, and, more recently, films about Benjamin Franklin, Alexander Hamilton, and Dolley Madison.
- Have actors perform the words in period documents on camera, but without costumes or makeup. This was the approach taken for the HBO film *Unchained Memories*, in which actors read the words of elderly former slaves, as documented by workers for the Works Progress Administration.

Another example: Who will tell the stories in your film? What will drive the narrative?

- In *Grizzly Man*, the narrative is driven by filmmaker Werner Herzog's quest to understand the life and work of naturalist Timothy Treadwell. In his voice over narration and his appearances on camera, Herzog makes his presence known and at times argues against Treadwell's views about the natural world.

- In *Enron: The Smartest Guys in the Room*, the point of view is omniscient, although it's derived to some extent from the book of the same title by Peter Elkind and Bethany McLean, both of whom are interviewed on camera. The narration, read by actor Peter Coyote, is anonymous and informational. This style is the most "traditional" for television documentaries. But the use of an omniscient narrator in this film makes a lot of sense: A few title cards could never have provided the kind of detail needed for audiences to follow the enormously complex story unfolding on screen. And while the filmmaker might have cast himself as a storyteller, there is no obvious reason to do so, and a number of reasons not to. (For one, the cast of characters is already quite large: three top Enron executives, the Enron traders, various whistle-blowers, and the two journalist/book authors.)

- In Nick Broomfield's *Kurt & Courtney*, a film about the death of rock star Kurt Cobain that paints an unflattering portrait of his widow, Courtney Love, Broomfield (like Herzog) makes himself and his quest to make the film the story of the film. But the style is noticeably different: Broomfield, much like Judith Helfand in *Blue Vinyl* and Michael Moore in *Bowling for Columbine*, is confrontational, in a style somewhat akin to televised investigative journalism.

- In the Academy Award–winning *Born into Brothels*, filmmaker Zana Briski appears on camera and speaks the voice over narration, but she's also playing an active role in the story unfolding on screen, whose outcome she does not know when the filmmaking begins. In other words, the story of the film is not the story about making the film; it's the story of her work with children in Calcutta's red light district and her efforts to open doors to education and opportunity on their behalf.

- *Murderball* is an example of a film that, like many documentaries, is a hybrid of vérité and other filmmaking styles. Although there is no narrator, the film is "narrated" in a few ways, including interviews (seen on screen and heard in voice over) and text on screen (e.g., *For the first time, Joe will face his former U.S.A. teammates.*). The filmmakers follow an ongoing rivalry between quadriplegic rugby teams representing the United States and Canada; they create intimate portraits of key players on the American team and of the American coach of the Canadian team; they combine footage of these top athletes in action with everyday footage—dressing, driving, dating—that rounds out our sense of them as characters; and they contrast these athletes, who have already been through physical and emotional rehabilitation following devastating injury or illness, with a young man for whom the shock of disability is still new, so that we can appreciate the distance the players have come. There is a "no limits" sense to this film's style, including its soundtrack, and that carries through to participants' willingness to share private moments. The filmmakers play no observable role on screen.

- In some of the more popular biography series on television, the focus is less on storytelling and more on a sort of narrated "scrapbook" approach to a celebrity's life, telling the key events in chronological order and building to emotional highs and lows, such as illness, marriage, or scandal. That these films work is less a tribute to storytelling than to the audience's interest in the subject. Like family photos (which generally fascinate the immediate family but no one else), they're of interest mostly because viewers care about the celebrities on screen, not because there's a particularly strong story being told.

The decision to even *tell* stories is one of approach, along with how to tell them. Michael Ambrosino, who created the long-running PBS science series *Nova* in 1973 (which was inspired by the BBC series *Horizon*), says, "We conceived *Nova* as a series that would explore and explain the way the world worked. We would use science as a tool, but we would primarily think of ourselves as journalists looking for the stories of science." The reason for the stories? "It's not possible to make a film about the crab nebula and have you be interested in it or understand it," Ambrosino says. "It *is* possible to tell the story of the dozen or so men and women who are trying to find out what was the core of the crab nebula. And in telling their story of discovery, you had a story that was understandable."

Some films contrive situations that then unfold on screen, becoming observational. For example, Alan Berliner invited a dozen other people named "Alan Berliner" to dinner at his New York City apartment, and included footage of the event in his film, *The Sweetest Sound*. Perhaps you want to include a demonstration of some sort. For a science series called *The Ring of Truth*, I was involved in arranging a sequence in which we drove a yellow rental truck 183 miles due south and charted the path of Antares at the start and end of our journey, in order to do a modern-day version of an ancient measurement of the Earth's circumference. Errol Morris filmed a teacup shattering for *A Brief History of Time*, so that he could play with the notion of it *un*shattering. (Morris also set up and filmed dominoes cascading to use as a recurring motif in *The Fog of War*. This stylized means of visualizing themes and concepts has become increasingly popular; it can be seen, for example, in the casino footage and magic act cut into *Enron*.)

There is an approach to consider for almost every aspect of your filmmaking. Will you interview people alone, together, inside, outside, or informally? Will the interviewer be on camera or off screen? If off screen, will the questions be heard at all by the viewers? Not every detail needs to be considered right up front, but, for example, if you're telling the story of a particular military unit, rather than interview members separately, there might be value in bringing them together and filming their interaction, provided it can be done in a way that feels natural. Nobody wants to see films in which one character interviews another about something they both already know: "Well, Jim, wasn't it a good thing that we invented that breathing apparatus?" "Yes, Pete; without it, many more lives might have been lost."

DOCUMENTARY OR DIATRIBE?

Some people decide to make documentaries because they're passionate about a subject and determined to bring others to their point of view. This can be a great place to start, but only if you can be open-minded as you explore the evidence, and honest as you present it to an audience. If you start out with a conclusion—"I want to show that animal testing is bad"—you're going to create a film that is either an illustrated lecture or a sham trial.

Instead, consider finding a hypothesis within the topic that you are genuinely open to exploring. "I can't imagine a single scenario in which animal testing is justified," for example, opens the door to conversation with a range of people (scientists, patients, animal rights advocates, and others) who may share your point of view, strongly disagree with it, or more likely fall somewhere in between. You don't necessarily need to put all or even most of these people on screen. You just need to do your homework, so that whatever story you tell contains the complexity it demands.

There is a difference between starting with a foregone conclusion and having a strong point of view, either as a filmmaker or within your film. For example, I was among the producers responsible for the multipart PBS series *Eyes on the Prize*, a history of the American civil rights movement. We did not set out to "show" that the movement was necessary and right, although I doubt any of us felt otherwise. Instead, our task was to explore the history and let it reveal itself—especially to younger viewers, who had not experienced it firsthand—through stories. We were continually reminded by the production executives that our ability to do so, effectively and well, lay in our willingness to let the evidence of history speak for itself, including giving a fair platform to those who did not (at the time) believe that the movement was either necessary or right. The resulting series would be far more complex and entertaining, and not coincidentally, it would better reflect the complexity of history.

Fairness

There is also a difference between being *fair* and being *balanced*. Look at Errol Morris's Academy Award–winning *The Fog of War*. The film offers a platform to the uncontested and at times seemingly self-serving views of its subject, former U.S. Secretary of Defense Robert S. McNamara. But that's the *point* of the film: Morris leaves it to the audience to decide whether they want to accept or discredit McNamara's words. This approach is fair because the rules of the film are clear. Had Morris somehow billed the film as a definitive history of American conflict in the 20th century, then obviously other views would have been necessary.

Being fair also means including the information necessary to an honest understanding of your subject and your argument. It does *not* mean including everything, giving everyone's point of view, or even, necessarily, finding an opposing point of view. *The Boys of Baraka* did not offer a menu of other alternative educational programs for at-risk Baltimore youth, nor were there critics arguing against programs like the Baraka School. *Born into Brothels* did not spend screen time telling you how or where Zana Briski learned photography or how she'd chosen the particular cameras the children in Calcutta were using, nor did the filmmakers include voices of people who thought, for example, that Briski shouldn't be interfering in a foreign culture. Even if such concerns exist, filmmaking always involves choices, and those concerns didn't necessarily impact the story being told.

Including the contradictory evidence that you uncover, when it *does* impact your central story or argument, can often strengthen that argument. In part, this is because it demonstrates respect for the audience's intelligence and inspires trust that they're not being manipulated. Look at *Super Size Me*, which is explored in greater detail in Chapter 7. Starting his 30-day diet, director Morgan Spurlock is critical but also somewhat ambivalent about McDonald's and a lawsuit that blames fast food for the obesity of two teenaged girls. He lays out the basic construction of his experiment on camera and brings in three independent doctors to measure the results. (Some critics have argued that the artificiality of this experiment stacks the decks against McDonald's, but I don't agree. Knowing the setup, the audience can and should bring its own skepticism to the table; the experiment is obviously extreme.) Throughout the film, Spurlock also allows interviewees with whom he might be assumed to be sympathetic—doctors, lawyers, school personnel, people on the street—to paint themselves (at times) as mercenary, misinformed, or ignorant. How difficult is it to understand that 64 ounces of soda contains a lot of sugar? Or to look across a lunchroom and notice that the teens you're feeding are eating nothing but high-fat, high-salt junk food? By the film's end, Spurlock has learned and conveyed a great deal of unflattering evidence against the fast-food industry, but his call for change is directed at consumers.

Deception

Film is a medium that we *experience*, both because of the range of senses involved (we see and hear events unfolding with our own eyes and ears) and the kind of storytelling that engages us both emotionally and intellectually. It is powerful and convincing, and if we are not on guard, we may be deceived by films that deliberately (or naively) distort or mislead. This is achieved, for example, by:

- Asking rhetorical and unmotivated questions that lead the viewer in a false direction;
- Presenting facts out of context or in a context designed to mislead. Suppose that I'm trying to convince you that Joe had his wife murdered, and as evidence, I tell you that he paid $25,000 to the killer. That sounds bad, until someone points out that the killer happened to work in a factory that Joe owns, and he earned the money in hourly wages;
- Presenting evidence out of context and/or mashed together in a way that creates a false impression;
- Creating false evidence, such as reports that sound like news reports, or documents that appear to be genuine.

It takes a certain amount of media literacy (and will on the part of the consumer) to tangle this type of film apart from those that are journalistically rigorous but address controversial issues that inherently face opposition. So how do we know, or teach, the difference?

- First, do what you can to determine not only who is making the film but also who is paying for it. For what purpose is the film made? Was it created by teenagers on a home computer? By a special interest or advocacy group? By a political think tank or political action committee? (Don't be fooled by what appear to be neutral or academic names—they're easy to make up.)
- Find out what else the filmmakers have produced. There is diversity in most filmmakers' portfolios, but if someone has made a career out of films that focus on alien abductions and conspiracies, the chances are good that the climate change film they're producing is not going to be scientifically rigorous.
- Look very closely at the film, and especially at what it presents as evidence. If a newspaper looks odd, find out if it is an actual publication. If documents are presented, can you read and confirm the agency issuing the documents; could you find them through independent research? Is the film asking unmotivated and leading questions? One example involves questions that are posed to suggest the validity of a hypothesis that simply can't be proven: "Could it be that these tracks were not made by humans or animals, but by the very aliens Dr. Smith claims to have seen?" Another involves questions that are not derived from evidence presented in the film, but serve to advance the thesis the filmmaker is trying to drive home. "Why were analysts so afraid of considering the alternative?" for example, implies that it's an established fact that analysts *were* afraid of considering the alternative, whether or not that is true.

Inaccuracies can (and do) find their way into even the best-researched films, but you don't want them to be there on purpose.

ARCHIVAL FILMMAKING

Say "archival films" and most people think of Ken Burns and *The Civil War*. Even though this is a great example of archival filmmaking, there are plenty of other films that use archival (or simply stock or third-party) footage and stills. Used specifically, *archival* and *stock* both refer to material available from public or private archives and/or commercial vendors. Used more generally, however, these words (and the term *third-party*) describe any imagery the filmmakers didn't create themselves. Home movies, amateur videos, surveillance tapes, and footage shot for public relations, education, or training, for example, might generally be described as stock footage.

Third-party footage (and sound) shows up in a wide range of documentaries. *Grizzly Man* wouldn't have been possible without the footage created by Timothy Treadwell himself. *Enron* includes pivotal audio recordings of Enron traders manipulating the power grid in California, sound the filmmakers discovered in the archives of a power company in Washington State. Alan Berliner has been collecting others' family photos and home movies for years, the visual history of people whose identities are unknown to him, and he used these eloquently in films such as *Nobody's Business* and *The Sweetest Sound*. The archival imagery in Jay Rosenblatt's *Human Remains* was selected not to tell any particular story, but because the men it captures on screen—including Mao, Hitler, and Stalin, known to history for the atrocities they committed—are seen doing disturbingly ordinary things, such as eating or playing with dogs and children.

How you use the archival material is also important. *The Civil War* used archival imagery (mostly still photographs) to illustrate and advance a powerful and thematically rich narrative. That series has also spawned a wealth of knockoffs. Take two parts archival material, the thinking seems to go, add one part emotional music and a dash of brand-name actors in voice over, and you've got a film. The missing element, too often, is story.

With archival films, the story is often driven by narration, with visuals playing a supporting role. In rare cases, however, where sufficient archival resources exist, the visuals may drive the storytelling. This was the case with two public television histories, *Vietnam: A Television History* (about the Vietnam War) and *Eyes on the Prize* (about the American civil rights movement). Both series covered events for which extensive news footage existed, with stories covered in depth and over a significant period of time. In developing *Eyes on the Prize*, executive producer Henry Hampton and his team decided that rather than present a survey of the civil rights struggle between the 1950s and 1980s, they wanted to feature a selection of stories from within that period and let them unfold as dramas on screen. Editors on *Eyes* often had sufficient archival footage to craft complete scenes that could then be augmented with modern-day interviews (conducted by the *Eyes* producers). Narration occurred only where it was needed to seam together other elements.

Producers of *Vietnam* and *Eyes* also followed rigorous rules for the use of this archival material. An image could not "stand in" for something else, and the rules of chronology and fact-checking applied to footage just as it did to interviews and narration. This meant that if you were telling the story of rioting in Detroit in 1967, you couldn't use a great scene that you knew had been shot on a Thursday if your narrative was still discussing events on Tuesday. Care was also taken with sound effects and the layering of sound onto otherwise silent film footage. "We sent all our silent archival footage to the Imperial War Museum in London, and they matched sound effects," says Kenn Rabin, describing his work as an archivist on *Vietnam*. If the footage showed a particular helicopter or a particular weapon firing, the sound effect would be of that model helicopter or that model weapon. "We were very careful not to add anything that would editorialize," Rabin adds. "For example, we never added a scream or a baby crying," unless you could see that action on screen.

Many historical films and series cover events for which there isn't as significant a visual record. Furthermore, the existence of historical visual material does not mandate its use; producers may decide to tell their stories using other means, such as recreations. But when historical stills and motion picture are used, how important is it that the images represent what they're being used to portray? This is a subject of some debate among filmmakers and historians. Producers of *The Civil War* grappled with this issue in making their series because the photographic record for their story was extremely limited. At a conference in 1993 ("Telling the Story: The Media, The Public, and American History"), Ken Burns presented a clip from *The Civil War* and then said that, with two exceptions, none of the "illustrative pictures" actually depicted what the narrative implied. "There is a street scene taken in the 1850s of a small Connecticut town, which is used to illustrate Horace Greeley's 1864 lament about the bloodshed of the Civil War," Burns offered. "There are Southern quotes over pictures of Northern soldiers. None of the hospitals specifically mentioned are actually shown, particularly Chimborazo in Richmond. . . . The picture of Walt Whitman is, in fact, several years too old, as is the illustration for Dix." Burns added, "There's not one photograph of action or battle during the Civil War, and yet nearly 40 percent of the series takes place while guns are actually going off. What do you do? What are the kind of licenses that you take?"

His question is an interesting one and still not sufficiently explored by filmmakers or the public. In the skilled hands of filmmakers who have the resources and commitment to work with a stellar group of media and academic personnel, the storytelling may override the limited imagery (see Chapter 17 for more discussion of this with filmmaker Ric Burns). But too often, and increasingly, substitutions are made not for historical or storytelling reasons, but because schedules and budgets mandate shortcuts. Not every image needs to be specific to time and place, of course. But if you're using archival stills or motion picture footage as visual evidence of the past, the images you select matter.

Another problem filmmakers encounter is that the cost to use commercial archival images (and prerecorded music, especially popular music) is often extremely high. In some cases, copyrighted music and images may be added by the filmmakers and featured in the soundtrack or on screen. But they can also be hard to avoid, even in the background. If you're filming a character as he's arrested and a radio in a nearby car is blaring the latest hit, you might be asked to pay large fees to use that snippet of song—or present the arrest without its sync soundtrack. At what point are rights issues hampering a filmmaker's freedom to document real life, or to explore the past and use material from the historical record? These are important issues that American University's Center for Social Media, among others, addressed in their November 2005 report, *Documentary Filmmakers' Statement of Best Practices in Fair Use*, available online.

RECREATIONS AND DOCUDRAMA

Many filmmakers use what are known as recreations to suggest the historical past, either to augment a sparse visual record or because the recreations better serve their storytelling (and at times, budgetary) needs. There are many ways to film recreations; it's a good idea to watch a range of styles to decide which works best for your film or determine an innovative new approach. You may choose to shoot partial reenactments—a hand here, legs marching, a wagon wheel. Human figures may be kept in the distance, as silhouettes against a skyline, or people may be filmed close up and asked to convey emotions. Entire scenes might be played out, whether by individuals who specialize in staging actual battles from the past, or by actors hired to perform for the film. You also need to decide what role recreations play in your film; will they be part of your evocation of the past, or will they play a central role in the storytelling? In Errol Morris's *The Thin Blue Line*, the recreations served to underscore the contradictory testimony of unreliable, self-serving witnesses.

Some films use recreations simply to make up for an absence of footage, or to avoid paying the high cost of rights, or because there are executives who believe that audiences would rather see actors portraying Roman guards and hungry Pilgrims and Chinese warriors. These recreations (or reenactments) may be based in part on the historic record: A director may have actors play out a murder scene, for example. But this means that the director is choosing a single version of the event, when other versions may be possible. Was the murderer really that angry? Did the victim actually see him coming? If the recreation involves dialogue and it is not based on any reliable transcript, that dialogue is invented.

Others, like *The Thin Blue Line*, use recreations to enhance the storytelling. In *Taxi to the Dark Side*, Alex Gibney includes a highly stylized scene to depict the interrogation of Mohamed al-Qahtani, with the methods documented in a 65-page log. The scene is included in a sequence that explores the history and science of torture strategies, and forces the audience to confront the bizarre methods applied to al-Qahtani. It's shot in a way that leaves no doubt that it was created by the filmmaker for the purpose of illustration or imagination; there is no mistaking it for actual footage of the interrogation. In *Waltz with Bashir*, the entire film is, by some definitions, recreation—the film is animated. This choice of style brilliantly underscores the nature of this film as memoir, allowing us inside not only the memories but also the dreams and hallucinations of various characters.

CHAPTER 7

Case Studies

If you want to figure out how something is put together—a table, a car, a sweater, a movie—you often have to take it apart, carefully; look at all the pieces, and *understand*, at a profound level, what it's made of, how it's fitted together, and how the component pieces work together as a single unit. That's what this chapter is about, but reading the results of someone else's efforts is only marginally as useful as doing it yourself. Authors in other disciplines do this, through a practice sometimes described as "close reading." They examine craft issues: how an author accomplishes something through dialogue, detail, pacing, the use of specific words, the rhythm of sentences and paragraphs.

Best-selling fiction writer Francine Prose wrote a book about close reading, titled, *Reading Like a Writer: A Guide for People Who Love Books and for Those Who Want to Write Them*. To some extent, this chapter, and in fact much of this book, might be called *Watching Like a Filmmaker: A Guide for People Who Love Documentaries and for Those Who Want to Make Them*. After reading these case studies, I urge you to spend some time—and it can take a while to do this carefully—watching, logging, and analyzing some films of your own choosing. As a bonus, consider this: The skills you develop in doing this well will prove enormously useful as you watch, log, and analyze your own works in progress to get a better sense of where they're working and where they could be made better.

GETTING STARTED

In some cases, a film's website may provide transcripts, which can be helpful, but is not essential, as you set out to study the work. (The PBS series *American Experience* and *Frontline*, for example, both provide transcripts.) Settle down to watch the film using some device that allows you to keep close track of the running time, even as you stop and rewind. You may be screening a DVD or you can screen from an online site, such as Netflix.

DOI: 10.1016/B978-0-240-81241-0.00007-1

Now, clear your schedule for a few hours, at least, to give this task some time and attention. Have a pad of paper and a pen handy, or split your computer screen so that you can see the film and type notes at the same time. Consider watching the film all the way through once, to gauge your general reaction to it. Without thinking too hard about it, which parts worked for you, and which didn't? How would you describe what the film is about? What's it made of? What's the story? What do you remember most? What are the elements of film storytelling—interviews, live action shooting, archival materials, etc.? If you had to describe the film's train, what do you *think* it was, based on this one-time run-through? Do you remember how the film began? Can you guess at where the act structure (if it seemed to follow one) had its breaks, and what drove the push from one act to the next?

Now, settle in for some closer viewing, starting from the beginning and planning to stop and start repeatedly.

- Make note of how long the film is. As a very rough guide, divide the total number of minutes by four. In films that employ three-act dramatic structure (or simply follow its rhythms), it's likely that in many cases—but by no means all—the end of the first quarter will roughly correspond to the end of the first act. The end of the third quarter will roughly correspond to the end of the second act. The end of the fourth quarter, or shortly before it, is the end of your third act, with the remaining film time spent (briefly) on resolution. (It's rarely this simple, but I find that it offers a good benchmark for beginning to map the structure.) Keep those benchmarks in mind as the film plays. As it nears the first quarter of its running time, do you see an act break? If so, does it relate to what you think the train is?

- In the film's open or tease, what are the questions that are set up? How does the filmmaker grab you and say: *This* is why this film is worth the next 20 or 60 or 90 minutes of your time, here's the journey we're going on, and here's why it matters?

- How is the film cast? Who comes on screen, what roles do they play in the story, and how are they different from each other?

- Do you have a sense of sequences, or chapters, that feel satisfying by themselves and also move you forward in the film? Are the sequences different from each other in terms of pacing, emotion, music?

- Every once in a while, pause the film to ask yourself some questions that specifically note your experience of the film as it unfolds. Ask yourself, *Whom or what do I care about at this point, and why? Where do I think the film is going, what do I think it's about?*

- How is exposition being revealed over the course of the film, and to what extent is its timing meeting your questions?
- How is this film handling the underlying chronology of its story? If it began in 2009 and went back to 1968, then returned to 2009, then went to 1973, then 1984, then back to 2009, did that movement back and forth in time feel motivated, and if so, by what?
- How is this film handling informational details that are relevant to the story but not necessarily filmic? (This is pretty much anything that, to a nonexpert, might be difficult to follow or perhaps care about if it weren't connected to a story that provides motivation and curiosity. It could be legal or political intricacies, details about corporate and government bureaucracy, background scientific or technological detail, etc.)

When you're done, take the time to make your notes legible, and then really look at what you've discovered and go back to the basics. What is the film's train? How many scenes are there, and how are they structured? How many people are part of the core cast? What is the arc of the story? If there is an act structure, what is it, and how do the individual act breaks and midpoint relate to that basic train that you identified?

CASE STUDY: *DAUGHTER FROM DANANG*

Daughter from Danang, nominated for an Academy Award in 2003, is roughly 78 minutes in length. As discussed earlier, the film tells the story of Heidi Bub, an Amerasian woman raised in Tennessee who travels to Vietnam to meet the birth mother who gave her up for adoption. Elements of the film include live-action shooting, archival footage and stills (including personal artifacts), and interviews.

Filmmakers Gail Dolgin and Vicente Franco shot in Vietnam for about a week with Bub and did additional shooting in Vietnam after she went home. After they returned to the United States, they conducted a follow-up interview with her. "Everything happened quickly, and we were really just gathering material," Dolgin says. "We came back with the story we had and then started doing research for the backstory of Bub's experience in the U.S., the babylift, and what the mother's experience might be, and it wasn't until after we accumulated all of that and started looking at it that we said, 'Wow, we've got a lot of material here, what do we do with it?'"

At that point, the filmmakers began approaching financiers, who wanted to know how the film would be structured. "They weren't asking for a script," she says, "but they wanted a clear sense of how we were going to tell the story." The filmmakers didn't want to tell a strictly chronological story, one that would begin with Bub's Vietnamese mother giving her up (in 1975) and move forward to the reunion (in 1997). "We were playing with the concept of memory; it's so capricious," Dolgin says. "Heidi's memories of her past with her mother—she says at different times in the film, 'I had such great memories' and 'The memories are so painful, they're all going to heal when I go to Vietnam.'" Because of this, they decided to structure the film around Bub's trip to Vietnam, using moments within the trip to motivate her memories of the past. "Working with that structure allowed us to figure out what story to craft out of this very complicated journey that we had all been on," Dolgin says.

The film took about a year to edit (Kim Roberts edited), and the final version offers an excellent example of three-act dramatic structure as applied to a documentary film. Note, however, that the timings and outline that follow are an analysis done by me, not the filmmakers. Dolgin says that the process of structuring their film was more organic, and that although they tried outlining material on the computer, "ultimately, having an Avid or any of the nonlinear (digital editing) systems, you can do so much of that trial-and-error with the actual material that it just made more sense to work that way."

Act One/Title Sequence

Zeroing the counter (00:00) at the first frame of action, the film begins with text on screen (with music in the background) that sets up basic information: In 1975, the U.S. government launched "Operation Babylift," through which over 2,000 Amerasian children were brought to the United States for adoption. Archival images of the war follow, as a voice over begins in Vietnamese, with English subtitles: "There were so many rumors. I was so frightened. If I didn't send my child away"—we now see the speaker, an older woman— "both she and I would die." Over more archival footage, we hear another speaker, revealed to be a young woman, as she remembers being torn from her family. "How could she do this to me? How could you just give up a child like that?" After some archival shots of airplanes, the title comes up: *Daughter from Danang*. Briefly, in this opening sequence, we've seen the inciting incident (the separation), the protagonist and antagonist (daughter and mother), and a foreshadowing of the conflict that will emerge between them.

After the title and opening credits, the film opens on a beach in Danang, and we learn more about Heidi's mother, who has missed her daughter for 20 years: "Finding her would be like giving birth a second time," she says. We learn that Heidi, too, has always hoped for a reunion, and is now getting ready to go and see her birth mother "face-to-face, for the first time in 22 years." This reunion is the film's train; it is the present-day narrative spine that drives the story forward. Once the train is under way, the filmmakers are free to take motivated detours into the past. Sitting on the airplane, for example—"going home," as she puts it—Heidi Bub tells us that the trip is bringing back memories, adding, "I was born in Danang, in 1968." The filmmakers use this opening to return to the past. We learn more about Bub's birth (her mother says Bub "had no father"), the war, and why her mother decided to send her away. Note that the filmmakers are only telling us what we need to know at this point. Later, for example, we will learn important details about Bub's father.

Bub's mother brought her to the orphanage, telling her she "must never forget" (6:02). This is the first big turning point; it also provides motivation for the filmmakers to explore the historic issues of Operation Babylift and what it meant in terms of U.S. policy. Among the storytellers in this section is Tran Tuog (T. T.) Nhu, identified as a journalist. She and her husband talk about their awareness, even then, that some of these "orphans" had families in Vietnam; through archival footage we see American social workers pressuring Vietnamese mothers to give up their children, a detail that adds complexity to the specific story of Bub and her mother. Nhu is not simply an expert in this story, but someone who plays a role in the reunion of Heidi and her mother.

A little more than 10 minutes into the film, Bub describes meeting her adoptive mother, with whom she moved to Tennessee, assuming an American identity. The sequence culminates with Bub being told, "If anybody asks where you were born, you tell 'em Columbia, South Carolina" (16:27).

But Bub's birth mother has begun searching for her daughter, and, by coincidence, gives a letter to an American who knows T. T. Nhu. Through Nhu, the mother's letter reaches the Holt Adoption Agency. In the meantime, Bub, at the age of 20 or 21, starts looking for her birth mother, and she, too, ends up at Holt. She contacts Nhu, and together they make plans to go to Vietnam for the reunion. This is the end of Act One, roughly a quarter of the way into the film. Note that once the filmmakers get the train under way, they are free to spend the first act on backstory, establishing who the characters are, how they became separated, and what it took to get to the verge of reunion.

Act Two

Act Two begins on the plane, as T. T. Nhu and Heidi Bub head to Vietnam. Bub begins to worry; she's been "101 percent Americanized" and has "no earthly idea" of her family's expectations. In this act, the filmmakers show how out of place Bub is in her native Vietnam; they set up her nervousness about meeting her mother, and her high hopes for what this meeting will mean. "It's going to be so healing for both of us to see each other," Bub says. "It's going to make all of those bad memories go away, and all of those last years not matter anymore."

At around 24:00, Bub and the filmmakers meet Bub's mother and other members of her family in Vietnam. Had this moment come earlier, the audience would not have been as prepared as they are, by this point in the film, to experience it. We are emotionally invested in the reunion because we've gotten to know something about Bub and her mother, and we're curious about the growing number of questions that remain unanswered: Where is Bub's adoptive mother? Who was her father? Are Bub's expectations realistic?

The reunion plays on screen for a while before the filmmakers use another interview statement to again motivate a return to the past. "I always wanted the feeling that someone would love me no matter what," Bub says. "And I never had that with Ann [her adoptive mother]." This time, the filmmakers' exploration of the past drives to a painful revelation: Escalating tension between Bub and her adoptive mother led to a severing of their relationship when Bub was still in college. By presenting this information here, the filmmakers have raised the stakes on the reunion currently under way in Vietnam: Bub has felt rejected by two mothers, so this reunion with the first has added significance. We carry this new information with us as we return to Vietnam, and the visit continues.

Act Two continues in this fashion, balancing the story on screen with events that have led to these moments. We learn more about Bub's husband and two children, and about her birth father, an American soldier. We also see a new complexity in the visit. Bub is getting homesick; she is overwhelmed by the poverty and lack of opportunity she encounters in Vietnam, and is newly appreciative of what her life in the United States has afforded her.

Mai Thi Kim and her daughter, Heidi Bub, in *Daughter from Danang.* Photo courtesy of the filmmakers.

At this point, events themselves raise the stakes on Bub's story, as her Vietnamese family begins asking her for money. T. T. Nhu, serving as cultural interpreter for the viewers as well as for Bub, explains that having a relative overseas can be an important lifeline to those in Vietnam. But Bub says she doesn't want to be anybody's salvation; she came here to be reunited (50:00). Tension continues to build as we realize that Bub and her family each have a very different under-standing of what this visit might lead to. Increasingly critical of her mother and feeling smothered by her family's attention, Bub finally says, "I can't wait to get out of here."

Act Three

The worst is yet to come, which is part of what makes the third act so strong. (Contrary to a common misperception, the stakes should continue to rise in Act Three, until the issue or conflict reaches its most extreme point. Only then, in the last minutes, should there be resolution.) T. T. Nhu has to leave, so a new translator is brought in to help Bub through a lengthy and painful family meeting in which all the misunderstandings come to a head. Bub's brothers ask her to bring their mother to the United States; then they suggest that she assume her "filial responsibility" by sending a monthly stipend. Bub is hurt, then outraged, even refusing to allow her mother to comfort her (63:36). Speaking to the filmmakers, Bub takes a position almost opposite to the one with which she began the journey: "I wish I could have just kept the memories I had—they were so happy. I wish this trip never happened now." She leaves Vietnam, and when the filmmakers visit her at her home in Rhode Island shortly afterward, she's not even sure she wants to write to her mother; "I wouldn't know what to say." Arguably, Act Three ends either when Bub leaves Vietnam (off screen), or here, at around 75:00. Although she's achieved her initial goal, to reunite with her birth mother, Bub has not succeeded in forming a bond with her or "erasing" bad memories. In some ways, the two women seem farther apart than they were before the story began, because their hopes for the reunion are gone.

Resolution

The resolution in this film comes in the form of a brief epilogue, which begins with a caption that reads: *Two Years Later. Bub and her children are seen visiting her adoptive grandmother.* In an interview, Bub summarizes her current feelings about her Vietnamese family. "I guess I have closed the door on them," she says, adding, "but I didn't lock the door. It's closed, but it's not locked." The ending, in part because of this ambiguity, is a satisfying resolution to the story that began the film.

CASE STUDY: *MURDERBALL*

Winner of the Documentary Audience Award and a Special Jury Prize for Editing at the 2005 Sundance Film Festival, *Murderball* is a terrific example of a modern documentary. Underneath an energetic soundtrack and some athletic competition is scientific information about spinal cord injury and an unsentimental look at disability. Like *Daughter from Danang, Murderball* generally follows a three-act dramatic structure. "During the shooting, we discussed fiction films, not docs," said co-director and cinematographer Henry-Alex Rubin, in the film's online publicity material. Citing dramas including *The Great Santini* and *Rocky*, he said, "We tried hard to follow an old screenwriting rule: show, not tell." The film has multiple protagonists and two story lines. The first and most prominent one is the rivalry between U.S. and Canadian teams, embodied by American player

Mark Zupan and Canadian coach Joe Soares, who is also American. The second follows newly injured Keith Cavill as he adapts to life as a paraplegic. The film is about 82 minutes long, and features vérité footage, interviews, and animation.

Act One/Title Sequence

The film fades up on a man in a wheelchair (later identified as Zupan) changing from jeans into workout clothes. There is no music or voice over, just natural sound. A credit interrupts the scene, and then the man removes his t-shirt and begins to wheel himself out of frame. In a series of vignettes intercut with credits, we meet three other men. Two tell stories that mock people's reactions to their wheelchairs: "They say 'It's good to see you out,'" one says, adding, "Where am I supposed to be, in a closet?" A third, with only partial limbs, is seen getting into a van. "What I can do that probably people don't think I can do," he says, "is I can cook, and I can drive." Finally, a garage door opens, and we see the first man (Zupan), sitting in a specialized chair, looking fierce. Beginning voice over, he says (in an interview that continues at a gym), "I've gone up to people, start talking shit and they're like, 'Oh, oh, oh.' I go, 'What, you're not gonna hit a kid in a chair? Fucking hit me. I'll hit you back.'" The musical soundtrack kicks in and soon we see wheelchair rugby players on an indoor court, smashing into each other until a chair tips over and players cheer. The title comes up: *Murderball* (2:55). This opening sequence has effectively introduced some but not all of the film's main characters (by attitude, not by name), and set an irreverent, tough-guy tone for the story to come.

Immediately after the title, two referees introduce quadriplegic rugby, developed in Canada and originally called "murderball." We see players' chairs being fixed up as a man (identified on screen as *Marty/USA pit crew*) talks about the gear involved. Zupan (still not identified) introduces the fact that the majority of players have had neck injuries, which motivates a drawn animation illustrating the location of the injury and the "rods, plates, screws" that are now inside. A match dissolve from the animation back to the scar on a player's neck transitions to the next important piece of exposition, one that anticipates confusion in at least some of the audience: "The biggest misconception," Zupan says, "is, 'You're quadriplegic? I thought they couldn't move their arms.' I'm like, 'No. I have impairment in all four limbs.'" Footage of a player on the court again dissolves to animation, as we learn that the higher up the neck is broken, the less mobility a person has. Quad rugby players are given a point value ranging from 0.5 to 3.5 points, "based on what you can move." (The four men we've met so far pose, and over their heads we see their numbers: 3.0, 2.0, 2.0, 1.0.) With four men on court at one time, the total ability can't exceed eight points.

Having set up some basics of the game (exposition), the film-makers then begin to introduce the players (more exposition), both through conversations with them and through brief onscreen words: *ANDY/Car crash/10 years ago, HOGSETT/Fist fight/13 years ago, ZUPAN/Car accident/11 years ago.* We get to know a bit more about Zupan through an interview with his parents (4:12), rugby colleagues, and some friends in a bar. Zupan is also shown clowning around with some guys in what seems to be a hotel lobby. When one falls backward, chair and all, an older, able-bodied couple standing nearby asks the cinematographer, "Do you want us to call security?" It doesn't matter when or where the scene was actually filmed. Its placement here is interesting because not only does it show Zupan acting playfully aggressive, it also shows that, as Andy remarked early on, "people say the dumbest things."

Six minutes into the film, the filmmakers get the first story, the U.S./Canada competition, under way. Through text on screen, shots of banners ("Wheelchair Rugby World Championship 2002 Gothenburg"), and shots of players, we learn that 12 countries are competing and that the United States has been on top for the last 10 years. Those are the stakes they need to defend.

Seven and a half minutes in, we finally meet Zupan's nemesis: *JOE/Polio/43 years ago.* Through visits to his home, where we see his trophy wall and hear from his nephew and wife, and through news reports, we learn that Joe Soares was arguably the best quad rugby player in the world. But he got older and was cut from the U.S. team, so he began to coach Canada (9:08) and took American plays with him. "U.S.A., learn a new way," he says without sympathy. Zupan responds in an interview, "If Joe was on the side of the road, on fire, I wouldn't piss on him to put it out."

At 9:55, Canada and the United States have both made the finals at Gothenburg. The filmmakers raise the stakes with text on screen: *For the first time, Joe will face his former U.S.A. teammates.* In other words, this isn't just any game. But, having increased the tension in the main story, the filmmakers now take another detour, to let Bob Lujano (now identified, but by name only—we still don't know how he lost his limbs) give more details about the rules of the game, with animation to help. The placement of this information is excellent;

these details would have been lost earlier, when there were too many other pieces of information vying for the audience's attention. Now, we know that it's team against team, man against man, and we're willing to take a moment to learn more about how this battle will be played. In addition, because these rules are fresh, the audience is prepared to just *watch* as the U.S./Canada match gets under way. It's fast and furious, with cameras mounted on and under chairs, and the editing (by Geoffrey Richman, with co-editor Conor O'Neill) is first rate. Through a combination of text on screen, wall clocks, and cutaways to coaches and the crowd, the filmmakers condense this close-scoring game. At 13:21 in the film, Canada wins. The Americans taunt Soares: "How's it feel to betray your country, man?" He appears to be hurt, revealing a new layer of complexity.

The film is far from over—we're only halfway through the first act—so the filmmakers need to quickly move the story and the stakes forward. Note that they did not set up a single goal early on and instead have been revealing a rivalry between the United States and Canada, and to a lesser extent between Zupan and Soares. Immediately after the win at Gothenburg, the filmmakers tell us (through text on screen) that the United States and Canada will face each other again at the 2004 Paralympics in Athens, Greece—so the rivalry has a new focus, a new goal. This motivates a cut to Birmingham, Alabama, to the Team USA training camp.

We learn that out of 500 players, coaches will select 12 to compete in Greece, although this is not a big source of tension in the storytelling. The camp seems to be more of an opportunity to get to know the guys better and, more importantly, explore the issue of disability. At 17:41, Andy introduces this shift: "Everybody who gets hurt thinks they're gonna walk again," he says, explaining that this hindered his ability to move forward. Hogsett talks about how hard the first two years after a spinal cord injury are. In quick shots, the filmmakers begin introducing a new location, a rehab hospital, and at 18:30, we're behind a young man with a large scar on the back of his neck; we then meet him, staring impassively at the strangeness of the hospital around him: he's *KEITH/Motocross accident/4 months ago*.

The casting of Keith is critical to this film. Without him, you see extraordinary athletes who are past the most difficult part of their journeys from injury to altered ability. "He anchors the film— narratively and emotionally—because without him, you don't see what [the other] guys lost," says Dana Adam Shapiro, the film's co-director and producer, in publicity material. At the Kessler Institute for Rehabilitation (an exterior shot of the building establishes this), the effort Keith makes to perform basic tasks—get himself into a sitting position, for example, or undo the Velcro straps on his shoes—shows, better than any words could tell, how far the rugby players have come. And interestingly, it's Keith's story, and not the rivalry, that structures the acts in this film. At the end of Act One, we see Keith at the start of his rehab journey.

Act Two

The second act (and this is my analysis, not necessarily one the filmmakers would agree with) begins as the film shifts back to its primary story line, the rivalry. Just under 21 minutes into the film, we see coach Joe Soares at his home in Florida. He's having a Super Bowl party, and for the first time, we meet his son, Robert. The relationship between this hard-driving, athletic man and his studious, musical son adds complexity to Soares's story, both personal and professional. Grilling steak, for example, he seems distant and demanding of his son; soon after, he tells his Canadian team that "in a year and a half, we've become the strongest family I've ever had, strongest second family. You guys are my boys." This sequence with Soares, his family, and friends lasts almost five minutes.

At about 26:30, the filmmakers turn their attention to Soares's rival, Mark Zupan. We see Mark in personal moments as well, swimming and hanging out with his girlfriend, which opens the door to the issue of sexuality after injury. The filmmakers cut to the hospital, where Keith asks a doctor if he'll be able to be sexually active again. His doctor, who's able-bodied, introduces an instructional video (hosted by the doctor); the filmmakers cut to their own footage of a disabled man talking about sex, followed by Andy Cohn and then Scott Hogsett, who articulates the question: "Can you do it?" For these guys, the answer is yes, and they (and Keith's doctor, in his video) offer details. This sequence also lasts a bit more than five minutes, and then the film returns to its train: the U.S./Canada rivalry (31:40), with text on screen: *Team Canada Training/8 months before Paralympics.* (Note the effective use of signposts in this film, occasional reminders about who, what, and especially when as the film returns to its train, to reground the audience in the story line.)

We don't stay at the training camp for long. A brief scene with Soares and his team as he tells them his theories on discipline motivates a cut to an interview with Soares, in which he reveals that his father was a police officer who used to hit Joe "really hard." His own treatment of his son, he argues, is "not even close." In the following scenes, we see Soares at an anniversary dinner with his wife, meet his sisters, and learn that a doctor is concerned about his stress. After a quick montage of his volatile coaching, text on screen announces that Soares has suffered a heart attack (35:00). He looks small and vulnerable in the hospital bed, but the filmmakers don't milk this moment unnecessarily; by 36:25, we know that he's out of the woods, and the scene shifts to Mark Zupan's 10-year high school reunion.

Note how long it's been since we've seen athletic competition—it's the train, but not the point, of this film. As structured by the filmmakers, the sequence about the reunion is really about Mark's accident (11 years ago) and the estrangement between him and the friend (Christopher Igoe) who was driving the night he was hurt. We hear from Zupan's classmates, parents, and Igoe. The sequence motivates an interview with Zupan, in which he remembers how hard it was for him when he first came out of rehab—which in turn allows for a smooth transition, at 42:15, to Keith, who is at the same point in his own recovery. After 10 months in rehab, he's going home. This is the film's midpoint (and note again that it's pegged to Keith's journey). The scene begins on a note of achievement but ends in frustration, as Keith realizes, he says, "what was once normal will never be the same" (46:12).

Cut to a banner (with the Olympic logo) setting a new scene: "USA Lakeshore Foundation Official U.S. Training Site." With six months to go, Team USA is making its final cuts. The selection is edited for some tension, but all of our characters make the 2004 team. A visit from some Camp Fire Girls gives the filmmakers an opportunity to tell us more about Bob Lujano. (Note that you don't have to introduce everybody right away, nor do you have to introduce everyone in the same way. Several recent documentaries, including *Spellbound* and *Born into Brothels*, also feature multiple protagonists. It's worth watching them to see how they handle introductions and the balance of story lines to avoid repetition.)

At 51:40, coach Joe Soares is out of the hospital. On a visit to his childhood home in Rhode Island, he tells us a bit more about himself. Born in Portugal, he describes himself as living the American dream— in other words, this adds even more texture to the fact that he's coaching Canada. But as we see him play with children at the house, we have a sense, confirmed by his sisters, that Joe is different since his illness; we see him bragging to childhood neighbors about his son. (A transformation like this, while important to good drama, can never be manufactured or overstated. If it happened, great; if it didn't, you aren't free to even suggest that it did.) Here, the change in Soares begs the question, does he still have the edge he needs to lead Canada to victory?

At 54:39, the scene shifts to Vancouver, Canada. Text onscreen continues the countdown: *3 months before the Paralympics/The US is facing Canada to determine the #1 seed*. This is the first we've heard about this interim match (we were aiming for the Paralympics), and it's a bit of a risk. You never want to have three versions of the same basic event played out in three locations: The stakes, style, and purpose of each should be different, and they need to build in importance. (For example, you wouldn't want to start with an Olympic match and then follow with two exhibition games merely to see the rivalry in action.) Here, the filmmakers skillfully use the match to remind us of the stakes and players and get us back into the game (we haven't seen actual competition for more than 40 minutes). First, they intercut a tense-looking Joe Soares and an equally tense-looking Mark Zupan, the core rivals. Then, they use a somewhat different editing style from the previous game, and this time, the U.S. team wins, so the power position as they go to the Paralympics has changed. In sync footage right after the game, Zupan reminds us that the Paralympics are still two and a half months away—this was just a warm-up. Finally, and a key reason to keep this sequence, about 58:00 into the film, the coach of the losing team, Soares, gets a call from his son, asking him to hurry home to attend a viola concert. The scene that follows visualizes, more than the conversations in Providence, that Soares has changed.

In the next sequence, about an hour into the film, the "A" and "B" stories come together elegantly, as Keith attends a demonstration about quad rugby led by Mark Zupan. Act Two ends as Keith tries out a specialized rugby chair (63:44).

Act Three

The filmmakers take advantage of a "US Olympic media summit" (a press conference) to add a bit more exposition about the Athens Paralympics, and Mark Zupan describes his visit to the rehab hospital and how "fulfilling" it was to see the response of one patient (Keith). The inclusion of this moment is nice, in part because it tells us that the sequencing of these events is real. From there, the film moves on to: *1 Month to Paralympics* (65:14). The filmmakers add some breathing room here, as the team plays a practical joke; they also erase what may be a confusion in the minds of some audience members about the distinction between Paralympics and Special Olympics. Then, with a week to go, we learn that Zupan has invited Christopher Igoe to see him play, pulling together strands of an earlier sequence. There's a bit of an interlude as Igoe makes his way to Athens (in part, perhaps, to give the audience a chance to remember who Igoe is and why this meeting matters).

At 71:00, it's "game on" at the Paralympics, the culmination of the film. The editing of this game is unusual: We see people scoring, the crowd cheering, and the score changing, but the natural sound has been replaced by a fairly quiet musical score. The effect is powerful; the music swells and natural sound returns gradually at the end, as tension mounts and Canada pulls ahead. At 75:00, it's over. Now, the filmmakers focus on the Americans as they are comforted by family and friends, followed by a bittersweet conclusion: Team USA didn't win the gold (they came in third), but neither did Team Canada. They came in second, after New Zealand.

Epilogue

We see the team traveling together, and hear quick voice overs of the guys' stories about how they became injured. Only gradually do we understand that they're addressing wounded Iraq war veterans at Walter Reed Army Hospital in Virginia. After a cheer, "USA Rugby!" (79:00), the film goes to black. Interrupting the end credits, the film-makers then show a series of "Where are they now?" vignettes of all the major characters, including Keith and young Robert.

CASE STUDY: *SUPER SIZE ME*

Nominated for an Academy Award in 2004, and one of the top-grossing documentaries of all time, *Super Size Me* is a science documentary that's funny, thought-provoking, and fast-moving. The film is probably best described as an essay, but there is a protagonist (filmmaker Morgan Spurlock, who won the Best Director award for the film at the 2004 Sundance Film Festival) and goal (to see what happens if he eats only at McDonald's for 30 days). He faces opposition not from an individual, but from the effect this diet may have on his health and well-being, which may force him to end the experiment early. From first frame of action to closing credits, the film is about 95 minutes long.

Act One/Title Sequence

The first frame of action shows children singing, invoking the names of fast-food restaurants. Following a text-on-screen quote from McDonald's founder Ray Kroc, a professional-sounding narrator (who turns out to be Morgan Spurlock) tells us that "everything's bigger in America." In a fast-paced, fact-filled setup, he defines the problem: "Nearly 100 million Americans are today either overweight or obese. That's more than 60 percent of all U.S. adults." He suggests a cause: When he was growing up, his mother cooked dinner every single day. Now, he says, families eat out all the time, and pay for it with their wallets and waistlines. He notes a cost: "Obesity is now second only to smoking as a major cause of preventable death in America."

Spurlock then introduces the lawsuit that inspired the film: "In 2002, a few Americans got fed up with being overweight, and did what we do best: They sued the bastards." Using a magazine cover and animation, he lays out the basics of the case, which was filed on behalf of two teenaged girls: a 14-year-old, who was 4'10" and weighed 170 pounds, and a 19-year-old, 5'6", who weighed 270 pounds. Sounding astounded, Spurlock says the "unthinkable" was happening: People were suing McDonald's "for selling them food that most of us know isn't good for you to begin with." But he offers evidence to show that we eat it anyway, millions of us worldwide. Returning to the lawsuit, he highlights a statement by the judge, which he paraphrases: "If lawyers for the teens could show that McDonald's intends for people to eat its food for every meal of every day, and that doing so would be unreasonably dangerous, they may be able to state a claim." Spurlock seizes on this challenge but also notes a question, a theme that will inform the entire film: "Where does personal responsibility stop, and corporate responsibility begin?"

At 3:48, we see him for the first time on camera as he sets out the design of his experiment: "What would happen if I ate nothing but McDonald's for 30 days straight? Would I suddenly be on the fast track to becoming an obese American? Would it be unreasonably dangerous? Let's find out. I'm ready. Super size me" (4:04). This 30-day regimen is the film's train, the narrative framework that, once under way, allows the filmmaker to take detours into issues that, on their own, would probably not have packed audiences into theaters worldwide. (It's also likely that a similar 30-day experiment in the hands of someone bent on "proving" the evils of fast food and McDonald's wouldn't have been as effective. Spurlock is credible as he takes us on this journey because he seems genuinely open to gray areas, as described later.)

After the opening titles, Spurlock spends time establishing a base-line for his own physical condition. Three doctors, a nutritionist, and a physiologist confirm that his health is excellent. They aren't thrilled by the experiment, but don't expect anything too terrible to happen in just 30 days. Roughly 10.5 minutes into the show, Spurlock adds a further wrinkle: Because more than 60 percent of Americans get no form of exercise, neither will he, other than routine walking. (This prompts a sidetrack about walking in general, walking in Manhattan, and how many McDonald's there are to walk by in Manhattan.)

At 12:03, we're back to the train as we meet Spurlock's girlfriend Alex, a vegan chef. She prepares *The Last Supper*, one of a handful of chapters named on screen over original artwork. A little over a minute later, the experiment gets under way, as *Day 1* is identified with text on screen. Spurlock orders an Egg McMuffin and eats. (Here, as in several places throughout the film, he breaks up blocks of narration with musical interludes. These breaks are important; they add humor and breathing room, giving the audience a chance to process informa-tion.) In a quick scene, we see Spurlock writing down what he's eaten. We need to see this record keeping at least once, because it's part of the experiment: The log provides the data the nutritionist uses to calculate his food intake. We then see Spurlock on the street, asking people about fast food. Interspersed at various points throughout the film, these inter-views also add humor and alter the rhythm of the film, while providing a range of what are presumably "typical" responses.

Around 15 minutes into the film, standing in line at McDonald's, Spurlock expands on the experiment's rules (he talks on camera to his film crew, and also in scripted voice over). After getting this additional exposition out of the way, he bites happily into a Big Mac (gray area—he enjoys some fast food). At 15:47, another piece of artwork, another title: *Sue the Bastards*. We see Spurlock again on the street conducting interviews, this time about the lawsuit. All three of the people consulted think the lawsuit is ridiculous—which at this point in the film may also be the attitude of the audience. Spurlock interviews John F. Banzhaf, a law professor "spearheading the attacks against the food industry" and advising the suit's lawyers. Spurlock gives Banzhaf's work a bit of credibility (to counter the man-on-the-street responses) by noting that people thought Banzhaf was crazy when he was going after tobacco companies, too—"until he won." Banzhaf adds an important detail about why McDonald's is a particular target: The company markets to children.

Another man worried about the children, Spurlock says, is Samuel Hirsch, lawyer for the two girls in the lawsuit. But look at the gray area in this interview. Over a shot of Hirsch, we hear Spurlock ask, "Why are you suing the fast-food establishment?" The shot continues, unedited, as Hirsch considers, smiling. "You mean motives besides monetary re—, compensation? You mean you want to hear a noble cause? Is that it?" The lawyer seems to consider a bit longer, and then Spurlock cuts away from him, and that's the end of Hirsch's time on screen. It's funny, but perhaps more importantly, this willingness to paint various sides of the argument in less-than-flattering light is part of what makes this film engaging. Audiences have to stay on their toes and be willing to not only see complexity, but figure out for themselves what they think.

David Satcher, former U.S. Surgeon General, introduces the problem of "super sizing," which allows Spurlock (and other experts) to explore the issue of portion size. In other words, Spurlock is building an argument and letting one idea flow to the next. Finally, it's just under 21 minutes into the film and we've been away from the "train" for about five minutes, so Spurlock drives up to a McDonald's, and text on screen announces *Day 2*.

Act Two

In the second act, the experiment really gets under way. Fortunately for Spurlock, he was asked on Day 2 if he wanted to super size, and by the rules he's established, he must say yes. (There might be a temptation, in a film like this, to let Day 4 stand in for Day 2, if it provided an opportunity like this. You can't. You don't need to give each day equal weight—some days are barely mentioned—and you don't need to show all meals each day. But the time line of these meals needs to be factual, as does the time line of Spurlock's health.) Watch how Spurlock condenses time in this scene: He starts out laughing, kissing his double quarter-pounder, calling it "a little bit of heaven." The image fades to black, and white lettering comes up: *5 minutes later*. Fade up: He's still eating. (The visual point, underscored by the card and by the screen time given to the scene, is that this is a lot of food, and for Spurlock, it's an effort to eat it.) Fade to black again: *10 minutes later*. Spurlock says that a "Mcstomach ache" is kicking in. To black, then: *15 minutes later*. He's leaning back in his seat. To black, then: *22 minutes later*. He's *still* forcing the food down. A cut, and we see him leaning out the window and vomiting. A meal that lasted at least 45 minutes has been effectively compressed into a sequence that's 2.5 minutes long.

At about 23:18, we see a new illustrated chapter title, *The Toxic Environment*. Experts and Spurlock introduce the problem of "constant access to cheap, fat-laden foods" and soda vending machines, compounded by a reliance on cars. After a brief health concern on Day 3, he cuts to Day 4 and takes a detour to further compare obesity and tobacco use, including marketing to children. This sequence is followed by another "meadow" (or musical interlude), in which we see Spurlock enjoying a McDonald's play area.

At 28:21, a new chapter, *The Impact*, explores the lifelong health implications, including liver failure, of obesity in children. At 30:38, Spurlock cuts to a 16-year-old, Caitlin, cooking in a fast-food restaurant. Here again, his ambivalence seems to leave some of the work to the audience. In an interview, Caitlin talks about how hard it is for overweight teenagers like herself because they see the pictures of the "thin, pretty, popular girls" and think "aren't I supposed to look like that?" As she's talking, Spurlock fills the screen with images of thin young women, until he's covered Caitlin's face. Just before she disappears, she concludes: "It's not realistic, it's not a realistic way to live."

Is Spurlock implying that Caitlin is letting herself off the hook too easily? This may be the case, because the scene is immediately followed (32:07) by a sequence in which motivational speaker Jared Fogle, who lost 245 pounds on a Subway diet, gives a talk at what appears to be a school. An overweight eighth grader argues, like Caitlin, that weight loss isn't realistic: "I can't afford to like, go there [to Subway] every single day and buy a sandwich like two times a day, and that's what he's talking about."

As if to offer a contrast, the film then cuts to a sequence about a man who did take personal responsibility for his health: Baskin-Robbins heir John Robbins. According to headlines on screen, he walked away from a fortune because ice cream is so unhealthy.

Robbins, a health advocate, runs through a litany of health-related problems involving not only his own family but also one of the founders of Ben & Jerry's ice cream. (This sequence, like the many shots in the film of fast-food companies other than McDonald's, helps expand the argument beyond one company to look at larger issues of food choice and health.)

At 35:09, it's Day 5 of the experiment. We see Spurlock ordering food but don't see the meal; instead, we follow Spurlock into his nutritionist's office, where we learn that he's eating about 5000 calories a day, twice what his body requires, and has already gained nine pounds. Hitting the streets again (about 37:00), he asks a range of people about fast food (they like it) and exercise (only some do it).

About a minute later, Day 6 finds him in Los Angeles, ordering chicken McNuggets. This meal motivates another look at the lawsuit and McDonald's statements about processed foods; Spurlock augments this with a cartoon about the creation of McNuggets, which he says the judge in the case called "a McFrankenstein creation."

Back to the experiment, Day 7, and Spurlock isn't feeling well. Within 30 seconds, it's Day 8, and he's disgusted by the fish sandwich he's unwrapping. Less than 30 seconds later, it's Day 9, and he's eating a double quarter-pounder with cheese and feeling "really depressed." He's begun to notice not only physical but also emotional changes. The following sequence, with an extreme "Big Mac" enthusiast, doesn't add to the argument but is quirky and entertaining.

With that, we return (at 43:00) to an idea raised earlier, the notion of advertising to children. An expert offers data on the amount of advertising aimed at kids, and how ineffective parental messages are when countered with this. Another expert points out that most children know the word "McDonald's," so Spurlock—in a scene set up for the purposes of the film—tests this out, asking a group of first graders to identify pictures of George Washington, Jesus Christ, Wendy (from the restaurant), and Ronald McDonald. He also uses a cartoon to demonstrate how much money the biggest companies spend on direct media advertising worldwide.

At 46:34, we're back to the experiment: *Day 10*. But once again, we leave the experiment quickly. By 47:02, a new illustrated chapter title appears, *Nutrition*. This sequence doesn't actually look at nutrition, but at how difficult it is to get nutrition information in stores. As John Banzhaf argues, how can people exercise personal responsibility if they don't have the information on which to base it? At 49:20 (roughly midway through the film), we're back to the experiment, as Spurlock gets his first blood test. He now weighs 203 pounds, 17 more than when he started.

Around 50:30, a new chapter: *It's for kids*. Spurlock takes the essay even wider, with narration: "The one place where the impact of our fast-food world has become more and more evident is in our nation's schools." This is a long sequence in which he visits three schools in three different states. In Illinois, the lunch staff and a representative for Sodexo School Services (a private company that services school districts nationwide) seem willing to believe that students make smart food choices, even though Spurlock shows evidence that they don't. In West Virginia, Spurlock visits a school served by the U.S. federal school lunch program. Here, students eat reheated, reconstituted packaged foods, with a single meal sometimes exceeding 1,000 calories. Finally, Spurlock goes to a school in Wisconsin, where a company called Natural Ovens provides food for students with "truancy and behavioral problems." The food here is not fried or canned, and the school has no candy or soda machines. (It's almost a shock at this point to see fresh vegetables and fruit and realize how brightly colored they are.) The behavioral improvements in the students here, administrators tell us, are significant. And, Spurlock notes, the program "costs about the same as any other school lunch program. So my question is, why isn't everyone doing this?" (56:02).

Over footage of the Wisconsin lunch line, we hear a phone interview in which the founder of the Natural Ovens Bakery is allowed to answer Spurlock's question: "There's an awful lot of resistance from the junk food companies that make huge profits off of schools at the present time," he says. To me, this is a misstep in an otherwise powerful sequence. Unlike several of the experts who've been interviewed, this man's ability to speak for or about "the junk food companies" hasn't been established. (I'm not saying it doesn't exist, just that it's not set here.) The information he conveys may be fact checked and 100 percent accurate, but to me, a better way to convey it might be through facts, such as how much money per year the fast-food companies actually make in the nation's public schools. (That companies resist being removed from schools is a point made, effectively, in the following scene, when the Honorable Marlene Canter talks about the Los Angeles Unified School District's ban on soda machines.)

At about 57:08—roughly 60 percent of the way through the film—Spurlock returns to the experiment. It's Day 13, and he's in Texas, home to five of the top 15 "fattest" cities in America. Day 14 finds him in the #1 city, Houston, but he quickly goes into a new sidetrack: a visit with the Grocery Manufacturers of America, a lobbying firm based in Washington, D.C. The group's vice president says the issue is education, teaching good nutrition, and teaching physical education. It's a bit of a thin transition, but this leads Spurlock to explore the fact that only one state, Illinois, requires physical education for grades K–12. Returning to the Illinois school, he films an exceptional program, and then for contrast, shows an elementary school in Massachusetts where physical education involves running around a gym once a week for 45 minutes. At 61:00, Spurlock suggests a reason for the issue, the "No Child Left Behind" education reforms of President George W. Bush, which an expert says explains cuts to "phys ed, nutrition, health." This, in turn, motivates Spurlock to ask students in a ninth-grade health class what a calorie is. They struggle to answer—but so do six out of six adults interviewed on the street.

At 63:02, it's Day 16, "still in Texas," but in about 20 seconds, it's Day 17 and he's back in New York. We learn that the experiment is getting to Spurlock; his girlfriend says he's exhausted and their sex life is suffering. The following day, the doctor says his blood pressure and cholesterol are up and his liver "is sick." He's advised to stop. We see him talking on the phone to his mother; they're both concerned. She's afraid the damage he's doing will be irreversible, but Spurlock reassures her that "they" think things should get back on track once it's done. Act Two ends here.

Act Three

At 69:26, Act Three (and again, as with the other films, this is my analysis, not the filmmaker's) begins with a look at the "drug effect" of food, with input from a new expert, a cartoon about McDonald's use of the terms "heavy user" and "super heavy user," and an informal phone survey. Spurlock learns that his nutritionist's company is closing, and uses this as an opportunity to explore the amount spent on diet products and weight loss programs compared to the amount spent on health and fitness. This motivates a transition to an extreme weight loss option, gastric bypass surgery, filmed in Houston (74:03). Note that this sequence may have been filmed anywhere during this production; its placement here in the film makes sense, because things are reaching their extremes.

The stakes for Spurlock have also continued to rise, which helps to make this third act strong. At 77:33, in New York, Spurlock wakes at 2:00 a.m.; he's having heart palpitations and difficulty breathing. "I want to finish," he says, "but don't want anything real bad to happen, either." More visits to doctors result not only in specific warnings about what symptoms should send him immediately to an emergency room, but also the realization that these results are well beyond anything the doctors anticipated. But at 81:20, Spurlock is back at it: Day 22. In short order, he sets out to answer a new question that he's posed: "How much influence on government legislators does the food industry have?" He visits again with the Grocery Manufacturers of America, before finally (at 83:26) attempting to contact McDonald's directly.

These efforts, ultimately unsuccessful, will punctuate the rest of the film. Spurlock gets through Days 25, 26, and 27 quickly. At Day 29, he's having a hard time getting up stairs. By Day 30, his girlfriend has a detox diet all planned out. First, there's *The Last McSupper*—a party at McDonald's with many of the people we've seen throughout the film. Then it's off to a final medical weigh-in. Fifteen calls later, still no response from McDonald's.

Resolution

At 89:34, Spurlock is nearing the end of his film, and essay. He returns again to the court case. "After six months of deliberation, Judge Robert Sweet dismissed the lawsuit against McDonald's," he says. "The big reason—the two girls failed to show that eating McDonald's food was what caused their injuries." Spurlock counters by tallying up the injuries he's suffered in just 30 days. He challenges the fast-food companies: "Why not do away with your super size options?" But he also challenges the audience to change, warning: "Over time you may find yourself getting as sick as I did. And you may wind up here (we see an emergency room) or here (a cemetery). I guess the big question is, who do you want to see go first—you or them?"

Epilogue

Before the credits, the filmmakers do a quick wrap-up, including information about how long it took Spurlock to get back to his original weight and regain his health, and the fact that six weeks after the film screened at Sundance, McDonald's eliminated its super size option. At 96:23, the credits roll.

PART II

Working with Story

CHAPTER 8

Research

Good documentary storytelling, with few exceptions, depends on good research. This is true for what may seem like a surprising range of filmmaking styles. In an interview with Jason Silverman, filmmaker Alan Berliner describes working on his personal documentary, *The Sweetest Sound*. "I began where I always begin, with a tremendous amount of research, with a passion to understand the total landscape of whatever subject I'm entering." Susan Froemke and assistants at Maysles Films, the noted vérité company, spent about six months researching poverty and looking for potential stories in several states, including Wisconsin, Maine, Iowa, and Missouri, before they settled on the stories and characters of *Lalee's Kin*, filmed in the Mississippi Delta. Filmmaker Jay Rosenblatt creates unusual documentary stories from bits of old films and "found footage." In press material submitted to the San Francisco Jewish Film Festival, Rosenblatt says that it took about eight months to do the research for *Human Remains*, a half-hour film about the banality of evil. In it, he presents black-and-white footage of five of the 20th century's most notorious leaders—Hitler, Mussolini, Stalin, Franco, and Mao—over reminiscences voiced by actors but scripted from actual quotes and/or factual biographical information.

Do all documentaries require research? No. Liane Brandon's memorable and deceptively simple film, *Betty Tells Her Story*, while evoking powerful themes, began when the filmmaker heard something of interest in a colleague's story and asked her to tell it on camera. Not everything has to involve experts and advisors and location scouting. But many films, if not most, do involve research to some degree. With that in mind, here are a few suggestions.

ASK QUESTIONS, DIG DEEPER

Whether you're looking for a story or finding the best way to tell it, a good film is one that surprises, challenges, and, often, informs. This means that the information going into that film needs to be surprising. All too often, documentaries just repeat information that everybody knows. The easiest way out of that trap is to stop and challenge yourself. "Energy equals mass"—what does that mean? The Apollo 13 space mission—why was it named Apollo? "Everybody knows" that Rosa Parks was the tired seamstress who didn't feel like giving up her seat on that bus in Montgomery in 1955, right? It's a nice story, this downtrodden woman who has reached her breaking point. What if you found out that she was an active member of the Montgomery chapter of the NAACP, a group fighting for civil rights? Suddenly she's not so much a victim of oppression as an activist who sees an opportunity to fight it. You're telling better history and bringing fresh details to an old story that everybody thought they knew.

DO YOUR OWN RESEARCH

One of the problems of faster and cheaper filmmaking is that original and up-to-date research is often beyond the scope of a project's resources and budget. It's much easier for producers to rely on a few articles or books rather than explore what's new in a field, who's doing innovative work, or what a more diverse group of storytellers might add to the audience's understanding of a familiar topic. The same tired experts are approached time and again to speak about the same subjects, in part because the producers have already seen them on TV and know both what they look like and how well they speak on camera. But why tell the same story again, particularly if you could explore a newer or more complex angle?

DON'T BE AFRAID TO ASK BASIC QUESTIONS

Although you should gain a thorough grounding in your subject, you can't possibly, in a few days or even a few months, become an expert. Don't, in the interest of appearing "professional" to your advisors or experts, fake an understanding that you don't have. If you're confused, speak up. Your expertise is in knowing how to communicate a complex subject to a general audience.

DO GENUINE RESEARCH

A historian I know received an e-mail from a company seeking what they said, at first, were "his thoughts" on the U.S. temperance movement. In the next sentence, they made it clear that what they actually wanted was his help plugging a hole: they envisioned a story of a 20th century trial involving a married woman abused (or murdered) by an addicted husband, a case that influenced activism, and were hoping he could identify such a case.

There are two problems with this. First, if their research (and historical advisors) were telling them that such cases played a significant role in the discussion of temperance, why hadn't multiple cases and names already been suggested? Second, although they seem to have identified the general area of this particular historian's expertise, they clearly had not read his work or they would have known that had he been asked, his expertise would have led him to suggest a different approach.

Although the resulting project may have worked out fine, what might these researchers have done differently? More homework could have led them to a clearer and more specific understanding of the issue they were trying to illustrate and to specific stories and scholars. Alternatively, if they were still fishing for stories that would illuminate the temperance movement, they might have contacted a range of scholars, whose work they had familiarized themselves with beforehand, and asked for help in identifying stories that the experts believed best represented the history, rather than vice versa.

WHEN DO YOU RESEARCH?

The amount of research you do, and when you do it, varies from project to project and depends, to some degree, on your chosen topic, your approach, and your strategies for fundraising. Some public funding sources, as well as some private foundations, require that your grant application include evidence that your film project is built on solid and current academic research. Projects that are funded "in house"—by public or commercial broadcasters directly—may be less rigorous in their up-front requirements, but producers will still need to do at least some research in order to effectively pitch their ideas and make their programs. Research generally is ongoing through the development of outlines and shooting treatments, and continues as needed until the film is complete. A flurry of fact checking often occurs in the last weeks of editing.

ADVISORS

The input of academic and nonacademic advisors can be crucial to a project. These people offer their insight and experience behind the scenes; some of them may also be asked to appear on camera as experts, if that fits the program's style. On any film that's intended to be the least bit authoritative about a subject, advisors can help tremendously by getting you up to date quickly on current research in the field and directing you to people, places, and content to be explored. They can help you to see how your film might contribute to the public's understanding of a subject and who, beyond a general audience, might be able to use the film (in classrooms, for example). It's important to seek out advisors and experts who represent a variety of viewpoints.

Good advisors—and they are often extraordinary—understand that they are advisors and you are a filmmaker, and that their job is to push for content and inclusion and yours is to try to tell the strongest and most accurate story you can. What a film can do best is excite viewers about new and complex material; it's up to library and web resources to satisfy the hunger you may create for extensive detail. You won't and can't do everything the advisors want, but if you have truly considered their expertise and understood their concerns, chances are you've found a way to address the concerns that also serves your purposes as a filmmaker.

When do you approach advisors? As filmmaker Jon Else summarizes, "You read the ten most important and widely respected books about the subject, and then you read the two fringe books at either end of the subject. Then you do the basic primary research; you figure out who are the ten important living people and what are the ten important available documents or pieces of stock footage. And then you call the experts." As mentioned, some of the people you'll be contacting as advisors may turn out to be people you want to interview. It's good to avoid confusing these roles initially, because what you need at first is background help. If someone asks whether or not he or she will also be asked to appear on camera, you can honestly say that it's too soon to tell.

Advisors' Meetings

On some larger-budget documentaries and documentary series, funds are raised to enable at least one in-person gathering of filmmakers, advisors, and invited experts. These meetings might take place as the funding proposal is taking shape, and maybe again as production gets under way. With *Eyes on the Prize* and other major series produced by Blackside, Inc., production began with what was called "school." Production teams, researchers, and others joined invited scholars and other experts in panel discussions that continued over a period of several days and were invaluable in setting out the work ahead. If you can afford them, in-person meetings spark an exchange of information and ideas that isn't possible when the filmmaker speaks individually to this advisor, then that one. Valuable information can result from their interaction not only with you but also with each other.

TELEPHONE RESEARCH

Some of your research, whether searching for people, fact checking, or just trying to get a handle on a subject, will inevitably be done by phone. Be as prepared as possible for these calls. Knowing as much as you can (within time limitations) about the person you're calling and his or her area of expertise will sharpen your questions and make the call more productive. Be careful to use a professional tone and respectful manner.

FACT CHECKING

Fact checking means being able to footnote your film. Any fact stated, whether by you as the filmmaker or by someone on camera, needs to be verified through not one but at least two credible sources. Even authors of highly reputable sources make mistakes, and bias and inaccuracy can be found in both primary and secondary sources. Have you ever been at a rally that seemed packed, only to hear it described on the news as a "small number" of protesters? Or sat through an afternoon in which the majority of speeches were credible and coherent, and the radio coverage featured a couple of speakers who clearly had no grasp of the issues? The reports may be factual, but they don't accurately represent the events.

Another example: A writer profiling an anti-poverty activist might point out that the activist grew up in a town that, she notes, is "a wealthy suburb of New York." The fact may be true, but 50 years earlier, the town was still quite rural and had not yet become a bedroom community for the city. And even then, the activist was from a family living well below the means of other townspeople. Yet the reporter has used factual material to create a false impression, whether intentionally or not, that the activist grew up wealthy—an impression that has a direct bearing on the portrayal of the activist's current work.

Suppose you're making a film about this activist's life. Because you're using multiple sources, you should realize that the picture being painted by this reporter doesn't match others that you're seeing. You should also be doing your own reality checks: Is it really possible that the description of a town in 2006 also applies to the same town in 1956? Furthermore, even if the majority of townspeople were mega-wealthy back in 1956, do you know that the activist's family was also wealthy?

Suppose you've pushed ahead without considering this, however, and have become attached to the idea of using the man's childhood in a wealthy town as a motivating factor behind his work on behalf of the poor. Maybe you've even talked to experts (unfamiliar with the activist in question) who explain that growing up wealthy can have this type of impact on children. So the information and motivation end up in your narration, whether they are accurate or not. This is a situation in which having advisors on your side can be invaluable. A biographer of the activist, if given a chance to read a treatment of your film or screen a rough cut, will respond to narration such as "He grew up in the wealthy community of X," and cry foul. This doesn't mean that you have to remove the fact; it does mean that you will need to put it into a more accurate context.

THE TELLING DETAIL

Facts are not just something to ensure accuracy; they can also be the lifeblood of the "telling detail" that will enrich and inform your story-telling. Facts can be a source of humor and irony; they can illuminate character, heighten tension, and underscore themes. As you do your research, begin to keep track of the details and tidbits that strike your fancy, as well as the ones that answer questions essential to your storytelling. Make sure to note the source material as completely as possible, so that (1) you don't have to track it down again and (2) you could track it down again if necessary.

STATISTICS AND OTHER FORMS OF DATA

Statistics must be scrutinized and put into context. It's always a good idea, when you come across a statistic you want to use, to trace it back to its source. Suppose you find an article in a magazine that says that a certain percentage of teenagers smoked in the 1950s. Somewhere in the article you may be able to find the source of that information, such as "according to the National Institutes of Health." You should always question someone else's interpretation of raw data, meaning that if you really want to use this statistic, you need to go back to the NIH data yourself. Maybe it was x percent of all 17-year-olds who smoked, or maybe it was x percent of 17- and 18-year-olds in

Philadelphia. People often misinterpret statistical information, whether intentionally or not. The interpretation may satisfy your story, but don't trust it until you can get it corroborated by someone with sufficient expertise.

CHRONOLOGIES

Chronologies are one of most helpful and least utilized tools of storytelling. A good and careful chronology, started early on, can be of tremendous benefit throughout preproduction, production, and editing. It can help you "see" your story in new and unexpected ways, and can open up possibilities for nonlinear structure while providing a key tool for ensuring that you remain honest. The level of detail and the range of information needed depend on the type of film you're creating. For a historical film, a good side-by-side chart that looks at your specific story in the context of its times can be handy. They can be created as a table in Microsoft Word, with a header row that repeats on each page. Take care as you input information; if you develop a habit of accuracy when you first note names, places, dates, statistics, and such, fact checking will be that much less onerous. It can also be useful to annotate your notes, even roughly: "Bennett p. 44," for example, so that you can return to the original source either to get more details or to check facts.

Chronology Format

There is no one format for a chronology. We did several for the six-hour PBS series *I'll Make Me A World: A Century of African-American Arts* (the series is out of distribution). The initial chronology was a grid, containing 10 columns, left to right (one for each decade of the century), and then six rows down (one each for literature, theater and dance, music, the visual arts, African-American political history, and American social and cultural events). As the series developed, separate chronologies were made for each story. The lives and vaudeville careers of Bert Williams and George Walker, for example, were charted by month and year alongside events in American history.

Most film chronologies will be much simpler. Table 8.1 is a sample of format, a research chronology (one page out of about 10) that puts the Miss America competition into context, at roughly a page per decade. With more complex stories, it can be a good idea to give each year its own row (block) in the table. (The example is of an in-house chronology, not anything shared with outside readers.)

Table 8.1 This research chronology (which covered a century) puts the Miss America competition into general context, at roughly a page per decade.

	U.S. History	Women's History	Social/Cultural	Miss America (story)
1920-1929	Jan 1920: 18th Amendment (Prohibition) goes into effect	August 1920: The 19th Amendment is ratified (women's suffrage) 1920: National League of Women Voters is organized 1921: American Birth Control League is incorporated, with Margaret Sanger as president	Post-war spirit and disaffection characterizes era that will be known as "The Jazz Age" "Bobbed" hair on women, symbol of political and social emancipation, popularized by film stars—Garbo's "page boy," Veronica Lake's "peek-a-boo," Louise Brooks' "Prince Valiant" 1922: Emily Post's "Etiquette" column debuts 1923-28: The era of blueswomen—Ma Rainey, Bessie Smith, etc. 1926: The "permanent wave" (hair care) is invented by Antonio Buzzacchino	September 1920: The Fall Frolic—which will become the Miss America pageant—is conceived by businessmen in Atlantic City. No beauty contest, but a Rolling Chair Parade and a masked ball. September 1921: The 2nd Fall Frolic includes 2-day "Inter-city Beauty Contest" in Atlantic City—16-year-old Margaret Gorman wins 1921: A number of children participate in the Bather's Revue—including a professional child actor named Milton Berle 1923-24: Women's and religious groups protest the pageant 1927: The powerful Federation of Women's Clubs demands that the Pageant cease
	1929: Stock market crash and subsequent economic Depression	1928: Amelia Earhart is first woman to fly across the Atlantic	1927: Al Jolson stars in first "talkie," *The Jazz Singer*	1928: Largest pageant to date, 80 contestants, but ongoing protest over scandal, loose morals, etc. Atlantic City Hotel owners withdraw support, and the Pageant is discontinued.

Why Bother with Chronologies?

A chronology helps you to keep track of a story, look for a structure within it, and find some telling details that might enrich it and prevent mistakes. A song commonly believed to have been popular among soldiers during the First World War may, in fact, have been written in 1919—which a good chronology will show you is after the war's end. By listing the major events in your story in chronological sequence, you can sometimes see possible points of attack—places to begin the story—that come late in the chronology but are the strongest focus for your film. From there, you can think about what else the audience needs to know from the overall timeline and when they need to know it. *Daughter from Danang*, analyzed in Chapter 7, is an excellent example of a film that carefully weaves in material from its underlying timeline over the course of the entire film.

The other thing a chronology gives you is an opportunity to see the bigger picture, allowing for you to offer your audience points of reference ("the Berlin Wall would come down the following month"), and a sense of the world surrounding your characters. For example, the first Miss America competition was held in 1921. Prior to that, according to scholars, beauty contests were held in the pages of America's newspapers. But this wasn't possible until the photographic halftone was invented—in 1880, I find out when I look that up. What else was happening between then and 1921? A flood of immigration and migration was increasing the ethnic and racial diversity in America's growing cities, sparking differences of opinion about what constituted an American feminine "ideal." Add to all of this the emergence of mass media and a consumer culture, and the stage is set for the first official Miss America pageant in 1921. But note the date. A year earlier, in 1920, American women had finally won the right to vote. Is this relevant? The truthful answer is, "Not necessarily." So while you can note the interesting dateline, you can't draw any conclusions about it. Cause and effect is a slippery slope; the fact that two things happen in succession does not mean there is a link. This is an excellent example of the kind of question you explore with your advisors, which is just what the production team of *Miss America: A Documentary Film* did.

Chronologies for Present-Day Films

Not every film is historical, but even a personal or diary film may benefit from some sorting through of what happened when. For example, Table 8.2 is a fictional chronology in progress. Imagine a film in which a young man, Jeff, decides to document himself as he tracks down and perhaps reunites with a father he last saw when he was 11. By the time this chronology is coming together, Jeff has begun to piece together some of his father's life after he left.

Note that not every detail is tracked, just a few key ones. Putting them in order on the page can be revealing: Lucy left Jeff's dad the same day his mom got remarried, for example. It can suggest ways of establishing time and the passage of time, from Windows 2.0 through Windows 98, 2000, XP, Vista, for example. Most importantly,

Table 8.2 Personal film, vérité

Date	Jeff/Filmmaker (Son)	Father	Other
1987		Father and mother meet—first date, mother thinks it was *Moonstruck*; dad thinks it was *The Untouchables*	Microsoft releases Windows 2.0 Prozac is put on the market
January 2, 2000	11 years old; parents sit him down, dad is moving out		Y2K proved to be a lot of nothing
May 2002	Unaware that his father is remarrying	Marries Lucy	
		Began driving trucks long distance	
Fall 2003	Mom remarries	Lucy leaves Dad	
March 2005		Begins treatment for kidney disorder; loses his job soon after	
Sept 2006	Starts college		
Sept 2009	Decides to make a film about his father for a senior project		
November 2009	Tracks his father down	Father needs a kidney	

it can help suggest nonlinear ways to tell this story. In this case, having located his dad and begun to communicate with him, Jeff decides he wants to see if he might be a match to donate a kidney. That suggests a stronger potential train than simply, "I want to reunite." Will Jeff's father accept his son's offer of a kidney? Will the son even be a match? Will his mother or someone else in Jeff's life talk him out of it? In answering those questions, the film might go back through the course of these relationships, and the chronology will be a useful reference.

Take the Time to Do It Right

I've seen many filmmakers, including student filmmakers, try to rush through (or avoid) making chronologies. They'll jot down a few details that are so vague they're essentially useless: *19th century, Ellis Island opens, thousands of immigrants*. This is usually a big mistake: If you don't take a little bit of time to be more specific in the beginning, it's almost certain that you'll be taking a *lot* of time to figure it out later, going back to those same sources over and over and adding to your chronology in bits and pieces. But beyond fact checking, the chronology is an important tool for finding, shaping, and sharing your *story* from preproduction through post.

PRINT AND INTERNET RESEARCH

The Internet puts unbelievable amounts of information into your hands almost too easily. But the Internet augments libraries; it doesn't replace them. Keyword and subject searches on the Internet are limited by your ability to come up with the right combination of magic words, spelled correctly (or the way they were misspelled by someone else), to find what you want, and if you don't come up with those words, you'll wind up empty-handed. Perhaps even more frustrating, web searches can land you at sites that are not sufficiently credible. Wikipedia, for example, may be a place to start—*Waterloo, what was that referring to?*—but never stop there. Go to more credible sources, from authors and publications you have reason to trust. Get articles and books. Read them.

If you can get books online, too, why go to a library? One reason is that libraries and bookstores are great places to browse for ideas. For example, you know you're interested in making a film about music, a musician, something along those lines. But what? Wander through the stacks of a library or bookstore and see what catches your eye. Another obvious argument for library research is that you can find material, such as magazines and newspapers, that predates the limits of most web databases. Also, even when you *can* find these articles online, what you lose is the ability to see them as their original readers would have, in the context of everything else on the page and in the issue. Along with your article on early 20th-century performer Bert Williams, for example, you might see the price of shoes and mattresses at the time, read reviews of whatever entertainment form was being offered, or look at how a mainstream paper discussed issues such as race, immigration, and gender. Best of all, not only do you get a better sense of the period, you also get ideas for visual storytelling and narrative context.

Be Organized

You'll need to keep track of the material you're citing. If you are taking notes on published text, make it clear that you are copying someone else's work. Note the source, put it in quotes, make the font purple—do whatever it takes to make sure that six months from now, you don't go back to this material, think that you've written it yourself, and incorporate it into narration, only to find out that you've lifted entire sentences from someone else. This is also true of material you cut and paste from the web. It is never permissible to use it without attribution.

A few other tips:

- *Note the source.* An article that's not referenced is a waste of everyone's time. On the copy of the document itself, note the bibliographic data. It's also useful to note which library you found it in and even write down the call numbers, or the specific page as well as the website. Otherwise, you may very well find yourself having to look it up again.
- *Be sure you've got the whole article.* If you're photocopying an article or printing one off a microfilm reader or the web, check to be sure that the entire piece is actually readable. If it's not, try again or take out a pen and fill in the gaps. If an article is footnoted, photocopy the footnotes. It's very frustrating to the producer to find great material in the body of an article and not be able to use it without sending the researcher back to the library.
- *Don't editorialize.* Do not, as the researcher, take it upon yourself to annotate the research you're compiling, unless you're asked to do so. Pages and pages of underlined and highlighted material can be annoying. Steer the production team to relevant passages, but let them form their own impressions.

- *Be organized.* For example, do your best to keep bibliographies in alphabetical order. It will save you from looking up the same source more than once, by mistake, as you go down the list.
- *Make use of file folders,* so that you don't end up with a massive stack of paper that you will find yourself sorting through over and over.
- *Give computer files relevant names.* There is nothing as useless as "France.docx," even if you think you'll remember what it is. "Francelocationscout1-17-10.docx" will tell you, six months from now, what's in that file and that it's different from "Franceinterviewlist5-17-10."
- *Neatness counts.* Research is a lot of work, and everybody gets tired. But you must take the time to write legibly, or at least to copy any scribbled notes within a short period of time, before you can no longer decipher them. And if you're keeping a research notebook, keep it current.
- A plea on behalf of libraries: *Never mark up a library-owned book or magazine.* Never bend the pages down, and if you must spread the book face down to photocopy or scan, do it gently.
- *Go a step further.* If you're doing research for someone else, get the material you've been asked to retrieve and then look through it. As mentioned, photocopy footnotes if they accompany an article. But then scan those footnotes to see if there's additional material you could pick up while you're at the library. Does a more current book by the same author come to your attention? If there's a reference to a primary source within a secondary source, can you dig up the original material? Come back with these unexpected treasures and you will make the producers very happy. Primary sources, especially, tend to be wonderful finds that take more than Internet digging.
- Again, *be cautious about what you find on the Internet.* An impressive-looking history of the civil rights movement might turn out to have been produced by Mr. Crabtree's eighth-grade social studies class; a scientific-looking report on the "myths" of global warming might have been produced both by and for the oil industry. Read everything with a skeptical eye.

VISUAL ARCHIVES

Depending on the story you're telling, you may or may not need to explore what's available in terms of stills or motion picture footage in the archives, whether public (such as the National Archives in

Washington, D.C.) or private (such as Corbis). Extensive visual research is most commonly done once a film is at least partially funded; the visual research becomes part of the overall research and development leading to a shooting treatment, and often continues as needed (or begins again) as the story takes further shape in the editing room. As with the print material, organization of your visual research is everything. Also remember that archival stills and motion picture footage, no less than print materials, should be subject to scrutiny in terms of its veracity and completeness. As discussed in *Archival Storytelling* (Focal Press, 2008), written with Kenn Rabin, even newsreels, which are often used by filmmakers as historical evidence, were at times heavily propagandized and even staged.

MOVING FORWARD

Research of every sort will be ongoing for most of the film's production, but there comes a point when the filmmaker has to decide that it's time to move to the next stage—production. This can be difficult: There's always more to learn, and the more you learn, the more you want everybody to know what you've found out. As Alan Berliner said about working on *The Sweetest Sound* (in the same interview that started this chapter), "one of the hardest things I had to do was let go of everything I knew—to accept that the film could not possibly contain everything I had learned about names."

CHAPTER 9

Planning

You've decided on the film you want to make and done enough research to determine that it seems feasible. Now what? This chapter is very broadly called "planning" to describe a range of activities that includes pitching, outlining, and casting your film.

PITCHING

A pitch is the core statement of your film's story, stated clearly and succinctly. It confirms to you and to others that you not only have a good subject, but you have a good *story*, one that you can tell in a way that will interest others. You'll be pitching your film, revising your pitch, and pitching it some more from the moment the idea begins to take shape until you are out in the world with a finished product that needs promotion. The good news is that pitching is the single best way to determine that you actually *have* a clear, coherent story as discussed in Part I of this book. If you can't pitch your story concisely—on an elevator, say, after you've discovered yourself by sheer luck riding up four floors with the head of acquisitions or a well-connected celebrity—then chances are you're still muddling through, and will be spending time and money on film elements you don't need.

On Pitching Well

An ineffective pitch introduces the topic but not the story, as in "This is a film about the ethics of genetic testing and about how some people face hard choices." An effective pitch does both. "This is a film about genetic testing in which we follow an actress making the tough decision about whether to be tested for the disease that claimed her mother's life." The pitch works because it compels the listener to ask follow-up questions: What will she do if the test is positive? Will she let you follow her through the process? What if she doesn't take the test?

Here's another example of a weak pitch: "Four years ago, Vietnam veteran Martin Robinson decided he would scale the heights of Mount Whatsit at the age of 53—with one leg. He succeeded, and in the years since has inspired veterans' groups across America." Where's the story here? There *was* a story (his efforts four years ago), but unless you have some plan for telling it now, what's holding the film together? A 57-year-old man standing before various groups of veterans. Not coincidentally, the problem with this pitch is that it does not suggest a train (Chapter 4). Your train is the skeleton on which you hang your story and by which you hook and hold your viewer; your pitch articulates the train.

In other words: *If you don't have a grasp on your train, you probably don't have a grasp on your story—and you won't be able to make an effective pitch.*

With that in mind, a better version of this pitch might be: "Four years ago, Vietnam veteran Martin Robinson became the first amputee to scale the heights of Mount Whatsit. Now, he's going back—and bringing two Gulf War veterans, amputees who thought their best athletic days were behind them, along with him." Not a bad pitch, especially if you can follow it up with good access to these people and some information about your own skills as both a filmmaker and a mountaineer (to show you'll be capable of following them up the mountain). In many cases, the pitch will be even stronger if you show a tape that introduces your main characters, allowing people to see that they're appealing and will work on camera.

On some projects, producers pitch their stories at in-house development meetings, not once but several times as the film or series take shape. We did this during the planning of *I'll Make Me a World: A Century of African-American Arts*. Rather than survey 100 years' worth of dance, theatre, visual art, literature, and more, the six-hour historical series presented two or three stories per hour arranged in a way that moved forward chronologically. The century's thematic arc, revealed in our research, helped producers and project advisors decide which stories best exemplified a particular era, and we were careful to include a range of artists and art forms. Here is the pitch for one of three stories, called "Nobody" for the purpose of quick reference (but not titled on screen), that was to be included in the series' second hour, *Without Fear or Shame*.

- "Nobody" follows Bert Williams as he teams up with George Walker and they head for the Broadway stage, where they face an audience whose expectations of black entertainment have been shaped by 60 years of minstrel traditions. Can they reject these stereotypes and still attract a mainstream audience? This story continues through the death of George Walker; we end with Bert Williams performing with the Ziegfeld Follies alongside stars including W. C. Fields, Will Rogers, and Fannie Brice—and yet, as actor Ben Vereen portrays him on stage, still facing intense racial hostility.

The other two stories in this hour were related thematically. One was about Edward "Kid" Ory and the rise of New Orleans jazz, and the other was about early filmmaker Oscar Micheaux. *Each* story was conceived of as having its own three-act dramatic structure. In the editing room, they were interrupted at key moments and interwoven with the other two stories, but in the planning stage, they were kept apart in order to see more clearly that they each had a beginning, middle, end, and arc. It's worth noting that this was also possible because these were historical stories to be built of archival material and interviews, so the structure could be significantly anticipated in advance. Our research, including pre-interviews, had made it clear which emotional moments we were driving toward, so that we knew which elements of an overall biography or history we wanted to emphasize and where we were driving to at the end of each act.

Pitching Out Loud

Giving a pitch in person can be tough. Too often, filmmakers load their pitches with parentheticals about all the information you need to know or they should have mentioned: "Okay, well, it's about this guy (well, okay, 20 years ago he won this amazing award for scientific research, but then he thinks someone ripped off the idea), so this guy was trying to (actually someone *did* rip him off, which sort of explains his motivation but I'm going to get into that later in the film), so this guy has been working to..." And so on.

The point is, if you're pitching out loud, it's a good idea to practice beforehand.

OUTLINES

Most filmmakers go well beyond the pitch when planning their films. The next step is an outline which, like the pitch, will continue to be revised and honed over the course of production and editing. The outline is where you begin to flesh out your train, by anticipating and sketching out the *sequences* and the order in which they'll appear. If you're using an act structure, that also will be made apparent.

An outline helps you to see, on paper, the film as you imagine it. It should begin where you think the beginning of the film is, as opposed to the beginning of the underlying chronological story. It drives to key moments that you anticipate driving to, and it ends where you anticipate the film ending up. It should begin to introduce the characters, scenes, and materials you will need to tell your story.

Why Write an Outline?

An outline is both a planning tool and a diagnostic tool. It lets you see clearly what job a sequence is doing in your overall story and what storytelling role your characters are playing. If there is redundancy or if there is a gap, you will be better able to see it in a couple of pages of outline than you will be watching footage on screen. Be careful to focus the outline as you intend (at least at the stage you're currently at) to focus the final film. Is the story about the expedition leader or about the group of retirees on the expedition? The parents waging a legal battle against commercialism in the public schools or the budget-starved principal actively courting soft-drink contracts?

As mentioned, the key difference between an outline and either a pitch or simply a research report is that an outline breaks your film into sequences. This helps you to clarify, in story terms, *why* you're filming one event and not another, one individual and not another. Trust me: It's worth doing. And frankly, you'll revise this outline (or sometimes, to get a fresh eye, start over entirely) before, during, and after you shoot and well into editing. As a consultant, one of the first things I do if I get involved with a film while it's being edited is to write an outline of the film that exists, which I use to help the filmmakers figure out what's working and what's not. This works because an outline can clearly show that two or more sequences are doing the same job, or that the first act runs for half the film, or that the film doesn't really get going until halfway through the second act.

What's a Sequence?

As introduced in Chapter 4, a sequence in a documentary is akin to a chapter in a book. It should feel somewhat complete by itself, but push you to the next sequence. It should add something unique to the story and the film: *this* is the sequence about force drift, *this* is the sequence about shock of capture, *this* is the sequence about "changing the rules" in the wake of 9/11. This doesn't mean that "force drift" doesn't get mentioned elsewhere, but that in one sequence in particular it will be introduced and looked at more closely. The single best way to understand sequences is to watch a number of documentaries and look closely at how filmmakers break stories into distinct chapters. Sometimes these chapters are labeled ("A Few Bad Apples" and "Shock of Capture" are examples of sequence titles in Alex Gibney's *Taxi to the Dark Side*, also discussed in Chapter 20). More often, you can identify a sequence through visual and storytelling cues. The film fades to black and then up again, for example; a sequence about getting the children to the beach and back gives way to a sequence about something completely different. A shift in rhythm, a change in music, the loud emergence of sync sound all may signal the start of a new chapter.

You anticipate and sketch out a sequence during the planning of your film by thinking like a storyteller. You "watch" the film in your head and listen to your gut. What *feels* like it should come next? What questions do you want to have answered now, rather than at some other time? What window does a character suggest opening up?

Those of you who are editors or have worked closely with editors will recognize that this is also how you often work when assembling and shaping footage into an edited film. In fact, outlines come in handy throughout the editing process. It's much easier to play with alternative structures on paper to quickly see them than it is to recut the whole film, only to find the flaw in the logic of the restructure. Does the fact that it seems to work on paper guarantee that it will work in the editing room? Unfortunately—and emphatically—no. But often, the exercise helps you and your team move toward a solution that *will* work.

Thinking about Sequences

What follows is a *very simple* version of an outline for a straightforward documentary, entirely invented for the purpose of illustration. The film is called *Zach Gets a Baby Sister*. The outline presumes that because this event was very contained, shooting was under way (the vérité scenes were filmed, but not many of the interviews) before the outline was written.

> Synopsis: This short video (estimated 20 minutes) follows a five-year-old boy, up to now an only child, as his entire world changes: His parents bring home a baby sister. The film views this event through the lens of childhood, and is intended to be both humorous and thought-provoking.
>
> ### Sequence 1: Tease
> (My first sequence will be the tease, which I anticipate being no more than 1-2 minutes long and highlighting maybe five funny and thematic moments from the film without *giving the best stuff away*.)

FILM TITLE: *Zach Gets a Baby Sister*

Sequence 2: "On the way"

Zach's getting ready to go to the hospital to meet his newborn sister. He's almost five; so far he's an only child; he's not sure what to expect, according to his parents, but they've been preparing him as well as they can. He climbs into his grandmother's car (this footage was shot) and sets out for the hospital. In the car, he talks about the baby and the fact that classmates of his have older and younger sisters and brothers. We use this discussion to cut to his classroom, a couple of weeks earlier, and the scene with the teacher talking about brothers and sisters; also, words of advice from some of Zach's classmates, vox pops. We return to the car just as it pulls into the hospital parking lot.

Storytellers (other than Zach): His teacher, his classmates, possibly his grandmother

Sequence 3: "Hello, baby"

We are in the hospital room with Zach's parents as they wait for Zach and his grandmother to make their way to the room. Zach's parents talk briefly about the baby, the delivery, their memories of Zach's birth.... Zach enters, and everybody makes a fuss over him. Then they settle Zach on his mom's bed. The nurse enters with a bundle wrapped in pink. Matt's dad is in tears as he looks at his son, and we follow his gaze: Zach taking in this odd little creature and then holding her, amazed, as she is set carefully across his lap. He is very, very serious. His mother asks if he has anything to say to her; his response is a whispered, "Hello, baby."

Storytellers: Zach's parents, his grandmother

And so on. This is not breathtakingly good filmmaking. But something to notice: Each sequence is a chapter. Each has a beginning, middle, and end. Sequence two thematically is about anticipation: We see that Zach has no idea what to expect, and the primary voice in the sequence is Zach's; we also see his school and his classmates. In terms of plot, the sequence gets him to the hospital, where he's going to meet his sister.

In contrast, sequence three is about Zach's parents, how they have tried to prepare him for the baby, how they have concerns. The primary voice in this sequence is theirs, whether or not the interviews are conducted in the hospital room or, more likely, at some other time. The point of view in this sequence is theirs, too, as they watch their son hold his sister for the first time. In terms of plot, this sequence begins with Zach at the hospital, and drives to him meeting his sister. In a 20-minute film, chances are good that this meeting is the film's midpoint.

Looking at these two sequences, I can anticipate what the next sequence should be. It does not need to do the job of getting Zach home that day, nor do we need to see his parents checking out (with the new baby). We can cut to the next best scene that tells the story we're telling. And our story is "Zach Gets a Baby Sister"—*not* "Zach welcomes a new baby home from the hospital."

So, for example, if the parents are planning a party, I might decide to film that. I can anticipate (and will be flexible if I'm wrong) that Zach will be excited that it's a party, and perhaps upset to discover that the attention is on his noisy, red-faced sister. This sequence would be about making adjustments, told from Zach's point of view.

Again, this is just an illustration. Take the time to look at successful documentaries and identify the sequences within them. Watch a range of films and film styles, from historical films (such as Middlemarch's *Benjamin Franklin*) to social issue films (compare the use of sequences in *Taxi to the Dark Side* and *The War Tapes*, for example) to traditional vérité. Sequences, also known as chapters, are structural devices that enhance, rather than limit, presentation.

How Many Sequences Should a Film Have?

There is no fixed number of sequences. If a film is 20 minutes long and your sequences run between, say, three and six minutes each, that's maybe five sequences. Also, to make your life a little more complicated, sequences sometimes have sub-sequences. You're in the midst of a sequence about a World Bank protest and you want to make a brief diversion into backstory: That's a sub-sequence. Just remember to get back to the main sequence you started, and finish it.

Historical Stories

Some funding agencies and commissioning editors require scripts—or at least detailed outlines/treatments—so that they can get a sense of what the film's approach and focus will be. Although these are possible for any type of film, they're easier to create in greater detail for films about events in the past. For example, here is a description of the first sequence in a short, three-act story about the transformation of boxer Cassius Clay into world heavyweight champion and political activist Muhammad Ali. Because this hour-long film had three stories in it—which were not interwoven—the opening sequence (the tease) was thematic, setting up the film overall. This example, then, describes the second sequence, the first in the story of Muhammad Ali. It was written prior to filming.

Sequence: "I Shook Up The World"

We begin the first act of our first story: Olympic champion Cassius Clay challenges World Heavyweight Champion Sonny Liston. Rumors are spread that Clay is spending time with Malcolm X, spokesperson for the Nation of Islam. Fight promoters want Clay to deny the rumors; he refuses, and after he defeats Liston, he publicly announces his new Muslim identity: Muhammad Ali.

PEOPLE: Edwin Pope, sportswriter; Kareem-Abdul Jabbar, student; Angelo Dundee, trainer; Herbert Muhammad, son of Elijah Muhammad

FOOTAGE: Archival of Muhammad Ali, Ali with Malcolm X, the Liston fight

Notice that people are identified by who they were at the time of the story; this is an excerpt of a sequence from *Eyes on the Prize*, in which the storytellers were witnesses to and participants in the stories unfolding. In this sequence, basketball legend Kareem Abdul-Jabbar is speaking from his perspective at the time, as a student. Angelo Dundee was Ali's trainer in this period.

Present-Day Stories

For films of events that will unfold as you shoot, it's still possible to draft an outline based on what you anticipate happening. If you intend to follow an eighth grader through a summer at basketball camp, you can do research to find out what the experience is typically like, and what scenes or sequences offer possibilities for meaningful interaction. Do the students board at the camp or go home at night? Do they tend to form close friendships? Are there one-on-one sessions with coaches? Is there much pressure from parents? Knowing these things can help you begin to think about what a sequence will *do*, as opposed to the specifics of what it *is*. If research has indicated, for example, that you want a sequence that you're tentatively calling "The end of innocence"—a sequence that looks at the commercial pressure on young phenoms—then you arrive on location with that focus in mind.

The same is true when considering the people you want to film. As you're doing the outline, you'll begin sketching in the names of people you need to tell your story, from those you "have to have" to those you'd ideally like. Sometimes, as you develop present-day or historical films, you won't know whom you want specifically, in which case they can be described. For example, "We need someone who was at the dance with her," or "We want to talk to janitors and others who keep the physical plant operating." An outline can help you see if your story or argument is building and if you have enough variety in casting and sequences, or if too much of your film is doing (and saying) the same thing. Over the course of filming, decisions about story and structure are bound to change, but for now you're taking the first steps in organizing your story into a workable film.

Whether or not your film is historical, present-day, or some combination of the two, this exercise forces you to think about your film's approach. If you want to follow a production of Wagner's *Ring Cycle*, for example, will you do it, as Jon Else did, from the perspective of union workers backstage? Or would you see the production from the point of view of its director, or a children's group trying to make sense of the opera as part of their efforts to stage a condensed version of it on their own in school? Is your point the many months it takes to mount a production, or the tension of running such a grand show over the course of a day? Each *approach* decision should be carried through in your outline, so that someone from the outside who reads it will have a sense of the film that you are making: its themes, plot, point of view, arc.

CASTING

Not all documentary filmmakers would call it "casting," yet all would agree that the people you see on screen—whether they're interacting with each other, talking to an off-screen interviewer, or acting as narrator or host—need to be researched, contacted, and brought onto the project with care. Decisions about who will be filmed and what they're expected to contribute to the storytelling are important. Even the people who appear through archival means, whether in archival footage or through a reading of their letters, diaries, and other artifacts of the past, are important to the overall casting of a story. In fact, how you cast your documentary is so important that some executives want to see footage of your main characters before they'll approve or commission a project.

When to Cast

In general, you begin thinking about casting even as you're considering a topic and story to film; it's part of the conception of a film's style and approach. If there are specific people whose involvement is critical, you'll need to cast them (or at least know that they would be available and amenable) prior to your inclusion of them in any pitch. After that, casting takes shape as the outline and treatment do, and you begin to know whom or what type of people you're looking for and why.

Whom to Cast

For a film that requires experts, it's wise to cast a range of viewpoints. This means that instead of just shooting "five experts" on a subject, you know how each of the five differs from the others in expertise and outlook, offering a means of adding complexity and balance to the overall film. There are only so many people an audience can follow in a half-hour or an hour, and you don't want all of those people talking about the same issues from the same perspective.

One way to think about casting is to regard each individual who appears on screen, whether as a character you're following or as someone you interview (or both), as having a *job* to do in the overall film. Sometimes they stand in for a particular aspect of an argument; sometimes they represent an element that you could not otherwise film. For example, you could get three people to talk in general about Title IX legislation in the United States, but it might be stronger to find a lawyer who fought for its enforcement, a female athlete who got a college scholarship because of it, and an athletic director who opposed it out of fear that it would limit resources for his school's football program. They may each know a little bit or even a lot about each other's areas of expertise, but it muddies the storytelling if they don't stick to the parts of the story that they best serve.

Along the same lines, if you're creating a historical film, you might want a biographer to stand in for Martha Washington, for example. He or she would be asked to comment specifically and only on your story as it relates to Martha. Without attention being called to it, the audience will learn this cue. When they see that expert, they'll know that—in a way—Martha, or at least her proxy, is now on screen.

Do Your Homework

A significant part of casting effectively is doing some research before you start indiscriminately calling around looking for experts or "types." The less generic the casting is, the stronger the film will be.

Casting Nonexperts

Sometimes you're not looking for experts but for real people willing to give you access to lives and situations that embody themes and ideas you've set out to explore. For their production of the 2005 film *Building the Alaska Highway*, Tracy Heather Strain, Randall MacLowry, Katy Mostoller, and "an army of interns" set out to locate men who helped to build the highway as part of their military service during World War II. Military records about the highway's construction had been among materials burned in a fire several years earlier, making the job of finding the men more difficult. The producers wrote down any lead they got, whether from program advisors or from names mentioned in books about the highway project, a feat in which more than 10,000 workers, often working in intense cold, constructed 1,500 miles of highway in just eight months.

Once they had names, they began poring through telephone directories. The producers gave the interns a sheet of questions to ask, reminding them to address these elderly veterans by their proper names. "They would do a preliminary pre-interview, and then Randy, Katy, or I would follow up with the real pre-interview," Strain, the film's producer and director, says. "One of the problems was that people thought we were selling something, so sometimes we got hung up on. We had to come up with a strategy for saying *Alaska Highway* early." The storytellers chosen—a diverse group of men whose memories of that long-ago time are clear and poignant—are a strong element in the film. Strain estimates that they ended up filming interviews with perhaps a tenth of the people contacted.

A stretch of the Alcan Highway, from *Building the Alaska Highway*. Photo: Library of Congress.

On-the-Fly Casting

A popular device in television advertising these days is to put a group of young people into a car with a camera and portray them as making a documentary, apparently winging it. They pull up in unfamiliar places, shout questions to strangers, and then move on. There are circumstances in which you might want to do this, but in general, this isn't an effective use of time, unless of course it's part of a thought-out film design. In *Super Size Me*, Morgan Spurlock effectively conducts a number of these "man-on-the-street" interviews. While not a random sampling, these people seem to represent the average person and his or her knowledge of fast food, nutrition, and in one case, the lyrics to a McDonald's jingle. This can be fun and effective.

Casting Opposing Voices

How do you get people to participate in a film when it's likely that the viewpoint they hold is contrary to yours or the audience's? A primary way is by making it clear that you are open to what they have to say, intend to treat them fairly on screen, and believe that their point of view, while you might disagree with it, is important to the subject at hand and the public's understanding of it.

Don't misrepresent yourself or your project just to gain someone's cooperation. If you want to explore the notion that the 1969 moonwalk was faked, don't imply that your film is a look at manned space flight. Does this mean that you can't approach credible experts on subjects that strain credibility? No. It means that you need to bring them with you, not trick them into participating. Give them the option of adding their credibility to the project, and then use their credibility responsibly. (If you are an expert and are approached for a documentary, do some homework before saying yes. A quick web search should tell you a bit about the producer and/or the series that will be airing the interview.)

Casting for Balance

Balancing the point of view of a film does not mean simply presenting opposing sides. In fact, it almost never means that. Two opposing sides talking past each other do not advance anyone's understanding of an issue. When the opposing sides are actually very uneven, such as when a majority of credible experts takes one position and a small (and often fringe or invested) minority disagrees, then giving these two views equal time and weight creates a false impression that the issues are more uncertain than they actually are. This is not balanced; it's inaccurate. Instead, you should look for people who can offer shades of gray, complexity, within an issue.

Note that casting for balance also means letting the appropriate people present their own points of view. This doesn't mean that individuals can't speak to experiences outside their own; a French historian whose expertise is Native-American education at the turn of the last century, for example, might be well qualified to discuss life on a particular Oklahoma reservation in 1910. It's more of a stretch to ask a biology major who happens to be protesting foreign sweatshops to tell you what goes on in an overseas sneaker factory, unless you limit your questioning to a frame of reference relevant to that person: "Why am I here? I'm here because I read an article that said ..." If your film storytelling requires that you convey conditions in the factory, you'd be better off trying to find someone who has witnessed those conditions firsthand (as a worker or owner, for example, or as someone who toured the facilities on a fact-finding tour) and/or a labor expert who has studied those specific conditions.

When you hear someone on camera talking about "them"—for example, "The people living in government housing thought we were being unfair to them"—it's likely you need to find individuals from within that community who can speak for themselves, or experts uniquely qualified to speak on their behalf.

Genuine Casting

During the closing credits of Robert Greenwald's *Iraq for Sale*, he and his production team are shown trying to get interviews with representatives of Halliburton, CACI, Blackwater, and other companies. They state that between June 8 and August 4, 2006, they sent out 31 e-mails and made 38 phone calls. But listen to the phone calls, and see if you think you'd respond. The time line is indicative: According to the filmmakers, they had not started the film before the end of April 2006, when they raised funds through an e-mail campaign. They were finishing production by August, which leaves little time for research or the kind of relationship building that is sometimes necessary when handling complex and controversial topics.

In addition, the phone calls do not come across as questions, but rather indictments. Greenwald tells one company, "We've discovered frankly quite a bit of very troubling material," and argues, "I thought letting people know that we found something critical would be fairer than just kind of trying to sucker punch them." In letters, he writes of wanting "their side of the story," and so on.

Compare the casts of this film and Eugene Jarecki's *Why We Fight*, which was on a comparable topic. Jarecki's cast is far more diverse in terms of points of view and organizational affiliation. The difference, I think, reflects each filmmaker's approach and intent. Both films are successful, but they speak in very different ways to different (if at times overlapping) audiences.

Expanding the Perspective

It's very easy, when casting (and especially when casting quickly), to go after the people at the top, the leaders and figureheads. Often, they are known to be charismatic and articulate. But they rarely represent the whole story or, often, the most interesting part of it. Dig deeper, and ask yourself who else might add perspective to a story. If you're talking to policy experts for a film on education, you might want to explore what a second-grade teacher would add. If you're doing a film about corporate scandals, an interesting perspective might come from a realtor trying to sell the homes of some former executives who are now in prison.

Be careful, also, to avoid perpetuating misconceptions about gender, ethnicity, or nationality. It would be incomplete and inaccurate in today's world (or yesterday's, for that matter) to portray it as less diverse and complex than it truly is (or was). You should reflect that complexity in your casting.

Paying Your Cast

The general rule in journalism is that if you start paying for stories, people will come up with stories for which they want to be paid. Some filmmakers may decide to pay subjects indirectly, whether through buying them groceries or making a contribution to a charity. Scholars and experts who appear on screen (and are not also advisors) are not paid by filmmakers, although this is currently under debate and some new precedents are being set.

CASTING HOSTS AND NARRATORS

There is a wide range in how and why people use on-camera hosts for documentary films. Sometimes a broadcaster will want the producer to use a celebrity, such as an actor, sports figure, or politician. With celebrities known to be involved in particular political, social, or health issues, for example, this can give the project added credibility. A celebrity's reputation—as a humorist, for example—can set the tone for a project. Finally, the involvement of a celebrity can help boost a project's promotion and raise audience interest.

Narrators (heard in voice-over but not seen as hosts) may also be cast for their celebrity, or they may simply be individuals with strong voices that carry, even when placed against music or sync sound. Remember that the narrator's voice also sets a tone for the film. Will it be male or female, or have an identifiable accent? How old do you want your narrator to sound? How do you want this person to come across to the audience? As an expert or a friend? Sounding humorous, somber, remote, or warm? Even an unseen narrator is part of the overall balance of voices that are heard.

TREATMENTS

Many projects, if not most, progress from an outline to some form of treatment prior to shooting. Information on what these are and how they're used can be found in Chapter 10, *Selling*.

CHAPTER 10

Selling

"Selling" in the context of documentary films can mean a lot of things, including negotiations that happen when a project is complete or nearing completion. This chapter is talking about selling as part of how you position your film to others. This might mean convincing a top-notch cinematographer to work with you, an executive producer to give you a "green light" (and resources) to start shooting, or a funding agency to give you a grant. It might also mean finding a convincing way to share your vision of how a story should be told with all the many people it takes, at all levels, to get a documentary made. In many cases, a way to do that is with a document known as a treatment.

TREATMENTS

A treatment is essentially a prose version of your film, playing out on paper as it will play out on screen. In some cases it's a short document written to ensure that the entire production team is on board with a film's story and concept. Even if it's only a few pages long, though, a treatment should demonstrate that the producer has a sense of the film's train and how it will be realized on screen. Even more than an outline, a treatment may be required by outsiders as a condition for providing funding. In that case, it should be polished, like a smart, high-quality magazine article. You can't expect outsiders, especially nonfilmmakers, to decipher an outline, and many outsiders are also not good at reading film scripts. A prose version of your film, though, can be a strong selling tool.

What Does a Treatment Look Like?

Usually, a treatment in documentary is analogous, in form, to a treatment for a dramatic screenplay. You don't talk *about* the story: You tell it.

A treatment for an hour-long film might be five pages or 25, depending on what you need. (For some examples, see the end of

DOI: 10.1016/B978-0-240-81241-0.00010-1

this chapter.) They should be double spaced, for ease of reading, and written in the present tense—a film story moves forward in time, even if the story is set in the past. The structure of the treatment should mirror the structure of the film. If you plan to start at the grave of a soldier killed in Iraq, for example, your treatment will also start there. If the film is driving toward a meeting between siblings who only recently learned of each other's existence, your treatment should also drive to that point, and not "give away" the drama of that moment by referring to it earlier. If, in your thinking about the film, you envision a three-act dramatic structure and the reunion as being a culmination of Act Two, the reunion should probably not appear until *roughly* three-fourths of the way through your pages.

People, places, and events should be introduced in screen order (meaning the order in which you think they will appear on screen), including a description of how information will be presented. For example, if you plan a sequence about the New York City marathon, it should be clear in the treatment when and how it occurs in your film. Does it start the film, or do you drive to it? If you're going to explore the history of the marathon, will you do so with archival material, interviews, or something else? There's a bit of a balancing act involved—a treatment is *not* a script, nor is it the finished film. You are merely trying to convey not only your story but also your approach: "We take this journey with Nils, sitting with him in libraries as he searches through old microfilm, traveling with him to interview elderly relatives and neighbors. Finally, we accompany him to the Venice airport, where the meeting with his long-lost brother will take place."

WRITING TREATMENTS FOR OUTSIDE REVIEW

When writing a treatment for outside review, you need to engage readers who may not be as familiar with your topic as you are. For example, a shorthand line intended for the in-house team might read: "Washington crosses the Delaware; military historians explain; Smith reviews the mythology." More careful and detailed prose might read, "Over Emanuel Gottlieb Leutze's famous painting, *George Washington Crossing the Delaware*, we learn through narration of Washington's triumphant crossing of the Delaware River on the stormy night of December 25, 1776. As our historians make clear, all had seemed lost for the Americans. Now, Washington and his army of 3,000 surprise Britain's mercenary forces at Trenton and capture one-third of the men. They also gain a foothold in New Jersey that puts a halt to the British offensive. It's a decisive moment in the war for independence. We return to the painting, as art historian Jane Smith compares the history to the mythology. The painting was completed in 1851, a full 75 years after the event."

Note that this example, which happens to be for a historical film, hasn't said what images you'll be weaving into and out of between historians; hopefully by this point in the treatment, it's clear how you're handling the war history. Nor does it list all the specific historians who'll be talking about this particular event, because by now the reader probably has a sense of which historians you've involved. You can't describe every image and every voice-over and every anticipated sync bite, or you might as well write the script. What you're doing is making the story and progression of events clear, and including the most important details: in this case, the use of the painting and the art historian. The same would be true if you were imagining a modern-day story for which you were seeking support.

Story, Not Images

Your focus is on story, not photography, which means that you don't want to spend time describing spectacular sunsets or what you're going to achieve with a helicopter mount. With that said, you can write a treatment that is (occasionally) cinematic. For example, "Work-worn fingers moving rapidly under the sewing machine seem to belong to someone other than the lively 14-year-old operating the machine." That sentence clearly is a close-up that widens out to reveal the person sewing. Or this, from *The Milltail Pack* (see sample pages at the end of this chapter): "The pack [of red wolves] is heading to a corn field just at the end of the road. In the brown, dry stalks of last month's corn live mice, rabbits and voles—tasty appetizers for the Milltail Pack." This is enough of an image to carry the reader through the exposition that follows. Using a different style, here is the first sentence of the treatment for *You Could Grow Aluminum Out There* (for the series *Cadillac Desert*): "In California we name things for what they destroyed. *Real estate signs whiz by the windshield....'Quail Meadows,' 'The Grasslands,' 'Indian Creek,' 'Riverbank Estates,' 'Elk Grove Townhouses,' 'Miwok Village.'* Before the Spaniards came, 300 tribes shared the Central Valley of California."

Note that there's a difference between writing to describe what you *know* you can see, and inventing it as if you were writing the treatment for a dramatic feature. A treatment for a dramatic feature might set a scene like this: "It's late at night. President Truman and his cabinet sit in a smoke-filled room, deliberating their next move." If this is how you're writing a treatment for a factual, historical documentary, either you're aware of stock/archival footage or stills of this scene, or you're planning to recreate it, based on historical evidence that supports your visual interpretation—who was in the room, how late at night it was, what was being discussed. In either case, it should be clear in your treatment how we'll be seeing what we're seeing. For example, "We recreate an impression of this meeting as we hear an actor reading from the president's own diary: It's late at night. He and his cabinet sit in a smoke-filled room. They are deliberating their next move." Or, "In black-and-white-footage shot by the president's niece, a young art student who happened to be with her uncle that fateful day, we see the late-night meeting, the smoke-filled room. A weary president and his staff, deliberating."

If this is a scene that you're *anticipating* for a present-day story— for example, you've gotten permission to film a corporation as it unveils a new product—then imagining a scene is permissible, if it is based on research and reasonable expectations. For example, "Our cameras accompany Heather Bourne as she strides into Gotham Towers and rides an elevator to the penthouse, where we'll see her present the new, and somewhat radical, ad campaign to the company's famously traditional board of directors."

Introduce People

You need to let readers know who people are. "Webster describes the carnage at the battlefield" is not enough for outside readers not already steeped in your subject. "Historian Victoria Webster, an expert on World War II military. . . ." Then, if you don't mention Professor Webster for another 10 pages, remind us briefly who she is, for example, "Historian Victoria Webster disagrees."

Quoting People

Suppose you know whom you want to interview, but you haven't spoken with that person yet, either in a pre-interview or a filmed interview. You should never make up quotes based on what you hope someone will say, even if you have a good idea of what it might be, if only because the world is small and if Professor X finds out that you attributed a statement to him that he hasn't or wouldn't make, the chances that he will cooperate with you in the future are slim.

Instead, there are a few options for sprinkling in quotes from sources you haven't spoken with directly. First, you can simply describe what someone will be asked about, for example, "Dr. Hunter offers an introduction to photosynthesis. . . ." Second, you can quote from the individual's published writing. Third, you can quote from interviews that others have conducted with the person. However, if you do any of these, you need to be clear that you have not yet contacted the person directly, and that he or she has not yet agreed to participate in the film. You might say, "Except as noted, quotes are taken from print material published elsewhere." *Suggestion: If you decide to do this, write a version of your treatment with footnotes, so that you can go back to this source if necessary. Remove those footnotes in copies for outside review; they're distracting and unnecessary for readers who are "seeing" your film on paper, not reading a research report.* Another possibility would be, "We have gained the cooperation of Dr. X and Reverend Y, but have not yet spoken with Mr. Z and Dr. P, who are also quoted here." In any case, quotes should be used sparingly. This is your treatment, not your script.

Unknown Information

Even the most polished treatments are written before all the pieces are in place; you don't know what you'll discover on the film shoot or what terrific visuals you'll find in somebody's attic. Most importantly, it's often the case that you're writing the treatment to raise money to do necessary research; you're doing the best you can with the resources you have, but you know that there's a lot more you need to learn before you can go out to shoot. One solution is to acknowledge these gaps by describing, in general terms, types or scenes that you believe you'll need. For example, "A trainer describes what it's like to work with thoroughbred horses and takes us through the paces of an early-morning workout." Or, "We are searching for an expert in queuing theory who can apply his or her theoretical work to the design of amusement parks, and we will find parents who know from experience that there is a limit to how long their children, and they themselves, are willing to wait in line."

Reflect the Work You've Done

Surprisingly, one of the most common problems I encounter when reviewing treatments intended for outsider readers (in particular, funding agencies) is that a treatment will seem to be based on an afternoon's worth of research, when in fact, the filmmakers have spent weeks or even months on the project and, in some cases, have shot a significant portion of the footage. Your treatment should sell your project and play to its strengths. Add the details that will make your efforts show. For example, "In an interview filmed last May on the steps of her home in Leeds, author Celia Jones offers her perspective on the housing crisis." Or "Our crew follows Mr. Smith down spiral stairs leading to a dusty basement filled with old newspapers, magazines, and a rare collection of photographs that he offers to show us." Provide enough detail to make it clear that you know your subject inside and out, even if you also know that there is a lot more you need to learn.

Tell a Good Story

An important trick of writing treatments is to convey your passion early on. You think you've found an excellent subject for a film—convince the reader. A good story, well researched and well told, goes a long way. As someone who's reviewed proposals, I can say from experience that many submitted treatments are little more than research documents, or, even worse, ideas that haven't progressed much beyond a basic topic. Treatments that attract attention are those that set up and deliver a compelling story, one that's informed by research and enlivened by something different—an unusual perspective, a new angle, unique access to people or places.

Tell a good story as best you can. Then run your treatment past someone who knows nothing about your movie, and preferably is not related to you, so that you get impartial feedback before you send your material to the people you're likely to need most at this stage—financiers.

THE SHOOTING TREATMENT

A shooting treatment, if you create one, is the culmination of your work prior to shooting. If you did a treatment to raise development and scripting funds, a shooting treatment reflects the research and creative thinking that those funds enabled. Usually, a shooting treatment is for use by the filmmaking team; if a preliminary treatment got you some development funds from a commissioning editor or executive producer, a shooting treatment may be required to get the go-ahead to head out into the field with a crew. It's the baseline guide to the elements you need to tell the story that you anticipate telling, a document that can be shared (as discussed by Boyd Estus in Chapter 11) with cinematographers, sound recordists, and others to help ensure that opportunities aren't missed.

SCRIPTS

Documentary scripts tend to evolve over the course of production. In the case of programs that are significantly driven by narration, the script may begin to take shape during preproduction, only to be significantly revised and rewritten during editing. In the case of scripts driven by character voice-over, or entirely composed of sync, a script may be derived from what is essentially a transcript of the finished film, in which case the "script" refers to the storytelling of the overall film.

Scripts for Fundraising

Some funding agencies require a "script" as a condition of granting production money. If you are already editing, you will be able to submit a draft of your script in progress (see Chapter 12 for information about working with scripts in the editing room). If you are still seeking funding for production, however, what you submit may be more akin to a very developed treatment or a document that is part treatment, part script. As mentioned, I find that for many reviewers, a treatment that adheres to the description above—meaning that it is not a research report, but clearly presents on paper the film as it will appear on screen—may be more effective as a "script" submission. When in doubt, always consult with the person requesting the materials. (Better yet, ask if they have samples of successful proposals and use those as models.)

TREATMENTS AS A CLASSROOM EXERCISE

I recently led a seminar that looked at the presentation of history on screen. It was a nonproduction course, and only a few of the students had film experience. I wanted them to evaluate the storytelling in others' films and learn how to apply it to their own (hypothetical) documentaries. For the first half of the semester, we screened and critiqued several historical documentaries as well as some dramatized (and fictionalized) histories.

During the second half of the semester, each student developed ideas and wrote a detailed treatment (20 to 25 pages) for a film on a subject of his or her choosing. To give them all a common set of ground rules, the topics and treatments had to suit guidelines for the PBS historical series *American Experience*. The series seeks "dramatic and compelling stories about the American past—stories about people both ordinary and extraordinary," according to its website, www.pbs.org/wgbh/amex/guidelines/. "We are particularly interested in stories that offer a unique or rarely seen perspective on our history and that have a clear narrative arc and strong characters. We are least interested in films that take a survey-type approach to history." Series guidelines allow for programs that raise issues that resonate to the present, but not for programs where the historical information is merely a bridge into "contemporary issues and conflict."

In the professional world, treatments for historical films can take many weeks, if not months, to research and write. My expectations for the students' treatments were scaled back to accommodate the realities of their academic schedules. I strongly recommended that they start with subjects for which at least one, if not two, secondary sources existed (preferably books that had been well reviewed), because that meant that professionals had done the time-consuming and highly skilled work of digesting raw historical data. I also wanted them to explore at least two primary sources, to have the experience of working with period documents and/or artifacts. Otherwise, my emphasis for the assignment was on turning a subject into a story, one exciting enough to draw and hold general viewers even as it offered historical evidence and complexity. I stressed that someone reading the treatment should enjoy the experience the way one enjoys reading a well-written magazine article, and that this "article" should give a good sense of the film as it would unfold on screen.

A few lessons learned from this approach in the classroom apply to the "real world" as well:

- It helps to do a quick academic web search to see where scholars stand on your story. Is there cutting-edge research or controversy? Don't find just any secondary source and go with it— find the *best* source or two, and then a couple of backups. (An excellent article in a reputable journal, for the purpose of this exercise, was also acceptable.)
- Students who have not studied documentary need to be reminded that creative arrangement in nonfiction is not the same thing as "artistic license" in fact-inspired fiction. In

fictionalized history, "artistic license" is the freedom (with some constraints) to create composite characters, to put real people into imagined situations and vice versa, or to mix fiction and nonfiction elements. This is not generally permissible with documentaries, although there are exceptions. Peter Watkins television "reporting" in *Culloden* is an example of this.

- Along the same lines, it's important to stress that "creative arrangement" (in other words, narrative design) does not mean sleight of hand—the stories presented must be factual, fair, and truthful. It also does not mean that the history being conveyed will be dumbed down. In contrast, the challenge is to find the core story and use that as a vehicle to make a film smarter—and at the same time, play to the unique strengths of audio visual media.
- Treatments are not theses. With some exceptions, historical documentary filmmakers don't come up with an original take on the history; they come up with original, compelling, and thought-provoking ways to present current scholarship (sometimes from a single point of view, more often from a range of perspectives) to audiences.
- Chronologies matter, and students who shortcut this part of the assignment find that it costs them in time and effort later.
- In considering their film's approach, students do better when they think not only about the kinds of subjects that interest them but also the kinds of films they like to watch. A historical film can be a mystery, a love story, an epic journey, a biography, or something else entirely; it can be humorous and unexpected.
- It's useful to remind students to pay attention to what excites them about the subject and what stands out as they go through books and articles right from the beginning—the kinds of things they find themselves telling their friends and families. This is often the material that gets bulleted in the film's tease and becomes the answer to "Why make this film, now?" and "Why should an audience watch?"
- Thinking simpler is always a good idea.

PLANNING AND PROPOSAL WRITING

For many filmmakers, raising funds is part of the planning process. If you get some money, you move forward and do more research. A little more money, and you can work on a shooting treatment or maybe start shooting. Perhaps you take some of that material to create a demo of the film in progress, and use that to raise more money.

With the caveat that fundraising is an area of expertise beyond the scope of this book, what follows are some tips for addressing the questions often asked by funders. As it turns out, the process of thinking these questions through, and answering them, is often very helpful in the kind of planning that can strengthen storytelling.

WHAT'S A FUNDRAISING PROPOSAL?

Proposals are the documents you submit in order to request funding from grant-making agencies, whether public or private. In general, the following are stages at which financial support might be available prior to the completion of your film: planning, scripting, production, postproduction, and finishing. The first two fall under the category of "development" and can be very difficult funds to raise. The easiest, arguably, are finishing funds, which are awarded at or after the rough cut stage. At that point, the financier can see your film, there are few surprises, and there is a higher likelihood that you'll be able to complete the project.

Although each proposal must be tailored to the guidelines and mandates of the particular agency you're requesting funding from, there are a few basic things that they'll usually want to know, whether in a letter of introduction, a three-page summary, or a 25-page narrative. They tend to include the following.

Nature of the Request

Who you are, what your project is ("a 90-minute program to be shot on digital video on the history of the can opener and its impact on American cuisine"), how much you're requesting at this time from this grant maker ("$X,000 for scripting" or "$XXX,000 for production of one hour of this four-part series"), what activities are to be supported for the amount requested, and what the end result of the grant will be. (For example, if you ask for a scripting grant, you should end up with a script or, in some cases, a production-ready treatment.)

Introduction to the Subject

A general grounding in the subject matter to be treated on film. In other words, this is not your film treatment and does not have to include detail about how you will treat the subject on screen. It's an overview of the subject, presented clearly and concisely, and written in a way that will hopefully bring the reader to share your conviction that the subject is interesting, relevant, and worth a commitment of resources.

Rationale

A more focused opportunity to convey the significance of the project and, in particular, its relevance to the financier. Another way to look at it is, "Why this project now? How will it advance public understanding and awareness of the topic? Why is it useful for this topic to be presented on film? In what way will audiences be served by this project?" A few carefully chosen facts often speak volumes when making the case for a film.

Goals and Objectives

What your project is designed to accomplish. There will be a handful of these; for example:

> **Goal:** *To explore the historical context in which Title IX legislation was originally passed and the inequalities it sought to address, and to evaluate the law's impact, intended and unintended, in the context of current efforts to repeal it.* **Objective:** *Viewers will better understand the complexity of Title IX legislation beyond the issue of school sports, and appreciate the social and political processes by which legal change is brought about.*

Related Projects

What other films have been done on the same or related subjects? How does their success (or lack of success) inform your approach to your story? How does your story build on or differ from these projects? As mentioned previously, the fact that a topic has been covered is not necessarily a deterrent, given all the different ways a topic can be treated and the different venues available. But you should demonstrate that you know what's out there.

Ancillary Projects

These are sometimes also called "related projects," which makes for confusion. An ancillary project is something that you're developing to bolster your film's shelf life and reach. These might include web-based materials, radio broadcasts, material for educational outreach, and/or material for community engagement, which uses media as the catalyst for action and discussion within and between community groups. At a time when the television landscape is cluttered with choices, including documentary choices, it's becoming increasingly important to financiers, especially those who support public television programming, that you demonstrate ways in which you will extend the impact of a broadcast.

History of the Project

Some information on how the project got under way and on the financial or institutional support you've received to date. Your passion for the project and your connection to the story are likely to come through here, because this is where you tell people how you got involved in the project, why the story appealed to you and/or seemed vitally important to tell, and what you've done, so far, to tell it.

Audience and Broadcast Prospects

Information on your target audience(s) and how you intend to reach them.

Organization History

Information about the organizations involved in submitting the proposal, including the production company and possibly the fiscal sponsor. As elsewhere, you may want to highlight those areas of your expertise that mesh with the interests of the potential financiers.

Project Staff

Information on the media team and academic advisors (where appropriate). If you or your media team aren't experienced in the kind of production you're proposing, consider taking on other team members who will add to your credibility. If it's your idea but your first film, figure out what you need to get out of it, personally and professionally, and then determine what you might be able to give up in the interest of getting it made. It's very difficult to get anything funded these days, so you need to do what you can to be competitive. (Alternatively, if you can afford to do so, you might work to get farther into the production before requesting funds, so that you have a film in progress that demonstrates your ability.)

Plan of Work

A detailed description of the work that will be done, and by whom, with the funding requested. Be sure that this plan of work doesn't exceed the scope or length of the grant period; if you're asking for scripting money, your plan of work generally shouldn't continue through production and editing (check with the individual agency).

Appendices

Résumés, letters of commitment, research bibliography, lists of films on this or related subjects, description of materials to be used, if appropriate. For example, for a film that will rely on archival footage, a list—even a preliminary one—of archival materials pertinent to the subject should be included.

Treatment

Many financiers want to see some form of written treatment in order to consider a request for scripting or production funds.

Budget

Financiers often want to see a breakdown of how you'll spend the money you're asking them to provide. They're also likely to want to see your entire production budget, to get a sense of how funds will be allocated overall.

A Few Extra Pointers

Much of the advice for proposal writing can be applied to the entire production, including the editing. From my own experience as a consultant and proposal writer and my experience as a proposal reviewer, here are a few tips:

- *Accuracy is important.* It's standard practice for potential sponsors to send proposals out for review by people who know the subject well. If you spell names incorrectly, get titles and dates wrong, or misrepresent factual information, it will (and should) be held against you. The proposal and the quality of work that goes into it are indicative of the film to come. Besides, the fact checking you do now, if filed carefully, will be useful later.
- *The storytelling matters.* The people reviewing your proposal, whether they're scientists, historians, mathematicians, or teachers, are as aware as you are that audiences don't watch a

film because the topic is important; they watch because they're interested in a story. So while reviewers will be on guard to see that you don't cut academic corners, they'll also be checking to see that you know how to attract and hold an audience's interest.

- *Good writing goes a long way.* Beyond the basics of spelling and facts, the proposal should present a coherent argument that flows from paragraph to paragraph. Be concise. Your readers are likely to be plowing through several proposals, and you don't want to trip them up with writing that's unedited, unclear, or ungrammatical.
- *Be your own first audience.* Ask yourself if you'd be interested in the film you're pitching, and if the answer is no, work on it some more.
- *Anticipate resistance.* If you are going to propose a history of the American soap opera as a way to look at important themes in American cultural and social history and women's history, be prepared for the reviewer whose first instinct is to laugh. Get some experts on your side and, with them, make your case. Answer the naysayers with solid research. Producers have gotten funding for films on all sorts of subjects that might not, at first glance, have seemed "suitable."
- *Arm people with what they need to know to understand the proposal.* A producer can sometimes get so close to a topic that he or she forgets that other people aren't immersed in the subject and may need either to be reminded or introduced to key characters and events. Assume that your audience is smart, but seed information throughout your proposal in a way that brings readers along with you.
- *Passion is important.* It comes across in the presentation of a proposal in subtle ways, but mostly it shows in the quality of the work—how thorough the groundwork was, how creatively the ideas have been transformed into a story, and how well that story is presented on paper.
- *Avoid overproduction.* Teachers are known to be wary when they receive papers with fancy, multicolored covers that clearly took hours to design and execute, because they doubt the same effort went into the actual paper. The same is true of proposals.
- *Avoid unfounded hyperbole.* "This is the most amazing story that the XYZ foundation will ever help to produce, and nothing that XYZ has done to date will have the kind of impact this film will have." This kind of language is always a turn-off for readers.

- *Avoid paranoia.* "While we are pleased to share this proposal with you, we ask that you keep it in strictest confidence as we are certain that others would grab this idea the minute they got wind of it." Foundations keep proposals in confidence unless or until they are funded and produced.

What If All They Want Is a Letter of Inquiry?

First, be grateful—it's a lot less work. Second, take that letter as seriously as you would a full-length proposal narrative. Look *very closely* at the mandate of the organization involved. And get to the point. Don't expect someone to wade through two pages of single-spaced prose to find out what you want. Hook the reader in the first paragraph with a compelling film project and a clear idea of why you're contacting that person's organization for help in getting it made.

SAMPLE PAGES FROM BROADCAST FILMS AND SERIES

In the pages that follow, I've included some sample pages of outlines, treatments, and scripts for programs that have already been broadcast. The samples reflect diversity in the program styles and the varied uses of the print material. The editing outline for *Lalee's Kin*, for example, was created for in-house use only. In contrast, the treatment for *Getting Over* (an hour of the six-part series *This Far By Faith*) was submitted to numerous public and private funding agencies, including the National Endowment for the Humanities.

ACT I, THE CENTRAL VALLEY PROJECT

FIRST CAUSES

In California we name things for what they destroyed.

Real estate signs whiz by the windshield...."Quail Meadows," "The Grasslands," "Indian Creek," "Riverbank Estates," "Elk Grove Townhouses," "Miwok Village."

Before the Spaniards came, 300 tribes shared the Central Valley of California...Maidu, Miwok, Patwin. A few weeks of flooding each winter fed the great marshes and seasonal lakes, but for most of the year—the seven month dry season when Indians moved to the cooler surrounding foothills—the Great Central Valley got, and still gets, less rain than North Africa. It was the American Serengeti.

Spanish maps.

Richard Rodriguez, or perhaps Maxine Hong Kingston or Jesse De La Cruz pick up the story.

The wet winters and dry summers unique to California had gone on for a hundred thousand years before Europeans came. A rich, complex ecosystem had evolved with such intelligence that the great condors, elk, delta smelt, cougars and bunch grass could survive in the natural cycles of drought and flood. Each carried genetic information for the next generation to thrive in arid land, and the next and the next. Bidwell saw 40 grizzlies in a single day, and Central Valley salmon ran in the millions. Muir, standing on a hill south of San Francisco looked 100 miles east toward the Sierra and saw "...a carpet of wildflowers, a continuous sheet of bloom bounded only by mountains."

---

[1] Program produced, directed, and written by Jon Else; page 4 of 40, episode three of *Cadillac Desert*, broadcast as *The Mercy of Nature*. © 1995 Jon Else, reprinted with permission.

HOUR THREE: *Getting Over* (1910–1939)

Tell me how we got over, Lord;
Had a mighty hard time, comin' on over.
You know, my soul looks back in wonder,
How did we make it over?

Tell me how we got over, Lord;
I've been falling and rising all these years.
But you know, my soul looks back in wonder,
How did I make it over?

"How I Got Over" (gospel song)

THE PRESENT:

"Where is hope? Hope is closer than we know!" declares the Reverend Cecil Williams, pastor of the Glide Memorial United Methodist Church in San Francisco.

> I want you to know this morning that this is Bethlehem! The rejected are here. The wretched of the earth are here. Poor folks, rich folks, middle-class folks. You can be yourself here. You don't have to run from yourself here. You don't have to put yourself down here. You can embrace love here. Where is hope? Hope is here! Amen!

Glide Memorial Church in the Tenderloin district of San Francisco, an area of tenements, crack houses, and shooting galleries, lies at what Rev. Williams calls "the intersection of despair and hope." Williams took over the church in 1966, when the congregation included about 35 people, nearly all of them middle-class whites. Today, it has 6,400 members and a reputation, as *Psychology Today* reported in 1995, as "an urban refuge for the spiritually disenfranchised...a faith steeped more in heart and soul than in scripture."

Powerful and influential visitors like Oprah Winfrey and President Bill Clinton speak of Glide as a model religious institution. Poet Maya Angelou, a parishioner for nearly 30 years, calls it "a church for the 21st century." Glide is San Francisco's largest provider of social services, offering recovery centers for substance abusers, domestic-violence workshops for batterers and victims, anger management classes for youth, job skills and computer training for the unemployed or those wishing to further their education. Its tradition of outreach is a hallmark of African-American religion, especially as it developed in the decades following the Great Migration.

3-3

On a Sunday morning, we watch as Rev. Williams evokes the past in his demands for the future:

> Faith and resistance are the fuels that power the train of freedom and transformation.…
> The train of freedom and recovery chugs on daily. Claim your place on this train. The
> freedom train is passing you by. Catch it. Then listen. Listen carefully. Those on the
> train are singing. Can you hear the voices of a New Generation? They are singing and
> shouting with unchained abandon. Lift your voice, raise your fist. You sing, too.

We will return to Glide throughout this program, as its ministry informs the historical events in this hour.
For now, we cut to:

THE PAST:

A train rushes by, seen in grainy black-and-white footage reminiscent of the early years of this century. A
woman can be heard singing softly, unaccompanied, as if comforting a sleeping child on board: *Plenty of*
good room, plenty of good room in my Father's kingdom. A few cars back, we catch a glimpse of a
window, the curtain drawn. Inside, a man's hand sets words to paper:

> I am writing on board a Jim Crow car…a horrible night ride.… Why does the negro
> leave the South?… You feel a large part of that answer on this train…and share for one
> night the longing of the people to reach the line…which separates Dixie from the rest of
> creation.

Everyone Is Welcome

The third hour of THIS FAR BY FAITH begins with the onset of the greatest internal population shift to
have yet occurred in the United States. In 1910, more than 90% of African Americans live in the South.
Between the turn of the century and 1930, nearly two million will make their way north in a mass exodus.
They are "led as if by some mysterious unseen hand which was compelling them on," reports Charles S.
Johnson, an African-American sociologist in Chicago at the time. A group of nearly 150 Southerners,
crossing the Ohio River, a divide "between Dixie and the rest of creation," kneels together and prays.

3-4

---

[i] Treatment written by Sheila Curran Bernard and Lulie Haddad; episode three of THIS FAR BY FAITH, broadcast as
Guide My Feet. © 1998 Blackside, Inc., reprinted with permission.

The Milltail Pack

At the edge of a dirt roadway which runs along a thick wooded area, three red wolves appear as dusk begins to fall. The leader of the pack is an old male in his twilight years with a thick auburn coat and a long nose. Though he's not as fast as he used to be, his gait remains quick, his eyes and ears alert. Close behind are two noticeably smaller wolves. They are siblings, a male and a female just turned three years old. The pack is heading to a corn field just at the end of the road. In the brown dry stalks of last month's corn live mice, rabbits and voles–tasty appetizers for the Milltail Pack.

At nine years old, the aging male is raising, in all probability, his last offspring. He's seen a lot of change over the years, and he's survived to tell the story of how a species on the brink of extinction came to be saved by a handful of dedicated humans and a branch of government. Known to biologists at the Alligator River National Wildlife Refuge in North Carolina as #331, this old male is living proof that predators and people can live together and flourish. The only remaining red wolf that was born in captivity and reintroduced into the wild, his life parallels the timeline of a unique government initiative.

In 1980 the red wolf was declared biologically extinct–in the wild. In answer to this, the US Fish and Wildlife Service implemented the Red Wolf Recovery Plan–an all-out effort to save the species using captive wolves. This was the first re-introductory program of its kind for any carnivore in the world! Against overwhelming odds and after countless setbacks, the program has managed success.

In 1987, a red wolf breeding pair was reintroduced into the Alligator River Wildlife Refuge, and by the next year their first litter of pups was born in the wild. Since then wolves have been introduced on three island sites, three wildlife refuges, a national park, and a number of privately-owned properties in North Carolina, Tennessee, and South Carolina. But it wasn't easy. The recovery plan had to insure genetic diversity, hope the wolves tolerant of people in a captive setting would shy away from them once wild, and enlist public support for reintroduction of a predator in their neighborhoods. And the ultimate goal of the plan, not yet realized, is to have a total population of 220 wild red wolves.

Today there are about 70 wolves living in northeastern North Carolina, and all but one were born in the wild. Number 331 and his brother, 332, were released when they were just under one year old. Running together they sought out a home range that was occupied by a resident male. They killed the wolf and began consorting with his mate, 205. Together the young males shared the area with 331 mating with 205 and 332 taking up with 205's daughter. But 332 was killed by a car leaving 331 the leader of the Milltail Pack. Like gray wolves, red wolves mate for life, but 331 lost his first mate several years ago. He then mated with his step daughter, 394, who was mother to the siblings he takes hunting today. Last year, she died leaving him without a mate and the youngsters without a mother.

The Milltail Pack ranges through farmlands, wooded areas, public roadways and along the banks of Milltail Creek in search of food. They mainly eat white-tailed deer, but their diet also consists of raccoons and small mammals like rabbits and mice. Similar to gray wolves, they tend to shy away from people and stay close to woodlands or farm edges that provide cover. In their home in North Carolina the habitat ranges from farmland to wooded areas including marshy wetlands, and even a military bombing range!

Before becoming extinct in the wild, red wolves populated the southeastern United States, but as man began clear-cutting areas for wood, drainage and farms, wolves and men came into closer contact. Fear and misunderstanding led to indiscriminate killings and bounties. In addition, as coyotes adapted stretching their habitat from western states into the southeast, they interbred with red wolves, threatening the wolves' genetic purity.

The Milltail Pack has lived through the successes and failures of the Red Wolf Recovery Plan and now stands on the threshold of a new debate. Can man use this program as a model for other species and can we learn from our mistakes? Despite the success of such re-introductory programs, there will always be opponents of predators. In 1995, gray wolves were reintroduced into Yellowstone National Park and today their fate is questionable because opponents to the reintroduction have waged a court struggle to have them removed. In North Carolina opponents to the Red Wolf Recovery Plan still threaten to shut down the program with lengthy court battles. Last year 11 Mexican wolves were released in Arizona after 16 years of planning, and today they are all dead—most were shot by angry ranchers. For conservationists and biologists these programs represent a chance for society to learn from our mistakes. Without the existence of top predators, prey animals go unchecked and often overpopulate areas. And not only is it important to save wolves because of their role as predators, but they are a leading symbol of wild nature.

Because red wolves were virtually extinct until 1987, little was known about their behavior. But biologists are learning that their social structure, feeding and breeding habits are similar to gray wolves. Ten years after reintroducing the first red wolves into the wild, their numbers are growing—evidence of their adaptability, strength and stamina. The leader of the Milltail Pack has survived to sire 4 litters and he and his offspring have a unique story to tell.

Wolves have been in the news for the past few years and are a hot topic. But little has been said about the red wolf or this recovery project. Most of the national press has focused on the gray wolves and their reintroduction to Yellowstone. While there has been regional press about the Red Wolf Recovery Plan, this film is the first documentary to offer an in-depth look at these beautiful animals and the circumstances that have brought them back into the wild.

Film Approach

This film offers an opportunity for a rare glimpse into the lives of a fascinating species, and the film's goal is to tell a success story. Using the Milltail Pack we'll chronicle the program from the early days of life in captivity, move to life today in the wild, and finally speculate about the future of the recovery program and these amazing animals. We have access to footage of wolves in captivity, footage of animals being released, and filming in the wild today. {In order for the biologists to monitor the health and movements of released wolves, most of the animals are radio collared which makes it easy for us to locate packs and differentiate between them.}

This film will take the viewer on an odyssey of survival through the eyes of an aging red wolf. Filming will include captive animals at the Alligator River National Wildlife Refuge, wolf capture and tagging, wolf release, and behavior of family groups in the wild. In addition, interviews with biologists who have been working in the program for 11 years as well as area farmers and townspeople will help illustrate how these wolves came to be accepted on both private and refuge land and how they've managed to survive. While the focus of the film is the red wolf, we'll round out the piece with a look at what's happening to the Mexican wolf and the grays in Yellowstone.

---

[i] Treatment written by Holly Stadtler; film broadcast on EXPLORER WILD as *America's Last Red Wolves.* © 2000 Dream Catcher Films, reprinted with permission.

Sample editing outline, *Lalee's Kin*[i]

AUGUST
A NEW SCHOOL YEAR BEGINS

LLW AND KIDS ON PORCH

    Intro kids

    Main flunked first grade

BOYS BATH – before school

LOST CLOTHES (night before school)

TELEPHONE GAME

FIRST DAY OF SCHOOL – LW brushes Redman's hair

PARKING LOT ADVICE – LLW and Redman

REGISTRATION – LLW and Redman

SAN'S HOUSE

    Supplies

DON'T NOBODY KNOW

SUNSET

    Praise Jesus

GRANNY CRIES ON PORCH

    No pencils

KIDS GET ON SCHOOL BUS/ARRIVE AT SCHOOL

REGGIE – If kids don't come to school first day we're not going to solve anything

    We have a test Oct. 1 and instruction begins now

    Someone has to be Level 1, but we don't want to be it

GRANNY IN SCHOOL

SADIE DILLS

COTTON FIELD

LALEE AND REGGIE RE COTTON PICKING AND PLANTATION MENTALITY

    R- Closed schools

---

[i] © 2002 Maysles Films, Inc., reprinted with permission.

VOICE 001: It is odd to watch with what feverish ardor Americans pursue prosperity – ever tormented by the shadowy suspicion that they may not have chosen the shortest route to get it. They cleave to the things of this world as if assured that they will never die – and yet rush to snatch any that comes within their reach, as if they expected to stop living before they had relished them. Death steps in in the end and stops them, before they have grown tired of this futile pursuit of that complete felicity which always escapes them.

Alexis de Toqueville

TITLE: THE DONNER PARTY

NARRATOR: It began in the 1840s, spurred on by financial panic in the East, by outbreaks of cholera and malaria, and by the ceaseless American hankering to move West. When the pioneer movement began, fewer than 20,000 white Americans lived west of the Mississippi River. [Ten years later the emigration had swelled to a flood, and] Before it was over, more than half a million men, women and children had stepped off into the wilderness at places like Independence, Missouri, and headed out over the long road to Oregon and California.

In places their wagon wheels carved ruts shoulder-deep in the rocky road.

The settlers themselves knew they were making history. "It will be received," one Emigrant wrote, "as a legend on the borderland of myth." But of all the stories to come out of the West, none has cut more deeply into the imagination of the American people than the tale of the Donner Party high in the Sierra Nevada in the winter of 1846.

INTERVIEW HS24: Human endeavor and failure. Blunders, mistakes, ambition, greed – all of the elements. And if you call the rescue of the surviving parties a happy ending, it's a happy ending. But what about those that didn't make it. Terrible, terrible.

Harold Schindler

INTERVIEW JK1: We're curious about people who've experienced hardship, who have gone through terrible ordeals. And certainly the Donner Party, you know, 87 people went through a crisis the likes of which few human beings have ever faced. And we're curious about that. It can tell us something

1

---

[i] Written by Ric Burns. © 1992 Steeplechase Films, Inc., reprinted with permission.

Sample page, script (two column), *Lift Every Voice*[1]

SERIES TITLE	*I'LL MAKE ME A WORLD: A CENTURY OF AFRICAN-AMERICAN ARTS*
NAME OF SHOW	*EPISODE 1: LIFT EVERY VOICE*

	Van Peebles: People always talk about the—the down side of
Lower third: **Melvin Van Peebles** **Filmmaker**	racism. There's an up side, too. The up side is that nobody thinks you're smart. They don't even know why they don't think you're smart. Don't woke 'em, let 'em slept. Just go ahead and do the deal you have to do. Racism offers great business opportunities if you keep your mouth shut.
clips of Bert Williams – *Nobody*	(hearing a few bars of *Nobody*) *When life seems full of clouds and rain* *And I am full of nothing and pain* *Who soothes my thumping, bumping brain?* *NOBODY.*
lower third: **Lloyd Brown** **Writer**	**LLOYD BROWN:** Bert Williams combined the grace of a Charlie Chaplin, imagery and all, and at the same time with a very rich voice too. And so he—he was...wonderful comedy.
lower third: **James Hatch** **Theater Historian**	**HATCH:** He has a...(laughing) song where he's obviously explaining to his wife who the woman was that he was seen with. And the refrain chorus line is "She was a cousin of mine." He has that line, I would say, six or seven times in the song: "She was just a cousin of mine." Every time it's different. Every time it's a new interpretation. (v/o) The man was a genius.
Stills of Bert Williams	**NARRATION 1: In the earliest years of the 20th century, Bert Williams was the most successful black performer on the American stage. But each night, he performed behind a mask he hated: blackface.**
Lower third: **Ben Vereen** **Performer**	**VEREEN** (v/o): Bert Williams didn't want to black up. But socially during that time, he had to. And he realized that. He was a very intelligent man…. We have to hide our identity by putting on this mask, in order to get things said and done. (o/c) But we did it. We did it. And today we don't have to do it. But we cannot forget it.

---

[1] Written by Sheila Curran Bernard; episode one of *I'll Make A World.* © 1998 Blackside, Inc., reprinted with permission.

CHAPTER 11

Shooting

Shooting with the story in mind means being prepared to get all the visuals you need to tell the story you think you want to tell, and being prepared for those surprises that are likely to make a good documentary even better. Who shoots, how, and with what, depends on a host of variables. Are you shooting on your parents' farm or in the middle of a political campaign in a foreign country? Is the event you're covering something that happens every day, or is it a once-in-a-lifetime opportunity? Are special skills or equipment needed to get the shots you need?

CREW SIZE

The actual configuration of a documentary crew can vary widely. At one end of the spectrum, a filmmaker as renowned as Spike Lee might set out with the kind of crew more likely to shoot a Hollywood feature than an independent documentary. "Normally when you shoot a doc, it's you as the producer, camera, an assistant (if you're shooting film), sound, and maybe a production assistant," says Sam Pollard, who edited and co-produced *When the Levees Broke* with Lee. "But when we flew out of Newark the day after Thanksgiving [in 2005], it was Spike, me, a line producer, three cameramen, four assistants, and six graduate students from NYU. Then, when we got to New Orleans, we got a location manager with his four location people, five vans, five drivers, a camera loader—I mean, it was like an army."

Filming the spectacular footage of birds crossing exotic skylines in *Winged Migration* took five teams of people, according to the film's press material, including 17 pilots, 14 cinematographers, and the use of "planes, gliders, helicopters, and balloons." (The DVD's bonus material includes a look at how this film was made. Most significantly, birds were raised from birth by humans upon whom they imprinted, and their flight is actually in pursuit of the "parent" bird riding, with a cinematographer, in an ultralight airplane. In some cases, birds were transported between locations.)

DOI: 10.1016/B978-0-240-81241-0.00011-3

At the other end of the spectrum are two- and even one-person crews. In general, working alone is not ideal, although there may be situations in which a project or scenes of a project can benefit. In making their film *So Much So Fast*, for example, Steve Ascher and Jeannie Jordan worked as a team, with Steve shooting. But Steve says they discovered that when Jamie Heywood (who'd been diagnosed with ALS) was alone with one or both of his brothers, "it worked out better if it was just me alone. If we were both there, Stephen's focus would get split." So Steve shot these scenes alone, eventually wearing a mic as he engaged the brothers in conversation.

Jon Else, who has served as a cinematographer on hundreds of films, says that with "very few exceptions," a minimum of a two-person crew is the way to go. "Working as a one-person crew involves such incredible compromise, you only have so much brain power, you only have so much muscle power," he explains.

Are you under significant time constraints? Vérité filmmaker Susan Froemke had just one day in which to film the making of the cast album for the Broadway hit *The Producers*, and her work could not interfere with the album's production. "We could have used four cameras, but we only had the budget for three—two in the recording studio and one in the control room," Froemke explains, adding that she hired three very experienced vérité shooters, Bob Richman, Don Lenzer, and Tom Hurwitz. She added, "You had to go in with people who are also filmmakers in their own right, because you couldn't be everywhere at once and there was almost no way to have a communication system because it would interfere with the recording process."

SHOOTING WITH THE STORY IN MIND

You want to go into the field with a clear sense of your film's story and approach so that you can maximize the quality and impact of what you get, and so you'll be better able to recognize and take advantage of those moments you couldn't possibly have anticipated beforehand.

Some films require more visual planning than others. As mentioned, watch the "making of" documentaries on the DVDs for *Winged Migration* and *March of the Penguins*, about the challenges of making those films. Read interviews with Nathanial Kahn as he discusses *My Architect*, and how important it was to him that his footage capture the power of the buildings that his father, a world-renowned architect, had designed. Each film demands its own type of preparation.

Thinking Visually

Will your film be dependent on interviews and narration, or can scenes and sequences be played without sound and still convey story? With live-action filming, unless a member of the core team is shooting, the best way to ensure visual storytelling is to involve your cinematographer and not to simply use him or her as a "shooter." Being able to frame images beautifully is not the same thing as being able to frame *meaningful* images beautifully. Boyd Estus, a director of photography whose credits include the Academy Award–winning *The Flight of the Gossamer Condor*, has shot both documentary and drama for venues including the BBC, PBS, Discovery Channel, and National Geographic. When a documentary producer calls him about shooting, Estus always asks to see an outline or treatment in advance, something that gives him an idea of the big picture—not only what's being filmed, but why.

In cases where a crew is filming an event, the sound recordist, too, should be in on the story, in part because he or she is often better able to anticipate, through listening to the conversations of key players who've been miked, where the action is going next. "They often will hear things that nobody else hears," Estus says, adding that when he shoots vérité, he also wears a headset so that he can hear the radio mikes directly. This can pay off in unexpected ways. For example, Estus worked on a series called *Survivor, M.D.*, which followed seven Harvard Medical School students over a period of several years as they became doctors. He was filming a student assisting in a heart operation when the patient, an elderly man she'd grown close to, died. Estus watched as the student walked off by herself, to the back of the operating room.

"By then, I knew her well enough to know she would have trouble [with the loss]," Estus says, and because he was wearing a sound monitor, he could hear that she was crying. He stayed in the distance but continued to film as the senior surgeon approached the student and consoled her, but also reminded her that as a physician, she had to balance her own feelings with the family's need for her professional guidance. She nodded, and together the doctors went to speak with the patient's family. Since the story was about the making of a doctor, the emotion shown by the tears was important, but not as important as the lesson—another step on the road to becoming a physician. The moment feels intimate despite the fact that Estus stayed several feet away (he shot the scene handheld until a tripod was slipped underneath the camera as it was rolling). "Normally I'm right on top of people, especially for that kind of shooting," he says. "But I didn't want to break the spell. And also, I felt the perspective was appropriate, the two of them meeting." Estus notes that, although at times like this he can be afraid to move a muscle for fear of interrupting the moment, at other times he's proactive in ensuring that he gets the coverage he wants.

What you shoot and how you shoot it involves more than simply documenting an event; it's a way of contributing to the story. "Think about what the scene is supposed to say, as much as you can, both before it and during it," says Steve Ascher, who coauthored *The Filmmaker's Handbook* (with Edward Pincus). He adds that the same applies "to the broader structure, in terms of how you go about deciding what to film, how much of it to film, and whom to film." In many cases, you may be filming a scene or sequence without knowing exactly how it will come out or how the overall story will ultimately be structured. "But you should be asking yourself, what seems important, who's compelling, how might the story be structured?" Ascher says. He notes that first-time filmmakers often have trouble projecting ahead like this. "They haven't done it enough to think about, what is a narrative spine, what is structure, how will scenes get distilled? They tend to overshoot and at the same time not shoot in a focused way that makes themes emerge."

If your crew understands what your storytelling needs are, they can help when the unexpected occurs. When Karin Hayes and Victoria Bruce left Colombia after their first shoot for *The Kidnapping of Ingrid Betancourt*, they left their second camera, a small digital recorder, in the care of their Colombian cinematographer. As they explain in Chapter 16, his own camera had been stolen during the kidnapping, and they wanted to be sure that if anything important happened, such as Betancourt's release, he would be able to film it. Unexpectedly, Betancourt's father died, and the cinematographer's brother covered not only the funeral but also the visit of Betancourt's two children, who'd been sent for safety to live with their father (Betancourt's ex-husband) in France. "That was the only time they were back in Colombia," Bruce noted. "So it was great that we'd left that camera there." The funeral sequence is one of the film's most powerful.

SHOOTING WITH THE EDITING IN MIND

It's important that footage be shot in a way that it can be edited. There needs to be sufficient coverage to give you options, and to let a scene play. You are not shooting news, where one shot per scene might be enough. Think of shooting your documentary the way you would shoot a dramatic feature: Within any given scene, you want wide shots, medium shots, close-ups, and cutaways, making sure that shots are long enough and steady enough to use. You want to be able to create visual scenes that give context and other story information. For example, if someone is talking or performing, you want shots of the audience, to let viewers know where the speech or performance is directed and how it's being received. You'll want exteriors of the performance space—is it a vinyl-sided church in the middle of a rural area, or the Kennedy Center in Washington? You'll want identifying markers, if they exist: the marquis, a handwritten sign introducing the speaker, a cutaway to a program. You want to see what people are looking at, the angles at which they see each other, their points of view as they look at the world. (Look at *Murderball* for an excellent example of this; the film was frequently shot from the point of view of those in wheelchairs.)

Note that you're not randomly shooting everything possible; you're making sure that you have visual information that conveys basic narrative information: what, where, how. You want to establish the time, place, and people, looking for visuals that might let you cut back on verbal information. Look for the telling details that reveal character, whether it's the cigarette burning untended or the pile of liquor bottles in the recycling bin. Look for shots that show how people behave in relationship to each other and how skillfully they handle the tools of their work. You might want to look for humor. And as mentioned, you need to be sure that you have a sufficient range of angles, shots, and cutaways that your editor can condense hours of material into a final film that tells a coherent and visually satisfying story.

Cinematographers try to "cover scenes to leave as many story-telling options as possible open," Jon Else says. "I have kind of written on the inside of my eyelids a list of basic storytelling shots that I have to have coming away from a scene, about a half dozen shots." These include the widest possible angle of a landscape or cityscape, a proscenium shot in which all the figures involved in the action are in the frame and large enough that their faces and actions can be seen, several angles on any process being filmed, and close-ups "on every single face of every person, both talking and not talking."

If there's a sign saying, "Joe's Orchard" or "The Henry Ford Motor Company," Else says, you want to get a "nice picture of the sign, preferably one picture with something happening in the foreground or background and one picture without anything happening." If there are time markers such as clocks, you want to get a shot of them. "A lot of it's cliché stuff, and 90 percent of the time you don't use it," he says, "but that one time you need to show that time has passed, the clock is invaluable." And finally, he notes that you want to be sure to shoot simple indicators of direction. "If you're next to a river," for example, "you want to make sure that you get a shot that's close enough that you can see which way the current's going."

For those who shoot in film, the cost of stock and processing seems to mandate careful shot selection. "I used to joke that there should be a dollar counter in the viewfinder instead of a footage counter," says Ascher, who shot *Troublesome Creek* (1996) on film and *So Much So Fast* (2006) on digital video. "In film you're really thinking ahead about each camera move, how you can it cut with the others, what will it mean. 'I'm now doing a close shot, I'm now doing a move from character A to character B.' People who learn to shoot with video often shoot more continuously, and it's a real problem. They don't stop the camera, they're not thinking about where shots begin and end, and sometimes that results in uncuttable footage."

Shooting Scenes

On location, as in the office and the editing room, film storytelling means thinking not only in terms of shots but also scenes and sequences. "We're trying to make scenes, because we're trying to make nonfiction films ... just like a feature film director makes a film," explains Susan Froemke, one of the leading vérité filmmakers in the United States. "I've got to get cutaways, I've got to get an end point of the scene, and I've got to get into the scene some way."

Main and Redman, from *Lalee's Kin: The Legacy of Cotton*. Photo courtesy of the filmmakers.

Froemke says that with observational filmmaking, it's not unusual to miss the beginning of the scene. "Often you're sitting waiting and something happens and you just miss that first line, she says." Froemke and Albert Maysles were in Mississippi filming *Lalee's Kin* when they discovered that Lalee (see Chapter 9) was very upset, but didn't know why. Froemke and Maysles began filming, and realized that a neighbor had informed Lalee that her son had been taken back to jail. "I knew that I didn't have a beginning to the scene. I had to get a beginning, but I didn't want to just ask Lalee, 'What's going on?'" Froemke says. At the time, there was no plan to narrate the film (eventually a few title cards were used), and so Froemke had to figure out how to nudge Lalee to get the opening line.

"That's, to me, a real skill that you develop after you've shot a lot of vérité and you know what you need to bring back to the editing room for the editor to be able to craft a scene together to tell a story," Froemke explains. "Lalee didn't know what [her son] had been taken to jail for. So what I did is, I asked Jeanette, Lalee's daughter, 'Why don't you call the police, to find out?' As soon as I said that, Lalee said to Jeanette, 'Why don't you call the police?' That allowed Jeanette to talk with them and then tell Lalee [as we were filming] what had happened. So that we did have a beginning to the story."

Capturing Backstory

With vérité filming, there is also the challenge of telling backstory. "Often over the course of shooting I'll just throw out a question," Froemke says, adding, "Especially if there's someone else around, and some comment about the past goes into a discussion about the present. You throw out a thought and let the subjects bounce that around and see where it goes."

CREATING VISUALS

Not all film ideas are inherently visual, especially those that concern complex or technical issues. If you haven't found a sufficiently visual story through which to explore these issues, it's likely that you'll try to find general visuals that will at least put some images on screen as your experts and/or narrator speak. For a story on educational policy, for example, you might spend an afternoon filming at a local elementary school; for a story on aging, you might attend a physical therapy session at a local hospital. This material is often described as "wallpaper" because the visuals themselves are generic, in that they're not linked to any particular character or story.

Generic or not, created visuals are often necessary to a film project, and the more creative you can be with them, the better. In developing a film on the controversial diagnosis of multiple personality disorder, for example, filmmaker Holly Stadtler and her co-producer came up with a variety of visuals. To demonstrate the concept of dissociation, they filmed a child in her bedroom, on the bed, playing near the bed, standing and sitting, and then combined these images in the editing room. The result is a portrait of the child surrounded by "alternate" versions of herself engaged in a range of behaviors. Stadtler also mounted Styrofoam heads (wig forms) on turntables and had them lit dramatically. "I wanted to have some footage I could cut to that wasn't specific and wasn't someone just sitting in a park or something," she says. To further explore dissociation and compare it to the common phenomenon of "highway hypnosis"—losing track of where you've been while you're driving—they combined point-of-view shooting from within a car (including a car going through a tunnel) to a more dizzying "drive" through corrugated steel pipe, shot with a lipstick camera.

Demonstrations may also be devised to advance your story or themes. Morgan Spurlock's *Super Size Me* is built around a demonstration, a 30-day diet that occurred only for the sake of the film. Spurlock interweaves this with a range of shooting styles. He travels to several different schools and school districts to investigate approaches to diet and physical education, for example. He films a man before and during gastric bypass surgery. He interviews people on the street, asks a family in front of the White House if they can recite the pledge of allegiance, and finds a man who's fanatical about Big Macs. All of these scenes had to be planned, and each element of the film had to be weighed against the other elements. It costs money to shoot, so you don't want to waste time filming scenes or sequences that duplicate each other, whether literally or emotionally, because if they do, as discussed in the following chapter, they're likely to be cut.

Visual Storytelling in the Wild

Creating visual stories out of nature and wildlife footage can be very expensive and time-consuming, but the results, as evidenced by the blockbuster hits *March of the Penguins* and *Winged Migration*, can be spectacular. These productions took considerable time, money, and technology. But what about the relatively lower-budget natural history documentaries that are popular on television?

Filmmaker Holly Stadtler produced *America's Last Red Wolves*, a half-hour film for the series *National Geographic Explorer*. Her approach to wildlife films comes, in part, from her experience filming a documentary about the making of *The Leopard Son*, a Discovery Channel feature produced several years ago by noted naturalist Hugo Van Lawick. "*The Leopard Son* started out being called *Big Cats*," she says, "a story about lions, cheetahs, and leopards in the Serengeti." Filmed on 35mm over a period of a year, the story evolved on location and in the editing room; the final film focuses on leopards, and the real-life drama of a young leopard coming of age. Stadtler spent several weeks on the Serengeti with the production crew and saw how Van Lawick captured natural behavior by "getting the animals used to his presence, staying with it and persevering, and not manipulating things in the environment. And so I became this purist," she says, "'This is the way to do it.'"

With the growth of cable and the decrease in the amount of money available for production, however, filmmakers must often find ways to make quality wildlife films that don't require the time needed to fully habituate animals to a film crew's presence. This can be a tricky business due to ethical issues involved in wildlife shooting. Concern has been raised over such practices as tying carcasses (or worse, maimed animals) down so that animals will come to feed at predictable spots. Stadtler also notes that some people object to filmmakers using vehicle lights at night because it can affect the outcome of a kill. "What I try to do is find a happy medium," she says. "For instance, there's no way you can get 25 feet from wolves feeding in the wild—they're going to take the carcass and go—or that you could get that close to a den site. We had a lot of discussion about setting up remote cameras that could be tripped by sensors, which I had done on *Troubled Waters* (a one-hour film for TBS), but you get a shot or two and the animal leaves."

Red wolves were once extinct in the wild; they were bred in captivity by the U.S. Fish and Wildlife Service and then reintroduced into the wild at the Alligator River National Wildlife Refuge in North Carolina, beginning in the mid-1980s. Some wolves remain in captivity, however, and Stadtler took advantage of this to get the close shots she needed. She and the crew masked the fencing behind the wolves; the cameraman stood about 25 feet away from the wolves on the other side, poking his lens through the fence and filming as a deer carcass was put out for the animals. "That's how we got some beautiful images, close up, of wolves," Stadtler says. "The only other way we could have done that is if we had, in essence, habituated the wolves in the wild to our presence, which would have required months of being there—and even then, I'm not sure how close they would have allowed our camera people."

TONE AND STYLE

Visual storytelling goes well beyond what you shoot: How you shoot, how you light, and how you treat the material in postproduction are also critical. Tone (Does the light convey something harsh and cold or warm and familiar?), point of view (From whose point of view is a scene shot? Is it from a first-person point of view, or is it omniscient? Is the camera shooting up at the subject or looking down?), and context (Does the subject fill the frame, or does he or she appear small and overwhelmed by the surroundings?) are all important considerations. Knowing at least some of the answers in advance can help you plan your production needs, including lights, lenses, and filters; whether or not to use special equipment such as dollies and cranes; and how specialized (and experienced) you might need your production crew to be.

SHOOTING FROM THE HIP

It can takes months, if not years, to raise enough money to do films the "right" way. Unless you're a name filmmaker, chances are that the path between you and that kind of movie will be littered, as discussed in previous chapters, with proposals, rejections, more proposals, more rejections, and the occasional but still too small grant. At least that's the way it is in the United States, where a relatively quick time line for a higher-budget independent project to move from idea to broadcast can be three to five years. Some very worthy films and series have taken considerably longer, and some equally worthy projects have never made the final hurdle to production. (This isn't full-time attention; it's not unusual for projects to go in fits and starts as producers intersperse development on one or more programs with additional, paying work on other films.)

So what do independents do if the story won't wait but early funding is likely to be difficult to raise? The answer depends in part on the filmmakers. Those who have significant experience and some resources may simply develop the film outline and start shooting. Their financial investment is limited to their time and out-of-pocket expenses such as equipment rental and travel, but since they themselves are experienced personnel, the resulting film is likely to be professional in quality. Those without significant shooting experience may choose to teach themselves quickly or do what they can and hire professionals to help. A powerful story, told well, can often overcome some cinematic rough edges. The converse is not true: A weak story shot spectacularly well is still a weak story.

INTERVIEWS

Before shooting, look at films that contain interviews and decide what you like or don't like about an approach and what you want to do in your own film. Do you plan to appear on camera along with your interviewees, as Judith Helfand did in *Blue Vinyl*? Do you want your interviewees to appear to be addressing the audience directly? Do you want to take a less formal approach to interviewing, asking your subjects questions as they go about their lives or filming them as they discuss specific subjects with each other?

Your answers to these questions will affect how you conduct and shoot your interviews. If you're not going to appear on camera, and your questions won't be heard as voice-over, you'll need to frame the question in a way that elicits a full answer, not just, "Yes. Sure. Oh, yes, I agree with that." You might want to ask the person being interviewed to incorporate part of your question in his or her answer, as in, "When did you know there was trouble?" Answer: "I knew there was trouble when. . ." In any case, you'll need to listen carefully as the interview is under way to make sure that you're getting something that will work as the beginning of a sentence, thought, or paragraph. If necessary, ask the question again, maybe in a different way.

Go into the interview knowing the handful of specific story points the interview needs to cover, and then include other material that would be nice to have or questions that are essentially fishing—you're not sure what you're going to get, but the answers could be interesting. Note that if you've cast the person you're interviewing in advance, you probably already know what ground the interviewee can best cover. It's rarely productive to ask everyone in a film the same 20 questions.

Conducting Interviews

Everyone approaches interviewing differently. Some people work to put the subjects at ease, starting with more "comfortable" questions before easing into material that's more touchy. As mentioned, filmmakers whose style is more confrontational may show up with the cameras rolling. Sometimes you're asking someone to relate an event he or she has told many times, and the story's taken on a polished quality that you want it to lose; it may take getting the person riled up, or challenging something about the story, to accomplish that.

Another strategy for interviewing, notes Boyd Estus, "is for the person asking the questions not to look at the interviewee as a source of information but to get them involved in a conversation, which often involves playing devil's advocate. 'I really don't understand why this is better than that. Can you explain that to me?'" Estus explains, "So the person's engaged, as opposed to spouting a pat answer."

The Interview Setup

Only rarely is an interviewee asked to speak directly into the camera, in part because few "regular" people can do it comfortably. (Filmmaker Errol Morris achieves this effect through an elaborate setup he devised, called an *Interrotron*™, in which the interviewee speaks to an image of Morris on a screen placed over the camera lens.) Most filmmakers, instead, sit opposite the person (or people) being interviewed and just slightly to the left or right of the camera lens. The person looks at the interviewer, and so appears to be looking just slightly off camera. Although some cinematographers work further away, Boyd Estus likes to position the camera fairly close to the interview subject, within five feet or so. "It does two things," Estus says. "If the person moves, they change size in the frame, which makes it more three-dimensional, whereas if you're on a long lens they're plastered against the background." More importantly, he says, this puts the interviewer in comfortable range of the questioner.

This kind of intimacy may also be enhanced by conducting the interview over a table. If both parties lean forward, they're very close, and their hand gestures will be in the frame. Estus notes that wooden chairs with arms (often found in academic institutions) can be especially good, because the arms tend to be higher than normal. "The gesture's in front of your face, and if you're leaning forward you look more energetic." You don't want the chair's frame or headrest to show behind the person, and as a rule, try to avoid chairs that swivel or rock.

Another decision to make is whether the interviewee should be looking slightly to the left or to the right. If, for example, you know that you want two people to be "answering" each other on film, you might want them to be facing different directions. This isn't always possible to do, but if it's a style you like, you'll need to plan for it in advance. You and your crew also need to think about the other visual content in the frame. "Part of the job is to sell the person so that the audience really wants to hear what they say," says Estus. "My approach is to try to make an environmental portrait, so that the setting the person is in and the way they look tells you something about them and the subject matter. In wide screen (16:9) television that's much more important because no matter how tight you are on the head, there's half the screen hanging there empty, and a wall of books doesn't tell you anything."

Additional decisions, stemming from the style of film and approach to storytelling, include how you light the interviews and whether you strive for some kind of consistency in look throughout the film (or series). How do you want the interviewee to come across? There are ways to light that will flatter someone's face and minimize the distractions that could leave viewers focusing on the appearance of an interviewee, rather than his or her words. What are your subjects wearing? For more formal interview setups, some producers ask subjects to bring a few clothing options. (For some films, a stylistic decision might be made to ask interviewees to dress one way or another; Estus did a series with gothic themes in which the interviewees were asked to wear black.)

The visual context of an interview and the visual cues contained within it can be very important to the storytelling. How tightly do you frame the interview? Some cinematographers will stay wider for expositional information and move in closer as the interview gets more intimate and/or emotional. What do the interview setting and subject's clothing convey? In *The Thin Blue Line*, Randall Adams and David Harris are interviewed in a setting that suggests confinement, and in fact both turn out to be in prison. Law enforcement people are all filmed indoors, in suits and ties. David Harris's friends are filmed outdoors, in casual clothing. Because Morris uses no lower thirds (on-screen titles) to identify speakers by name, these visual cues serve as a form of identification.

If you've filmed someone involved in his or her work or at home, you probably have footage that advances our understanding of the character (we can see that she is confident as she works very complex machinery, or that he is devoted to his children) even as we hear who the person is. But it's still common to see typical and uninformative introductory shots of the interviewee—"Walking into the Building" or "Entering the Office" or "Working at the Computer." Even some films that are otherwise excellent resort to these shots. In hindsight, there are almost always better alternatives.

Interview Styles

Interviews need to have an energy and immediacy about them, as well as credibility. They also need to serve the story being told. Watch a range of interviews and you'll see that they can be very different. Is the interviewee talking about a subject from a distance of time, or is he or she speaking as if the event is ongoing? It's not only experts who talk about subjects; people often shape stories after the fact, especially if they've told them before, and it creates a kind of distance between the storyteller and the story, which is sometimes desired, but not always.

CHAPTER 12

Editing

Many of the storytelling issues covered elsewhere in the book come into play again in the editing room. On the majority of films, story and structure do not truly come together until the editor begins to assemble and pare down filmed material. Several versions of the film may be cut before the best point of attack is identified; you may be cutting toward one ending for weeks before you realize that, in fact, the film ends on an even earlier and stronger note.

Although every project is different, the basic editing process is that you screen everything and make a long assembly of your footage, which is then honed into a rough cut, a fine cut, a picture lock, and finally, a script lock. The assembly includes the material you've shot to date as well as archival material, if any. (Often, you're working not with original archival footage but with "slop" dubs, such as preview reels or stills you might have shot quickly in the editing room. Later, when you know what images will stay in the film, you negotiate for rights to use this material, order broadcast-quality duplications, or arrange for broadcast-quality filming of still material and artifacts.)

As the editing progresses, you work toward a rough cut. This is a draft of your film that is significantly longer than the final show will be. But your general story and structure are in place, and you have some, if not all, of your elements on hand. The rough cut stage is often the best time to reassess major issues of story and structure and experiment with alternatives; this becomes more difficult as the film is fine-tuned. By fine cut, the film is almost to time. (For example, a film that will end up being 57 minutes long might be 63 minutes at the fine cut stage.) Major problems, hopefully, have been worked out. If there is narration, this is the time to begin polishing it. And for the movie as a whole, this is the time to make sure the facts are accurate. Picture lock means that all the images are in place and to time. Script lock means that any outstanding issues of narration or voice-over are

DOI: 10.1016/B978-0-240-81241-0.00012-5

resolved and that the material can be recorded and laid in without further changes.

Jeanne Jordan and family in 1960, from *Troublesome Creek: A Midwestern*. Photo courtesy of the filmmakers.

GETTING TO ROUGH CUT

The interaction between producer, director, writer, and editor (or some combination of these) differs with each project. Some teams watch the rushes (the raw footage) all together and discuss which interview bites work, which scenes are strong, and how material might be assembled. Some editors screen the footage alone because they want to evaluate the material without being influenced by the producer's ideas of what worked or didn't work on location. "I really like to just look," says Jeanne Jordan, an accomplished editor (see Chapter 15). "I don't want people to even tell me 'This was a difficult interview' or 'I didn't get what I wanted.'"

As you screen the footage, you're watching for moments that affect you in some way, whether emotionally or intellectually. Look for scenes and sequences that can play on their own, interview bites that seem strong and clear, material that has the potential to reveal themes and issues you want to raise, and the special moments that you hope audiences will discuss with each other at work the next day. "I'm looking for emotion, that's always my first thing," says editor Sam Pollard (see Chapter 23). "Then I'm looking for some tension and opposition, because that's going to always make those sequences work the best. And if I feel none of those elements are in there, then I figure I've got to convey another type of feeling. Maybe this is a moment where you just sit back and listen to some music; maybe it's a moment to be somewhat reflective. You've got to know what the material says." Each person will come away from a first screening with his or her own favorite moments; this memory of what was strong in the raw footage will be useful as you shape and trim the material into a coherent story, all the while working to retain the energy it held in its raw state.

Some editors work from a written outline of scenes and sequences, especially if the film consists primarily of live action, such as cinéma vérité. If there is a significant amount of interview material, whether or not there is to be narration, the producer may also take transcripts of the interviews and cut and paste selected bites into a "paper edit." If the project was shot to a script or a script-in-progress, that working script will be adjusted to reflect the actual material on hand. In either case, rough narration can be written to seam together disparate elements, make a transition clear, or hold a place for a sequence that's still to be shot. In many editing rooms, "scratch" narration is recorded and cut in against the picture, to better evaluate its effectiveness.

As previously discussed, what works on paper won't necessarily work on film. The juxtaposition of two interview bites and two filmed sequences might read very well, but there may be something about the way a phrase is spoken or the scene plays out that makes it less than powerful on screen. This doesn't mean that you shouldn't do paper cuts; they can be a faster and easier way to "see" an edit before realizing the changes physically. But since a good portion of the paper editing won't work on film, it's also useful to know why you're suggesting a particular change, in addition to what it will be. Perhaps you pulled a bite because it conveyed two specific points; if your choice doesn't work, the editor might be able to satisfy those points in a different way, either through a different bite, a combination of bites, or perhaps through a scene that he or she has just edited that makes the interview bite unnecessary.

The editor, meanwhile, may be assembling scenes, whether from live action or archival footage, shaping them individually, and putting together the strongest beginning, middle, and end possible before sequencing them into the overall film. The editing process tends to be very collaborative. A producer or director coming into the editing room to watch a cut in progress can often see links and transitions that the editor may not have seen, or he or she may see something in what the editor has assembled that will spark a realization that additional material—a piece of artwork, a fragment of music, a different interview excerpt—is needed. It's a give-and-take process, with everyone in the editing room putting themselves in the role of viewers as well as storytellers. Ultimately, there has to be a single person who makes decisions, usually either the producer or director.

Transcripts

If you've conducted interviews or filmed scenes with a lot of relevant discussion, you should get them transcribed, accurately and thoroughly. Not a summary ("Dr. Fisher talking about gravitational forces ..."), but an exact transcription of what is said, including the "um, um, he said, he said, um, well, let me back up by saying that what gravity is not, is...." This will save you a lot of time later, because you're likely to go back to these transcripts repeatedly during the editing process in search of story solutions, and an inaccurate or incomplete transcript can mean that you assemble a scene based on what you think someone said, only to find out that it's close but not what you need, or that it's great but the answer took forever. Some filmmakers will also transcribe scenes that have a lot of dialogue, such as a meeting, press conference, or conversation.

In the case of foreign language interviews, filmmakers in the field often rely on quick translations to get a sense of what's being spoken. In the editing room, particularly if no one on the team is fluent in the interview language, it's good to get an accurate and detailed translation as soon as you can, but no later than rough cut. You don't want to fine tune a film to interview material that doesn't say what you think it says.

When viewing the interviews, make notes on the transcripts to help you remember what someone's energy level is like, if there are problems such as flies or a microphone in the frame, or whether someone sneezes. Some portions of the interview may be usable but only as voice-over; others may be useful as information only. Better to write it down once than to go back to the same bite three times in the course of the editing session because you forgot that there was a reason you didn't use it in the first place. (You're also writing down time code that corresponds to the transcript, so you can find material quickly.)

Another reason to transcribe interviews is that it's unfortunately very easy to cut up someone's words, assemble them with other interviews, and eventually lose track of what the original answer was. I always try to make a point of rereading the transcripts as the editing nears completion (or if I'm hired to help on a project late in the editing stage), for three reasons: to make sure the interviewee is not being misrepresented; to make sure that some terrific material wasn't overlooked earlier when the story was somewhat different; and to look for color and details that might be helpful to narration, if there is narration.

The Paper Edit

Don't go out and buy a commercial screenwriting software program; these are designed specifically for dramatic feature films and serve that function well, but they're of little use for documentaries. Most documentary filmmakers seem to use Word or WordPerfect (files cross these platforms without much difficulty), using them to create scripts that are formatted in either one or two columns.

If two columns are used, one is for visuals, the other for audio. With a single-column format, visuals, if mentioned, are put in parentheses or italics. In either case, narration and interview bites should stand out from each other; for example, the narration might be in bold, or the interview bites indented. On films with significant interview material, whether or not there will also be narration, it can be helpful to create a separate block (whether you're working with one column or two) for each interview bite that's pulled, so they can be quickly moved around. Some filmmakers also use the outlining function to keep sequences intact, again, so they can be quickly rearranged.

The first paper edit is usually an *assembly script*, in which you put all of your selected scenes and interviews into the order in which you think they'll appear. The next target draft of the script is a *rough cut script*, in which you're honing everything down and fine-tuning structure. Every team has its own way of working, but often the director, producer, editor, and writer (if there is a separate writer) are collaborating, so that changes made either on paper or on video are communicated back and forth.

Editing Interviews

As you trim sync material, be careful to mark the script in some way so that you know an edit was made. Not only will this help to ensure that you remember which parts of the statement were constructed (in a way that remains truthful), but it will also help if you go back a month later hoping that the entire statement is on camera, only to discover that it has three different cuts in it. For example, here's the pull as it appears in the assembly script, with no edits:

> CHARLIE: (beginning v/o) He was selling auto parts, used auto parts. Besides, embezzlement's a white collar crime, he's a blue collar guy—well, not really, he's not working with the auto parts, he's more the manager of the store, driving to work in his, oh, what was it, Tercel, his blue Tercel, shirt and tie and all the while I guess he's thinking nobody above him would miss that thirty thou.

The edited bite as it might appear in the rough cut script, with the excision noted:

> CHARLIE: (beginning v/o) He was selling auto parts, used auto parts.// and all the while I guess he's thinking nobody above him would miss that thirty thou.

Juxtaposition

The juxtaposition of two shots, or two sequences, adds meaning that is not necessarily contained in either of the elements alone. This works to your advantage, but it's also something to guard against if the juxtaposition creates a false impression. If you cut from someone saying, "Well, who was responsible for it?" to a shot of Mr. Smith, you are creating the impression that Mr. Smith was responsible, whether you meant to or not.

Entering Late, Exiting Early

As you edit, try to enter a scene at the last possible moment and leave at the earliest possible moment. This doesn't mean chopping the heart out of a scene or losing its context, but it does mean figuring out what is the most meaningful part of that scene, and what is just treading water on screen. Suppose you've filmed a sequence in which a mother goes to the grocery store, chats with a neighbor or two, fusses with the butcher over a choice cut of meat, waits in line at the checkout counter, drives home, prepares a meal, calls her college-age daughter to the table, and then watches with dismay as her daughter storms off, angry that her mother has not respected the fact that she is a vegetarian—a fact that the mother says she didn't know.

Where you enter and exit this scene depends on what the scene is about. Is it about the mother going to tremendous lengths to make her daughter feel welcome at home, perhaps because of a recent divorce or the daughter's expulsion from school? Or is it about a chasm between mother and daughter and their inability to communicate even basic information? If it's the former, the scenes in the grocery store help to establish the mother's efforts to please; if the latter, the grocery store scenes aren't really relevant. You could convey their lack of communication with the following shots: the mother puts the steak on the table; the daughter refuses to eat it and storms away; the mother is left looking at the steak.

Where do you end the scene? Again, it depends on where your story is going. If the story is about the fuss the woman made to please her daughter, you might end it with the reversal: the daughter rejects the food and storms away from the table. But if it's about the communication between mother and daughter, you might want to go a bit further and see what happens next. Will the mother try to find some other way to reach the daughter, perhaps by cooking a vegetarian meal?

Again, you don't want to cut scenes to their tightest in terms of the action; you want to focus them so that their meaning and their emphasis in your film's narrative are clear.

Sequences

Review the discussion in previous chapters about sequences, because construction of these is an important part of getting to rough cut. You want to be sure that each sequence does a unique job in the film, advancing the overall story while also varying the rhythm, tone, and emotional level of the film. Be sure to let each start properly and come to a satisfying close. These are your chapters, the breadcrumbs that entice people to keep watching.

Anticipate Confusion

In general, audiences are willing to do quite a bit of work to figure out what the story is and where you're going with it—that's part of what makes viewing a good documentary an active rather than passive experience—but eventually, if they become too lost, they'll give up. A good storyteller anticipates the audience's confusion and meets it in subtle and creative ways, skillfully weaving information in where and when it's needed and not before. It may take some effort to bring a general audience up to speed on what those gadgets actually do or how certain laws of physics work. But armed with that information and an understanding of how it furthers or frustrates the efforts of the protagonist to reach a goal, solve a mystery, unlock a secret, or prove a theorem, the audience can be one step ahead of the story. Those moments when the audience "gets it" just before you, as the storyteller, give it to them, are enormously satisfying.

Just as you want to present information at the moment it's most needed, you also want to be careful not to clutter a story with too much detail. Many film stories get diluted by details that the filmmakers are convinced are "important," although they are not directly relevant to the story at hand. If you're telling the story about a candidate's political campaign, for example, you might not want to spend a lot of time looking at his business career. If there's something about his career that he's promoting on the campaign trail—he wants to bring his cost-cutting strategies to the job of managing a state budget, for example—then it might be relevant. Otherwise, it's taking up space that you need for your story.

Be careful, though, that you don't "cherry pick" your information, selectively using only those details that support your argument or "take" on a story and ignoring those that contradict you. It's possible to be factually accurate and still create an overall story that is fundamentally dishonest. Choosing some details from a person's life as a means of focusing a story is not the same thing as selectively leaving out information you don't want the audience to know. Ultimately you'll be found out, and it weakens your film and credibility.

ROUGH CUT TO FINE CUT

As the film moves toward completion, footage is dropped and hard decisions must be made. Is the story working as filmed, or is new material needed? Does the story that was set up at the film's beginning pay off at the end? Is it being told for maximum audience involvement? Is this the kind of film that people will talk about? Will it keep an audience watching? If the filmmaker hopes to convey important but difficult concepts, are those concepts being communicated accurately and well? To get the film to a broadcast length, would it be better to delete an entire scene or subplot, or should time be shaved off a number of scenes?

One way to begin answering these questions is by showing the film to an impartial audience. Often this is done at rough cut and, schedules and budgets permitting, again at fine cut. You want to invite people who don't know the story and aren't necessarily interested in it, as well as people who know the story better than you do. If, in previewing your film, you discover that the message you think you're sending is not the message being received, there's a problem. As simple as this seems, it's not uncommon for filmmakers to simply decide there must be something wrong with the audience: "I've said it clearly; I don't know why they're not getting it." Or they fear that if they "pander" to an audience, they will be toning down their "message." It doesn't work that way. If one person doesn't get your film, maybe it's just not that person's cup of tea. If two people don't get it, fine. But if a significant portion of an audience has missed your point, your point isn't being made.

Screening Tips

You want to invite a manageable number of filmmaker colleagues, scholars, and a general audience of "others" to these screenings. If you have a very small screening room, it may be necessary to show the film more than once to get an adequate cross-section of reactions. Before the screening starts, make sure everyone has paper and pencils for note taking. You or an appointed moderator should explain what stage your film is at, mentioning, for example, that it's running several minutes long, that narration is provisional, and the footage has numbers and other information printed on it that will be gone by the time it reaches broadcast or it plays at an upcoming festival. In other words, it's a work in progress, and their input and help are extremely valuable to you. Make it clear that you will be asking for their reactions, both positive and negative. Ask them to please stay in the room for a few minutes immediately after the film ends. Then dim the lights, but not so low that people can't see to scribble occasionally in the dark. As the film plays, notice the audience's reactions. When do they seem intent on the story? When is there a lot of shuffling and coughing? Is there laughter? Are there tears?

After the film ends, ask people to jot down their first impressions, anonymously if they'd prefer. Then start the discussion, with you or the moderator asking for broad impressions—what worked, what didn't, what was surprising or confusing or fascinating. After a while, move on to specific questions agreed on by the production team, such as, "Were you confused by the transition to France?" "If you had to cut eight minutes out of this film, what would you cut?" "Did you understand that Dan was more concerned about Marcie's health than about his job?" Concrete responses can be very helpful.

Two important points. First, during a feedback session, the members of the filmmaking team should be quiet. Don't answer questions, offer explanations, or defend any aspect of the filmmaking. You are there to receive information, period. It will waste the opportunity afforded by this valuable audience if you take 15 minutes to explain why it was important to keep the sequence with the demolition derby in, or to explain the backstory that left this audience mystified. Even if it kills you to sit there and listen to people debate subjects that you know the answer to, restrain yourself. You're not there to educate this audience on the topic or show them that you do know more than was up on the screen; you're there to get a good sense of what actually was on screen and where it needs work.

Second, take any and all suggestions, say thanks, and keep going. You know, and your entire production team knows, that you can't possibly afford to shoot another four interviews, as the guy in the corner suggests, or that cutting out the trial sequence would make your entire film irrelevant. After this audience goes home, however, consider *why* these suggestions were made. Nonfilmmakers don't always know how to articulate a problem, and they can't be expected to know how to fix it. You can and do. If your audience thinks that you're missing significant interviews, is there information that those interviews would add that you could convey in some other way? If you believe the trial sequence is critical and they think it's disposable, what's wrong with it? Is it edited badly? Is it in the wrong place? Is the narration not effectively setting it up so the audience can see its relevance?

You don't have to take anything that anyone says as marching orders. But you do need to pay attention to which elements of your film are working and which will send your audience racing for the remote or the door.

With that said, it's your film. Know when to trust your gut. Understand that there will be a degree of criticism that is not about your filmmaking but about your ideology. Someone doesn't understand why you would even give the skinheads a chance to speak. Someone else thinks it's invasive to stay focused on the woman sobbing because her son has blown his mind on inhalants. This is useful information to have, because it anticipates some of the criticism the final film might receive. But if the issue is not one of fact or clarity but of style, the choice is yours to make. Hear that people don't like it, but decide for yourself what makes you and your team comfortable.

The same is true of scholarship. Tell an accurate story, but don't feel compelled to tell everything. It's sometimes difficult for scholars who care deeply about their subjects to see that the entire section on primate behavior is only six minutes long or that you decided not to include a certain letter that Albert Einstein wrote. Accept the criticism and really consider whether or not it would enrich the story you have chosen to tell on film. If not, file this information away for use later in the companion book or website, if you're creating these, or for the teachers' guides and other educational and community engagement components of the project. Your film is successful if it appeals to a wide audience with a strong story and motivates part of that audience to go to the library or the web for more information.

FINE CUT TO PICTURE LOCK

The process as you get down to the wire is more of the same, looking backward as well as forward. It's often very helpful at this stage to go back and reread initial outlines and treatments to see if you've lost a story thread along the way that might prove useful. You might also reread transcripts to see if the changes that you've made to the structure are better served by interview bites you didn't pull because you were looking at a very different film back then. It's even useful to look back into research files, to make sure there aren't details and other tidbits that might speak volumes. And, of course, you are by now immersed in the task of making sure that everything that will end up on screen has been fact checked, not once but twice.

Fact Checking

Fact checking means going through your script line by line, finding the information that needs to be verified through at least two credible sources. If you can't confirm a fact—and it happens—find a way to write around it. Maybe you don't need to say that 25,000 bikers rode into town. If your sources all agree that it was "over 20,000," then say that instead.

What needs to be checked? Pretty much everything:

- "Brilliant and fearless, Admiral Marks now seized command of the troops." *Brilliant* and *fearless* both need corroboration, as does *seized command*. You don't want to find out after broadcast that Marks was widely considered a coward, or that command was thrust upon him when the admiral before him came down with food poisoning.
- "The senator was *exhausted* and *frustrated*, convinced now that the bill she'd *authored* would not be passed." Exhausted and frustrated need to be confirmed, and you should have solid evidence that at this point, she truly was convinced of the bill's failure, and that she had authored it and not simply supported it. (Confirming an emotional state depends on reliable reports from reliable eyewitnesses, recorded as close to the event as possible.)

You need to fact check interview and sync material as well as narration. For example, an auto manufacturer says, "Forty percent of the tires we got in had the problem. They all had to go back." He's the expert, but you find out that in fact, 25 percent of the tires were sent back because of the problem. You can't hide behind the argument that "He said it, I didn't." As the filmmaker, you are incorporating the statement into your film and, therefore, it will be your statement as well. In this case, the line has to go. Of course, if the falsehood is deliberate, and that's part of your story, or if it's clearly a lie and therefore reveals character, you don't need to cut it. But when it is presented as significant evidence to support the argument you're making, then it must be accurate. However, there is also some room to maneuver. For example, if you've confirmed that 38 percent of registered voters in Millville voted for a rise in property tax, and the mayor says, "I don't know, about a third of the voters wanted it," that's probably close enough to use.

FILM LENGTH

If you're creating a film for which you have a specific venue in mind, length is something you want to plan for from the beginning. A theatrically released film will tend to run around 80 to 90 minutes or longer. A film for broadcast has to meet the length requirements of the programmer, leaving time as needed for series credits, packaging, and, in some cases, commercial breaks. The subject and story, too, will suggest appropriate length. When I'm helping people to develop ideas, one of the questions we ask ourselves is, "How much time would it take to tell this well?" If a subject seems to demand three hours, do we reasonably think we could raise money to produce it (and convince programmers to give us a three-hour television slot), or do we want to narrow the focus and try to create an hour-long film that might appeal to the commissioning editors of an existing series?

It's usually better to resist the temptation to leave your film long. Filmmaking is about making choices, and among the most important choices you face is what to include and what to leave out. If your story feels complete in 45 minutes, padding it with extra footage won't make it a longer story; it makes it a 45-minute story that took an hour to tell.

THE OPENING SEQUENCE

The opening sequence is also sometimes called a tease. By tease, I don't mean the little advertisement for your film that may run in advance of the actual broadcast program. I mean whatever comes up at the very first frame of action, usually before the title. The tease may offer highlights of the film to come, or it may get your film's story under way, as is the case with the opening to *Man on Wire*, directed by James Marsh (Chapter 22), or it may highlight the film to come, as is the case with *Jonestown*, directed by Stanley Nelson. In either case, the tease contains within it the DNA of your film: the themes, arc, characters, and *raison d'etre*. You, as the filmmaker, have two minutes, maybe a couple more, to grab your viewers and say: Look at this. Here are a few reasons why this movie is worth the next 30 or 60 or 120 minutes of your time.

It's a good exercise to study the opening sequences of some top films to see if you can identify the bullet points, perhaps three to five, that the filmmaker has chosen to grab your attention and say, "Not only is this story interesting, but here's why it *matters*." In thinking about your own films, think back to the key points about your project that you share with others. I like to suggest that people imagine that they're home for a family gathering, and everybody's talking at once and there's probably a game on the television and food to be prepared, so getting people's attention may be tough. What are the headlines that'll make those around you stop and listen, at least for a few minutes?

As noted, *Man on Wire* begins at the chronological start of the film's train. In that film, we see the van approaching the Twin Towers, and notice that it goes past a cemetery. We learn from Philippe Petit's girlfriend at the time, Annie, that he "could no longer carry on living without having at least tried to conquer those towers." We can see that this movie is going to be presented as a heist film; we can tell that it is heavily dramatized, but that its storytellers are the men and women who were actually present at the time. A quick shot of a television in one of the scenes, with archival images of U.S. President Richard M. Nixon, sets the general time period. By the end of the film's open, they are inside the building, and the story of this film is under way. In this case, the opening sequence is actually a full sequence, in that it not only teases the film's story but also has its own beginning, middle, and end.

In contrast, the opening moments of *Jonestown: The Life and Death of Peoples Temple*, directed by Stanley Nelson, provide a tease of the film to come, but the sequence is not complete in the sense of having a beginning, middle, and end. While the film's train gets under way (the mass murder-suicide that occurred on November 18, 1978), what we see and hear are essentially bullets of the film's themes and questions. We learn that "nobody joins a cult," which helps to set out a film theme. We see a charismatic but disturbing leader, and understand that a community that once held promise for people somehow became nightmarish. And we learn that just a day before the tragedy, Jonestown had still seemed vibrant. The audience can't help but have questions: How could this happen? Couldn't something have been done? Who was this leader, and who chose to follow him? And so on.

NARRATION SCRIPT

When it comes time to record narration, your narration pieces are generally numbered and then isolated into a script of their own—a *narration script*—which is often a single-column, double-spaced document, with very wide margins to the left and right for ease of reading. Don't put the narration in all capitals, because this makes it more difficult to read.

PROBLEM SOLVING

Every film has its own problems, but the following ones seem fairly common.

No Story

You have scenes and sequences that are interesting but aren't adding up to a coherent whole. One reason for this may be that there really wasn't a clear story to begin with. What you can do at this point is take a step back and return to the earlier stages of the process. Looking realistically at what you have and what you know, do you now see a truthful story in the material? Do you have enough footage to support that story? You may need pick-up material to fill in the gaps, but you also may be surprised to find that you are heading in the right direction and just need to do a bit of housekeeping. You also may need to drop favorite scenes because they don't serve the story that you've now identified. If a shot or a scene or even a sequence is a distraction rather than an addition, it's got to go, no matter how expensive it was to shoot or how difficult it was to get. The same standard should be applied to interview material. If you didn't plan ahead but instead simply shot a few available experts, it's very possible that there will be redundancy and somebody's interview will be dropped. (If you end up cutting people out of a show, do them the courtesy of letting them know before the program is aired.)

You Start One Story and End Another

A related problem is that the film starts one story and then drifts onto a different track. As previously discussed, creating a new outline can help you to decide which of the stories you want to tell and have the footage to tell. Be careful not to bend material to tell a story other than the one for which it was originally shot. Footage of Sally's graduation party should not be substituted for the engagement party you didn't film. Find a way to use the party footage to make a more generic point, if need be.

Too Many Characters or Story Threads

You didn't want to give up the incredible research you did or the wonderful people you found, so now you find yourself telling the stories of eight people, all with different goals but perhaps a common thread—maybe they're all recent college graduates looking for work. But your film is only an hour long and everybody is getting short shrift, or audiences can't keep track of which person was having trouble with his neighbors and who was being investigated by the Immigration and Naturalization Service and which one was going to move her business to Seattle. You may need to make choices as to which people best embody the themes you are trying to convey or the policy issues or areas of discrimination you want the audience to know about. You can also get distracted by too many details within an overall story. No matter what style film you're making, you need to keep track of the one primary story you're telling, folding in additional threads (or subplots, backstory, etc.) as they serve that one story.

Too Many Beginnings or Endings

The film opens with a look at the farming industry and the cultivation of wheat. The narration offers some information as to what's being presented, and the audience thinks, "Oh, it's a documentary about farming." Then it seems to start again with a look at the processing of wheat into bread. "Oh, it's a film about food as big business." But then it starts again, and gradually it becomes clear that your film is really a look at the health issue of wheat intolerance or sensitivity. An unfocused opening is a fairly common problem, so it's good to watch out for it, asking yourself as the story unfolds, "What do I think this story is about at this point?" The primary story you're going to tell should start soon after your film begins, and it should be possible, from the way that story is launched, to anticipate—not to know, but to anticipate and be curious about—how it will end. In this case, the remaining details of wheat farming and the baking industry can be folded into that overall story.

Where you end your film is also very important. Appearing to end it, and then ending it again, and then ending it again can dilute a film's overall power; furthermore, there's generally just one ending that will truly bring a satisfactory resolution to the story you set out to tell. Resolution does not mean things are resolved; it means that you've reached a conclusion that satisfies the questions and issues initially raised in your film's opening moments.

Not Enough Breathing Room

In the rush to cut a film down to time, to get everything tight, and to make every point, it's possible to trim interviews or scenes into oblivion. The production team doesn't necessarily notice; they've been looking at this guy day after day and week after week, so they know what he's going to say, they've heard it before, and the joke is no longer funny. Or they realize that they can say in two lines of narration what that scene takes nearly two minutes to convey. It's important to resist this—you need the energy that real people bring to a film and the enthusiasm they bring to their storytelling. While radio and television news reports may cut interviews or scenes into fragments, you generally want to let material play for a reasonable period of time.

Insufficient Casting

You may discover, in editing, that an important voice is missing, or that someone you've interviewed is filling a storytelling role that would be better filled by someone else. If possible, you might shoot an additional interview, trying to match its tone and look to your film's style. Otherwise, you need to find another way to bring this point of view forward, such as through archival voices or the way a scene is edited. It's also possible, as your story becomes more focused, that you've neglected to ask someone important story-related questions. Depending on how significant the problem is (and the size of your budget), you can either do another interview with that person, intending to either replace one with the other or somehow use both (although cutting directly between them may prove difficult), or you can work to match the audio enough so that you can use the pick-up material as voice-over.

Occasionally, an entirely new sentence can be crafted from someone's existing interview, a sentence the person never uttered but one that you think he or she would agree with. If you really want to do this, and it's your only option, you must run this new sentence past the person and secure permission to use it.

GETTING UNSTUCK

Even the best creative minds get tired. You try six ways of cutting something and it still doesn't work, or the editor thinks it works one way, the director hates it, and the producer is thinking that now might be a good time to get that law degree. Assuming that you have at least something strung together in sequence, take a step back and try throwing all the pieces up in the air. This is easier done at rough cut than fine cut, but it's a useful exercise in any case. You've got a story and structure that maybe aren't great, but they're fine. Open the door, for a short period, and let everyone throw out the craziest ideas they can think of, without anybody becoming scornful or arguing about why it won't work and that it's already been tried. "What if we started where the film now ends? What if we held off on the fireman's story until after his wife is in the accident? What if we told the story from the child's point of view, and not his parents'?"

Just throw it all out there and then try a few things. Maybe none of them will work. But in the difference between what was boring and safe and what is outrageous and stupid, you might see new opportunities. In other words, two wrong answers may lead you toward one that's right. You can't do this indefinitely, and at some point whoever's in charge has to make the final call. But what you end up with might be really interesting.

BE YOUR FIRST AUDIENCE

A mark of a good storyteller is the ability to look with fresh eyes—the audience's eyes—at material each time a new cut is available, and to honestly assess its weaknesses. If you see problems, don't ignore them. Audiences are uncanny in their ability to see that one flaw you thought you could gloss over or the transition whose absence you thought you'd masked with some fancy music and images. At the same time, you can't cut a film or tell a story with a critic on your shoulder. Don't second-guess yourself; that's not what this process is about. Instead, ask yourself every step of the way, "Is this interesting? Would I keep watching? What do I care about here? Who am I worried for? Am I confused? Where do I need more information?"

Chances are, if it works for you—the editor, producer, director—it will work for the audience.

CHAPTER 13

Narration and Voice-Over

Narration is not the worst thing to happen to a documentary, but bad narration might be, which might explain why so many film-makers want to avoid it at all costs. We've all seen films that were talky, preachy, hyperventilated, and dull. But there's also narration (or extensive voice-over commentary) that makes films funny, sarcastic, spare, poetic, and elegant. *Enron, Super Size Me, Grizzly Man,* and *Born into Brothels,* among many recent films, have effective narration. *Enron's* narration is the most traditional, in that it's spoken by an unseen per-son, the actor Peter Coyote, who has no identity in the film other than to provide information that moves the story along. *Super Size Me,* narrated in voice-over and on screen by filmmaker Morgan Spurlock, is packed with what would be considered traditional narration: facts and figures about nutrition, health, the food industry, and more. *Grizzly Man* is narrated in the first person by filmmaker Werner Herzog, whose voice-over tells of his journey to explore the legacy and death of naturalist Timothy Treadwell. *Born into Brothels,* although narrated by Zana Briski, does not refer to her role as the film's producer and director (with Ross Kauffman), but to her involvement in the story, as a photographer helping a group of children in the brothels of Calcutta.

Narration or voice-over, if done well, can be one of the best and most efficient ways to move your story along, not because it tells the story but because it draws the audience into and through it. Narration provides information that's not otherwise available but is essential if audiences are to fully experience your film. "When docu-mentary makers dive into fairly complicated historical policy or legal and legislative issues," notes filmmaker Jon Else, "narration is your friend. It may mean that you have only two or three lines of narration in a film, but something that might take 10 minutes of tortured inter-view or tortured vérité footage can be often disposed of better in 15 seconds of a well-written line of narration."

DOI: 10.1016/B978-0-240-81241-0.00013-7

POINT OF VIEW

When crafting narration, it's important to choose the point of view from which to tell the story, for example:

- First-person narration is when the narrator speaks of him- or herself. *I needed to find out.* This point of view is generally limited to what the narrator knows at a given point in the story.
- Second-person narration may be found more often in print than on screen. It has the narrator addressing the audience as "you," as in, *He asks if you want a soda, and you say yes.*
- Third-person omniscient is the most commonly used form of narration; it is written using "he" or "she," and the narrator can slip in and out of anyone's thoughts or actions. For example, *The mayor was well aware of Smith's plans. And from his campaign headquarters, Smith knew that the mayor's response, when it came, would be fierce.* Most often, this narration is described as "objective," meaning that it is limited to factual information that can be observed or verified. However, as discussed in the first chapter, it still has a point of view, no matter how balanced or neutral it seeks to be.
- Third-person subjective uses the "he" or "she" form, but is limited to the same point of view as first-person narration. In other words, I might describe the writing of this chapter as *She sits at her desk and types, wondering if she'll meet her deadline.*

Beyond the narrator's point of view, there is also a point of view in the words being spoken. Even if you've chosen an omniscient narrator, you want to be careful not to jump back and forth between points of view, but instead situate the viewer. For example, if you begin to narrate a Revolutionary War battle from the point of view of the advancing British, you don't want to suddenly switch to the American side without signaling to the audience that you've done so. In other words, the following (imagined) scene is confusing: *British forces prepared their charge as the Americans assembled near Boone Hill. General Washington ordered his men, a ragtag group of 300, to stand firm. The soldiers advanced, a force of nearly 2,000 in territory that offered little resistance.*

Told from the American point of view, the scene might go like this: *The Americans were assembled near Boone Hill when they got word that British forces were advancing. General Washington ordered his men, a ragtag group of 300, to stand firm, as nearly 2,000 British soldiers advanced toward them.*

From the British point of view, it might go this way: *British forces prepared to charge on the Americans who were assembled nearby. A force of nearly 2,000 men, they had little difficulty with the terrain as they approached Boone Hill, where General Washington was waiting with a rag tag force of about 300.*

Obviously, your writing should fit the visuals. But it's very easy in a case like this to quickly lose track of who's fighting whom or who's advancing where. One way to help, as the filmmaker, is to maintain a consistent point of view.

VARIETY IN NARRATION

At times, filmmakers "narrate" films without speaking, through the use of text on screen. This usually means using either title cards (text on a neutral background) or lower thirds (text over a scene) to add information that's not otherwise evident. This technique is generally used in films that are strongly vérité (action unfolds on screen) and is always used sparingly. Filmmakers who use title cards generally use them to set up the film and then, on occasion, to establish time and place or to bridge sequences.

For example, the documentary *Spellbound*, about a group of children who compete in the National Spelling Bee, sets up the story with a brief series of cards that immediately follow the film's title. The cards come on in the following order (numbers are added here for clarity and do not appear in the film): 1, joined by 2, both off; 3, joined by 4, both off; 5, joined by 6, both off:

1. *Across the country, 9,000,000 children compete in school and city spelling bees.*
2. *Only 249 qualify for the Nationals in Washington, D.C.*
3. *Over two days of competition 248 will misspell a word.*
4. *One will be named champion.*
5. *This is the story of eight American children*
6. *who, one spring, set out to win the National Spelling Bee.*

These effectively set up the story to come; later, text on screen briefly introduces the protagonists, for example: *Perryton, Texas* (over an establishing shot of the town) is followed shortly after by *Angela* (over an establishing shot of Angela).

When to narrate, how to narrate, who should narrate—these are important storytelling decisions, driven in part by the content of the film and the style and tone adopted by the filmmakers. Compare the narration in *Enron* with the lack of narration in a film like

Spellbound. Enron, based on the reporting of *Fortune* magazine's Bethany McLean and Peter Elkind, seeks to give general audiences an understanding of a corporate financial scandal that was enormously complex. The narration is relatively spare, but it helps the filmmakers weave together a complicated body of evidence derived from interviews, news reports, audiotapes, video coverage of hearings, and more. In contrast, *Spellbound* does not set out to provide a wealth of complex factual data, but instead seeks to let viewers inside the homes and lives of selected children as they prepare for a national competition, and then follows them there to see how they do.

As mentioned, Werner Herzog's voice-over in *Grizzly Man* is an important part of the film's story. The film begins with an intriguing excerpt of Treadwell's footage. Then, like the title cards at the start of *Spellbound,* the first words we hear from Herzog set up the premise of the film to come:

> *All these majestic creatures were filmed by Timothy Treadwell, who lived among wild grizzlies for 13 summers. He went to remote areas of the Alaskan peninsula believing that he was needed there to protect these animals and educate the public. During his last five years out there, he took along a video camera and shot over 100 hours of footage. What Treadwell intended was to show these bears in their natural habitat. Having myself filmed in the wilderness of jungle, I found that beyond a wildlife film, in his material lay dormant a story of astonishing beauty and depth. I discovered a film of human ecstasies and darkest inner turmoil. As if there was a desire in him to leave the confinements of his humanness and bond with the bears, Treadwell reached out, seeking a primordial encounter. But in doing so, he crossed an invisible borderline. . . .*

Herzog plays a number of roles as the film's narrator. Sometimes he provides basic exposition: *Timothy grew up with four siblings in Long Island . . .*or lends his expertise as a filmmaker: *Now the scene seems to be over. But as a filmmaker, sometimes things fall into your lap which you couldn't expect, never even dream of.* Perhaps most interesting are Herzog's challenges to Treadwell. At times, these are simple statements of contradiction, for example: *Treadwell saw himself as the guardian of this land and stylized himself as Prince Valiant, fighting the bad guys with their schemes to do harm to the bears. But all this land is a federally protected reserve. . . .* But Herzog also argues directly with the Treadwell we see on screen, as when Treadwell mourns the killing (by other animals) of a bear cub and then a baby fox. Treadwell says, in his footage: "I love you and I don't understand. It's a painful world." In voice-over, Herzog responds: *Here I differ with Treadwell. He seemed* *to ignore the fact that in nature there are predators. I believe the common denominator of the universe is not harmony, but chaos, hostility, and murder.*

Former Enron CFO Andy Fastow, in *Enron: The Smartest Guys in the Room*, a Magnolia Pictures release. Photo credit: AP Worldwide.

WHEN IS THE NARRATION WRITTEN?

When you write narration varies from project to project. In general, if you are using narration to seam together visual images, interviews, and perhaps archival material, the final narration (or voice-over) won't come together until you're editing. You may assemble other elements first, such as filmed footage, archival material, or interview bites, and then rough out narration as needed to help move the story along. Sometimes you need to write "into" a talking head, which means that your words are needed as a kind of setup, to make the meaning of the upcoming interview bite more clear. Sometimes you need narration to set the stage for a scene that can then play out on camera without interruption, or to make a transition from one sequence to the next.

WHO WRITES THE NARRATION?

Film writing is a different skill than magazine or book writing. While some prose writers make the transition successfully, not all do. Writing to picture—writing words that will be heard rather than read—and structuring a film story within the confines of the time allotted, whether 30 minutes or eight hours, are specialized skills. Just as a great poet might be a terrible screenwriter, a great print journalist might not write a good movie.

On many documentary projects, the film's producer and/or director is also the writer (meaning the individual responsible for story and structure, regardless of whether there is also narration), and in that role also writes narration. At other times, a person identified as the writer may be involved in the project through development, production, and editing, and will therefore take primary responsibility for narration. It's also not uncommon for an editor to rough out pieces of narration as he or she works, which will then be polished in collaboration with the film's writer(s).

Occasionally, a writer is asked to join a project solely to write and/or polish narration and make it stronger. This kind of wordsmithing can make a positive difference if the film is otherwise in good shape. But keep in mind that polished narration cannot mask underlying structural and story issues. If there isn't a strong writer on the team, consider bringing one on, even part time, much earlier in the process.

Note that if you plan to hire an actor or other celebrity to narrate your film, you may also need to fine-tune narration to suit their unique voices and identities.

WRITING TO PICTURE

The camera pans across a sepia-toned still photograph of a wagon train on a dusty road. To the side, an old farmer stands, watching as the wagons pass. The shot ends on a hand-painted sign tacked to the back of one of the last wagons: *Califna or Bust.* As you watch this shot on screen, which line of narration would be more useful to you?

- *The wagons set out along the dusty road.*
- *On August 4th they set out: four men, five women, and eight children determined to find gold.*

Which narration breathes life into the photograph, and which just states the obvious? Narration should add information to picture, not simply describe it. Above all, narration should advance the story.

Here's a second example, from a film that follows a group of college friends as they face their first year in the job market. In a live-action scene set in a private home, a group of young women sits down to a fancy dinner. One of them, dressed in an expensive-looking suit, sets a roasted turkey on the table. Which narration is useful?

- *Donna is the most vivacious of the group, and the most fashion-conscious.*
- *Donna, who graduated from Harvard Law School, hopes to pursue a career in advertising.*

Obviously, what you say depends on what the audience needs to learn. But we can tell from watching the scene that Donna is vivacious and well-dressed. We can't tell from looking at her that she went to Harvard Law School. That narration adds to picture.

Here is another approach that people sometimes use, believing that it will create a sense of tension:

- *Donna, the organizer of this gathering, would soon learn that her life would change in ways she couldn't imagine.*

What exactly does this add? Are you on the edge of your seat wondering how Donna's life will change? No. This sounds like it's intended to build tension, but it's just words. Tension comes from the story, not a narrator's hints.

Just as you should write to picture, you should never write against picture. A common mistake people make is to write in a way that sets the film up to go in one direction, when in fact the images are going somewhere else. Here's an example. We see a group of executives sitting around a table, talking. Narration: *The board decided to hire a consultant, Jane Johnson.* Cut to a woman talking. Wouldn't you assume it's Jane Johnson? If it's not, it's going to take a moment to readjust your thinking, to figure out, well, if it's not Johnson, who is it? By then, you'll have missed at least part of what this woman has said.

Suppose the woman that we cut to is on the board of directors, and she's explaining why they're hiring Jane Johnson. The edit makes sense. But the narration gets in the way. Try again. We see a group of executives sitting around a table, talking. Narration: *The board decided that a consultant was needed.* Cut to the woman from the board, who explains, "We were spinning our wheels. And so...." It's a minor difference but an important one.

Words and picture should work together, each adding to the build-up of your story. Words should also accurately identify the picture. This can be frustrating to filmmakers when the visual record is limited. Suppose, for example, that you are telling the story of a man and woman who met in Ohio at a USO dance, the night before he was shipped off to fight in the Second World War. But the family only has photographs that were taken five years later, after the man returned from the war and the couple, now married, had a child. No footage exists of that particular USO dance or even of the club in which it was held. Can you use footage of another USO dance, from another state and another year?

Of course you can, but your narration should avoid creating the false impression that the audience is seeing the real thing. For example, suppose the editor cuts in footage of a USO dance held two years later in a different state. The narration says, *On February 2, 1942, at a USO dance in Columbus, Ohio, Tim finally met the girl of his dreams.* The audience may think, "Gee, isn't that amazing, there was a film crew there to capture it." I think it stretches credibility, and if the audience assumes that this couldn't possibly be the USO dance on the night in the city, they will see your footage for what it is—wallpaper. From that point on, the archival value of the footage is diminished, and the rest of your material becomes a bit suspect, deservedly or not.

There is an alternative, using the same scene, with the same footage. Open the narration wider, as in this example: *USO dances were held in gymnasiums and hospitals, canteens and clubs throughout the U.S., and it was at a dance like this that Tim met the girl of his dreams.* You're not writing as closely to that one particular image; at the same time, you're offering a valuable reminder that your characters are just two people caught up in a time and a situation that's bigger than both of them. The footage is no longer generic wallpaper, but illustrative of an era.

Writing to picture also means that the words you choose work in tandem with the visuals. Here's an example. You are making a film about a team of cyclists competing in the Tour de France. You need to introduce Ralph Martinez, riding for the Americans. In the scene you're narrating, it's early morning and the cyclists are gathered in a village square, drinking coffee or juice, eating pastries, and psyching themselves up for a day on the Tour. The specific shot starts close on a croissant. A hand wearing a bicycling glove reaches in and picks up the pastry; the shot widens and pulls back as we follow the pastry up to a rider's mouth, and see that it is a young man (Ralph) perched on his bike, sipping coffee as he laughs and talks with teammates. Some narration options:

- *Pastry and coffee start the day for Ralph Martinez and his American teammates.* Too "on the nose"—we can see the pastry and coffee for ourselves.
- *Ralph Martinez, getting ready for his third tour, is riding with the American team.* This won't work, because the words "Ralph Martinez" will fall too soon, probably when we're still looking at a big glob of jam on a croissant. You want your narration to roughly mirror the picture and to arrive at Ralph when the visuals do.
- *Riding with the Americans is Ralph Martinez, in his third Tour de France.* This might work—it's hard to tell until you see and hear it against picture. Note that you don't need to say "team" because it can be assumed. Chances are that by this point in the film you also won't need to say "de France." You want to be as economical in word use as possible. Better to have a moment for natural sound than to keep yammering away at the viewers.

Writing to picture can be difficult, especially for those who resist rewriting. While a film is being edited, nearly everything is subject to change. A scene needs to be cut down to give another scene more time. An archival shot needs to be changed because the rights to it aren't available. A sequence is moved from the last half of the film to the first half and therefore needs to be set up differently. From the assembly through to script lock, narration is a moving target. You must be willing to make changes. When enough changes pile up, the editor or someone else on the production team will record a new scratch narration track and lay it against picture. As you'll discover, at least some of these revisions will need further revising. Eventually, though, the script will be locked, the picture will be locked, and the narration will be finished.

WRITING NARRATION TO BE SPOKEN

Narration scripts are, by design, written to be spoken out loud. Every word counts. Important words should stand out in a sentence or paragraph. Sentences should be short and written in an active voice. Phrases should be reviewed to ensure that they don't create a confusing impression, such as *Mark left Philip. Underneath the house, a skunk was waiting.* Reading it, the meaning is clear. Hearing it, you wonder if Mark left Philip underneath the house, or if the skunk is going to catch Mark unaware. *The remains were sent to the local anthropology lab. There, they believed Dr. Smith could provide vital information.* The remains believe something about Dr. Smith?

You also need to avoid tongue twisters and quotation marks; audiences can't hear the irony when a narrator says, *Eleanor was "sorry," but no one believed her.* On paper, a reader could reasonably figure that Eleanor had made an apology but it was taken as false. To the listener, it sounds like the narrator has determined that Eleanor is in fact sorry, but no one believes her. There's a small but important distinction. (For the same reason, you need to be wary of words that sound alike but have different meanings, and of conjunctions, such as "shouldn't," which may be misheard as "should.")

The solution is very simple. Read your narration out loud, even as you're writing it. You will find it far easier to hear the rhythm, feel where the strong words are falling, and get a sense of what's hard to say or where words are superfluous. Then read it aloud again (and again, and again) against picture.

If you are the film's final narrator, at some point you'll have to record the actual voice-over. As you watch documentaries, pay attention to the narrator's tone. Morgan Spurlock's upbeat energy pumps up the narration of *Super Size Me*. Al Gore brings two separate tones to his voice-over in *An Inconvenient Truth*: one is the public voice that lectures on climate change, and the other is a more private, intimate voice in which he talks about his life and family. Actors hired to record voice-over for films tend to aim for clarity and neutrality in their tone.

SOME GENERAL GUIDELINES FOR NARRATION

Reapply the Rules of Grammar

As with proposal writing, narration writing must be grammatical. Common problems include dangling and misplaced modifiers, dangling participles, a confusing use of pronouns, a lack of parallel form, incorrect or inexact use of common words (such as *fewer* and *less*; *but* and *and*; *since*, *like*, and *as*; and *might* and *may*), and use of nonsequiturs. Some excellent style books are available, including *The Elements of Style*, a classic by William Strunk, Jr., and E. B. White; *The Associated Press Stylebook and Libel Manual*, edited by Norm Goldstein, and *The New York Times Manual of Style and Usage*, by Allan M. Siegal and William G. Connolly.

Use Anticipation

Narration needs to follow the arc of the story, not lead it. In the film's opening minutes, you want to set up the questions that will drive your story forward. You then want to anticipate the audience's needs and almost intuitively seed information in, just as—or just after—the question or confusion begins to flicker in the viewer's mind. Pay attention as you watch a well-made film, and you'll notice this happening. You turn to a friend and say, "I don't understand; I thought she couldn't run for governor," and seconds later, the narration answers your question: A loophole in electoral law had worked to her advantage.

Avoid Stereotyping

Use the most gender-neutral terms available (e.g., *firefighter* rather than *fireman*, *police officer* rather than *policeman*). This is important for two reasons. It more accurately represents the world in which we live, and it's a step toward acknowledging (and involving) an audience of diverse backgrounds.

Avoiding stereotyping also means being careful of "code" words (saying "suburban" when you mean white or middle class, for example) and watching out for an overlay of judgment based on stereotypes, such as "She was pushing 40, but still attractive." Whose point of view does a statement like this reflect? "Pushing 40" implies that this is an unbelievably ancient age, and the "but" is a dead giveaway that nobody on the production team could imagine anyone over 25 being worth a second glance. Stereotypes—dumb jock, dumb blonde, little old lady, "not your grandmother's store"—have no place in documentary narration. Mothers-in-law run corporations and countries; "geezers" set foreign policy and rob banks.

Watch Out for Anachronisms

If you are telling narration from a point of view within a story, stay within the boundaries of that point of view. This means respecting the limitations of your character's frame of reference, including time and place. An example of narration that fails to do this comes from *When Dinosaurs Roamed America*, an animated series from the Discovery Channel. Narrator John Goodman is speaking from the point of view of a dinosaur, trying to size up a new beast he's encountered. *The raptor's never seen a dinosaur like this before,* Goodman says. *Is it a predator, or is it prey? No other creature in the world looks like a half-plucked turkey and walks like a potbellied bear. Still, an oddball can be dangerous.* This narration has the dinosaur comparing what he sees to animals he has no knowledge of, since they won't exist for several million years. For the audience, the comparison may be valuable, but its use here pulls us out of the story. To use the comparison, the producers should have acknowledged the leap in time by moving— even briefly—outside the raptor's point of view, for example: *The raptor's never seen a dinosaur like this before. Scientists today say it probably looked like a cross between a plucked turkey and a potbellied bear. To the raptor, it just looks odd—and oddballs can be dangerous.*

You also want to be careful, when speaking of the past, not to impose your 21st-century values, assumptions, and knowledge.

Limit the Number of Ideas in Each Block of Narration

Your narration should convey only the story points needed to get to the next sync material; if you go too far or include too many points, your audience will lose track of the information and will be distracted or confused by what follows. For example, here's a piece of narration from *Not a Rhyme Time*, a program from the *I'll Make Me a World* series: *In the spring of 1967, Amiri Baraka was scheduled to address the Black Writers' Conference at Fisk University in Nashville, Tennessee. Gwendolyn Brooks was also on the program.*

The tension in the film comes from the fact that Baraka represents the new Black Arts Movement, and Brooks—a Pulitzer Prize–winning author who publishes with a large, mainstream publisher—represents the "establishment." The interaction of the two will help to spark Brooks's transformation, which is the focus of the story.

Look at what happens if we go too far and turn the corner with this narration: *In the spring of 1967, Amiri Baraka was scheduled to address the Black Writers' Conference at Fisk University in Nashville, Tennessee. Gwendolyn Brooks was also on the program. She had prepared to read her poem, "The Life of Lincoln West."* Suddenly the focus is on this one particular poem, and the power of the narration is lost.

This is probably one of the most common and most serious narration mistakes people make. Say less, say it better, and say it in the best possible way to advance your story, including the one being told by the pictures.

Foreshadow Important Information

The American troops battling the British in the Revolutionary War were promised in July of 1776, when the fighting broke out, that they would all be discharged by December 31. Don't wait to tell the audience this until it's December 31 in your film's chronology. Tell them in July, when they won't think it matters; remind them in September, when the war is dragging on. That way, when winter sets in, it will be on their minds—just as it must have been on General Washington's mind—when the troops are tired and demoralized, and there's no way that Washington can keep his word.

Understand the Different Roles Played by Narration and Sync Material

It's all too common for filmmakers to use talking heads to do work that is better done by narration, and vice versa. Sometimes, this happens because the casting is weak; everybody talks about everything, nothing is differentiated, and they all might as well be narrating.

Ideally, your interviewees should be advancing the story through the lens of their own expertise, experience, and point of view. This is information that is more valuable, in some ways, than narration, and it's certainly more personable. Using these characters to convey information that narration could convey just as well is something of a waste. Conversely, if you replace too many of your talking heads or too much of what they say with narration, you risk pulling the heart and soul out of your film. Even people who are resistant to talking heads would prefer a good visit with an enjoyable character to narration.

Except in films where the filmmaker's investigation, at least in part, drives the film, narration is generally not the best way to contradict an interviewee. The subject says, "No one knew about those documents," and a disembodied voice interrupts, *No one knew? It seemed unlikely.* So how do you contradict people on screen? You find another interviewee to offer a rebuttal, or you film scenes that contain evidence contradicting the interviewee's statement. Let the individuals, facts, and story speak for themselves, and trust that audience members can decide the truth for themselves.

Use Words Sparingly and Specifically

Screen time is a precious commodity, and you want your narration to be as spare as possible. Don't waste good airtime on words that are little more than filler, such as *Salinas. A town of working people, it hardly seems the place for a murder. But on January 14, 1998, the owners of a house discovered something that would change that impression forever.* A quick check shows that Salinas is a city of around 123,000 people, and that in the 20 years before the homeowners discovered a body buried beneath their house, a total of 218 people had been killed in Salinas, including 18 in 1997. The narration pumped emotion into the story, but it's not useful or even accurate.

The perceived need for hype—most often on commercial television—often seems to lead to imprecise writing. *In rural Michigan, a search for a missing man ends in cold-blooded murder.* Well, actually, it doesn't. If the search ended in cold-blooded murder, then someone involved in the search would have ended up dead. What happened is that a missing person case is revealed to be a murder case—the search for the missing man leads to a corpse. Why not say that?

Using words sparingly also means choosing the best word to describe what you mean, being careful of nuances. Does a teenager walk across the room or saunter? Does a CEO say that he doesn't have numbers for the fourth quarter, or does he admit that fact? Has the world leader made an impassioned speech or launched into a tirade?

Was a nation's capital liberated, or did it fall? Was it a conflagration—a term that has specific meaning among firefighters—or simply a bad fire? Choose your words carefully, and be sure the meaning you want is not only the most exciting, but also the most accurate.

Along these lines, try to avoid the slogans of others, whether you agree with them or not. For example, rather than adopt the phrases "pro-life" or "pro-choice," state that someone is either for or against abortion rights.

Use Telling Details

A well-placed detail can convey a tremendous amount of story information. If there were any doubts about the need for a campaign to register voters in Selma, Alabama, they were dispelled in *Eyes on the Prize* by this fact: *More than half of Dallas County citizens were black, but less than one percent were registered* [to vote]. Details can set a stage where visuals are insufficient, as in *The Civil War* series: *Sherman began his march. Sixty-two thousand men in blue were on the move in two great columns. Their supply train stretched 25 miles. A slave watching the army stream past wondered aloud if anybody was left up north.* And details can convey tone and wit, as in *Troublesome Creek: A Midwestern*, narrated by filmmaker Jeanne Jordan: *Like a lot of families facing a real crisis, we immediately stopped talking about it.*

Put Information into Context

Your narration needs to move the story along, which means it should not only impart facts, but also make it clear how they are relevant to the story you're telling. *The 390 people in the club now fought their way to an exit* is interesting, but I have no way of knowing if that's a lot or a little. If the club is Madison Square Garden, it's a very small crowd. In contrast, *390 people—nearly twice as many as the club could legally hold—fought their way to an exit* tells you that laws were broken even before disaster occurred. The same is true for motivation. *The mayor called a late-night meeting* may not advance your story as well as *Hoping to avoid the press, the mayor called a late-night meeting*. Motivation must be fact checked, however. Never guess at what someone was thinking or feeling, unless your narration makes clear that it's speculation, as in, *She might have been concerned not to hear from him; perhaps that's why she got into her car that night.*

If quantity is important to convey, offer it in terms that are comparative, rather than giving specific numbers. *From head to tail, the dinosaur would have been half as long as a football field.* Comparisons and context are also useful when discussing quantities from the past. It's common for filmmakers to imply that someone "only making $5 a day" in 1905 was being exploited, without finding out what this amount meant at the time, what it might buy, and how it compared to other incomes at the time.

As you add this context, keep in mind that you're building toward story events. You need to remind the audience occasionally (not constantly) what's at stake, what information we know, and where we're going. *The board will stop hearing testimony at 9:30. At that point, their vote will decide the future of this regional school system.* Offer gentle clues about the outcome as we move forward. *He had gambled everything, and he had lost. As Ransom's troops trudged wearily north.* . . .

Get Off the Dime

Like the story itself, narration needs to keep moving forward. It's surprising how often narration repeats the same information over and over, especially to remind viewers that they're seeing something for the first time, or that it's very dangerous, or that no one knows what's around the next corner. If you've told us once that a particular military unit is untrained and untested, don't tell us again; build on that information as you move the story forward.

Don't Drop Names

If people are worth mentioning, they're worth identifying. The first time someone's name comes up in narration, let us know who the person is, even if you think that we'd have to be living under a rock not to know. You don't have to go into a lot of detail, just enough to remind those who know and inform those who don't: *Noted composer Leonard Bernstein once said.* . ., or, *He was filmed in performance by cinematographer Gordon Parks.* . . .

Along the same lines, try to anticipate words that your audience may be unfamiliar with, whether they're spoken by the narrator (and a more familiar word can't be substituted) or spoken by an interviewee or someone on camera. If the word's meaning is not clear in the context, you may need to set it up. For example, suppose the historic artifacts you're presenting on screen include a bill of sale for a frigate. You might set it up as, *That day, the general placed an order for a new sailing ship, one outfitted for war.*

Put Lists in an Order That Builds (or Descends)

This is fairly straightforward. You want your paragraphs to pack a punch. Look at the following line of narration from the series *Liberty! The American Revolution,* describing the British invasion of New York in 1776: *30,000 troops. 10,000 sailors. 300 supply ships. 30 battleships with 1200 cannons. It is the largest seaborne attack ever attempted by England until the 20th century.* What's great about this is that the build is not by number but by power; in fact, the numbers decrease from 30,000 (troops) to 1 (attack). But the power goes from men to supply ships to battleships, and news of the force that's about to hit the newly independent states is delivered with a sentence that jumps the chronology and lands us, very briefly, in the present. It's very effective drama.

Use an Active Voice

You want your narration to be as active as possible. For example, *A decision was made to allow Coca-Cola to advertise on school property.* Who made the decision, and how? A more active way to say this is, *By a vote of 4 to 1, the school board decided to allow Coca-Cola to advertise on school property.* (Obviously, if we're watching a scene where we know it's the school board, and can actually see four hands up and one down, you won't say this. But if we're seeing a shot of the hallway with soda vending machines all lined up, you want narration that helps that shot along.)

Help to Differentiate among Similar Things

Narration can play an important role in getting a viewer through a succession of battles, or medical interventions, or political gatherings. Since you've been careful to film a series of events that build on each other, and not just three or four examples of the same thing, your narration may be needed to simply make that build a little more clear or fill in the details. *The operation on Bill's knee had only improved mobility. Now Dr. Fishman needed to add cartilage....*

Do the Math for Them

If you write narration that says, *Born in 1934, she was 18 when she met Mark,* there are viewers who will be so distracted trying to figure out the year she met Mark (1952) that they'll momentarily lose track of your story. Whether it's calculating profits or age or elapsed time, it's best to write it in a way that doesn't make the viewer do the work. This is not an issue of involving the audience in the story, it's a matter of not wanting to distract them from it.

Avoid Hype

If a story is truly astonishing or an event is truly chilling or a person is really sinister, that fact should become evident through the story or character or event and the way you present it. The cheapest and worst way to try to pump emotion into a piece is through adjectives and hyperbole. Frankly, audiences become skeptical when narrators begin to sound like overcaffeinated salespeople. If your story is really good, it will sell itself.

Know When to Stop Narrating

Prepare the moment, and then let it play. If you're building toward the battle of Waterloo or a lifesaving operation or a statewide volleyball tournament, get us there and then let it play for a bit. Audiences need a respite from the talking; they need time to feel those moments of humor or pathos or fear. Anticipate those moments and build them in, whether it means a moment of silence or a moment with music or just action and sync sound. This is also true when the information is very complex and needs to be processed, or when it's very funny and the audience needs time to laugh.

CHAPTER 14

Storytelling: A Checklist

Here's a list of questions to be asked at each stage of production, and especially as you near the end of the editing process:

- Given a choice between your film and the latest sitcom or indie drama, which would you choose? Are you telling a compelling and dramatic story and giving the viewer a reason to watch?
- Does your film involve the viewer in a story unfolding on screen, rather than talk at them?
- Are there interesting questions being asked and answered throughout, offering mystery, intrigue, and suspense?
- Are you offering new information and an unusual perspective, or just rehashing tired, unchallenging material?
- Have you grounded viewers in your story so that they can anticipate where you're going and will be surprised when you take unexpected turns?
- Are you in the driver's seat of your film, steering toward emotional and intellectual highlights? Have you created moments of discovery for the audience, allowing them to reach their own conclusions before having them confirmed or denied?
- If there is backstory in your film, have you gotten a story under way that motivates the audience to want to go there?
- If your subject is complex or technical, have you gotten a story under way that motivates the audience to want to understand it?
- Have you "cast" the film carefully, with a manageable group of characters who fairly represent the complexity of an issue and not just its extremes? Or, if your focus is the extremes, have you made that context clear?
- Do individual characters stand out and play differentiated roles in your overall story and film, or is their presence generic?

DOI: 10.1016/B978-0-240-81241-0.00014-9

- Does the story that was set up at the film's beginning pay off at the end? Can you articulate that story in a sentence or two?
- Does the film seem like "just another documentary" or is it something that people might want to tell each other about the next day?

PART III

Talking about Story

With each edition, some interviews from previous editions have to be dropped. Please see the first edition for an interview with Susanne Simpson, and the second edition for interviews with Jon Else, Kenn Rabin, Per Saari, and Onyekachi Wambu. Included in this third edition are the following:

Steven Ascher and Jeanne Jordan (Massachusetts) were asked about their two feature-length documentaries, *Troublesome Creek* and *So Much So Fast*, which they describe as "nonfiction novels."

Victoria Bruce and Karin Hayes (Maryland and New York) discuss their first collaboration, *The Kidnapping of Ingrid Betancourt*, a feature-length documentary.

Ric Burns (New York) describes his experiences as a filmmaker who specializes in long-form historical documentaries, including the multipart series *New York: A Documentary Film*.

Brett Culp (Florida) is a celebrity event filmmaker who brings a documentary approach to his work, capturing the stories of families, communities, and corporations.

Nick Fraser (London) is the commissioning editor of *Storyville*, an international documentary strand of the British Broadcasting Corporation.

Alex Gibney (New York) discusses his theatrical documentaries, including the 2007 Academy Award–winner *Taxi to the Dark Side*.

Susan Kim (New York) has written plays, graphic novels, children's television, and documentaries, and talks about the fundamentals of dramatic storytelling as applied to the production of the award-winning *Imaginary Witness: Hollywood and the Holocaust*.

James Marsh (Copenhagen) discusses his 2008 Academy Award–winning documentary *Man on Wire*.

Sam Pollard (New York) has served in a variety of roles as a filmmaker, but we spoke at greatest length about his experiences as an editor and co-producer of two documentaries with Spike Lee, both for HBO: *4 Little Girls* and *When the Levees Broke*.

Deborah Scranton (New Hampshire) discusses "virtual embedding" in her direction of the documentaries *The War Tapes* and *Bad Voodoo's War*, filmed in part by soldiers in Iraq.

CHAPTER 15

Steven Ascher and
Jeanne Jordan

Steven Ascher and Jeanne Jordan have been making documentary and
fiction films for more than 20 years. This husband-and-wife team have
made many films together, and are currently (in 2010) finishing the
feature documentary, *Raising Renee*, about artist Beverly McIver and
the promise she made to her mother to care for her developmentally
disabled sister, Renee. Jeannie's credits include serving as series producer of PBS's *Postcards from Buster*; co-producing and directing *Running with Jesse* for the PBS series *Frontline*; editing two films for the
acclaimed series *Eyes on the Prize*, and editing dramatic films including
Blue Diner, Lemon Sky, and *Concealed Enemies.*

Steve Ascher's work has appeared on networks around the world,
and his films include the documentary *Life and Other Anxieties* and the
drama *Del and Alex*. He is the author of *The Filmmaker's Handbook: A
Comprehensive Guide for the Digital Age* (with Ed Pincus), a best-selling
text now in third edition, which *The Independent* called a "filmmaking
bible." Steve has taught filmmaking at MIT, and both he and Jeannie
have taught at Harvard and in master classes around the world. Their
website is www.westcityfilms.com.

Discussed here are two of their feature documentaries. *Troublesome
Creek: A Midwestern*, about the Jordan family's struggle to save their
Iowa farm, won the Grand Jury Prize and Audience Award at the
Sundance Film Festival in 1996 and was nominated for an Academy
Award. *So Much So Fast*, which premiered at Sundance in 2006, is about
the events set in motion when Stephen Heywood was diagnosed with
ALS (Lou Gehrig's disease). I spoke with the filmmakers separately for
this interview, conducted in 2003 and updated since.

Troublesome Creek *documents the Jordan family's struggle to save their
Iowa farm. You began the film after receiving a phone call from Jeannie's
father, Russ.*

STEVE: Russ called and said he thought this would be his last year of farming. If we were going to call ourselves filmmakers and not make a film about this, there was something wrong. To be able to do a story like this, to have that kind of access—I thought of it as both an opportunity to tell this story and also for Jeannie to be able to tell some of the wonderful stories she'd been telling around the dinner table for years about growing up in Iowa.

He felt that he'd have one more year of planting and harvest followed by an auction. [The Jordans' plan was to auction off their livestock, equipment, and personal belongings in order to pay off their debts and keep the land itself, 450 acres.] That gave us the possibility of a narrative spine. It would have been much harder if not impossible to just make a film about day-to-day life on the farm, and be able to get into the kinds of issues that we did. We filmed four times over the course of about a year and a half.

How did you plan for the visual storytelling? Did you write up outlines, a treatment?

STEVE: We had to write up various things in order to raise money, but they were never really part of our thinking. With stories like this, in part you're following events and the events dictate what you're filming. But you have in your mind certain themes that you're interested in. In this case, the year on the farm, which included all the tasks that had to be accomplished—planting, harvesting, preparing for the auction, the auction. Then there are themes about Russ and Mary Jane, their marriage and their raising of children; there were themes about Jeannie's childhood; and themes about the changing landscape all over the Midwest, all over rural America. You're kind of advancing all of these fronts together, and you shoot things that can work toward them.

At the start of the film, there's a sequence in which a cat jumps from the roof of a barn into the arms of Jeannie's brother, Jon. It serves as a metaphor: as Jeannie says in voice-over, "My family in a nutshell—incredible luck, incredible timing, and teetering on the brink of disaster."

STEVE: That's a real tribute to editing. We had been filming for over a week, on the first shoot, and nothing had happened. We filmed mostly just goings-on at the farm. A cow had died, and we were doing a stakeout, waiting for the rendering truck to pick it up. Just waiting, for hours. And then we heard people shouting, and there was this cat on the roof. At the time we were just incredibly depressed. If the big event is a cat on the roof, we're really in trouble.

JEANNIE: Plus, when the cat jumped, we were moving the camera. I saw the cat jump, and Steve got the end of the cat jumping. But we didn't get the cat jumping. So it was a disaster. We filmed the wrong thing and we didn't get the climax of it. But in *Troublesome Creek*, I cut every inch that we shot. So I just went at that. I thought, I'm going to see if I can find a way to make "missing the cat" work. I know we have "after missing the cat," and I know we have "before jumping," so let me just cut it and look at it. And I realized that missing it was part of the story and the metaphor, and that the metaphor was unbelievable. The fact that Jon would even walk up there and say, "Come jump into my arms, little kitty," was absolutely a thing about my family that's always driven me nuts. Totally unrealistic, and it worked.

Once I got it cut and realized it was a metaphor, I also realized that if this were the first thing you really saw in the body of the film, it would set you up to be ready for anything. I knew—because we'd been trying to raise money for the film for years at that point—that people had the most prosaic, small-minded reaction to what farming is or what people who farm are and that I had to fight that.

STEVE: The problem with doing a film like this is as soon as people hear the words farm or farm documentary, their eyes glaze over. "Oh, it's another farm film, and it's going to be sentimental," or "It's going to be, 'Oh, poor farmers.'" And when they actually see it, they're stunned to find out these people are funny, they're intelligent, and the film is doing all sorts of things that they just didn't expect. Our hope was that the film would resonate with universal themes and become something that's about the passing of time, and about a marriage, and about the history of America.

You shot only 27 hours of film footage, in 16mm, for a program that runs about 88 minutes. That's very conservative.

STEVE: That was mostly imposed by budgetary problems. Every time we'd get out there, we'd budget a certain amount to shoot, and invariably we would have shot that amount halfway through the time. And then we'd have these agonizing meetings up in the bedroom trying to decide how much more stock we could order, which we knew we couldn't afford to process. Most of the footage of the film we never saw for about a year. [It was stored in the freezer at their home in Massachusetts until they could process it.] The joke was that instead of having dailies, we had yearlies.

Would you shoot it in video today?

STEVE: Probably we would, but at the time we felt strongly that the landscape of Iowa and the texture of the farm would only come across in film. The beauty of the landscape, the feel of the animals, and the smells, and the corn in the summer—all of those things are an important part of why farmers do what they do, because it's such a tough life. That had to come across, mixing the financial tension and strain with the rewards of being a farmer; it played into the structure of the story. So we made sure that the seasons were very much a part of the film. Ultimately, we blew the film up to 35mm. There's no comparison between the beauty of the 35mm image even to 16mm projection.

But by the same token, there were a number of scenes that we missed or gave short shrift to because we were so limited in the amount of film we could shoot. In a typical evening, we might shoot a roll or a roll and a half of film. That's 10 minutes or 15 minutes of material, which is hundreds of dollars.

You filmed the Jordan family during an extraordinarily difficult time. Were you ever concerned that the filmmaking would add to their burden?

JEANNIE: I have a very political family. The farm situation, the farm question, was something I was raised dealing with, a really viable big political issue in this country. So trying to capture what it was that we felt was so tragic and shortsighted about it, through what was happening to us, I knew they'd all be behind that. I also knew I wasn't going to betray them in any way. I wasn't going to show anything that they didn't want me to show or say anything that was a breach of their privacy.

The only time that I felt bad was when we asked my parents to go to Rolfe, where I grew up. [The filmmakers bring the Jordans to a farm they'd rented for several years before taking over the family property.] I knew that the house had fallen apart, and they didn't. It was very painful for them. So when we edited it in, I asked them if they didn't want that there. My mother wasn't talking by that time [because of illness], but she agreed with what my dad said, which was, "If you don't see what eventually will happen, you don't understand what you're talking about. You can say farmers go out of business and farms go away. How do they go away? They fall apart. They tear them down." And he said, "You have to show something like that; this is as good as anything else."

STEVE: They never asked us to stop filming. We're very careful, even with subjects that we've been filming for years; we still feel very hesitant about what we film and when we're being intrusive. In Jeannie's family the most you would get might be a look of "Why are you filming this?" or, as we approached the time of the auction, one of the reasons that Jeannie becomes more of a character on screen is that her sisters were saying, "You don't think you're going to be able to just film this without helping, do you?"

The idea that you can respect the privacy of your subjects and still present an honest story might surprise some filmmakers. Do your students ever ask about that?

JEANNIE: It's not so much that they ask about it as that I tell them. A lot of students do personal films; that's kind of what all of our first instincts are. Lots of times they'll have crossed the line. A young filmmaker I know did a film about her mother dying of cancer, and it was very raw. Her mother was a very beautiful woman who, when she knew she was being filmed, would get really done up, as much as she could. But sometimes her daughter would walk in the room filming, and her mother wouldn't be prepared for it, and she'd complain a bit. One of the things I said to the filmmaker after I looked at one cut is, "I want you to look at this through your mom's eyes. And I want you to look for moments where she looks good. As much as you can tell the story with those, I think that it will still work and you don't have to embarrass her. You don't have to make her feel like, "Oh, I look so horrible." Her mother probably wasn't going to see this film, but still, it's trying to instill that kind of respect. We all have a natural instinct to protect, but I think that a lot of students, when they're young, think that means you're not being honest; that you have to show something bad or raw to tell a good story.

The stories in Troublesome Creek—*both the overall story of the Jordan farm and the individual stories that Jeannie tells, such as "Daddy Date Night" (in which she recounts nervously preparing for one-on-one time with her father, even writing out talking points in her hand)—manage to be both very personal and universal.*

STEVE: When I think of the universals that mean the most to me in the film, they're about time and family connections and the passing of history, a history that means so much now but will be completely gone in a certain number of years. You're looking for true moments. Part of it involves giving the audience room to think and images that are suggestive of those themes. The drive from the house to town, the shot is out the back, facing backward, and you're seeing this beautiful plume of dust that was kicked up, backlit by the sun. And I remember shooting it, hanging out the car door, and thinking it was beautiful, but it's also clearly a visual metaphor for leaving the past behind. And it's while Jeannie's narrating this wonderful Daddy Date Night story.

As their daughter, are you revealing information to your parents, through this film, for the first time?

JEANNIE: Yes, absolutely. Mother knew that I was scornful of her Polly-anna-ish view of the world, as in the scene of me giving her shit because she thought that Charlotte at the bank was her best friend. But Daddy, we were all scared of him when we were little. We aren't anymore; he's mellowed incredibly. But he was moody, he was worried, and he was just a formidable guy. He was also 6-foot-4 and has those eyebrows. So in doing the film, the one thing I could not do is depict our childhood without some hint of that. So there were two places in the film: Daddy Date Night and the Bergman reference. ["Russ came to the idea of optimism late in life," Jeannie says in narration. "The Russ I knew growing up could give a Bergman film a run for its money in the Moody Darkness Department."] But if you say something good right afterwards, which is, "He's completely turned around and is the optimist of the family," he comes away from it thinking, "I'm the optimist." But he noticed the other. We were visiting Steve's mom and stepfather. We were sitting on the porch on Martha's Vineyard, and my dad said, "Bergman." I said, "He's this Swedish filmmaker, makes really, really, depressing films, but really good films." And he said, "When you were little, did you think I was like that?" And I said, "You were like that Daddy, I didn't think you were like that." Then we had a really interesting talk. One of the things I asked him was, "Did that hurt your feelings?" And he said, "No, because everybody seems to like me anyway, who saw the film."

Tell me about the westerns that we see the Jordans watching throughout Troublesome Creek.

JEANNIE: The first time we were there to shoot, it was like, they're going to watch TV every night. They're not going to talk about anything. This is a disaster. And then part of us started realizing, wait a minute, what they're watching, by and large, are westerns. We decided we could use that as a metaphor.

STEVE: Russ loved westerns, and the whole issue of his struggle with the bank is informed by clichéd storytelling notions of good guys and bad guys, cowboys and farmers, and making a stand against your enemy. *Lonesome Dove* was on the night before the cattle auction, and it felt like some incredible piece of serendipity or fate that this story about the end of the West would be on the night that Russ was about to shed the cowboy part of himself. When you're a farmer with animals, you're partly a plant grower and you're partly an animal wrangler. And this was going to be the end of his wrangling days.

Troublesome Creek is narrated by Jeannie. Did you always know that she would narrate?

STEVE: Jeannie thought that hopefully the film could stand on its own without narration. In the end, the narration is a very important part of moving the story along and giving you access to layers of knowledge and storytelling that go into the past, that you just can't film. Jeannie would sit down and write stories about, for example, Daddy Date Night. She'd write a few pages and then she'd give it to me and I'd pull things out of it, and then she'd rephrase them and place them; it's a kind of an organic back and forth. Collaboration can be hard, but there's so much about how you interpret the material and what's really going on in a scene, and what does the audience need to know and when, that it's very hard to make these films alone.

I think of the film as both biographical and autobiographical. And it's always walking the line between "as seen through" Jeannie's eyes, she's narrating; my eyes, because I'm shooting; but also seeking to make that presence disappear at moments when we want the audience to just be immersed in Russ and Mary Jane's story without thinking about the perspective from which you're viewing them.

The film also conveys a strong point of view without becoming a rant.

JEANNIE: To be a political film, *Troublesome Creek* had to be charming. You had to like these people, to identify with them. If I had ranted, which was in me to do, I would have lost a part of the audience because the bias would have been too obvious. The bias is obvious, but it's tempered. I'm not positive I'm right. I had to show that I was angry that there are only three million farmers left, but I'm not saying I know how to fix it or whose fault it is. It's history; it's just happening.

STEVE: As partners, Jeannie and I had very different perspectives on what was going on. Jeannie had lived it and knew it intimately, and I was from New York and didn't know anything about farms. So we combined an insider's and an outsider's perspective. The film by turns takes you deeply inside the family and then steps outside and looks at the story in a more distanced way. I think that's a way that you can take a personal narrative and help the audience to see it in larger terms.

We felt that the film's biggest influence would be if it were a compelling narrative that people would want to watch. All of the other issues emerge from the story and are there to be talked about. We took it around the Midwest, and the fervor of the discussions that would come after the film—it raises the questions to a level that people feel passionate about. We saw that as its biggest kind of political contribution.

Is that why you avoided some "traditional" documentary elements, such as interviews?

STEVE: We didn't want to do interviews. We absolutely did not want any expert testimony about anything having to do with farming or economics that would make it seem like that this was a subject being studied as opposed to a subject that was being lived. At one point, [though] we felt we had to sit Russ Jordan down to try to get him to tell us his side of the story—

JEANNIE: —Steve and I had this whole list of questions to ask him—

STEVE: —And the result of that is the banker joke that he tells. And that's it. That was his response to, "How are you doing? What do you think is going on with the bank?"

JEANNIE: That's denial, but it's a good way to do it. At least it's funny.

Wendy, Alex, and Stephen Heywood, from *So Much So Fast*. Photo courtesy of the filmmakers.

So Much So Fast *begins with a prologue, a transition from* Troublesome Creek. *We learn that after you'd shot the film, Jeannie's mother, Mary Jane, was diagnosed with ALS. Five years after her death, in 1995, you began filming the Heywoods: one brother has ALS, and the other quit his job to start a foundation and find a cure.*

STEVE: When Mary Jane got ALS, there was nothing you could do about it, and it was hard to even find out anything about it. This was in the very early days of the Internet. By 2000, everything had changed. There was a real explosion of research, and the Internet made it possible to find out what was going on anywhere in the world. We had been looking around for a way to do something about ALS that wouldn't just be about somebody being sick and deteriorating, and in the Heywoods we saw the possibility of an extremely vital story with a lot of growth. And also, they're a very dynamic family, and very funny. That was very important to us, that we could get at the story with a lot of black humor.

When we first talked to the Heywoods about filming, we talked about how close we needed to be in order to do this story. Actually, Jeannie said first that Mary Jane would never have let us make a film about her illness, and so we totally understood if the Heywoods didn't want to do it. Which I thought at the time was perhaps one of the worst pitches ever made to a film subject! But Jeannie also talked about how we're really asking to become members of their family, in a certain way. And given the amount of time we spent together over those years—which included a lot of time of not filming—we did become very intimate. We went on vacation with them, for example. A small portion of the time was filming, but most of it was just hanging out and eating and doing all of the other things that you do.

How did you decide how much of the illness to show, and what to leave out?

STEVE: Stephen Heywood welcomed us filming anything. At one point, he started gagging, before he got his feeding tube. And I put the camera down and went to try to help him, and afterward he said, "Why didn't you keep shooting?" And my feeling was one, I can't shoot when somebody's in that kind of distress and I might be able to do something, but also, I just really didn't feel that that was something the audience needed to see. We're already asking the audience to see and think about things they normally might turn away from.

In becoming close to your subjects, do you risk losing your perspective, your objectivity? How can you be inside but also outside at the same time?

STEVE: I would say that *So Much So Fast* is much more about intimacy than it is objectivity. I don't particularly believe in objectivity; I believe that you can give a truthful account and an account that may be balanced in various ways, but I don't think objectivity really comes into it. That said, both Jeannie and I are capable of both being very close to the people we film and stepping back when we need to. We were both deeply involved with the Heywoods' lives, but at various times would say, "We're making a film here, we can't play a role." There's a scene in the film where Jamie is quoting Melinda, from couples counseling, where she said, "These people are making a film about us and they were wondering when I was going to crack." And I know that I never had that conversation, which is what I tell Jamie, and he thinks that Jeannie did, but she didn't. We wouldn't take sides in that way, because it would be inappropriate. But we decided that we had to leave that scene in, even though it deeply misrepresents our relationship. We felt that film subjects are often misquoted and have no control over what is said about them; we might as well subject ourselves to the same treatment. And we couldn't narrate our way out of it.

Jeannie once talked with Jamie about the prime directive from *Star Trek*: When you go back in time, you can't move a rock on a planet or you'll change its history forever. And Jamie said, "Well, you can move the rocks on my planet anytime you want."

In contrast to Troublesome Creek, *you shot* So Much So Fast *on video. Was that a storytelling choice?*

STEVE: Yes. With *Troublesome Creek*, we had defined the story in such a way that we were only going to shoot for a certain period of time. Whereas with *So Much So Fast*, it was much more open-ended. There were many more story lines that we were following: Stephen Heywood's experience with ALS; the foundation growing from three people in a basement to a multimillion dollar research facility; the family itself; and aspects of ALS separate from any of those things. All of those different story lines called for a much higher shooting ratio.

How many hours did you end up shooting?

STEVE: About 200. But for a project that was shot over four years, that's still not extraordinarily high.

Did you find it took longer to edit than Troublesome Creek?

STEVE: It does take longer to edit, in that you've got a lot of stuff to wade through. And also, in this case, we were following different story lines and trying to do them all justice. At one point we had a really interesting cut that was about 2 hours and 15 minutes, but our feeling was that it was just too much to sustain the emotional arc. The executive producer at German television, one of our backers, said, "You really have three films here, that are individually interesting but no one person could follow them all." Which kind of supported our feeling that the film had to be 90 minutes or less, given the intensity of what you're watching.

What were the three films, and how did you choose between them?

STEVE: One of them was about the family, one was about the foundation and the business of trying to run this nonprofit research organization, and part of it was the science. We gave a lot of priority to the family side of it. But we're hoping people will see this film in a lot of different ways. It's partly a topical film about an orphan disease and how people cope with it. But it's also about time and life, and we hope that audiences will find themselves in the film, and see the metaphors that are there for them.

As you approach material in the editing room, do you think about act structure?

JEANNIE: Act structure? No. I tend to be a natural storyteller; it's something I kind of grew up with. I start from the beginning of the footage, and I'm cutting whenever I see any kind of a story. The story might be Wendy, Stephen Heywood's wife, gets tired of watching [their son] Alex try to open his sippy cup and goes over and opens it for him, but there's a whole back and forth between them. I'm probably not a good person to talk to on some level just because I really don't want to think about the big picture until I have all the little pictures together.

Isn't that the same as editing sequences?

JEANNIE: It is, it's making sequences. And I'm stringing them together and then I'll get Steve to come in and we'll watch them together. So that whatever reactions I have already in my mind, he'll have his own. Because he had his own to begin with, because he shot them. So we just kind of leapfrog over each other and try to sneak up on whatever is in the material that the other one doesn't see.

In contrast to Troublesome Creek, *Steve is the narrator of* So Much So Fast, *and in addition is occasionally heard and even seen on camera. How did that come about?*

STEVE: When filming the men, it worked out better if it was just me alone. If we were both there, Stephen [Heywood]'s focus would get split, and it just wasn't working. So I would shoot them and have these conversations—much more conversations than interviews. Initially I didn't even mic myself, but Jeannie encouraged me to do it. And then, because the conversations took on the importance that they did, she felt strongly that I should be the narrator, to continue that voice and be the audience's access to the story.

You're currently producing a third feature-length documentary, about an artist who's assumed responsibility for her mentally-challenged sister. What's it like to create these kinds of films, which you describe as "nonfiction novels" because of their complexity and layering.

STEVE: I remember when we started *So Much So Fast*, the first time we went out with equipment—after not doing that kind of filming for a long time—we looked at each other: "Are we really going to do this again?" It's a tremendous commitment, and you have to develop this incredible kind of symbiosis with your subjects, where you're getting close to them. On some level you feel kind of parasitic, that you're living off their life in a certain way. In another way you feel invisible because you're filming all of this, but you don't know if they see you as a person or as a someone who's making the film. Those are questions along the way. But the reason to do it is you end up with a kind of film that you can't get any other way.

I think for both Jeannie and me, it's a matter of needing to really get on the inside of something, to be able to tell a story with that detail and deep knowledge. Having wrestled with those issues over that length of time makes for a much deeper film, and there's also the throughline of time, how the world changes over time. As much as we'd like to finish these films faster, they get a tremendous amount of power from showing life unfold.

Any last words of advice on storytelling?

STEVE: Think before you shoot, know what it is you're looking at, and have a sense of what you want a shot to convey. Shots don't just happen; they're an expression that is concocted between the camera, person, the subject, and serendipity. And you should always be thinking, "What is it that I want to take out of this scene, what do I want audiences to see?" You're always putting yourself in a seat in the theater when you're shooting, or you should be, and thinking, "What am I revealing? When do I want you to know that this character is sitting over here or that this person is frowning?" And that's a calculation that you're doing both when you're shooting and you're editing. How to structure a scene to reveal things.

JEANNIE: Be respectful of the privacy of who you're covering, especially if you're making personal films. Even if you're doing a very intimate film you can do that. Unless there's some real evil that you're dealing with, I think that people need to be careful and respectful of whom they're shooting.

CHAPTER 16

Victoria Bruce and Karin Hayes

Although their fathers had been lifelong friends, Victoria Bruce and Karin Hayes did not meet until shortly before they began their first film, *The Kidnapping of Ingrid Betancourt*. At the time, Victoria was a science writer with a master's degree in geology, and the author of *No Apparent Danger* (HarperCollins, 2001), about a tragic expedition into a volcano in Colombia. Karin, a graduate of the University of California in Los Angeles, was working as an associate producer in Washington, D.C. Their plans to document the Colombian presidential campaign of Ingrid Betancourt changed when Betancourt was kidnapped by guerrillas in February 2002; instead, the filmmakers told Betancourt's story through her family's efforts to continue her campaign and ensure her safe return. Their feature-length film, *The Kidnapping of Ingrid Betancourt*, aired on HBO in 2004.

Bruce and Hayes also produced *Held Hostage*, a 48-minute film about three Americans who worked for a private military contractor and, like Betancourt, were being held by Colombian guerrillas. At the time this interview was conducted, in June 2006, the contractors and Betancourt remained in captivity. They were rescued on July 2, 2008, and HBO reacquired the rights to air *The Kidnapping of Ingrid Betancourt*. In a joint deal with CNN, the film aired on *CNN Presents* just days later (both HBO and CNN are owned by TimeWarner).

In the meantime, Bruce and Hayes completed *Pip & Zastrow: An American Friendship*, a feature-length documentary that premiered at the 2008 American Black Film Festival in Los Angeles, and won the Target® Filmmaker Award.

In August 2010, Knopf will publish a nonfiction book by Bruce and Hayes, with Jorge Enrique Botero, *Hostage Nation: Colombia's Guerrilla Army and the Failed War on Drugs*.

DOI: 10.1016/B978-0-240-81241-0.00016-2

In 2002, Ingrid Betancourt was a senator in Colombia, campaigning for president and calling for reform of a corruption-plagued government, in a country that had endured 40 years of civil war. How did you first meet her?

VICTORIA: Ingrid had a deal with HarperCollins to do the English version of her autobiography, *Until Death Do Us Part*, which was first published in France. So she came here to go on book tour. A year before, I'd gone on book tour, and I had this wonderful publicist who knew that I'd fallen in love with Colombia when I wrote my book and that I wanted to do something positive, to show a positive side of Colombia. He was also the publicist for Ingrid's book tour, and he called me up and said, "Vicky, you have to meet this woman."

So I read the book and thought, "This is great." Because here's a way to put a face on Colombia, the face that I saw, which was bravery and beauty and compassion, which Ingrid encompasses all of. So I met with Ingrid for an hour, in January 2002. She was running around doing all these interviews. I didn't really have a feel of what I wanted to do with her, I thought maybe a magazine article. Somebody suggested maybe a film, a documentary. So I met with National Geographic Television and tried to interest them in the idea of following Ingrid on the campaign trail. National Geographic has some kinds of series where they have journalists out in the field, and I was thinking I would do something like that, with me as the journalist. They seemed interested, but a couple of weeks went by, so that wasn't happening.

It's already January 2002, the campaign is under way, and the presidential elections are in May. So I imagine you had to move quickly. Is that when you called Karin?

VICTORIA: I had met Karin twice by then, and I knew she spoke Spanish. [Karin attended both the University of Guadalajara and the Universidad de Costa Rica before going to UCLA.] And I knew she knew how to make films, so I called her.

KARIN: I read Ingrid's book and just thought, "I have to do this; this is an amazing woman." At that time I was on contract still; I was an associate producer at Cronkite Ward and had a couple more months in my contract. But Vicky and I met in New York and we were trying to decide in what style we were going to do the documentary. Because initially she was thinking, journalist. And I was thinking about *The War Room*, that vérité style, like in the campaign headquarters.

At this point, she's a free woman, and you're planning to tell the story of the campaign?

KARIN: Yes, we were going to follow her on the campaign trail: Here's this woman running for president in Latin America, a woman who started her own political party, who's been very controversial in Congress and the Senate; she's led hunger strikes, she's pointed out all of the corrupt people in Congress, she's made a lot of enemies, and she's just taking Colombia by storm—or had the potential to. So we thought how fascinating it would be to follow her through these little towns and see people's reaction to her campaign.

Did you have any funding?

KARIN: No, [not] with all of this really happening in such a short time. The next thing I remember, I saw on CNN that she'd been kidnapped. [In February, Senator Betancourt was kidnapped by the Revolutionary Armed Forces of Colombia (FARC), a guerrilla group with whom the government had been negotiating.]

VICTORIA: We had talked to her right before that. Ingrid knew we were coming; it was sort of going to be more set up. "Well, if you want to go see the FARC, we'll see the FARC, if you want to do this—" because this was before the peace process broke down. There were a lot of journalists meeting with FARC in those days, and so we could have driven a bus through FARC territory. That's what we were planning on. And she said, "I'm going down to meet with the FARC on the fourteenth." And actually we have footage from that; we didn't shoot it—

That's the meeting in your film, with everyone around the table?

VICTORIA: That's the meeting at the table where she says, "No more kidnapping." And that was nine days before her kidnapping. So we knew she was going there, we were setting up, getting ready, and we were planning on going a couple of days later than we ended up going. But when she was kidnapped we just went into Plan B. Karin was still working, so I had to go down by myself.

From your press materials, it sounds like Karin gave you, Vicky, an all-night crash course in video production. You had Karin's PD150, your own video camera, and some rented sound gear....

VICTORIA: She tried to make me bring a flak jacket. My pack's already too heavy—

KARIN: I was there with a mixer, explaining how to use a mixer in case she had to. And she said, "You've got to record this so I can remember how to do it." So we're filming my explanation of how to use the mixer and we're testing all the mics and all this.

VICTORIA: And white balance, I didn't know what that was. . . .

KARIN: I was trying to give her the crash course, some basics, and then when she was down there we would talk. And I'd ask, "What'd you guys get?" and she'd tell me, and I'd [suggest], "What about this and this?" She's really good at interviews and knowing how to get the story, and I was more about the technical: "Did you get shots of this," and b-roll, you know—

VICTORIA: And our cameraman [Cesar Pinzón] didn't speak any English. I speak a little bit of Spanish, and we got a great fixer [Mayra Rodriguez] who became our associate producer on the film, who was wonderful. But it was a little bit scary, for me.

KARIN: And she was shooting second camera.

VICTORIA: I shot a lot of second camera.

KARIN: And then the cinematographer used my camera. And then one of the best things was, she left her Panasonic one-chip camera down there when she left Colombia, after that first trip, so that if anything happened to Ingrid—

VICTORIA: We figured she'd be released, we really did. And that would be a happy ending, and they'd have a camera to shoot with. Because our cameraman didn't have his own camera—

KARIN: It was stolen when Ingrid was kidnapped; he'd given it to the sound guy, our sound guy [who was present but not held]. But with the camera we left down there, he captured the whole funeral scene—

VICTORIA: The father's funeral, and the kids calling Ingrid on the radio. We wouldn't have had the kids in there at all, because that was the only time they were back in Colombia. So it was great that we had left that camera there. And it was the brother, the cameraman's brother, who shot it; the cameraman was out of town.

After she's been kidnapped, the family decides to continue the campaign without her, carrying a life-sized cardboard torso of Ingrid around with them. Given the changed circumstances, why do you think they continued to allow the film?

VICTORIA: They were surrounded by media because they were running a campaign. So it wasn't like we came into their lives during a crisis time and no one else was around.

KARIN: Many times, we blended into all the other media that was there. It was like a blur to [her husband] Juan Carlos, I think. And it was only in the very end, I remember the last day, we bought dinner for Juan Carlos and took it to his house, a kind of wrap-up. And he said to us, "Wow, I'm really going to miss not having you guys here. Because it's been company for me."

VICTORIA: Not that we'd really even talk to him very much. We'd ride in the car with him; he kind of always had us around. The hardest thing for me originally going down there was meeting Juan Carlos. When you first meet him you're like, "Oh please, he's going to be a drag, this can't be our main character." I mean, on camera, he's not dynamic, he sort of mumbles. We only did one sit-down interview with him. That was it. The rest was just shooting. We didn't want to sit him down again. You didn't have to ask him, "How're you feeling today, Juan Carlos?" Which is the question he was getting all the time.

Juan Carlos Lecompte and cardboard figure of his wife, from *The Kidnapping of Ingrid Betancourt*. Photo by Ana Maria Garcia Rojas, courtesy of the filmmakers.

KARIN: He's a little closed off. Hard to get to know.

VICTORIA: But when you cut the film together, then the human being comes out. Trust that the character will come out in your shooting, if you spend enough time with them.

KARIN: But also, I was kind of hypersensitive about not wanting it to become sappy, to show every scene that [Ingrid's mother] Yolanda's crying in. I mean, she was strong, but at some point in most of our footage there was a point where she usually broke down. But I didn't want to be...what's the word? Exploitative. I didn't want to put in crying just to pull people's heart strings. I really wanted to be honest with it, not force it.

VICTORIA: The kids hang up the phone [after leaving a voice message they hope will reach their mother, via radio], and then it immediately goes to this happy music, and it's campaigning again. We made a real conscious decision to pull you out of that: It's sad, and then, onward.

In terms of vérité filming, were there ever times when you intervened? I'm thinking, for example, of the powerful image in which Juan Carlos appears to be holding his wife's cardboard hand.

VICTORIA: We have so much of that, we had so many shots. Our cinematographer was very good. Sometimes he would cut off audio in the middle of somebody saying something wonderful, it drove me crazy, but when he had a good shot he would be on it. That's the way Juan Carlos carried her, and sometimes he'd just look at her, and sometimes he'd touch her. The one thing we did ask him to do is ride his motorcycle. It's not pivotal, it's sort of a transition, the end of the act, coming down before the election.

You were there in March, and again in May, for the election?

KARIN: Sixteen days for the first shoot, and then ten days for the second. And in between that time, we thought, okay, March/April, we're going to cut a trailer together, and we're going to get funding, we're going to get grants.

VICTORIA: So we could go back in May and have the money. That didn't happen.

So you really didn't become part of the family while you were there—you blended in with the media instead, and weren't there for that long.

VICTORIA: We've become closer to them after, especially Karin. But we were there for four weeks, total.

In all, you filmed about 100 hours of material. Tell me about the process of editing it.

VICTORIA: That's another thing; we didn't realize that we'd have to learn how to edit until we came home with the second batch, and we were like, "Now what do we do? We still have no money." My ex-boyfriend gave me $15,000, and we spent that on the first shoot.

KARIN: And then the second shoot, we just said, "Okay, we're each taking this much out of our savings, and the rest we're putting on credit cards."

VICTORIA: We ended up being able to pay it all back, but after our second film. With Ingrid we would have broken even, because we've had international sales.

KARIN: We thought we'd hire an editor, but we had no money. We started doing the transcribing ourselves as soon as we got home. We had said we wanted to have the film done before she'd been kidnapped for a year.

VICTORIA: The goal was to apply to Sundance and Slamdance.

So you taught yourselves Final Cut, and worked on borrowed computers in Karin's parents' dining room?

KARIN: We bought Final Cut and we bought six Final Cut Pro books, and then we sat down and just started cutting. And we had already started trying to collect all the interviews from radio that Ingrid had done in English [during her book tour].

VICTORIA: The reason we did that is because, okay, here we have all this footage, but who cares about Ingrid? We have some campaign footage, but you're not going to like her much; you don't even know her. So Karin started contacting all of the media outlets where she'd done interviews, to get the tapes from there, and that's where we ended up cutting her whole audio narration from.

KARIN: We had five different interviews to cut from. *Fresh Air* [NPR] was probably the longest; it was an hour. The others were maybe half hours.

And you also use some stock footage—home movies, campaign footage, etc.—that you got from a range of sources.

VICTORIA: Some of the campaign footage was shot by Cesar. And then we got a lot from Colombian television. Cesar was really connected; he had seven brothers working in TV, and so he was able to negotiate and get us the Colombian stock footage for very little. I think we ended up paying for 14 seconds (20-second minimum) of CNN that cost us $1,800. But most of the footage and audio, Karin and Cesar negotiated, we got for very little.

So this is late in 2002, and you spent about three months editing, still without any financial support.

KARIN: Four months, maybe. To January, because we were up to the last wire.

VICTORIA: We used to put sticky notes on our computer, that said, "How's Ingrid's life?" Because we'd get so miserable, start complaining to each other. Neither of us had boyfriends; we had no social life; we used to sit by each other, at 3:00 in the morning, editing.

KARIN: And another thing we did is, I think it was Vicky who came up with this idea, the Shoeless Children's Fund. And whoever complains next has to start contributing—

VICTORIA: —a dollar.

KARIN: And whoever complains the least gets to choose the charity.

VICTORIA: The Shoeless Children's Fund. We still say that every once in a while when one of us starts complaining too much.

Did you hope your film might make a difference?

KARIN: We were really hoping that it would have some kind of effect. And mobilize people in a way. We [recently] got two calls, Amnesty International wants to screen it in Chile and Bolivia. So it's starting to get out there. But in terms of mobilizing in the U.S., I mean certainly the people who have seen it, the overwhelming response is "What can we do?"

VICTORIA: But they can't do anything.

KARIN: That's the hardest thing.

VICTORIA: Write your congressman or something.

In the fall of 2002, I was at an industry gathering where Vicky did what audience members are never supposed to do—it was a panel of commissioning editors, and when they opened the floor for questions, you pitched your film. The audience was a bit riled, but an editor at HBO asked to see you.

VICTORIA: "What's the question?" Well, I did PR for NASA, so I have a PR background. I was really nervous because I knew I was going to do it. I told Karin I was going to do it.

KARIN: From the very beginning, when I was imagining where did I want my film to be, and what style did it need to be, I was thinking HBO.

VICTORIA: And then I wouldn't give her [HBO] the tape, that was the best. Because it was going to be playing at Slamdance, so I told her to come see it. That's what they tell you, that you never should give a screener. You should never let them sit alone with a TV on a bad day. Get them in a room with other people, get audience reaction, a full house, and then you get your distributors to watch your film.

The film screened in competition at Slamdance on January 23, 2003, a few weeks shy of the first anniversary of Betancourt's kidnapping. The title was Missing Peace. *When and why was it changed?*

VICTORIA: After Slamdance, HBO acquired the film for two years. They wanted to do some reediting, and we worked for another two months with their editor, Geof Bartz. The most important thing they changed was that they wanted you to know that Ingrid was kidnapped up front. We had a slow build of getting to know this woman. And Sheila Nevins [said] that you will care so much more about her time with her kids in the home video if you know she's going to be gone soon. It's brilliant.

It's a really nice first act. Once you've made it clear that she's been kidnapped, you build a sense of who she is and what she's doing, and she herself, in voice-over, narrates. At the end of the first act, the story returns to the kidnapping, and she's no longer in the picture—except as a cardboard cut-out.

VICTORIA: I think that's just sort of a "gimme" storytelling—that's what happened to everyone around her, that's what happened to her family. To keep bringing her back wouldn't have had that effect. And I think that we also realized that this isn't a story about a woman, it's the story about a man. Really. And it became the story of Juan Carlos, how he changes from a guy who never votes to a guy who's a huge political animal at the end.

KARIN: We still see her and how she's in it, but it's about him and the family and the campaign and what a family of a kidnapped person goes through, even though she was in an extraordinary situation, being a presidential candidate. Here's Ingrid, and she's a face for all of the hundreds of other people who are kidnapped and the 50 to 60 people who are being held as political hostages now.

Betancourt was still in captivity when your film was released, and remains in captivity as of now, June 2006. Were there steps you had to take to ensure that the film didn't make her situation worse?

VICTORIA: We let her family watch it [before it was done]. Typically I would recommend that you not let your characters watch your film, but we didn't know what things were scary politically. They definitely didn't want to make the current president look bad, whoever was going to win, because that's their only hope to get Ingrid out. Some people said, "Are you making her so high profile that the FARC's going to think she's even more valuable, and keep her kidnapped longer?" But the family themselves, and especially Juan Carlos, a former advertising man, were always of the opinion, "Keep it in the media, keep it alive, keep the story alive." And it has turned out that the family is very supportive of the film. But at the time I think they were very worried; it's a very personal film about their family.

Did you intentionally use dramatic three-act structure for the film? The first act ends, as mentioned, with the kidnapping. The second act drives to election day. The third act continues through to the outcome—she doesn't win, but she does get enough votes to save the party she's founded. And then we see the videos released by the kidnappers, to prove that Betancourt is still alive.

KARIN: Vicky's really good with storytelling. She wrote her book, she was a journalist. And for me, I knew about the three-act structure, and I knew that it had to have an arc, our story. And that's what I was focusing on.

VICTORIA: We got a lot of advice from a lot of friends; we would have people watch rough cuts along the way.

KARIN: There was one point when we had some friends of ours who had gone to film school, and they came and sat with us at one point for like six hours, until 3:00 in the morning, going through our film, bit by bit, the rough cut, advising us on how we're editing. And I remember they sat down with me and said, "Karin, you have no second act. There's no character arc, nothing. It sucks. You have to do something."

And then after HBO acquired it, there was the additional editing, in New York.

VICTORIA: We'd go up there and see what Geof was doing, and he would send us things.

In some of the reviews I've read, people have taken the film to task for not offering more time to the other political candidates, or to FARC. How did you decide to just give a platform to Ingrid, and not, for example, let her assertions about corruption be challenged?

VICTORIA: We did interview all of the other candidates, except [Alvaro] Uribe; we interviewed him after the election because we couldn't get an interview previous. And the reason that we didn't put them in—I mean, we didn't have her specifically attacking any of the candidates. There was something in one of her audios that said, "I saw how all of the Congress was bought by so-and-so's money." And if you listen to the audio very carefully that "all" was taken out and we found a "some" somewhere in her audio and stuck it in there, for legal reasons.

A lot of times, some very strongly opinionated Colombians or even Americans will say, "You didn't tell the FARC side" or "You didn't tell the paramilitary side." And you say, "Colombia is such a complicated country. There's just no way to do a political story and a personal story." But then we did *Held Hostage,* and so now we tell people, "Buy our next film." Because we cover the drug dealers, the paramilitaries, the guerrillas; these are all the factions. To me, it's not hard, because I feel like I'm more of a storyteller. You can pick one side. This is a narrative and that's Ingrid's opinion.

KARIN: I think that in doing documentaries there's that freedom, because you can choose how you want to tell your story. People challenge us and say, "Ingrid did this, and Ingrid did that, and she wasn't all this good." Well, that's fine, because everyone's going to have their own opinion on that. We wanted to make a film where people would see the story, maybe it would inspire them to find out more about her, find out more about Colombia. The next step is for the audience. It's not up to us to say, "You must believe this, you must believe that." You need to think about it and make your own decisions. We're telling one story.

VICTORIA: If you are an activist, as many documentary filmmakers are, a way to really touch people is by finding a human story. Rather than an issue piece. I watched *China Blue* [produced and directed by Micha X. Peled], which is about the Chinese garment industry. And they actually got inside one of the sweatshops and lived with a 13-year-old girl who works there, followed her from her hometown. It was extraordinary.

You're onto a third film collaboration. What's the secret to a successful partnership?

KARIN: I think we both bring different things to the table, which is a good thing. Someone was asking me once, how do we figure things out, like if we both disagree on how something should go. And I would say that if either one of us has a stronger argument for why it should be this way, then the other one says okay, fine—

VICTORIA: Or is more passionate about it—

KARIN: —More passionate about it, we'll say fine, we'll try it that way—

VICTORIA: We always tried it the other person's way.

CHAPTER 17

Ric Burns

Over the past two decades, Ric Burns and his company, Steeplechase Films, have produced numerous award-winning films and series, many for the PBS series *American Experience*. His credits include the six-part series *The Way West*; films on *Coney Island*, *The Donner Party*, *Ansel Adams*, *Eugene O'Neill*, and *Andy Warhol*; and *Tecumseh's Vision*, directed with Chris Eyre for the 2009 PBS series *We Shall Remain*. Most recently, he completed *Into the Deep: America, Whaling & the World*, which is described as "the extraordinary story of the American whaling industry from its 17th century origins through the golden age of deep ocean whaling in the late 18th and early 19th centuries, and on to the industry's decline in the decades following the American Civil War." The film premiered on *American Experience* in May 2010. Before founding Steeplechase, Ric and his brother Ken produced the nine-part PBS series *The Civil War*, which premiered in 1990.

Ric and I talked in 2003 as he was completing *The Center of the World*, an eighth and final episode of his acclaimed series *New York: A Documentary Film*. The first seven episodes were completed shortly before the attacks of September 11, 2001. The eighth explored the history of the World Trade Center, and premiered on PBS in September 2003.

Of the ideas that cross your desk, how do you decide which to make into films?

For me, in the bundle of words "historical documentary filmmaker," there's no question that the word "film" is the most important. And that's because of how powerful and dreamlike film can be. Certainly the experience of film that I value most is an experience of being taken to some very deep place by the flow of light and shadow and sound and words and music, which are the elements of film. It's always about contrasts. Visually, thematically, emotionally. Think about the Donner Party. Read a one-paragraph account of the Donner Party, and if it's accurate, you'll feel that interplay of brightness and darkness. In one of the biggest years of the American dream, 87 people go west thinking they're going to find paradise and end up in a terrible nightmare. Say the words "New York" and try not to have in your mind, very swiftly,

DOI: 10.1016/B978-0-240-81241-0.00017-4

the New York skyline. Its most powerful moment is at twilight, where it's both tremendously, luminously shiny and also powerfully black and dark.

In choosing a story, the pilot light goes on when you sense that this is material that will allow you to exploit that dream power of film. Use that basic feeling to ask yourself, well, what's the story here? What's the structure of a film that will penetrate and elaborate the story? And in the case of New York, I think the most gratifying thing about working on that project—which sprawled to 14.5 hours, and now we're working on another two-hour film about the World Trade Center—is that, at the very center of it, a very simple, provisional explanation revealed itself as to, why did New York become such a shining and dark place? And that was that at the very beginning it was founded as a relentlessly commercial colony, unlike the religious colonies that were its rivals at the time.

From there, how do you focus a historical topic that's broad and complex?

Every step along the way you ask, "What's absolutely crucial to telling the story? What advances the story?" You've got to start with the Dutch [settlers]; you understand that. Then there are the English; you don't spend that much time with the English—they did some things that were different, but many things that were the same. So you apply the basic narrative yardstick, which is: try not to tell any story more than once. So there's only one riot. There's only one fire. There's only one burst of skyscrapers. There's only one war. In other words, always find that moment where the nature of the particular story you're telling is caught at its highest arc. Tell the story of the draft riots of 1863, the most catalytic and, to this day, the worst instance of civil unrest in American history.

You try to be as severe as possible as you go through the chronology of your subject matter. Ask, "What are the central themes that structure the material? Which are the moments that elaborate those themes most powerfully?" And you use those central themes as a kind of divining rod to show you—amongst the literally infinite amount of material, in the case of something like New York—where the gold lies. Where's the stuff that's most powerful? Where is the stuff that most embodies the themes, elaborates them, and drives them forward?

How do you define theme, and how do you handle themes in your work?

Theme is the most basic lifeblood of a film: This is what this thing is about. The story is the vehicle and the theme is the tone and emotion; theme tells you the tenor of your story.

Theme makes you see and feel the correspondences between different elements of your story. How do Harlem in the 1920s, the explosion of mass media, Al Smith, the stock market rise, and the skyscraper wars all correspond with each other? Theme is, in a sense, vibrating through all of them. At its worst, the theme becomes a kind of cookie cutter which causes everything to look the same. At its best, it makes you understand the metaphoric relationships between things which are, on the surface, more or less dissimilar, more or less alike. Al Smith's pursuit of the presidency, F. Scott Fitzgerald's pursuit of Zelda and the great American novel, a modest investor's pursuit of wealth, and somebody else's pursuit of the highest building in the world all stand in a corresponding metaphoric relationship to each other, which doesn't mean that they all mean the same thing. You understand them as resonating within the same ambiance, and that can't help but make each of them more powerful.

Not all historical documentaries explore themes; some present a story or situation without that added complexity.

What I know from my own work is that if you do it quickly, you can't possibly get the themes. It's one thing to understand the theme and write it out on the back of a matchbook. But then to actually cause the theme to flow through the film, that's really difficult. First, you find the right theme. That can take a while. You articulate it correctly, in relationship to the actual material, the research, the stories, which can take another while. Then you have to stitch it together in such a fashion that the theme actually stands up and walks like some Frankenstein monster. That's where so much of the work of filmmaking, in the writing and editing, takes place. And you keep comparing what you've done to what you intuitively know it could be and should be.

When and how does the storytelling take shape?

You create your first description of what the film is. Sometimes it's in the form of a letter to a colleague, sometimes it's in the form of a two-page proposal to get seed money. But every iteration in some sense is a version of the film, and you try to give that iteration as powerful and intense an articulation as you can. And then, when you move to the next articulation—longer, more detailed, more structured, more intense, hopefully more involving—you don't abandon the previous iteration. You use it as the point of departure. And as you do that, it begins to vary. Not four episodes, but five; not one hour each, but two. In my case, it's never shifted in a way that has retroactively obliterated the original intuition; it elaborates it. It's very much like rolling a snowball down a variegated hill. The snow is sort of wet here and dry there and dirty here and pristine there, and as you move, the snowball acquires its own eccentric shape and velocity. But it's always growing organically in relationship to the material and the hillside that it's moving down.

When there's a potential to research indefinitely, how do you know when to stop?

I think any successful creative project exists within an oscillation between obsessiveness and decisiveness, and you can't abandon either. The obsessiveness that makes you keep on looking for more material, another photograph, shoot another interview, delve deeper, is in a sense always there. A metaphor might be Odysseus strapped to the mast, listening to the sirens singing, and what they're singing is, "There's more stuff here. There could be more material. There must be more." But you create a structure in which you're not only Odysseus strapped to the mast with his ears unwaxed, you're also a disciplined crew moving forward, making decisions. "We're going to use this and go with it." Anytime anything works, you never let go of it. And that's the decisiveness. You say, "Right. It really works." Always rare. That's not to say that at some point you don't discover in the process that the things you like best are no longer going to fit. But you hold on to them, and by holding on to them, they take up space and begin to delimit what you can do.

Do you write a draft of the script before you shoot?

It's really happening in tandem. For example, right now we're working on a biography of the World Trade Center, an eighth episode to *New York*. We have a very clear outline of what the film is, and a kind of a treatment that's about 50 pages long, a corralling of the material likely to be in the story. But it's not a script. It's a chronologically arranged treatment of what feels like the principal historical materials, an iteration that has enough structure in it to tell you where the themes of the film are going to emerge, where they develop to their highest point, and where they transform.

Armed with that, you can do interviews; you know how to craft questions. And you can always go out and shoot live cinematography, whether it's cinéma vérité shooting or live shooting of landscapes. The ideal thing is to do at least some of the production, in addition to interviews, while you're doing the script, because you're going to find that there's material you didn't expect.

For example, everyone knows of Philippe Petit, the man who walked on the tightrope between the Twin Towers. What I didn't know until doing an interview with him was that he's going to be a huge part of the film, not just a little five-minute moment halfway through. Here was a man who in 1968 conceived, sitting in a dentist's office in Paris when he was 18, the fantastic ambition that he wanted to be a high-wire artist and walk between the two towers of the World Trade Center, which had not even been started. When he did it, in August of 1974, the buildings were reviled for their brutality and their kind of inhuman scale in lower Manhattan. And suddenly here was this slender, unlikely Frenchman, dancing on the edge of nothing, as crowds of New Yorkers looked up in astonishment. That juxtaposition of fragility and power—and sort of vertiginous aerial theatricality—is the essence of a crucial aspect of the World Trade Center. So you discover that this person you thought was a little footnote expands to become part of the psychological center of the film.

Six months ago, if someone had said, "Will you interview Philippe Petit?" I would have said, "Probably." But luck is a residue of design. The design comes from that intuitive conviction that the story is powerful, and from the themes that you articulate on the basis of that conviction. That design then allows you to go out in the world and chance, so to speak, upon all sorts of elements: interviewees, places that you might shoot, quotes from a book, episodes of the history that you knew nothing about. And that's why that interplay between obsessiveness and decisiveness is so crucial.

Tell me about your process of editing.

The analogy, I think, is writing, by which I don't mean to say that it's verbal. You're trying to create a sequence that is as powerful and intense and engaging a sequence as you can. And in a way, that's what writing is. You start out with a sentence, and then you elaborate it into a paragraph, a few pages, a treatment, a script. And all the while you're collecting material for the film. When you sit down to edit, in a sense, you're writing—not with words and ideas alone, but with words and ideas, images, interview moments, spoken material, archival newsreel footage, sound, music. You're still trying to sequence them, still trying to elaborate that sequence, which, like a five-word summary of your film on paper, sings a little bit and has some shape to it and engages somehow.

Do you use a dramatic act structure?

I think that that's a very sophisticated way of thinking about it, which probably one does whether one knows one is doing it or not. If you get to the point where you're actually driving forward the process of creating a story—and it's getting better—that's what you do. We have a very simple, very homely formula, which came up in the editing room of *The Civil War* 15 years ago, which is, just give and take away. It moves by the old structure of contrast. Now, if those contrasts were simply alternating back and forth, the film would be completely repetitive, like a red light going on and off and on and off. So that dynamic of giving and taking away has to itself have an arc of change in it. A value is posited, you care about something, some problem is put in its path, and it develops and transforms over time.

And your protagonists aren't necessarily human. In the series New York, *the city itself is the protagonist.*

Right. You have to be true to your subject. A mistake that's often made is to confuse the component parts of a subject for the subject itself. Say, for instance, you were doing a film about the West, the conquering of the American West in the second half of the 19th century. Immediately, the building of the transcontinental railway, the Battle of Little Bighorn, George Armstrong Custer, Sitting Bull, or the events leading up to Wounded Knee—all those stories, events, people, moments, clearly compete to be part of your story. But what can happen is you can be seduced into thinking that your film is really about that person or that moment or that thing. It may very well be fine to spend all your time talking about George Armstrong Custer. But if you've determined that you're doing a film about The Way West between 1845 and 1893, you can't take the cheap and easy solution of just being beguiled and distracted by the most dynamic, dramatic, component part. And I think that what happens in historical documentary films very frequently, to their detriment, is that the people who make them get diverted and don't stick to their guns, which is "I started with this subject. There's only one hero to this story."

That's the most challenging thing, I find, in doing these films: The part is always seductive and the whole is very elusive. Yet it's the whole which is your subject. It's the thing that creates coherence and narrative trajectory, relates incidental components to deeper themes. It's the whole that gives you dramatic movement. Not a kind of dramatic movement that keeps you penned within the circumstances of a local story, but dramatic movement that sends you arcing out across a vast amount of space and time. And if you discover that there's even as many as two heroes, you've got two stories. You've got two films.

How do you ensure that a film is balanced in its storytelling?

One big difference between a certain kind of written history and historical documentary films is that the former can afford to be discursive and self-qualifying and nuanced, without jeopardizing, necessarily, their power. The latter, films, cannot afford to do that. In my view, the way complexity gets into film is not by trying, at the same time, to say something is five different things, but by over time showing the many different facets of something.

I gnash my teeth at academic historians who seem to have dipped into 10 minutes of a film and say, "You claim that New York is all about commerce and greed. Doesn't that seem a powerfully capitalistic position to be taking?" Well, right, there are those moments where that was the facet of New York that we were holding up. Because film is, in certain ways, a reductively simple medium. It wants you to be transfixed at every moment by one simple thing. So how do you get complexity? Not simultaneously, but consecutively. You get the banker now, and then later you get the labor leader. You get the poet here, and later you get the master builder. When you're with the poet, don't say, "And at the same time, there was a master builder and there was a politician." To try to do more than one thing at once compromises the intensity, which is the promise of film's engagement with the audience.

I think viewers, filmgoers, and TV watchers understand that film works best by engaging you very powerfully in a sequence of "nows." Now we're here, and now we're here, and now we're here. New York turns out to have the logic of capitalism, but also the logic of alternatives to capitalism. It's a place about building fantastic public works, but it's also a place about stopping the building of fantastic public works. It's about powerful men who rule for 50 years, and about 144 disenfranchised women who in their fiery deaths catalyzed tremendous social change. It's all those things. And I think that what filmmakers are always vulnerable to is that any moment extracted from the flow of a film seems to be reductive. If it weren't reductive, it wouldn't work as film.

Do you think about what you want the audience to take away from a film?

The illusion that film performs, when it's powerful, is it gets people to confuse the experience of the film with the experience of the past—to get audiences to almost unconsciously confuse the aesthetic experience they're having as the film unfolds with their imagination of what it must have been like to be there in the past. In a way, I think that for historical documentary filmmakers, that's the way you animate the past. By creating, paradoxically, a present, which is the film that you're watching now, which is so aesthetically and psychologically and emotionally and intellectually engaging, ideally, that people say, "Right, that's the past. How amazing Coney Island was at the turn of the 20th century." But, of course, it's not the past. And that's the great poignancy of historical films. You're using the elements which history has handed down to us, or which we have created in the present, to stand in for those things.

The thing I've always found most difficult to describe about filmmaking, which I think is the most important thing, is that you must get people to believe in the existence of something other than what they're seeing on the screen. They have to believe that beyond that frame they're looking at—up above it, off to the left where they can't see, before the moment they're looking at, after the moment they're experiencing—there's something more. If you do that, which is, I find, very difficult to do, then what you see is that people are transfixed. They're not just looking at a shining screen. They believe that these are real people, real events, real moments, caught in a whole dynamic which is infinitely mysterious and dense, and they're not sure where it's going, but they sure as hell care about the outcome.

Which means you've engaged the viewers; they're active, not passive.

Right. It's easy to tell people what a story is; it's very difficult to tell a story. When films simply tell you what the story is, they're basically two-dimensional maps rather than four-dimensional universes. Storytelling is "once upon a time." It's a ship that comes around a corner, and you can see it and you're somehow thrilled by it, caught in the "now" and a whole bunch of potential futures which haven't yet occurred. You're saying, "What's going to happen here?" When films tell stories, when they engage you in the process of a story, then they work.

In terms of the ethics of using archival material, are there guidelines as to what you will or won't do in your work?

I think there's kind of a contract which any film or filmmaker establishes with the viewer. And that is you, the viewer, trust me. I will always use the thing that's closest to the truth that I possibly can. Now, that may turn out to be not very close at all sometimes. The purity of the intention of the filmmaker is crucial. And the intention is double—the truth, but the intensity of its presentation as well. If you're on the Donner Party trail, which took place 150, 160 years ago, there were no cameras there. Therefore, if a shot of a wagon train—which is, in fact, a still shot from a film made by the Church of the Latter Day Saints in the 1940s—works and is not a lie, it's because a moment's reflection will tell people there were no shots of the Donner Party. So why do we believe it? Because we're being taken there by an assembly of story elements: verbal elements, facts, artifacts, quotes, interviews, shots that are plausibly, clearly, demonstrably, from the route.

I think that there's a way in which you can be absolutely faithful to the archival elements and ruin a story. There are historical documentary filmmakers who apparently believe that having the original photograph is all you need to bring somebody into the truth and to make the film powerful. That's nonsense. It may well be that the shadow of a hand of a live actor, at a certain moment, will bring you closer to the truth of Abraham Lincoln than all the Brady photographs in the world. Conversely, maybe it won't. Maybe the reenactment will be terribly done. So it really has to do with the ingenuity of the filmmaker. Sometimes, you might actually choose to use an element that's less historically authentic, because it works better and is therefore a better thing to do. The essential purity of the intention of the filmmaker—to tell you the truth but to bring you intensely into the dynamic of the story—is being honored.

What about the underlying research?

Not only do you do book and archival research, but you always work closely with academic advisors. Tampering with the facts is absolutely inconceivable. It doesn't mean that you don't make a million mistakes, but you fact check and you change it. When filmmakers begin to play fast and loose with a fact, they begin to rupture the essential contract that they make with the audience. Even though the audience can't quite tell where or how or why, they may not have that knowledge, they swiftly and intuitively understand that somebody's bullshitting them. You need to feel the integrity of a film. It's solid. It's well wrought. It's made of materials that seem apt. It's well balanced. We bring an enormous amount of expertise, we viewers of films, when we sit down and let the lights go low. And in that sense, viewers are the best critics of films.

How do you begin to think about visualizing a subject for which there is no photographic record?

[Photographer] Alfred Stieglitz formulated the idea that a photograph was not an objective representation of an outer external reality but was an equivalent of an inner state, an emotional state. And I think that film, being a sequence of images, is in a sense simply a more elaborate version of that. Sometimes a plethora of available archival visual imagery can make you think that that's what the movie is, and not pay as much attention to the fact that it's always about finding an equivalent. When you're obliged to invent the imagery, it in a sense focuses you on what your job should be anyway.

The great example of this is Custer and Crazy Horse. The most photographed American of the 19th century, except for Abraham Lincoln, is George Armstrong Custer. And there's no photograph of Crazy Horse. I'm not convinced that it was easier to bring the emotional reality of George Armstrong Custer to life just because there were all those photographs. With Crazy Horse, you were obliged to go to landscape shots and modest recreations to find the psychological resonance. There was no easy way out.

Will you talk about the rhythms of editing, how you know when to fade to black for a moment, or when to let a sequence play?

The units of construction of films are scenes that have beginnings and middles and ends and their own rhythms and climaxes. In a story like *The Donner Party*, when you've had one climax, you need to fade out and have that moment of emotional pause and closure. Film is essentially musical, like any temporal art form. It's all about incremental progressive effect of all the events that make up the flow. Do you need a beat? Will the flow become too relentless if there's not that pause? Do I need to receive the information I was receiving in that last scene at a slightly statelier pace, or do I need to speed it up? What you're trying to enhance, it seems to me, is the axis of clarity and the axis of emotion. Because the two are totally related. The clearer the event, the more powerful the emotional impact of it.

What I love about the final phases of making a film is when you can just feel everything is exactly right. Not that there couldn't have been something else which was also right, but that given what you've chosen to do, it's right. The language, for example—that there's no gap between articulation and understanding. That's what makes these scripts so mind-bogglingly difficult. It's not the concepts or research that are the challenge, it's finding the articulation within the flow of this particular film. What are the words that are clear, in the simplest, best way for this moment in this film? I think of that line of Geoff's [Geoffrey C. Ward] from *The Civil War*: "The spring rains had washed open the fresh graves from the year before." You're done. You could come across the same historical fact or moment and articulate it differently, and maybe that different way would be just as good in its own context. But you're done.

CHAPTER 18

Brett Culp

Brett Culp is not, strictly speaking, a documentary filmmaker. Known as a celebrity videographer/digital storyteller, he is an event filmmaker, someone who specializes in crafting stories from key moments in the lives of individuals, families, communities, and even corporations. Based in Tampa, Florida, Brett's client list includes best-selling novelists, professional athletes, rock stars, actors, and ambassadors. His work has been featured on radio and television networks and programs including *Entertainment Tonight*, Martha Stewart Radio, ABC News Denver, and Lifetime; and in print publications including *Modern Bride* and *US Weekly*. His company has won two dozen awards from WEVA International, the world's largest organization of wedding and event videographers.

It was through WEVA that Brett and I met in 2008, when he arranged for me to talk about documentary storytelling at the group's annual expo. In planning for this third edition, I thought it would be interesting to turn the tables and ask him to explain how he brings storytelling strategies to the range of nonfiction projects he creates.

You launched your business in 1998, shortly after you graduated from college. Can you tell me how you got started?

I have a journalism degree with an emphasis in public relations. In my college years, people started to find out that I knew how to do video, and started asking me to film weddings, and do photo montages, and make a video that told the story of their parents for their 25th wedding anniversary, and things like that. And I realized, "Hey, I can make a living doing this, working for people almost as a commissioned artist"—which is really, at the end of the day, what I am. I'm not a guy selling entertainment to the masses; I'm a person that someone commissions to come in and create something special just for them.

Most of my projects have an audience of a couple hundred people. And then once that production has been shown to those people, frankly, in the years to come it has an audience probably of about 10 people that will actually watch it again and again. But every year that goes by, they cherish it more.

DOI: 10.1016/B978-0-240-81241-0.00018-6

It's interesting that your clients call your work "wedding movies" rather than simply wedding videos, because they're more than just documentation. You're not the A/V guy.

That's correct. In fact, that's one of the things I have to specify from the very beginning. I don't show up with projectors and mixers and all that stuff. I'm trying to walk into any environment and find out what it is about the environment that stimulates me as a storyteller. It's not like I don't have a plan; I do have somewhat of a plan. But I'm walking in with my eyes and mind wide open.

First dance, from a private wedding movie by Brett Culp. Photo courtesy of the filmmaker.

I kind of feel like videography is the jazz of the digital filmmaking world; every time it's a little different. To say that every wedding video is the same is like saying every person is the same. Every person is unique. Weddings are the same if you only look at them on a surface level, like an A/V person would. But if you start to look at them as family stories, you've got a bride on a path and a groom on a path, and a wedding is a celebration of a collision, a merging, a joining of two stories—two cultures, in many cases—together. It makes it almost even more interesting when a wedding is multicultural, and [you're] trying to figure out all those traditions, all of those family values, and then seeing—almost uniformly, at the end of the day—that when you get down to it, all those families value the same thing: the happiness of their children and their story being fully realized in their lives. I get to see it even more than the guests do, because I'm really thinking about: "Who are these people, and where did they come from, and how are they coming together?" And so it's fun. It's really fun.

But again, I never know what I'm going to get till I get in there. I can do months of preplanning work, but every time I try to do that, it's like I put blinders on myself. The more preplanning I do, the more I find that I've lost sight of the improvisational nature that makes my work most powerful.

What size crew do you tend to have covering an event, to ensure that you don't miss those moments that are so crucial?

The vast majority of our work is filmed with two cameras. I have one camera that's run by my assistants: They're locked down on a tripod, in a position where they can see most of what's going on.

So, a master shot.

It's a master shot, that's exactly right. And then I roam around almost like a photographer would. I used to shoot the traditional way you're supposed to shoot, which is to lock two cameras down on tripods and A/B roll it in the editing room. And then I started watching these photographers that were roaming around, not having to create four seconds, five seconds, 10 seconds of continuous clear movement. And I said, "I want to be like [them]. I've got this master shot that I can always cut back to if I miss something. I'm just going to move from place to place." You've got a ceremony [that's] going to last 25 minutes. Except for things like the vows and the rings, I've got 25 minutes to roam all around and get shots of parents and kids, and wide shots and close-up shots, and shots from this angle and with this depth of field. That's where the plan comes in. In my mind, I always have 30 options of anything I could do at any given time. And I think the skill that I've developed over the past decade, at least to some extent, is to be able to choose the best option at any given moment. What's the right thing to do right now? And then I do it.

As you consider events, you break them into three elements: client, plot, and mood. Can you talk about that?

Yes. We start with understanding the client. When I'm in a prewedding meeting—I even do this during the sales process when I'm trying to understand a client—I will say to them, "What's important to you about this? What does this wedding mean to you?" Sometimes a dad of the bride will say something like, "I want her to see on the outside what we feel on the inside." Or, "I want her to have an experience, in this eight hours of her wedding, that's like the way we feel about her."

That gives me a touchstone that I can use to then move to the plot section. I remember [director] Peter Jackson, in the commentary for *Lord of the Rings*. They had to cut all this stuff out, and he was saying he couldn't figure out what to cut and what to keep in. And he said, "At the end of the day, I just decided, if it doesn't affect Frodo, it doesn't stay in." And that's kind of the way we work, too. I walk away from a wedding with 10 hours of footage, and I'm going to be distilling it into a 20-minute movie. What stays in and what doesn't stay in? When I get into the plotting stage, if I know my client and I really understand what this wedding means to them and to the really important people [there], then that becomes my touchstone. I can look at each piece of the wedding and even—I look at a best man's toast, and maybe he gives a 10-minute toast. I'm only going to keep 45 seconds of it. What 45 seconds do I choose? Well, the 45 seconds comes back to the touchstone. Where is the moment where he says, in his toast, something that connects with the story of what this wedding means to the bride and the groom, and what their story is?

So in your analogy, Frodo is the theme; it's the film's theme that you've pulled from the family, basically?

That's correct.

And you're discovering it organically, through listening. You're not coming in from the outside and saying, "We're telling this story. We're imposing a story."

That's exactly right. As a filmmaker, I'm truly going in with no agenda. I am not coming in as a storyteller with my own voice. I am coming in to try to hear their voice, and then try to use my skill and experience and know-how to communicate *their* story in whatever way is most effective for them. Someone that really knows me and my work can probably identify a piece that I did versus a piece that some other event video producer did. However, what I want more than anything else is for the audience to hear the voice of the people. I want to be invisible.

Is there a chance that your take on a family or the underlying theme of a wedding is wrong? Have you ever had to adjust your initial concept as you spent more time with people over the course of an event?

I've never had an experience where I have mis-seen the core story. I have at times adjusted things. There have been times when a client has seen a finished product and said to me, "Oh, there was this element that was really important to us. Could you include it in the video?" And then it's clear that I didn't understand how this connected [to the] core story. So that does happen. But I can't remember a time, after [witnessing] a person's entire wedding, that the core story wasn't clear. Most people have events that are thoughtful; they have frankly done a lot of the research for you. They have spent time thinking about: "How can we make this special? How can we make for our guests a unique story of our event?" So they've done a lot of research, and sometimes you just end up asking questions. For instance, we did a wedding where the first thing that happened was, 10 different people walked down the aisle, each with a candle in their hand, and placed it in an empty part of a candelabra. There was no explanation of what that meant; I had to find out later that it represented, to them, someone who had passed away. It represented that person being there. Once I understood that, I could weave that element into the story.

How much in advance of an event do you get involved?

It totally depends. Some of our clients, we get very involved. The vast majority of the time, I am walking in with very little information, seeing faces for the first time. They're jet setters, they're in Switzerland, they're here and there. And they hire a planner, and the planner is meant to take care of all this. That happens a lot, with the affluent clients, where I don't even meet the bride and the groom until the day of the wedding.

When I can, I like to go to their party the night before [the wedding]; sometimes I'll even just go like I'm a guest. Just to watch people, how they interact, what they do, overhear what they say. Walk up to a guy—he doesn't know if you're from the other family or you're a friend of whomever—and just kind of ask questions. "You know them, what do you think about them?" I start to learn things, totally off the record, that help me.

It sounds as though as you're shooting, you're also listening for story—but the event is under way, so you also have to be sure you're getting the material you need to tell that story. How do you do that?

I take what I know about the people... I'm trying to think if I can give a specific example that would make it clear—

There's Andrew's Bar Mitzvah, for example, a 10-minute film posted on your website. I had a sense that your theme was family and tradition, which is expressed very early on, when Andrew's father talks about his own bar mitzvah, and that of Andrew's grandfather.

That's a good illustration. That was in Dallas, and I had very little information about that event until I came into it. I am listening all day. And so when I heard Dad say that from the bima, when he came up to congratulate and bless his son, my mind immediately went to: "Okay, he is right here on the stage, in front of all these people. He is revealing an element of *his* story to the audience. Now, how does that connect to Andrew's story?" Because this video isn't about Dad's story; it's about Andrew's. But I can't tell Andrew's story without partially telling Dad's story, and Dad's given me a thread. It's almost like you're looking at a sweater and you're thinking: "How can I take this sweater apart?" And then you see a loose thread and you say, "Aha! You've handed me something." And I'm looking for that all day, for somebody to say something, do something that will be that loose thread. And before we started editing, I remembered what Dad had said, and e-mailed him: "You said this in your speech. Can you get me photos for that? Because I would really like to incorporate that into the video." And of course he did, because it was important to him.

One of the things I'm also looking for is anomalies, anything that's out of the ordinary. And I know immediately, because I've done hundreds of weddings and I know all the traditional stuff. So, I see a bride trying to insert this strange-looking pin, like a pin a man would wear on his suit lapel, into her bouquet. Okay, that's weird; there's something there. That's a loose thread. And so I walk over to her—and I've got the camera rolling. I've developed a way that I can work with my viewfinder out, and she's making eye contact with me and doesn't even know if I'm filming. And I say to her, "What is that you're putting in there?" And she says, "Well, you know, my father was a policeman for 30 years in Boston, and he passed away. I'm putting this pin in here to honor him." Well, that gave me an element of that story that's got to get in.

I see 10 people walk down the aisle with 10 candles, and I say, "Okay, that's unique. What does it mean?" And I think that's where, long term, having a clear sense of wedding stories helps me significantly. When I did my first Indian wedding, I couldn't tell where the loose threads were. It all looked unique.

To what extent do you engage with the people you're filming? I'm thinking, for example, about another moment at Andrew's bar mitzvah. Two men, one balding, joke about who can keep a yarmulke on his head. And then Andrew's teenaged sister jokes that she has "yarmulke envy." Was that something you happened to capture, or having filmed the two men, did you ask her about it?

That's exactly what I did. Because I'm also kind of a personable guy, I can walk up to people with the camera rolling, *à la* Stephen Colbert, and just say some little snippy little thing about the yarmulke. And I cut myself out. But then they just start talking, and they're comfortable. Those little interview things, particularly when we're trying to be funny or silly, I'm definitely directing it. I'm keeping it open enough that they can be themselves, but I'm directing it in certain ways.

Take another example. When I'm filming a wedding, the bride will put on the wedding dress, and if her mom is in the room, I'll say, "Mom, how does she look?" I know what she's going to say. But I want to capture it. And then she'll kind of look over at me and say, "Did you just record that?" Or she won't even know I recorded that, and I'll just slide away, because I'm working with this tiny little camera with a little shotgun mic on it.

In thanking his mother, Andrew says, "I know these past couple of years have been hard for both of us." I had a sense that it's included for those who know what he's referring to, but it's also general enough that it's not airing family issues.

Exactly. It's walking that line between—Because I'm commissioned by the client, I'm not there to do an exposé on his family. I'm coming in with the mentality that no matter what goes on behind the scenes, life truly is beautiful, the world is beautiful, you are beautiful, and you are a beautiful story. I'm going to uncover that.

Now, in that, I'm not going to so candy-coat it that the reality doesn't come through. So like you said, we're going to address the reality that there's been some hard stuff going on, but we've all stuck together and we're all okay, and life is okay. Part of the way to do it, in that story, was to bring out the humor, was to bring out these people's levity, lightness, happiness—at a level that I don't often do. But it was appropriate for them.

Another thing that seems unusual about your work is that the structure is often quite fluid. You might start a wedding story at the reception, for example, which takes place after the ceremony. With Andrew's bar mitzvah, you begin and end with the ceremony and keep returning to it, but you're folding in the events of the day leading up to the ceremony and the party that followed it.

Yes, definitely. My goal when I'm filming is to capture as many things that point to the core story as I can, and then my goal in the editing room is to try to find an emotional flow.

When I first got into the wedding business in particular, what I loved about weddings was that there was this up-and-down flow of emotion throughout the day. There was drama and tension before the ceremony started; and then the ceremony would start and it was kind of formal and holy; and then after the ceremony there was this great relief and joy and happiness; and then you moved into the first dance, and it went into romance; and then the best man gave his toast, and it got light and humorous again; and then you did the father-daughter dance, and everybody got all somber and emotional again; and then they'd open the dance floor and do the hora, and everybody was like "Oh! Oh, this is amazing!" And then you send the bride and groom off at the end of the night, and there's this sense of relief and joy. This is what every great story does: it has texture, and the moods go up and down in terms of their tone. I started to plot that as a storyteller.

And mood is the third element, after client and plot.

My goal is to pick those moods and to say, "Okay, I want to start this video like this, and then I want to move to this mood, and then to this element of the story, and then to this element." I gather the sections that will allow me to do that. So with Andrew's story, I said, "I want to start it out dramatic, family-oriented, emotional, and then let's make it light. So how can I best do that?" Well, let's start with Dad. Let's let him set the tone of the family, and then we'll go to something light, and we can just go right into that preceremony time where they're all just kind of laughing. And then we'll do the ceremony, and then there'll be the release from the ceremony, and everybody having fun. Then in the end, let's come back and bring it full circle to the idea of the family and the tightness of the family. And I said: "What element do I have that can be my storytelling thread, my train through that?" And I realized, that's Andrew's speech in the ceremony.

So that's where it comes from. It's never random. It's always: "How can we take those moods up and down to keep it interesting, entertaining, but also tell the story in a beginning-middle-end kind of environment?" It's like documentary in those terms of hunting for the story, trying to find it, using more than one approach, using frankly any approach that I think will be effective as a storytelling tool.

How long does a project like that take to edit?

Postproduction time varies from project to project. Andrew's finished video took about two days to edit, but most projects are more complex, and some have required several weeks of work by multiple editors. Many of the events we cover span multiple days, and often we create custom animated closings, openings, and transitions.

I've noticed that sometimes you do "morning after" edits, short films that people can watch when they gather for brunch the next day, for example. But you must approach the editing of those quite differently.

Absolutely, yes. There are many, many things that we cannot do with a turnaround edit, in terms of deep storytelling. What we do for a quick turnaround or a same-day edit (or an instant edit, whatever you want to call them), is that as I'm shooting through the day, I'm giving tapes—because I'm still using tape—to my assistant, and he captures them. And the other thing about weddings is that there are down times. When they're eating dinner, I can have my assistant watching to make sure somebody doesn't get up and give an impromptu toast. But I can leave the room for 30 to 45 minutes, and go downstairs and start identifying clips. And then we'll start to clean those clips up, color correct them, put some effects on them, put them in slow motion, and rearrange the order to match what we want. Doesn't take that long.

Let's move on to your corporate work. There's an example on your website for a company, and you unexpectedly begin by interviewing a lot of children, asking what they think makes for a good party.

One of the best ways to get people to really look at their [own] story with fresh eyes is to surprise them. That video was for a conference of event professionals. My goal in that was twofold: The kids would obviously have fresh eyes to see things that the professionals wouldn't see, and it's just fun. Every time I do a corporate project, my goal is for it to be infotainment, where you're being entertained while you learn.

Classic corporate videos are not very exciting because they're too stiff. We're doing more corporate work right now than we've ever done before, I think because people are starting to see that the story-telling process—identifying a corporate story and then helping people feel part of it—is an essential part of a corporate event. Our corporate work is connected with videos that are shown at events. [Clients] want the attendees to walk away feeling connected on an emotional level, not just a mental level. If I can do unexpected things to bring that through, then I will.

You've said that companies often think that a mission statement is the same as a company story, but that it's not. Part of your task with corporate clients is the same as with wedding clients: to listen for the story.

That's exactly right. I go into a corporate event with the same approach as I do for a social event: The real story that's in there is powerful enough. You don't have to make up one. And in fact, if you make up one, people ain't going to buy it. These Toyota commercials that they're playing right now? It doesn't feel authentic. I don't know what they could do instead, frankly, but I don't think anybody's buying this.

People today are so savvy. I watch *Abbott and Costello* with my kids, these old TV shows. And they keep the old commercials in there. We look at them today, and not only are they silly from a production perspective, but you listen to the message, and you're thinking to yourself: Did this actually convince anybody? There's a clip that says, nine out of 10 doctors say this cigarette is healthier than another. Who's really buying any of that? But they were, at some level. I think today people are far more savvy about being manipulated by video and film storytelling. They can see your message; they can see if you're being preachy from a mile away. And sometimes they're willing to swallow it, and sometimes they're not.

We just finished a corporate project for a big medical company. Essentially, one smaller company had just been bought by [this bigger company], and this was the first national meeting where this company was going to be there. We were talking about the video and about: "How can we make these two groups cohesive? How can we make them feel like the other's not the bad guy?" Because there had been layoffs, there had been some redistribution of territories for the sales reps, so even the guys that were the old guard, some of their stuff was getting messed up. It was getting messed up for everybody. So, how can we convince them that this was a good thing that this happened, when there are so many reasons to feel that it wasn't?

Their first approach was, "Why don't we write a script and have people talk about, 'This is good because of this and this, and look at how it will affect the bottom line....'" And I said, "No. No, no, no. They won't buy it. That's a brochure. Let's bring these people in, and the first day of the convention, let's get a cross-section of people from the new company and the old company, and let's interview them. And let's just let them be real. We'll set it up like a Mac commercial, with the clean white background. Let them dress in casual clothes and talk about what they love about their job, what they love about the company they've been part of, their good experiences. Not contrived, just real stuff. And then let's also let them talk about their lives and who they are, what they value, and why they do what they do every day. Why they get up in the morning, and what their family means to them."

And so we created these four segments that played during the general sessions each morning. That was a crazy instant edit too, because I filmed these people Sunday morning and we had to play the first clip Monday morning, and then Tuesday morning, Wednesday morning, and Wednesday afternoon. But the vision of it was, you were hearing from real, authentic people talking about what it really meant to them. And you say, that's like a wedding—that's exactly right. "What does this wedding mean to you?" "What does this company mean to you?" "What does this organization mean to you?" Because I really believe that if you can get to the heart of meaning—what does it mean to people—then you can find the story.

You describe your work as "stylish storytelling with a documentary edge." For clients who might not otherwise know, how do you explain what that means?

I use the word "documentary" because in the world of events, particularly the wedding world, there are kind of two styles. There's the "cinematic" style and the "documentary" style. The cinematic style makes your wedding look like it went through the Disney factory. Everything is done to make it look magical, like it was the perfect fairytale event. And then the documentary style is much more just real: exactly what happened, kind of like a reality show—you and I both know how close reality shows are to documentary, but it has that flavor to it. And so when I say that it has a documentary edge, it would probably be closer, though not near as nice, to say that it has a reality show edge, where things don't always go perfectly. This glamorous necklace that the mom put on, she reveals to me that she broke it three times, trying to get it on right, in the week before the wedding, and kept having to take it back to the jeweler. Well, that adds an element to it. Instead of just seeing Mom as this glamorous lady, every time you look at that necklace, you think, "Oh, that's the necklace that broke three times. She was such a klutz."

I think that's what most modern people want. They want their life to be beautiful, they want their wedding to be beautiful, but there's that element of reality involved that they want. I'm still doctoring it, to where the people come across at their best and most beautiful; they're going to look like great people. And that skews me away from true documentary.

Where your work is more like documentary as opposed to reality television is that it's structured more creatively. Reality shows tend to be chronologically driven: it starts and goes.

That's true. It is chronological, and they do pump up the reality volume in the editing room, the dramatic volume, as much as they can, even to the point of lies. And I don't do that.

How do you think about ethics, about truthfulness, in your work?

For me—because so much of my work, rather than being script-driven, is interview-driven, sound bite–driven, it's listening to what people are saying and letting them speak—the challenge is that I can choose to leave somebody in or out. Take Andrew's bar mitzvah. If Grandpa had said to me in an interview, "We have the perfect, close-knit family," and that's a nice sound bite, I probably would have used it. Now, [that may not] be true. But it's true to him, or he's just willing to lie in the video. One or the other.

There were a couple of things that got said in those corporate videos that I was describing, where there were snickers from the audience. Not big ones but small ones, where somebody said, "I think this company's just a wonderful dadadadada," and some disenfranchised, disgruntled person went, "Yeah, right. That ain't true." Now, was it untrue? Was it a matter of perspective? Was it a lie? That is a difficult line for me.

However, going in and deciding on an agenda and promoting that agenda in the face of overwhelmingly different facts and perspectives is dishonest, disingenuous, and a disservice to your audience. I would never walk into a story and try to make something that wasn't there true, just because the family wanted me to. I have had people walk into my office and say, "What's important to me about this wedding is this and this and this," and then I show up at the wedding, and that's not real at all. I would have to be a total liar. And so I find a different angle than the angle they wanted.

What's your advice for people who seem to think that the possibilities for storytelling are more limited for shorter projects, whether for use by a school or a family or a local historical society?

So many videos that are boring—and you talk about that local historical society video; I've been in the midst of those kinds of proposals and discussions as well. A collection of facts in chronological order does not make a story. What makes a story is when you are able to take those facts and figure out how they connect with the universal human condition, what it is to be a human being. And when you can do that—when you can find a way to take whatever story that you're telling and connect it back so that a person who's seven years old or 80 years old, a person that lives in rural Kansas or New York City, they can all look at that and see a piece of themselves in that story—then I think you tell an effective story.

You take Andrew, for example. Everybody on some level has a relationship with their father. On a scale of 1 to 10, it's either zero (they have no relationship, but that affects them) or 10 (they have a delightful, wonderful, engaging relationship for them). One way or the other, when they hear Andrew's dad tell the legacy of their family, it touches the human condition. It's a universal. And the more we can, as storytellers, really touch those universal things, the more we can take any instance, any circumstance, any collection of data, and create a story that's engaging to people.

That's what we've been trying to do with companies. We've been trying to say: Look, you can give me as many statistics as you want, and you can tell me the history of this company, but that's not a story. You've got to take what you're doing and talk about how the toothpaste you're making, medical products you're selling, whatever it is, the construction sites you're building—how does that connect with the human condition, and how is that making life better for people?

CHAPTER 19

Nick Fraser

Since 1997, Nick Fraser has been series editor of BBC Four's acclaimed international documentary strand, *Storyville*, which each year presents up to 50 outstanding films from all over the world. Roughly a third of the films are bought as completed films, while the rest are "prebought" or commissioned jointly with other broadcasters. (For example, *Storyville* co-produced *So Much So Fast*. The film's credits read: "A production of West City Films in association with WGBH, ZDF/ARTE, BBC, with support from TV2/Danmark." In the United States, the film aired on the PBS series *Frontline*; in the United Kingdom, it aired on *Storyville*.)

Prior to joining the BBC, Nick was a commissioning editor at Channel Four and operated his own production company, Panoptic Productions. A former print journalist, he continues to be a contributing editor at *Harper's* magazine and is the author of books including *Evita: The Real Life of Eva Peron* (written with Marysa Navarra), *The Voice of Modern Hatred*, and in 2006, *The Importance of Being Eton*.

The list of films presented on *Storyville* is extensive, and includes *Trembling before G-d*, *The War Room*, *Why We Fight*, *My Terrorist, Me & My 51 Brothers & Sisters*, and *Murderball*. Since this interview was conducted in 2006, the list also includes *Gonzo*, *Roman Polanski: Wanted and Desired*, and *Barbados at the Races*, among many others.

There is quite a range of film subjects and styles on Storyville. *You've said that the requirement is that films "should all be strongly narrative." Do you explain to filmmakers what you mean by that?*

I don't. There's a backlog of *Storyville* they can go to, to figure out what we've shown. But I think it's bad for me to say, "Well, this is what I want." It's rather irritating, because it means I spend a lot of time saying what I don't want. We don't want films that are flat and look like current affairs. We don't want illustrated scripts. We want films where the narrative is important, and what you discover comes from what you see.

I like the dictum of D. H. Lawrence, when he said that you should always trust the tale, not the teller. I think that when documentary

DOI: 10.1016/B978-0-240-81241-0.00019-8

films have a very strong ideological point of view, they're not very satisfactory. I have no objections, necessarily, to strong ideological points of view, but it seems to me when a film is put to the service of a point of view—and it can be ideological, or it can be a point of view that comes over the script that's prewritten—you feel pushed into conclusions, and you feel the filmmaker decided what they wanted to say before they set out to make the film. So I would say I'm interested, firstly, in people who have a desire to tell a story because they wish to find out about something themselves. That just accords with my temperament: I tend to write articles or books because I want to find out about things, because I really don't know what I think about them. I may feel ambivalent; nothing wrong with feeling ambivalent.

You've compared today's documentaries with the New Journalism of the 1960s and 1970s, the nonfiction narrative prose of writers such as Norman Mailer, Truman Capote, and Tom Wolfe.

That's right. Documentaries are probably the most interesting form of nonfiction at the moment. It seems to me that with the exception of *Vanity Fair* and *The New Yorker* in North America, there's been some sort of decline—and *Harper's*, obviously I love *Harper's*, I'm a contributing editor—there's been some decline in the value given to long pieces of reportage. About 30 years ago there were far more pieces. They've been replaced by blogs. Blogs constitute instant controversy and opinion. And although I used to be in the business of instant controversy and opinion, I now find it sort of tiresome, because there are too many opinions. I think one should try to shed opinions in life, rather than acquiring them.

What appeals to me about documentaries made at the moment is that they do, consciously or not, seem to hark back to this moment in the late 1960s when everything seemed possible in the long-form story. That you could send a good writer out, whether it was Joan Didion or Norman Mailer or whomever, you could send them out to cover a story and they would come back with something remarkable. Well, you can do the same now with digital video cameras. It's a niche market, documentaries, but probably a broader niche market than journalism was in the 1960s. More people can be lured into seeing good documentaries than could be lured into reading *Esquire* in 1967. I want to get this right: It is a sort of democratic medium, but alas, at the moment these films are not reaching wide enough audiences. They should be, but they're not. But more and more good films are being made each year. And obviously the funding of these films has changed; a lot of private money goes into them. They're made with an eye on cinemas; they're not destined solely for television.

And if they do go to television, they don't go to the usual outlets like PBS or the networks as they might have done 20 years ago. They go to cable channels, satellite channels, and they will go over the Internet on demand. That will be the way these films will be distributed in a very short time, I imagine.

*Steve Ascher and Jeannie Jordan (*So Much So Fast*) describe their films as nonfiction novels, because they're shaping a narrative that's layered and textured.*

That's exactly what they are doing, and it's exactly what Norman Mailer prescribed. *Hoop Dreams* is a good nonfiction novel; *Guerrilla: The Taking of Patty Hearst* is just excellent. Numerous films that come out each year are great nonfiction novels. And they exist, if you like, at the boundary between the long piece in a magazine that you love to read on a plane, and the nonfiction novel. And that's a very good place for documentaries to be, in my view.

How important do you think journalism training is for documentary filmmakers?

In terms of actually getting stories right and knowing whom to trust and all that, it seems to me that's largely—I hate to say instinctive, but if you're well educated and ambitious you can figure that out. You can read a book about ethics, or you can go out with an executive producer who'll tell you what you can and can't do. If you invent everything, people are going to figure it out quickly.

A film like *Hoop Dreams*, its journalistic standards are impeccable. And yet it's not just a piece of journalism, it's something bigger, it's got bigger ambitions. Journalism makes use of characters for journalistic purposes. People exist in a story because they've been shoved into the story to back up the point of the journalist, or as source material for the story. In documentaries, it seems to be the other way around. You go with the characters and then the story builds itself around them.

The other similarity between New Journalism and the kinds of documentaries seen on Storyville *seems to be one of authorship. But not all documentaries are authored to the same extent; much of the documentary programming that dominates commercial television, for example, can feel sort of mass produced.*

Right. However, I think that authorship can be defined in a lot of ways. I think Robert Greenwald's films *(Outfoxed, Wal-Mart)* are authored; they're very journalistic. It's said to be a question of recognizable voice, but whose voice, and is it in the film? You can't be dogmatic about it. Sometimes it's very explicit. Sometimes the author has to be on camera, like Michael Moore. Other times, the films are very authored, such as the Ascher/Jordan films, but you rarely see them. You have the commentary [e.g., Steve narrated *So Much So Fast*], but even if someone else read the commentary they'd still seem like very personal, authored films.

In a way, it's very confusing, this discussion about authorship. A reason for this confusion comes from film theory, which is obsessed with auteurs and fiction. That's probably a very bad mold for a documentary, which is a hybrid of film and journalism. And just as you can be an author in a number of different ways, writing a nonfiction piece, so you can in a documentary.

Hunter S. Thompson, in *Gonzo: The Life & Work of Hunter S. Thompson,* a Magnolia Pictures release. Photo courtesy of Magnolia Pictures.

Do you see differences in storytelling across nationalities?

Yes, absolutely. Documentaries are more ambitious in America at the moment, because they can't go on television always. I mean, if you're guaranteed a place on a mainstream channel in Germany or Britain or

France, and it's a place in the middle of the schedule, well, what you're going to be asked to do is something for quite a big audience. So you tend to make something that's quite explicit, quite comprehensible—a bit like what you were talking about earlier, a bit like Discovery output or PBS output—some of PBS output, not all of it. But if you're an American, you don't know where it ends up, so you tend to make a different calculation, like, "What am I saying, and will people want to watch the film?" And that brings you to start every film from scratch, in a way. To say, "What is the point of what I'm doing?"

If you look at the totality of output from the United States, it's extraordinarily rich. And—I'll probably be shot for saying this—one of the reasons it's so rich is that it's actually reasonably hard to get commissioned to make a documentary in America. So that, coupled with the fact that they can get interest and they can get private money, means that people have to struggle and they have to be very ambitious. Or they have to be very rich. And that means that you get a certain winnowing out of people who are just doing hack work. I mean, there's a huge amount of hack work on American TV; there's enough hack work to keep one going until infinity, but it's not on the whole in the field of documentaries.

I also think that the American tradition that we were talking about, of 1960s New Journalism and direct cinema, is very rich. And in addition to that, I think Americans are disposed toward empiricism. You really do have this preparedness among very intelligent American filmmakers to spend forever on a subject until it's absolutely right, and that's why their films are very good. Very enduring. And why I love them so much.

I think that there are many good documentaries made in Europe. The subsidy system works both ways. Sometimes it's very good for films to get funded easily, and you don't have to suffer to make them. And other times it means there's a certain orthodoxy, you have a machine set up for commissioning documentaries and all documentaries conform to what the machine is used to getting. So the machine tells you, we believe in innovation, but actually they're churning out the same form of innovation every year.

I think there are good French documentaries, there are good German ones—I thought *Darwin's Nightmare* was very good. There's less pressure to make documentaries in Europe, because to be absolutely blunt about it, the European media are less crass than the American ones. I discovered a website [complaining about] my complacence and elitist views when I said I thought the BBC did a good job being impartial. But the fact is that it does. There is a crisis in news and reporting in Europe, but it's not as acute as the crisis in America. I think the crisis in America is why these very talented young people are being impelled to make documentaries, as a sort of compensation for the failure of what they call mainstream media.

And at the same time, it seems, the market for documentaries crosses national borders, so filmmakers need to work to create stories that will appeal to different cultures, lifestyles, viewpoints.

But I think it isn't so much down to national cultures; it's down to the receptiveness of documentary producers in each country as to whether they want to do this, whether they get it—the notion that you're not just making these films for a group of lefties in a smoke-filled cinema at a festival. That these films have to cross frontiers, and they have to deal with what is limited, what is special, what is often minute, what is local, but at the same time they have to go around the world. They really have to do that.

What I like about documentaries is they're very pluralistic. I'm not asking for a whole lot of documentaries to be made from the neo-con political position. But it seems to me that somehow, sometimes documentaries suffer from the fact that most of the people that make documentaries agree politically with each other. And I think the strength of filmmaking, like journalism, is that people should be unpredictable in their views, or they shouldn't have perceived views. They should actually rather look at things than have views about them. I mean, do we care that Cartier-Bresson was a lefty? No, we don't at all. Or Robert Capra. Well, ultimately I know what the filmmaker's views are, but that doesn't always translate into their documentaries, and they're much more subtle and richer because they're about narrative.

Al Maysles is great on this subject; he expresses it far more beautifully than I ever can, because he has an interest in human nature that's very rich. All his films, their lasting appeal comes from the fact that he loves his characters. I think it would be fine if he hated some of them as well as loving some of them, but he only loves them. And I think that's more important than ideology. Ideology, political positions—they go out of date in a week. No one can remember, what did Michael Moore really want to say about George Bush [in *Fahrenheit 9/11*]? All people can remember is the little goat book. All they can remember about Wolfowitz is licking his comb. The rest of the ideological stuff, you probably go back to it now and say you agree with only half of it.

Among the films you've commissioned are A Cry from the Grave *(1999) and a sequel,* Srebrenica: Never Again? *(2005), both written, produced, and directed by Leslie Woodhead. The films concern the 1995 Bosnian massacre at Srebrenica. I've read that you originated the project, sending articles about the massacre to the filmmaker and helping to shape the film through the questions you asked.*

I spent a lot of time with Leslie, because I was interested in the massacre at Srebrenica, and I thought the story was going to be very difficult to do. It was very politically sensitive, a huge subject.

What sorts of questions do you ask when you're working with filmmakers?

Quite basic journalistic questions: who, why, what, when, and where, really. I think that the most useful thing I can do is to ask people simple basic questions about what they're doing. "Why would you want to make a film about this subject? What's the point of the narrative? Why did you choose this situation and the subject? How does the situation and the subject you chose translate itself into this narrative?" If you chose to examine the film from this point of view, you have to tell me why. A lot of filmmakers, including Leslie, are very savvy at figuring this out. I mean, Jehane Noujaim—both *Startup.com* and *Control Room* are very well thought out. She tells me that she has no idea what she'll end up with when she starts filming, but this is hard to believe. When you get a pitch from her, it usually lasts about five minutes, but she knows exactly what she wants to do. The characters seem created in a very solid way, very early in the process.

This might surprise many new filmmakers, who still seem to have the misconception that documentaries are spontaneous and unplanned, not "discovered" until late in the editing process.

You should know much earlier what you're doing. You should know why and how you're telling the story. I mean, there are many, many films about Chinese factories. But if you're going to a Chinese factory, why are you filming the Chinese factory? What are you trying to tell people? There was one film we showed, *Made in China* [distributed as *A Decent Factory*], which is about a Nokia supplier in China. And what they filmed was a visit to a factory by a Nokia ethical consultant and a Nokia executive.

[According to material on Storyville's *website, French filmmaker Thomas Balmes was approached by YLE in Finland to take an "anthropological" look at the Finnish corporation, Nokia. He says he spent 18 months "filming boring Nokia meetings all over the world" before he met Hanna Kaskinen, Nokia's environmental expert. "She was just starting to push the Nokia management to take a new position with ethical issues," Balmes told the BBC*

Four interviewer. "I found it very interesting because it touched on the issue—can you be a capitalist and be ethical at the same time?" He also notes that he was in the right place at the right time: "Hanna was about to do Nokia's first ever ethical assessment." And so the film took shape and gained international co-production support. The story—the film's train—is deceptively simple: Balmes follows Nokia executive Kaskinen and English consultant Louise Jamison to China, to visit the factory of Nokia's major charger supplier.]

As soon as he said, "That's what I want to film," I could see the film. I could see why you would go around a Chinese factory in the company of these people looking into whether the Chinese factory conforms to European safety and health requirements, and whether that would be a comedy or not. And in fact the film was very funny, though a lot of people didn't get the humor. Somehow filmmakers manage to tell you, through an image or a description of the situation, that that's why they want to approach the story. And that tells me what the story's going to tell the audience.

Because you see a point of view?

Not so much a filmmaking point of view, but you see what they want to look at. You get a phone call from Cartier-Bresson, and let's say he is in the middle of Russia and he says, "I'm doing a sequence in a worker canteen, and there are people dancing there." You'd say, "That's great," and then he'd come back with 20 frames, and one of them will be that immortal picture of two peasants dancing in the middle of the canteen. And you'd know enough [when he called] to know, well, that's going to work very well.

This is the difference from print journalism: You'll be told by reporters what the story is about; documentary filmmakers are telling you what they see. My background is writing, but I write differently now because I've learned a lot from documentary filmmaking. My writing's become much more visual, and pieces are constructed more like documentaries, with scenes in them. I think it makes them easier to read.

What do you see when you walk into Big Edie and Little Edie's house in Southampton [in Maysles Films' *Grey Gardens*]? You see these crazy people at the top of a staircase in their funny clothes. But what you really see is this extraordinary performance put on by the daughter and the mother, not only for themselves but for the camera. And if you get a phone call from Al Maysles saying, "They were singing today, it was a wonderful day," you know it's fine. What you're getting is the situation and the way the filmmaker is filming it, not the paraphrase of what it's all about.

In considering projects for support, you've said that while filmmakers can come to you just with ideas, it helps, especially when it comes to filmmakers whose work you don't know, if they've shot at least a few minutes of material.

You should always have tapes, because if you don't send tapes, if it's all bits of paper, it's very hard to know what you want to film. Again, the analogy is, if you're commissioning a Magnum photographer to go somewhere, you want a piece of paper saying this is where I want to shoot, but you'd also like some work from the Magnum photographer that tells you how they're going to look at what they want to film.

What do you look for in a reel?

Often the problem with reels is that they're edited to look like TV shows. So you think, well, that's the subject, and it could be turned into a TV show, but you don't know how good the film is going to be. In other words, they shouldn't be too slick—or, they should be slick, but [you want] to edit them so that they look like the final film. Tapes can be much rawer, but something attractive on them tells you what the impact of the final film would be.

Among the topics covered in submissions you receive, do you get a lot of misery?

Much too much misery. You just can't supply a diet of unrelieved misery. "Miserabilism" is the handmaid of "reportorialism"—you've got to find other ways. And when you do cover things like the Iraq war, you've got to find interesting ways into the subject. For us to do a film about the horrors of Baghdad—a film we showed, called *The Liberace of Baghdad*, is very funny. And very telling. [Filmmaker Sean McAllister spent eight months filming Iraq's most famous pianist, Samir Peter, playing for journalists and others in a hotel bar.] But it's also seductive because you can watch it for a whole hour and 10 minutes without being too depressed. Absolutely unadulterated dollops of misery are no good, and audiences stay away from them.

How do you see documentary changing, in terms of both filmmakers and audiences?

I think that you can reach sizable audiences through the documentary form, because if the story is very attractive, people are prepared to sit down and watch it. I'm encouraged by that. It seems people don't have problems watching them; they don't find them difficult. You don't necessarily want to read a book about something; you should be forgiven for not wanting to read a book about the Iraq war because it's so depressing. But you're prepared to go to your local movie house and watch a film about it. Or better still, you'll watch a miraculously good film like *My Architect*, which does so many things: It tells you about architecture, about growing up, about being abandoned by your father. And I think these films have easily found a niche audience. It's not a big enough audience—for commercial purposes in America it's just about big enough, but it should be larger. The only thing that stops the sector being precarious, making documentaries, is that the cost is falling. That's not necessarily a wonderful thing for documentary makers. They can make cheaper films, but they may not get rewarded for doing them. I worry about people devoting their lives to documentaries; they don't make a lot of money at it. But I think you can survive if you're clever; there's money from lots of different sources around.

CHAPTER 20

Alex Gibney

Filmmaker Alex Gibney founded Jigsaw Productions in 1982, and in the years since has produced films with partners including Participant Productions, Magnolia Films, Sony Pictures Classics, ZDF-ARTE, BBC, and PBS. The company's website notes that Gibney is "well known for crafting stories that take an unflinching look at the political landscape of America." His recent films include *Gonzo: The Life and Work of Dr. Hunter S. Thompson*; *Taxi to the Dark Side*, the 2008 Academy Award winner for Best Documentary Feature; and *Enron: The Smartest Guys in the Room*, nominated for the 2006 Academy Award. For both *Enron* and *Gonzo*, Gibney won the Writers Guild of America award for Best Documentary Screenplay.

A new documentary, *Casino Jack and the United States of Money*, premiered at the 2010 Sundance Film Festival. At the time of this interview, in March 2010, the film had not yet been released. Alex himself was in a taxi, en route to catch a plane from New York to Los Angeles.

I wanted to talk particularly about Gonzo, Taxi to the Dark Side, *and* Enron. *At first glance, these are difficult subjects: a deceased writer, torture, accounting. How do you approach a subject, and how do you begin to find a story within it?*

In the case of *Taxi*, I was approached to do a film about torture, and initially reluctant because it was a very difficult subject and I wasn't sure the subject would be a film. And so I looked for a story, and Dilawar's moved me very much, the way [*The New York Times* reporters] Tim Golden and Carlotta Gaul had told it. It had a strong emotional heart, and in a peculiar way, connected up this man [in Afghanistan] with Iraq, Guantánamo, and indeed Washington, just by following the threads. The people who were in charge of Dilawar's interrogation in Afghanistan are then sent to Iraq just before Abu Ghraib. Once Dilawar dies, they send the passengers in Dilawar's taxi to Guantánamo, as if to suggest that they'd really stumbled on a conspiracy, when these guys were nothing but peanut farmers. And then you get some sense that the Dilawar story was actually heard in Washington,

D.C. And so finding ways to have that central story feather throughout the film, even as we're dealing with McCain and Bush and Cheney and all of that other stuff, was critical. It's one of the reasons I picked that story.

The father and daughter of Dilawar, in *Taxi to the Dark Side*. Photo credit Keith Bedford.

In the case of the other two, it was more about finding the themes inside the stories, and the characters are so rich. And even in the case of *Taxi*, to find the characters *around* the story of Dilawar, who was dead, that was hard. But that's where the stories, I think, get good. It's fleshing out great characters and seeing how they perform in action, just like a movie.

Are there strategies for how you do your research?

I have characters in my films who are journalists, so to some extent, I'm being introduced to subjects by people who have done a tremendous amount of research already. I want to honor that rather than pretend that I found it, when in fact they did. We also do a tremendous amount of research ourselves, so that at the end—and particularly if we're taking somebody on—nobody can say that there's anything that's factually inaccurate.

Yet I also want to take that journalistic rigor and find a visual language, when telling a story, that will create what [filmmaker] Werner Herzog called the poet's truth rather than the accountant's truth. That's why I have an argument sometimes with people in the audience who stand up and say, "Why don't you just give it to us straight? Why don't you take out all this junk?" I feel like what they're really asking me to do is to show somebody at a blackboard with a pointer, going point by point by point through a story. I don't find that very compelling. It doesn't do what film does best, which is to engage people emotionally.

In other words, the subject itself is not a good movie—or a good book, for that matter. You have to put it together in a way that tells a compelling story if you want to reach an audience.

That's right. What I do is similar to doing a nonfiction book. The best nonfiction books, in my view, are like good fiction in terms of their storytelling and their sense of narrative momentum. I lead the audience (hopefully) through some kind of unexpected emotional journey; this is where narrative issues come into play.

In the case of *Taxi*, a lot of viewers have told me that they came to identify greatly with the soldiers and liked them. And then at the end of the film, they found out they're the killers, that they were convicted. And that was a blow to viewers, but they couldn't go back to where they might have been if they had known that information to begin with, and say to themselves, "Oh, now I think they're bad guys." They couldn't do that. "No, I like these kids." That's something more profound.

Knowing when to reveal information is part of the skill of good storytelling—too soon and it's meaningless, too late and we don't need it. How do you know when to fold in new information?

It's a really hard thing. With *Taxi*, we had to discover some of that in the storytelling. The film wasn't quite working for a long, long time. One of the things we realized was that we revealed the [prison] sentences of soldiers a bit too early in the film; it was toward the end, but not sufficiently close to the end. Once we revealed the sentences, the audience felt like the story was over and we'd better wrap it up. But we still had a lot of story, and that was just dead wrong. So we had to shorten the film and also move the section of the soldiers being sentenced further down, where it made sense in terms of expectations of narrative structure: Oh, we've concluded their story, so the film must be about to end.

Do you run test screenings periodically during the editing?

Yes, particularly when we get close. I'm doing that now on a couple of films. And it's really important, because you learn a lot about what people don't get, who they like, who they don't like, obviously whether it's too long.

Where do you find your test audiences? Who's in them?

Usually it's a combination of friends and a few acquaintances or friends of friends. It's generally a reasonably friendly audience with a few strangers thrown in. But even in that audience, you can feel the room when you watch the film, and the reactions that are consistent among the viewers are the ones you most likely want to listen to.

There was a woman, Amanda Martin, who is the blonde executive [in *Enron*], and in our original cut she ended the film with a kind of confession, in effect saying, "I was human," meaning she was deeply tempted to become corrupt. But nobody wanted to accept her in that role. They're thinking, "Human? Screw you. You profited from this company." They weren't prepared to hear that from her, because they saw her, very pretty, in this very opulent house, dressed in very expensive clothes. But they *were* prepared to hear it from that younger kid [former trader Colin Whitehead]. We thought the ending was beautiful, but they hadn't seen in Amanda what we had seen in the cutting room. They could only reference what was in the film. So we took that bit out and put the kid in at the end, and people were much more comfortable with that.

Alternatively, you would have had to go back and restructure the film to get the audience to the point where they would have accepted her.

Yes, and I don't think there's anything wrong with that. Also, peculiarly, what ends up happening—and this is the hardest part to accept as a filmmaker—is that the story you create has unexpected dimensions that you never imagined. And rather than extinguish them, you're better off embracing them.

Can you give me an example?

Well, there were a lot of thematic issues I wanted to explore in *Enron*. And they were very meaningful in broader social context—for example, how the banks were complicit in Enron's fraud. We have some of it in there, but we had to take a lot of it out because it was just stopping the narrative. None of that stuff would matter if people weren't going to be riveted by the story. So it had to go by the wayside.

There is another example, in *Taxi*. There was a sequence which I love, which is now in the DVD extras. It was one of these weird side trips you take. [There was a] hunger strike at Guantánamo when we were there, and there was a desperate need to figure out how to break the strike. One of the things they were going to do was force-feed the prisoners who were on hunger strike, so they needed a way of restraining them. And lo and behold, some enterprising soldier at Guantánamo found this website called www.restraintchair.com. It turns out that there was a sheriff in Denison, Iowa, who was manufacturing restraint chairs to help calm people who were whacked out on crank, until they could reason with them, and to do so in a way that was not hurtful. So out of the blue, this sheriff gets a call from Operation Enduring Freedom saying, "We'd like to order 50 of your restraint chairs." That was a big order for this guy. I found that sequence to be funny, and I went out and visited with him, and we had a great sequence about it. But ultimately, once we got to the death of Dilawar, there was very little interest by the audience in exploring that kind of dark humor in the film.

I had other Catch-22 moments in the film that, bit by bit, I had to excise because they couldn't see—I had been immersed in this subject and had developed a kind of gallows humor that a doctor develops by being in an operating room all the time. But the audience couldn't go there. They wanted to experience the anguish without irony, and I couldn't rob them of that. So we had to eliminate a lot of that material that ultimately was distracting.

And just to clarify, that's a different kind of omission than, say, leaving out the negative side of Hunter S. Thompson's life, the pain he at times caused his family, just because you want to present a positive portrait of him.

Right. I'm not Hunter Thompson's press agent. Interestingly enough, in the case of Hunter—and we talked about this a lot in the cutting room—I think his bipolar nature, the way he would vacillate between dark and light, the way he would be wonderfully generous and also very cruel, I think that allowed him to appreciate the essential contradictions of the American character in a way that somebody who's more balanced probably couldn't.

I wanted to return to the analogy between your films and nonfiction books, because you've also noted that in your films, as in books, you can hear the voice of the author.

Yes, in terms of the style. Likewise, in a film, you have to find a visual language to carry the story. And that language should be different, in my view. There're some people like Ken Burns, whose visual language is the same no matter what story they're telling. The archival imagery may be different, but the style is exactly the same. To me, I think you find a style that fits the subject.

How do you? How do you decide upon a visual language for a particular film?

In *Gonzo*, we were wrestling with the fact that the guy's a writer. And a lot of the visual style—that scene of the motorcycle at the beginning of the film, it's overlaid with a kind of paper texture that's meant to evoke, in an emotional way, that this is a kind of written story, even though we're out there on a motorcycle with the surf. The other thing we were playing with was this blend that Hunter investigated between fact and fiction. He liked to rocket back and forth between them. He was a good reporter, at least early on. And then he would occasionally, for dramatic effect and also for thematic value, fly into fantasy. With something like the taco stand scene, we visualized it. That's a passage that's from the book [*Fear and Loathing in Las Vegas*], done in a way that felt true to their experience.

That's an interesting example, because the visuals are created to look a bit like home movies, while the audio, as you note on screen, is an "Original audio recording by Hunter S. Thompson & Oscar Acosta, Las Vegas, 1971."

Even though it's fiction, it was much more realistically shot than some of the other material we used, which was nonfiction. We were playing with that mixture of fact and fiction that Hunter liked to investigate. [That] was one of the reasons we decided to shoot his wife Sandy against green screen. [Still and motion images of their history together play behind her as she's interviewed.] She became the person that knew him the longest throughout his life. So rather than shoot her in a living room or a yoga studio—she's now a yoga teacher—or something, there was something literary to me about seeing different backgrounds behind her, as if she were a character, literally, in a fiction or nonfiction narrative. So that she didn't have her own space; she was inside this guy's story. It wasn't about, "Where are they now?" It was about, "Where were they then?"

That's a kind of visual choice you have to plan for ahead of time.

Yes, you do. Sometimes you stumble into that stuff, but you do have to think about it beforehand. In *Enron*, we thought about it a lot beforehand, and certainly in *Taxi*, too. The way we shot the interviews of everybody who was at Bagram, the guards and some of the prisoners—they were shot against a painted backdrop and lit with high-contrast lighting, where you have one side of the face in light and one side of the face in dark. That was meant to do two things: to signal the moral ambiguity of the guards, but also, in a story that's so complicated in terms of who's military police, who's military intelligence, who's the prisoner, it was meant to convey one very simple idea, which is: anybody who's photographed that way came from Bagram. And also that dark lighting had a kind of prison vibe, so that you create a sense of place. We had to think that out ahead of time, or else it never would have worked.

How much do you put on paper before you shoot? Do you have a basic narrative skeleton?

Yes, I think it's fair to say that I have a narrative skeleton ahead of time. Not too detailed, but at least a sense of the story that is going to be told. And then I go out and try to talk to people, and occasionally shoot stuff on location, as in *Taxi*, because that was a story that in some ways was still unfolding. So I went down and shot a sequence in Guantánamo, for example. And then of course the story changes, and you have to reckon with that. But if you don't at least give it some contour up front, then you don't have enough focus, I think, to really dig in.

Do you write a treatment?

We usually have a treatment, but it's not very long. It's maybe three or four pages, like a general sense of structure. And with that in mind, I go out and get stuff. And sometimes I see an opportunity to get something that wasn't in the plan, and I get it just because it seems like it might be great material.

There is a certain kind of filmmaking where you wade into an event and you just observe. But even there, it seems to me, you're being influenced by your own preconceptions—what you know, what you're hearing off camera—and you begin to focus on things that interest you. There was a lot about Enron that we could have gone into but didn't, because I had a sense of what to tackle, what would be a good story. But, that having been said, you do improvise a lot, based on material.

Early on in my career, I had a much more rigid idea about what to look at and cover, and what I was interested in. I would tend to make the material fit my idea of the story. The problem with that is that sometimes you end up using a lot of rather weak material, instead of looking at what you've shot and realizing, "Man, this is strong," and finding a way to include that material. If there's not a kind of balance between those two things, then either the film is all great material but no narrative thrust, or it's all story and theme and no heat, no passion. The key is finding the right balance.

In the case of *Enron*, we didn't know exactly who was going to talk. If Rebecca Mark had talked to me—she was the woman who, among other things, had done the Bhopal initiative, which was a big power plant they tried to make happen in India—the narrative might have taken a slightly different direction. Also, halfway through the film [production], we discovered the California audiotapes. We spent much more time on the California story than the authors of the book did, and the reason is that those audiotapes told us something about the culture at Enron that was so powerful, and something that you couldn't do on a printed page. Part of what makes them powerful is *hearing* the kind of "frat house" attitude of the people [Enron traders] laughing while the California grid goes down.

In Gonzo, *the imagery is often quite unexpected. We see an actor as Thompson, for example, sitting at his desk in Woody Creek, Colorado and writing about the attacks on 9/11, as the attacks are seen—impossibly and very stylistically—through the windows in front of him. Or we're looking at a still of Thompson holding a gun, and it suddenly becomes animated.*

It's looking at that in a playful way. Hunter really pushed the envelope of that kind of storytelling. As a filmmaker, I was trying to say right up front, "Beware." So when you see that photograph of him shooting his typewriter in the snow and suddenly it becomes live, and you see the typewriter jump and then it snaps back into the photograph, that was a way of saying: "Watch out. Everything is not what it seems. There's a kind of playful manipulation of reality going on here."

When Hunter does his riff in the campaign trail book about Edmund Muskie being addicted to Ibogaine, I don't think he really intended to fool his audience into thinking that "Oh my God, Ed Muskie is eating Ibogaine!" It was a playful, satirical way of saying to people, "This guy looks like and acts like he's a drug addict. That's how bad he is." So again, it's stretching the form, but in a way that, at its best, Hunter could do without violating larger notions of truth. I think later on it became sloppier in Hunter's writing. But in his prime and in some of the best pieces later, he really used that to great effect, where there was great, real, factual material, but then there was a lot of playful stuff. And I think he laid out the rules so that you as the reader could get it. We tried to play with that a little bit in the visual storytelling.

You also lay out the rules. The dramatizations (or reenactments, or recreations) are styled in a way that distinguishes them from actual archival materials, for example, and when something is real—the taco stand audio, for example, or the Enron traders on the phone—you make that clear as well.

I think that's pretty important. Sometimes I get criticized for recreations in my films. People say, "Why would you do such a cheap trick?" or something like that. Like the suicide of Cliff Baxter in *Enron*. I have a pretty careful explanation for why I did that. It may fool somebody at first, but then it's very quickly revealed what's happening, so there's no attempt to deceive the viewer. I think that's terribly important, because the idea of faking something and pretending it's real is really a big, big problem. [Audiences] need to have a sense of trust that the filmmaker's done their best to show you what they think the truth is.

There are different ways to the truth, and different kinds of truth. That's why every filmmaker needs to have a different kind of an approach, a different set of rules. You let the audience in on those rules right off the bat; you signal people. If you do that and you follow those rules, then everything is fine, because then the audience gets comfortable with what you're doing. The way *Enron* starts, both with the Tom Waits music at the beginning and also with that recreation, it lets people know this is not a *Frontline*, so you shouldn't see it that way. The idea of creating a film that looks and feel like a *Frontline* but then mixes artificially recreated footage with regular archival footage and pretends they're the same—that's hugely problematic.

The actor Johnny Depp "narrates" Gonzo, but only in the sense that he is reading from Thompson's work in voice-over—so he's really a stand-in for Thompson, and we know that because you also filmed Depp reading with the book in his hand.

Right. That was a play on a lot of different things. Here's the guy who played Hunter [in the dramatic feature *Fear and Loathing in Las Vegas*], now reading Hunter. It also signaled to people in a very simple and clear way—because clarity is another thing that I'm kind of a nut about—that all the narration you hear from now on will be the undependable narrator of Hunter Thompson, as read by Johnny Depp.

What are your thoughts about current efforts to articulate some sort of formalized understanding about documentary film ethics?

That's made me a little bit uncomfortable. If there's some committee that decides what's right, I could find myself on the wrong side of that committee. I think the thing to do is to make people think long and hard about why it's important not to fool the viewer. But I would hate to go back to the old days where—I did a *Frontline* a long time ago. There was a prohibition against using music; music was considered a manipulation. And of course it *is* a manipulation. But it seems to me to be a pretty good storytelling device, and part of what you're doing is telling a story. There are many fictional methods that I like to use. The key is creating a grammar so that viewers know you're doing that, and don't believe that you're showing them a *Frontline* when you're not.

The reason I put in the recreation of Cliff Baxter right at the top was because I felt that—First of all, you don't know yet that it's Cliff Baxter. It could be any executive. But you're riding alongside somebody who's listening to a Billie Holiday song ["God Bless the Child"], which happens to be very carefully chosen. It's the kind of song he might have listened to late at night on the radio, but it's also about how the rich and powerful screw the weak. You're on the seat next to this person, smelling the cigarette, hearing the water going down his throat, and then he kills himself. And that's very intimate—"Oh my God, somebody's just killed himself!" That's a very powerful human emotion. Then, when [the film cuts] to the archival footage, "Cliff Baxter was discovered dead today," blah-blah-blah, you realize, "Okay, that was just a recreation. Now we're in the real world." What I tried to give to the viewer is a sense of identification with that executive, so we're not there the whole time wagging our fingers at the Enron executives and creating too great a distance between them and us. We see the human dimension of this story in a way that's very emotional and palpable. And to me, it's perfectly legit.

*That gets to a different aspect of your storytelling, which is that part of being fair as a filmmaker—not balanced in some phony way, but fair—is to allow for complexity, which includes seeing more than one side to a character or a point of view. In an interview you said, "I always take my cue from Marcel Ophüls (*The Sorrow and the Pity) who said something like this: 'I always have a point of view; the trick is showing how hard it was to come to that point of view.'" Can you explain?*

There's another quote that I like a lot, too. [George Bernard] Shaw once said, "Showing a conversation between a right and a wrong is melodrama. Showing a conversation between two rights is a drama." A political science professor of mine would say, "Embrace the contradiction." All those things to me mean that if you find somebody that you think is kind of a bad guy, and then you only show that stuff that fits your preconceptions of who that person is, or the role they're playing, [that's] a kind of melodrama. Much more powerful is a drama, in which that bad guy is actually, in person, kind of a nice guy. Or you're surprised to learn, for example with the guards [at Bagram], these guys who beat a young kid to death, are young kids themselves who, in their own way, are nice guys that have been brutalized by the experience. That, I think, shows a kind of hidden dimension that connects us all together, which is part of what filmmaking and storytelling is all about. It doesn't necessarily undermine the moral outrage, but it makes it tougher to point at people and say, "They should wear the black hat, and I wear the white hat."

I try not just to preach to the choir. A lot of times people will come to seeing your point of view, or at least to appreciating your point of view, if they feel that you have respect for theirs. You may not agree with it, but at least you have respect for it and have tried to reckon with it. I think that's important, because otherwise we're just in some kind of endless loop of crossfire from the left, from the right. Ugh. What could be worse?

There are a couple of very pragmatic things I want to talk about. The first is the way that you visualize scenes, creating a strong sense of place.

I like the idea of creating visual beds, particularly in a complex story. An example would be the strip club which [Enron executive] Lou Pai used to inhabit. We shot it in a way that emphasized numbers, and we cut it to music by Philip Glass. We tried to shoot a sense of the place of the California trading floor too, and find music and a shooting style that would convey the frat house atmosphere, to portray it from their point of view. So those are two examples. [Someone else] could have done it very differently.

The other is sequences, which you sometimes name, such as "Shock of Capture" in Taxi to the Dark Side. *Your films are built on sequences, each of which has a unique job to do in the overall film, and each—while different from the others—moves the film forward.*

That's right. I find that helpful, and then if you vary the manner of the sequences, too, it keeps the audience fresh. You keep moving from one place to another, like you're on a journey. It's like a bus tour: We're leaving the Grand Canyon, and now we're headed for the Rockies.

And you've arrived at the airport! Thank you so much.

Delighted. I rarely get to talk about form. When you're a documentarian, the curse is, you almost always only talk about the subject, which is okay, but in terms of documentaries in the last 15 years, I think one of the great things that's happened is that the form has just exploded, which I think is really exciting.

CHAPTER 21

Susan Kim

Susan Kim is a prolific writer of books, plays, dramatic and documentary films, and children's television. For the stage, she wrote the adaptation of Amy Tan's *The Joy Luck Club*, as well as numerous one-act plays that have been performed at the Ensemble Studio Theatre and elsewhere, and also published. A five-time Emmy Award nominee, her television writing includes more than two dozen children's series. Her documentary credits include *Paving the Way* (1997), a 60-minute film for PBS for which she won the Writers Guild Award; *The Meaning of Food* (2005), a three-hour series for PBS; and the feature-length *Imaginary Witness: Hollywood and the Holocaust* (2007), which explores the 60-year relationship between the U.S. movie industry and the horrors of Nazi Germany.

Most recently, Susan Kim and Elissa Stein published the nonfiction book *Flow: The Cultural Story of Menstruation* (St. Martin's Press, 2009), and she and Laurence Klavan completed two graphic novels, *City of Spies* and *Brain Camp*, both of which will be published by First Second Books in 2010.

Susan serves on the faculty of the low-residency MFA Program in Creative Writing at Goddard College, which is where we met in 2008, as advisor and student.

The film I particularly want to talk to you about is Imaginary Witness, *which you wrote (as co-producer), and Daniel Anker directed and produced, along with Ellin Baumel. How did this project come about?*

It was back in 2001, and AMC, American Movie Classics, had a commissioned series, Hollywood and the Blank, Hollywood and Blank. So it was Hollywood and Islam, Hollywood and Vietnam.... How does the commercial narrative machine of Hollywood tackle complex geopolitical, historical subjects? And they approached Danny Anker to do Hollywood and the Holocaust. AMC's budgets were quite small, and I think their expectations were very much for it to be a clip show. The schedule was really tight. The budget was very small. And from what we saw of what they were doing, it was what you would expect.

DOI: 10.1016/B978-0-240-81241-0.00021-6

I met with Danny right after 9/11, maybe two or three weeks after, and you could still smell the smoke, even in Danny's apartment near Lincoln Center. We spent half of the conversation talking about the attack, and it was sort of clear to us that—part of it was just pure emotion—this was much bigger than just a clip show, and we don't want to do a clip show. We spent a lot of time talking about, "What are the fictional movies about 9/11 going to be like?" We just immediately started thinking about [the film] in very alive and current terms, as opposed to, say, historical terms. And I think that alone made it seem very, very urgent. From the beginning, the conversation became about: "How is this a current story? What are the issues we're dealing with today? This is not just some dusty subject that happened in the 1940s. This is actually something that has relevance."

All of us were in agreement that we didn't want to do it "trash and cash," one of those quick-and-dirty money jobs. We wanted to do it carefully. And Danny became this incredible warrior of this film, because it was extremely difficult. We had a lot of conflict with AMC, because the schedule was crazy. He started raising outside money, and we just slowed down, because we all thought, okay, this needs a lot of research. We did a ton of reading, all the books and articles we could find, and a ton of screening. And we discussed and argued and screened together for the longest time before we actually started digitizing footage and talking about interviews. Also, we had a fantastic researcher in D.C., Julie Stein, who was pulling material from the Library of Congress and National Archives and feeding it to us.

One of the things that comes through in the film is a very clear evolution, a transformation of the relationship between Hollywood and the Holocaust over this 60-year period. Is that something you discovered through this research?

Absolutely. It was a very cumulative thing. Early on, I drafted a really bad, really preliminary kind of shooting draft. And it was just sort of trying out different structures. For a very long time, we thought the movie moguls' trip to visit the camps in postwar Germany was going to be the wrap-around story. That was one of our earliest structures. When Bruce Shaw, the editor, came on and he started digitizing and laying out the roughest bones, we all kept saying, "We don't want to do chronological. We want to do something more clever." We wanted to impose a sort of a brilliant structure. But the more we started filling in the chronology—I think it was understanding that the chronology was not just a simple schematic device, but that there was extraordinary complexity within the chronology. That if you take it from 1933 until 2001, it followed a psychological arc in terms of the survivor community. There was a business relationship arc, certainly, between Hollywood and Germany in the '30s and '40s. Things like Israel and identity politics in the '60s and '70s. All these things started playing more and more of a part that we could not have anticipated. The miniseries *Roots* was really important in terms of laying the groundwork for the miniseries *Holocaust*.

It took a very long time. We were sort of reading and transcribing and interviewing. There has been some good, interesting literature. Annette Insdorf has written *Indelible Shadows*. Judith Doneson—she was going to be our advisor, and then she died fairly early on in our preproduction—wrote a book called *The Holocaust in American Film*. And there's a wonderful book *Celluloid Soldiers* [Michael Birdwell], which took a look at Warner Bros. and the run-ins they had with conservatives in Congress about interventionism versus isolationism. So it was cumulative. It was sort of like a gesso, just layer after layer after layer, and going back and finding out more and more things.

And then of course the interviews, as you know, inform the direction of your research. All that material got transcribed. I would start sticking pieces of transcript into my drafts while the editor was also starting to do his assemblies. We would all get together, and he would show us what he had assembled, and I would distribute my script, and then we would argue about it, and then Bruce would occasionally take some of what I'd written and try to make it work. And then we would say, "What are we missing? Do we need another interview here?" A lot of times, the interview subjects would mention resources that we didn't know about or hadn't heard about. So we would then go back into research, or we would get more films in, or we would research another person to interview.

I think you have 21 people that you interview on screen. How did you go about selecting them?

There are the obvious people, there are the clever people you interview toward the end to stitch together, there are the people who make the points you want them to make, and then there's sort of the marquee people. You weigh all these different things. Annette Insdorf was someone we obviously wanted. Even though I would say her angle tends to be a bit more European than American, she could certainly speak about it with great authority. So she was one of those "we've got to have." We very much pursued Elie Wiesel, and came very close to getting him, but he was ill, I don't believe he was in the country, and we didn't. That was a big disappointment. But Thane Rosenbaum's a colleague of Wiesel's, and Danny had heard him speak, and we knew that he would make Wiesel's argument: that it was commercializing the Holocaust to film it, and that there's an ethical quandary involved and something obscene about fictionalizing it.

Obviously someone like Steven Spielberg was a big "get." Rod Steiger, in terms of content, he said something very actor-y, but it's really effective. Same thing with Fritz Weaver. He was in *Holocaust*; he played the patriarch in the family Weiss. They're not necessarily adding heavy academic or historical substance, but they're certainly adding the Hollywood flavor, which was also part of the film.

Neal Gabler was one of the last people we interviewed. He screened the film, and we said, "We need you to pull together some things." They really were advisors, all of these people. They came in and screened the film several times, talked to us at great length: "Well, you made that point; you could make this point." And we *really* let these people talk on camera, which was a luxury that AMC would not have allowed us to do on the original budget and schedule. I think Neal Gabler said that he's used to being interviewed for two hours for a documentary and then seeing an 11-second bite go by and that's it. That was a real pleasure about working on this film.

The team used documentary footage to convey the history itself, and the Hollywood footage only to convey the Hollywood approach to the history. Was it difficult to make that work?

I really can't speak highly enough about our editor, Bruce Shaw. Bruce is very creative and thoughtful. And of course later, the whole concept of using documentary to inform us on screen becomes a thematic point.

Such as?

Certainly with, say, *Sophie's Choice* and the use of survivor testimony to inform the detail and the verisimilitude on screen. Certainly with *Shoah*, and the detail Spielberg used in *Schindler's List*. That was very much based on testimony from survivors.

But just visually speaking, it was a lot of back and forth and playing with things. Often it would be the three of us—Danny, Bruce, and me—sitting in the edit room. And I would be writing, and Danny would be researching something online, and Bruce would be editing. And occasionally one of us would say, "Hey, take a look at this," or "Stop, stop, stop. Can we use this?" And it was just a lot of arguing. It was kind of fractious, like the pervasive smell of Chinese food and burritos and a lot of yelling, because it was very delicate.

Because Imaginary Witness *contains both, it's interesting to compare the raw power of actual Holocaust footage with the different kind of power that comes from fictionalized accounts.*

I think you say that as a filmmaker and filmgoer, with more of an understanding of what's involved. I've seen the film many times, and I'm always intrigued to see people sobbing at *Sophie's Choice*, the scene where she has to choose between her children. I'm very dry-eyed at that point. But I am [continually] blown away by the reunion moment from *This Is Your Life* [a reality program that aired between 1952 and 1963], when Hanna Kohner [a survivor] is reunited with her brother. To me, the difference between Hollywood emotion and real emotion, documentary emotion, is just so vividly different.

One of our big decisions, something we went back and forth on, was whether or not to use actual atrocity footage. There's a very brief glimpse of a skeleton in an oven. It was from the section on *Judgment at Nuremberg* and that film's use of documentary footage. I personally thought it was obscene; I thought that we couldn't use it. But there's a sequence in the documentary where the newsreel footage is finally brought back to Hollywood for the first time. And we just have details of a film projector running, and a voice-over describing what it was like to watch it. We don't actually show the footage.

It's interesting that as the decades pass, the Hollywood dramatizations became increasingly graphic.

Yes. You can see Dan Curtis doing his incredibly graphic *War and Remembrance*, where you have piles and piles of skeletons. And then you have the Einsatzgruppen shooting all these naked people; they're tumbling into a ditch and it's extremely graphic. I think it does have a teachable value for people who don't understand the scope of it. But again, to me, knowing the production history a little bit, I know those are all extras from a nudist colony. You can tell these are plastic skeletons. You can see the show business to it; I think I can. But at the same time, I see the value of it. You need to use strong tools to tell a story.

With such a wealth of material to choose from—60 years of Hollywood moviemaking, plus all the documentary material and interviews—how did you decide what to leave out?

Ultimately—and this is something getting back to dramatic writing—you want everything to serve the story. There are times when something is really fascinating, but it sort of spirals off into [another] direction. For example, when I think of films that I wish we could have included, there was a screwball comedy called *Once Upon a Honeymoon* [1942, with Cary Grant and Ginger Rogers], where the couple accidentally go into a concentration camp because they're mistaken as Jews. And it's done as a wacky comedy. I really wish we could have used that. There was a really good film with Kirk Douglas called *The Juggler* [1953]. But you get these clips, you screen the film really carefully, and it doesn't support the structure of the act. Perhaps there's a larger point you're trying to make, and it does not support or challenge it in a way that moves the argument forward.

Documentary film, although I think any good film or any piece of art, frankly—the greatest work is ultimately interactive because it causes you to think and argue, and it doesn't necessarily give you a sealed package. I think anything good has complexity to it. But at the same time, you should be telling a story; you should have a point of view. And it's always that delicate balance about: "Are we sealing this too hermetically? Is there no air in this beat? Are we giving this moment the complexity that it needs, and the detail and the ambiguity it may demand? Or is it just amorphous?" And that's a really difficult thing. It's like: "Is this contributing to the ultimate shape?" There should be a sense of cohesion and vision, or point of view, in the finished piece, whether it's a marble sculpture, a documentary film, a play, a nonfiction book, or a magazine article.

Imaginary Witness looks very critically at its subject. With a film like this, how do you avoid it somehow coming across as a celebration?

The most important thing that we were trying to do in *Imaginary Witness* was pose larger questions. If you do that, by definition, you're not going in a celebratory direction. Celebration implies catharsis, closure, finality, that something has been won. And I think the themes that we were trying to explore are ones that are still active and alive, even when applied to other atrocities and other things that Hollywood attempts, on occasion, to grapple with.

You've described Imaginary Witness *as coming together very organically, and at the same time, it's built on a three-act structure. To me it sort of illustrates a basic point about structure, which is that it's a tool for understanding and shaping the film that exists, as opposed to a formula imposed from without.*

And it's funny because "structure" itself sounds so rigid. It sounds like everything has to fit to a T-square. But of course that's not true. Beautiful structure is like anything. Every great thing has its own structure that works, and it's not necessarily something you can apply to every film, but it makes sense within that film. So you're right. You can look at something and say—for example, with me when I'm working on a documentary, I will write something that to me makes great sense on paper; it's beautifully structured on paper, and we start putting it together, and it's so boring! It doesn't work. So then you start ripping it apart and asking those questions about: "Do we subvert the structure? Do we play with the chronology? Do we shift the perspective so we're not looking at it from this point of view, we're looking from that point of view? Have we misidentified the central event? Is that not the real point of this? Is there something else going on subtextually that we have not been aware of, and that is slowly starting to emerge?" Anybody who understands structure can argue this a lot of different ways. You can give the same raw footage to 10 different filmmakers and they can come up with 10 terrific films that are quite different, which is something that always fascinated me.

You've written a lot of television for children, some of it nonfiction, or at least with documentary elements. Do you approach storytelling differently when you're writing for young audiences?

I've written a lot of *Reading Rainbows,* [which] is a magazine format but often has documentary elements. And I also wrote and produced several episodes of *Really Wild Animals,* a natural history series for children that was produced by National Geographic for CBS. It's a little different because you can't assume that the attention span is there to follow these long, twisting threads over the course of a half hour. You're not necessarily going to have the same kind of setup and payoff, and stories cross-cutting the central story. With children, I tend to be much more modular; more basically educational. Like: "These are the different layers of a rain forest; these are the animals that live in the—." You basically say what the structure is going to be, and then you take them through it. And obviously the bells and whistles are a little more vibrant with kids: humor, animation, songs, jokes. Also, comparative visuals if you're working with young kids. Film editing is hard enough for a very young child to follow, because sudden visual juxtapositions are confusing.

You and Laurence Klavan have two graphic novels coming out this year, both written for middle school children. They're fiction, but one, for example, is inspired by a real-life story, the discovery of a Nazi spy ring in New York City. For documentary filmmakers whose work is sometimes compared to creative nonfiction, or nonfiction novels, the graphic novel seems like another creative model—certainly as we saw with Ari Folman's Waltz with Bashir, *an animated documentary memoir.*

Some of the most successful and effective graphic novels are [grounded in] nonfiction. A lot of them are memoir. I'm thinking of *Palestine* by Joe Sacco, and *Persepolis* obviously has documentary elements, but it's still a memoir. And *Stitches, Epileptic, A Drifting Life.* . . . They're so strongly drawn and so heightened, it's interesting for documentary filmmakers to take a look at them. They're like storyboards; they're so visual.

What do you say to filmmakers or dramatists who resist the notion of story as being contrived?

I'm always intrigued by people who don't have a taste for it. I have a student this semester who was attacking narrative, attacking theater as being fundamentally conservative. "Why do we have to read the stupid *Poetics*? I am sick of plot. I am tired of character. Why can't we explode them?" She said that all other art forms have transformed radically since, say, the ancient Greeks. She said you cannot look at painting today and say that it's at all based on the same precepts of, say, a Renaissance painting, even though of course they're using the same tools—color and composition and subjects and brush stroke. The rules have been completely exploded, and it's fine. She said, "Why can't drama have the same revolution? When people bend theater"—someone like Richard Foreman or Lee Breuer and Mabou Mines—"it always gets ghettoized."

My argument is, that while much of *The Poetics* is not germane because we live in a different era, there is something about the power of tragedy to effect catharsis. Drama is a really effective form, a really ancient form, and a powerful one. One of the first things children do is play act. They respond to fairy tales—the good guy, the bad guy, the antagonist, the ending—really strongly. The unconscious mind attempts to make narrative every night when we sleep. If we are very bothered, we will have dreams that are rife with subtext and symbolism and thematic development and conflict and strong emotion. I think that's just the way we as humans are neurologically and culturally structured. So I think there is something inherent in the dramatic form that's really powerful. And I think that's why, as storytellers, as people who want to make documentary or write plays, it behooves us to understand the potential of that structure.

I was thinking about *Hands on a Hard Body* yesterday, and I was thinking I don't particularly like marathons or dance-a-thons or endurance things. I would not last holding on to a truck for 48 hours. But that movie has stayed with me. The story actually was very simple: You had a very clear sense of character; there was a real beginning, a real dramatic action, and a real ending. And a surprising person wins, and people flame out. And even though, going into it, I wouldn't have necessarily thought that was an exciting story, I was really captured by it.

Spellbound is another example of a film like that. I'm going to spend 90 minutes watching kids spell?

Exactly, exactly. Or *Man on Wire*. These films where you're thinking, "Okay, I could see watching that for 20 minutes." And then 90 minutes later you're sobbing or applauding or jumping back because you want to see something again.

So how would you explain how that's done?

I think part of it is, if you love the story—if you really are emotionally and intellectually compelled by the story—then you start finding the complexity and the nuance. It's all specificity and stakes. Whether you're writing dramatic fiction or doing something that's nonfiction, the more specific you are—and if the specifics serve the dramatic action, and it's a good story to begin with—that, by definition, puts you ahead of nine-tenths of the pack.

People don't want to see a statement. They want to see action. And action is a fight; it's people fighting for what they want, and you don't know who's going to win. This is why people watch sports. For example, *Man on Wire*. We know that Philippe Petit is going to successfully walk across the World Trade towers, but if you break that into the separate battles of his achieving that, you don't know how each thing is going to turn out. And each step is full of surprises. You don't spoon-feed the information to the audience. You let it develop, so that there is suspense: Is he going to get up the stairs or not? Is the guard going to wake up or not?

How would you articulate that in terms of Imaginary Witness?

That there are real setbacks. Each act has different things going on that are very high stakes. Certainly during the 1940s itself, you could argue that thousands and thousands of Jews were being killed every day in the concentration camps, and was the United States going to do anything? Unless you're a historian or you've read a lot about the period, you don't necessarily know what's going to happen.

I think a lot of it has to do with narration; it's a heavily narrated film. I can understand why a lot of documentary filmmakers veer away from narration, because I think at its worst, it is what I'm talking about, a filmmaker spoon-feeding the audience. In an ideal world, it's merely giving you just enough to keep you up to speed with what's going on in the film. It should not stand apart from the film. It should not be imposed on the film. It really should be part of the film. And we phrased each of our acts as a question. For example, the question of, "What was going to happen to the tales of the survivors?" People were dead. Germany was trying to rebuild. Liberal voices in the Hollywood Jewish left wing were being silenced because of HUAC [the House UnAmerican Activities Committee]. So you pose those questions, and you don't answer them until you earn the answer.

CHAPTER 22

James Marsh

James Marsh is the director of *Man on Wire*, which won the 2008 Academy Award for Best Documentary. Based on the book, *To Reach the Clouds*, by Philippe Petit, the film tells the story of how Petit, at the age of 24, conspired with a group of friends and strangers over a period of eight months to plan and carry out an illegal and astonishing high-wire performance: On August 7, 1974, Petit spent nearly an hour walking, dancing, kneeling, and even reclining on a wire that connected the north and south towers of New York's World Trade Center, 1,350 feet—nearly a quarter of a mile—above the ground.

Marsh's other documentary credits as director include *Troubleman*, a look at the last years and death of singer Marvin Gaye; *The Burger and the King*, based on a book, *The Life & Cuisine of Elvis Presley*, by David Adler; *Wisconsin Death Trip*, based on a book of the same title by Michael Lesey, which looks at the strange fates that befall residents in a small Wisconsin town during the economic depression of the 1890s; and *The Team*, co-directed with Basia Winograd, a vérité film about a homeless soccer team from New York that competes in the first Homeless Soccer World Cup in Austria.

His dramatic films include *The King*, a theatrical feature based on a script he wrote with Milo Addica, and *1980*, the second film in the dramatic trilogy *Red Riding*, based on a series of historically inspired novels by David Peace and adapted for the screen by Tony Grisoni; the series aired on the BBC's Channel 4 in 2009.

How did your collaboration with Philippe Petit come about?

Most of the documentary films that I've made have been inspired by existing books, and *Man on Wire* is no exception. The way into the story for me was through this very personal, very idiosyncratic, very detailed memoir that Philippe had written. That gives you quite a strong sense of his character and what you're going to be faced with when you begin to start collaborating. So I read the book very carefully, and I had a very awkward phone conversation with Philippe, who's not the best approached on the phone; he's much better when

© 2011 Sheila Curran Bernard. Published by Elsevier, Inc. All rights reserved.
DOI: 10.1016/B978-0-240-81241-0.00022-8

you meet him in person. But we agreed to meet on the back of that awkward phone conversation.

What I gleaned from the book is that he is an absolute control freak—and would have to be, to be doing what he's spent his professional life doing. So in our first encounter, I just wanted to offer this idea of him being involved in the making of the film. It was his story, and I needed to entertain the ideas he had about how the film was going to turn out. Now, that was pragmatic on my part. To invite input would be much better than for it to be negotiated in that first meeting. So it was a long lunch with lots of wine and conversation, and then he called me just five minutes after I'd left the meeting, saying, "Let's do this together." It was a very spontaneous act, which is the best part of Philippe's character; he just trusts his instincts and feelings and goes with them.

And so that became a very long, intense, and often quite antagonistic collaboration, which ended up with a piece of work that I think reflected both the story and all the ideas that the story threw up, but it wasn't an easy process. Philippe, like many people, had seen lots and lots of films—he loves films—and there's a sense that if you've seen a lot that somehow you can make them. And that's quite difficult, when you're dealing with someone who's very beholden to their own opinions and ideas. When we didn't agree, I had—as the filmmaker—a greater responsibility to the film to do things the way I thought were best.

With the subject of the film so involved in its creation, there is the risk that it will become a vanity piece, but that doesn't seem to be the case here. The portrait of Philippe that comes through is complex and not always flattering, and of course the film is much more than just his story. It's also the story of his many collaborators and their relationship to Philippe and each other.

It was a very slow process of trying to, stage by stage, suggest that I felt the film needed to have elements of reconstruction and evocation. It wasn't generic reconstruction, but was based very specifically on the recollections of people that were there. Philippe quite vehemently resisted that for quite some time. That was particularly true of two Americans who got involved late in the adventure, both of whom bailed on him, in a certain kind of way, as it unfolded. He was violently against them being in the film. Of course, as a director you ought to tell the story with all the available voices you have, and the very fact that they betrayed him, as he would see it, made them very interesting to me. They were there, they saw things, they were part of the team.

So those were quite difficult obstacles that were overcome through dialogue and time. And to be honest with you, I just persevered to get my own way, and that feels like part of the job of a director in this kind of project. I do feel there's a responsibility to tell the story, the narrative, as well as I can. My job is to make a story that fascinates me as available to people as possible. And Philippe, to his great credit, saw that I had to make the film that I was seeing and to pursue the things I needed to pursue—even though he didn't necessarily agree with them, even when the film was finished.

So you're expanding on characters who may have been mentioned in the book, but aren't front and center.

These characters are referred to in the book, often in very disparaging terms. But it felt to me that what I needed to construct was a kaleidoscope of narrative. To give you a good example, there are two teams involved in getting the equipment into each tower, and then up each tower, and then across each tower. And therefore if you eliminate one team from that, you're losing half the story. Just on that very basic level, you need these other points of view. The drama that plays out in the tower where Jean-Louis is, in a sense, is equal if not more striking than what plays out with Philippe. And of course, therein lies dramatic conflict as well: you've got a group of people who aren't necessarily friends—there is lots of disagreement—going on this venture where a man's life is at stake.

It felt to me very obvious that people needed to represent themselves and be allowed to have their recollections, even if they were in conflict with other people's recollections. What's interesting about *Man on Wire*, as is often the case in documentaries, is that the most unlikely and preposterous details—that you think, "That could never have happened that way"—checked out! And everyone agreed on the most unlikely things that happened. It's very pleasing to confirm the most outlandish facts of the matter. That's what makes documentaries so special; you can't argue with something that happened. It happened. There are facts here. And when people agree on those, those really unlikely ones, it just makes the documentary almost transcend fiction.

Do you have a general approach, as a filmmaker, when you start with books? Wisconsin Death Trip, for example.

That was a much more imaginative interpretation of a book that, in its own way, doesn't look like you can even film it. There was a film I made in the '90s called *The Burger and the King* that was also based on a book, *The Life & Cuisine of Elvis Presley*, an Elvis Presley cookbook. And that was a starting point for a very detailed, written treatment.

Philippe Petit, in *Man on Wire*, a Magnolia Pictures release. Photo courtesy of Magnolia Pictures.

That was also true of *Man on Wire*. I had a 60-page outline for that film, which organized the structure of the film, which for documentary is quite unusual. It has various timelines and you're flashing back and overlapping them, which is quite difficult to pull off in a documentary film, so I thought it was good to organize it on paper. And that feels sort of antithetical to the practice of documentary as some people see it—that you're writing out the story before you've discovered it—but for me, it's very good to have. If you've got written source material that appears to be quite reliable, there's no reason why you shouldn't try and organize it as a narrative and lay it out for yourself and the people who are going to invest in film.

And, of course, in the course of making the film, you have to be very alive to new discoveries, things that might change the architecture that you've already created. I'm doing that now on a film I'm working on, called *Project Nim*—I'm not sure that will be its actual title. It's the story of an experiment to try and make a chimpanzee human, and based on a book as well [*Nim Chimsky: The Chimp Who Would Be Human*, by Elizabeth Hess]. And in this case, I found that the book is only half the story. By reaching out to people who didn't speak to the author, I'm finding a very different story. We've gone quite a long way away from my written script or outline.

I do find books, generally, a very good source material for the kind of work that I like to do. I'm not an observational filmmaker, or a filmmaker who wants to follow a story as it unfolds. Would that I could. I think it's actually quite a lot harder than what I do.

Given different types of source materials and subjects, how do you decide what approach you'll take, or what genre it might be? Man on Wire, *for example, is something of a heist film.*

I think it's not so much a genre, but a question of the *tone* of the film that you're doing. In Philippe's case, the tone is set by the protagonist, the main character, and how he sees himself, how he presents himself. It's a very important part of the story. So *Man on Wire* does have this heist movie kind of structure, and indeed elements that feel more fictional than a conventional documentary but that emerge from the theatricality of Philippe's personality. It felt like a very good extension of how he told the story, to construct the film that way.

The story that I'm seeing in *Project Nim* is about mothering and female nurturing. The chimpanzee has a series of human mothers that look after him; each one has a bad ending with him. To me, the essence of the film was the struggle to nurture and mother this alien life form, and to project onto it lots of human emotions that the chimpanzee doesn't either understand or will exploit in some way. So that sets a tone for a film that's about the experiences of these women, emotionally. That's what the focus is. And so the genre, for me, is same as the tone: What level do I play this at?

Would "theme" be another word for what you're calling "tone"?

To some extent, yes. But tone is the amalgamation of how you cut the film, how you score the film, how you emphasize humor over sadness, or whatever—where you put the emphasis. I think the scoring of film is perhaps the crudest part of that. You can see documentaries where the score feels very generic. It doesn't feel that it has its own personality; it feels like it's meant to grease the wheels. Scoring—or not scoring, which is equally important and equally a part of what you're doing in a film—is something that some documentaries do in a way that doesn't feel thought out. I'm very mindful of what score can do. And that's the crudest expression of this idea of tone that I'm getting at.

But theme is part of that, too. In *Man on Wire*, the ideas of the film were ones that I can't even control, because of the response that people are going to have based on later events. [The destruction of the towers in 2001, which is never mentioned in the film.] That's also probably true of the film I'm doing now on the chimpanzees. I think men and women will respond to this film very differently. So it's something you're trying to be mindful of, how it might be perceived, without making that the main thing that you're doing. You have to ultimately create something that you can stand to watch and that addresses your curiosities about the subject matter. That feels to me to be the first thing that all good documentary films have: You feel like the person who's made that film has pleased themselves, to some extent.

You're credited as writer on some of your documentaries, but there's no writer credited on Man on Wire, *and yet you just talked about writing a 60-page treatment.*

I wasn't allowed to have one, nor do I see [the need]; I feel it's somewhat of a vanity. And I don't understand how anyone who's directing a film would hire a writer to then write it, but you see it a lot on documentary credits and clearly that works for certain filmmakers, but would never work for me. I assume that as a director of a documentary, you're very actively involved (although of course that's not always the case) in the treatments for a film, the way a film is constructed before you shoot anything, and also you're very, very actively involved in the editing, where you're, in a sense, writing the scripts for it after you've shot it. I co-edit, essentially, although I don't take a credit for that either. It's because I feel like it should be implicit. The words are given to you by your contributors, but you're definitely, in some real sense, authoring and writing the film in the cutting room.

You hear stories of directors who don't come to the cutting room that often. I'm there every single day for the whole duration of the edit. And before I do the edit, I would've done a first cut myself at home, and worked on the structure. And that's not in any way to diminish the role of my editor [Jinx Godfrey], who's someone I've worked with for 13 years on practically every project I've done.

When it comes to dramatizations, how do you decide which moments in a story should be dramatized, and how?

Because of the nature of this kind of filmmaking, everything—every shot, every scene—has to be intentional. In certain documentaries that isn't the case at all. Clearly, the moment you make an edit, a documentary ceases to be real, whether it's an observational film or a film like the films that I make, which are very constructed. I think that the way to use reconstructions is to make them incredibly specific. In *Man on Wire*, they're written scenes. They're not just illustrations or generic shooting of locations or wallpaper imagery to get you across the talking heads or provide a cutaway. In this kind of filmmaking, you can and should be very precise about the images that you're going to use to tell the story.

In *Man on Wire*'s case, [the dramatizations] were evoked by the dialogue, by the interviews. I shot all the interviews first, and then spent three or four months editing them together before I shot anything else. When we had a structure that worked in the cutting room (and was very much like the structure I had worked out ahead of time), we had a fairly tight film; it was an hour and 45 minutes at this point. It was a little loose, but not very loose. I scripted and shot the reconstructions very specifically around the evocations of the words that were used by the contributors. So it was completely sourced on their memories, but of course it was my imaginings that ended up on the screen, very much tied to and informed by the dialogue. And throughout those reconstructions, you'll be hearing voice-over from the contributors, because that's where they came from: They were inspired directly by them. And I think that's important, in this kind of filmmaking. One isn't looking just to shoot general shots to toss into a film, to cover up the absence of imagery or archive. They should have a different and more singular purpose than that.

Some audiences weren't able to separate the reconstructions from the archive. I found that to be both flattering and utterly baffling at the same time, because it felt to me there was a clear feel and texture to them. And also, there's a progression in the way the reconstructions are organized, so that they start being reasonably realistic and they become much more abstract as the story unfolds, as if the characters had gone to some other place—and indeed they had: They'd gone to the top of the world, the World Trade Center. And I thought that was pretty clear, but it wasn't to some people, and I wasn't troubled by that. I think as long as the film is working on a narrative level, then how they reflect upon the elements you've used doesn't really bother me one way or another.

A.O. Scott of The New York Times *described your reenactments as "witty," and I thought that was a great word for them. But is that something a filmmaker can aspire to, or do you need to be born witty?*

I think it's perhaps the same point. The tone of those reenactments was based on the tone of the interviews, and the recollections were often quite witty, particularly Philippe's. They were flamboyant and sometimes self-parodying and sometimes self-aggrandizing. Philippe's story is playful, but with the most profound dimensions to it: questions about the nature of beauty and art, testing your personal limits, the absence of the Twin Towers, and so on—there are big, big ideas in this story. And that tension between the fanciful nature of the quest and the objective, and the fact that it is on one level totally pointless and on the other level totally profound—the idea of walking between those Twin Towers, why would you want to do that? Well, that's not a question I would ever ask him or myself. The "why" is completely the wrong word to use for that.

Other than the presence of Philippe himself on screen, were there other reasons that you felt this should be a documentary rather than a drama?

I never thought of it as a feature. Firstly, it wasn't what I was invited to do. And secondly, it felt to me that because of the nature of the story and because of the nature of the people involved, it would be vastly better as a documentary. Once [I met] Philippe, there was no question in my mind that this would be much better expressed as a documentary.

We'll see whether that's true, because there may well be, as we speak, an attempt to make Philippe's life story, and indeed that part of his life story, into a very expensive movie. But it feels like it's very hard to improve on the real people telling you the real story in this particular case.

A lot of documentary work in the past few years—not only your work, but also Waltz with Bashir *and* Gonzo *and other films—strikes me as pushing against the boundaries of the form while also striving to remain truthful. What is your take on the balance between creativity and truthfulness?*

I'm not sure I'm the best person to resolve that argument, not that you're asking me to. My responsibility with *Man on Wire*, with that subject matter, was to make the best possible film experience out of that, because it was such an experience for those involved. Here's this completely blank, empty canvas for a hundred minutes and you need to fill that canvas in the best way you can, tell the story as you see it. Now, another filmmaker would have made a very different film out of *Man on Wire*; they could have seen very different things in the narrative or very different emphases. So for me, it's obviously a very personal interpretation of the story. And that's true of the film I'm making now. It's, in a sense, my version of the story. By definition, it's selective. It ignores certain things and stresses other things, but that's true I think of any documentary film.

My issue with something is when it isn't true and you're trying to make it true, then that's wrong. But if you've established something as best you can to be a fact or the truth, and you dramatize it or you visualize it in a certain way that isn't completely literal-minded, that's fine. *Waltz with Bashir* is a very good example. It's an extraordinarily good film—it's one of my favorite documentaries of the last decade—and I think it truly is a documentary because it's based on a series of collective and personal experiences of a very extraordinary moment in history, and the events themselves. That film seems to critique the very notion that everything is subjective: This is how I remember it; it might not have been that way. That I think is a brilliant example of a documentary truly pushing against the form, both in its visuals and methods.

Can you talk about rhythm, and the role it plays in successful film storytelling?

I think the key to all good filmmaking—whether they're documentaries or features, and I've made both—is to understand the rhythm. How the story unfolds, when you stop and breathe, when you gallop forward, when you bombard with information, and when you have one single striking fact that you want to expose. And that comes, I guess, from really knowing the subject matter inside out. You know where the emphasis should be and what the real story is, the dramatic story.

With *Man on Wire*, I read everything I could read—I read all the newspaper reports, I had preliminary interviews with all the people involved—to really understand the story. And then when you do the interviews, you have to construct them really, really carefully. I don't just randomly sit down and ask questions. I'll spend a day planning out an interview, where I will very carefully work through the questions and when to ask what, when to ask the difficult questions. So the rhythm of the film gets established at that very point of the interview. Awkward ones will have their own rhythm, where you feel like you're leading the person through their memories and recollections, trying to give them space to reflect, trying to occasionally almost ambush them with questions that are going to throw them—all those kinds of things that you organize at the point of interview. That's certainly even more true with the film I've just done, *Project Nim*, the chimpanzee film, which is a much more complicated story and therefore I have to know it much, much better.

You're trying to be a conduit of what really happened, and looking to establish the ebb and flow of a story and the turning points. If you get it right, then the film is going to work. It's that simple. I've gotten them wrong; I know what a film looks like when you haven't got the rhythm right and it doesn't quite hang together.

In terms of the footage that you discovered that Philippe had shot but not processed—that was the footage of training out in the fields?

A film crew spent a week with him at his parents' home in France, as he was preparing for the World Trade Center break-in and walk, and documented some of these preparations. There were nine or 10 rolls of film that were shot over two or three days. And Philippe had kind of hoarded the negative of that film. So we processed it, and that's when I realized that I might have something a bit more extraordinary on my hands.

Why?

Because I saw in that footage—You can see the essence and spirit of what this is all about. A group of young people who know no fear, or know a little fear, but not enough to stop them doing something reckless and dangerous. And just the playfulness of that footage. And also, you're seeing some of the real solutions being found for real problems. That footage, for me, became the emotional center of the film: I felt I could anchor the film in spirit with what it was really like to be part of Philippe's merry band of ne'er-do-wells at that time. That footage gave me that, in a beautiful way. The sun is shining, people are galloping in meadows, and everyone is there who needs to be there. You see them all looking handsome and attractive as young people. It was just an amazing gift, that footage.

And it gives an arc to these relationships, adding depth especially to the stories of Jean-Louis and Annie—

And it shows you how much they care about what they're doing. It's not just some frivolous game that's being played. There's a lot of focused discussion and obsession from people like Jean-Louis and Annie, who know what the stakes are: It's their best friend whose life is potentially at risk by doing this. You get to glimpse the stakes as well, because of the intensity of the relationships that you see in that footage.

In storytelling terms, when did you first find out about this footage and how did it change what you were already doing?

Philippe alluded to it very cryptically as we were discussing the project initially, and then didn't really let me see it for quite some time. It was almost as if I had to prove myself to him before he'd let me see it. It came after we'd started shooting the film. He finally let me—We went to his garage and there it was. And then it was processed, and I remember watching it at DuArt as they were grading the negative transfer, my heart leaping, and thinking, "Oh my God! This doesn't change the film but it enriches it and illustrates it in ways that I could never have expected." At the moment, I knew that the film had become profoundly better. You could see things that, up until this point, I thought we'd have to somehow create or verbalize in order to evoke. Even better still, what I was seeing really sunk up with what I felt the film was about. Had it been different, I would have had to change my views and ideas about making the film the way I was making it. But there it was.

Looking at the list of documentaries you've done, it's very eclectic. I'm curious about how you pick a topic and how you find a story within that.

It's an interesting question, not one you ask yourself very often. It feels to me that I'm just looking for subjects that personally fascinate me. When I was younger, I did specialize in films about rock music and the rockumentary. But I always try to get involved in something that I haven't quite seen before, at least in the way I'm seeing it. You want to do something that feels like it's going to be an original contribution to the form, if you like, both by virtue of subject matter and [that] you've got a potentially original way of telling that story. Something that intrigues you and draws you in on a very personal level, and you feel that you can do that for other people too: You can draw them into what's made you so fascinated in that subject matter.

Also, you have to know that you're going to live with something for a year or so, and so you need to find subjects that open up and open up and open up, so that the ideas that lurk around them and beyond them and are activated by them feel strong and substantial. For *Man on Wire*, you've got the whole future tense of the buildings [the Twin Towers] to reckon with, and how what Philippe does has interesting tensions with what is going to happen later on. In *The Burger and the King*, a preposterous story about Elvis Presley eating himself to death, I felt there were really interesting stories about what it's like to grow up in the Depression, what that does to your mentality, what it's like to be able to have anything you want whenever you want it.

I read that you started out as an assistant editor and have said that editing is a good way to learn about directing.

Yes, I think it really is. When I worked at the BBC, I'd make little five- or 10-minute films for an art show, and you had to edit those yourself as well. It's a great way of seeing and having to reckon with your mistakes as opposed to passing them off to somebody else to deal with. That's a good way—and a painful way—of not repeating your mistakes.

Also, I think it makes you very mindful of what a film actually is. A film is a constructed piece, even if it's the best Frederick Wiseman observational film—and he's the best practitioner of that kind of film-making. His films are remarkably and brilliantly constructed to be the way they are; they're heavily constructed in the cutting room. I think he calls them "reality fictions," which is a great title. Even though you would think that his work transcends all those accusations about documentaries being pure, and being about real experiences, and not [shaped] with other elements and reconstructions and on and on, he's the first person to admit that that's not the way they are.

I'm surprised that more editors don't become directors. Personally, I always wanted to be a director; I was trying to find a way in, and that's the way I did it. Editors tend to be, I think, quite private people. I'm a much more gregarious person, and so editing would not have been what I wanted to do, but it was a brilliant way of going to film school, if you like. And editing is the thing I find most rewarding about the filmmaking process.

You recently directed 1980, *the middle film in the BBC's* Red Riding *series of three feature-length films set in Yorkshire in the 1970s and '80s. I'm wondering whether your documentary work influences your approach to fiction?*

It does. And in fact that film opens with what is essentially a documentary montage of news footage that has very clear and overt references to a real-life case in England. But I think what documentaries have given me is a really good sense of structure, because in a documentary you often have to find that structure, to find how the story's going to work in a dramatic way. Structure is a thing I'm absolutely obsessed with in documentary filmmaking. Is the structure working? Do things lead to other things the way they should? Is there cause and effect in my narrative or in my characters' actions? And that's enormously beneficial when you analyze a film script. It means that you can approach a film with a better sense of what it's going to be like, because documentaries are so slow to come together in the cutting room and you always try to figure out how to be more efficient and get to the end point more quickly.

Also, in documentaries, there's the constant frustration of low budget; you're quite restricted on what you can do and how you can do it. So that's why I love making [dramatic] features, is that you get to play more. You can use more complicated film grammar, in terms of what shots you can do and the time you're given to do them. So I find that quite liberating.

You have such an international perspective on documentary—you're from Cornwall, you lived for many years in New York City, and now you're in Copenhagen. How are the storytelling approaches different across boundaries, or the same, and how are they changing?

That's a very intriguing question; I wouldn't know where to begin on that. I grew up in the U.K. and became a documentary filmmaker within the BBC, essentially. Many filmmakers from England have worked for the BBC or worked within the BBC. So definitely the U.K. tradition of documentary filmmaking is the most important part of my earlier career. And I was fortunate enough when I was younger to work on *Arena*, an arts film series where you had an hour to make a film about a famous artist or some kind of artistic phenomenon. The series had absolutely no ground rules and it was run by crazy people who would let you do almost anything if they felt it was going to be a good film. They would encourage you to experiment. And that, to me, was the most formative part of my career, working for two very maverick producers. It was a completely anarchic environment, but so much brilliant work came out of that, much more so than if you were in a locked-down office and made to do a nine to five job with a film.

So I was sort of steeped in British TV; every week you could see two or three really good, very well made documentaries. And within that, there were many great directors who you would be able to imitate initially, and then find your own voice. It was only later on I discovered the great masters of American documentary filmmaking: the Maysles brothers, and Pennebaker, and particularly Wiseman, who's so far away from what I do and yet the filmmaker that I almost most admire in the world, because of the rigor of what he does. He gets something that I think no other filmmaker has gotten so regularly and consistently in his work. His portraits of institutions and people within them are just breathtakingly profound and beautifully edited. And so that became a later influence on me.

I think that the feature documentary in the last 10 years has really emerged as a very credible form in world cinema. In American cinema, I think documentaries are way more vigorous and exciting than what's going on in independent [drama] at the moment. There's a whole movement in American documentary filmmaking, that may be because journalism itself has been so poor in the last 10 years. We've been through a period of time where questions needed to be asked on a very basic level and documentaries have been doing that.

But not only that. You can see a film like *The King of Kong*, which is about something altogether nonpolitical. I love that documentary. You can see *Waltz with Bashir*. It feels like a very, very good time to be making documentaries. And increasingly, feature films—the Bourne films [*The Bourne Supremacy, The Bourne Ultimatum*] are taking some of their energy from documentaries. And [director Paul] Greengrass is a documentary filmmaker, lest we forget. We're blessed to live in a time where documentaries are very much part of the culture and are having an impact on the culture. And people are doing very interesting things with them, [which] wasn't true so much in the '90s. It's definitely over the decade that this movement has emerged and can be defined clearly for what it is.

Is there anything that I haven't asked you that, as you're thinking about storytelling or you mentor younger filmmakers, you try to convey?

The thing that should be thought about most in any film is the structure: how things relate to each other. We talked about that and it's my big obsession; I'm just obsessed with it.

So with a film like Man on Wire, *that has a very complex structure built around multiple story lines and flashbacks, are there strategies for keeping track of it all?*

You can't play with structure until you've really got a grip on the story that you're telling. That's true with a narrative film as well. I think some of it came, for me, from making *Wisconsin Death Trip.* What I'd liked in the book [is that] it had no given structure—it was completely formless and chaotic. But a film *has* to have some kind of structure, even if the structure is terrible—and there are films that have terrible structures and usually they're terrible films. That was such a struggle to make that film work, if it works, to flow and to feel like an experience that you could watch and lose yourself in. It was that film, by its very formlessness, that made me really conscious of structure and how important it was to good filmmaking.

If you're going to try a structure that isn't linear or isn't just one big long recollection, you have to really know your story inside out. And also, the structure has to serve the story. With *Man on Wire*, it was very clear to me that most people who were going to see the film would know the outcome—or would guess the outcome. And therefore, one had to structure it that way, to create suspense and live in the moment, [to invite] the audience into the gripping unfolding of this unlikely story. It was all worked out on paper, ahead of time, that it should have this structure. Not in the cutting room.

Feature films can be very helpful, if you watch, as I do, feature films all the time and you enjoy the structure. I just watched *Citizen Kane* again. It has an amazingly good structure, that. It's been imitated endlessly, but it's a brilliant, formal piece of filmmaking, so beautifully structured. I admire that more than anything else in a film: a well-structured piece of storytelling. It's about telling a story the best way that you can.

CHAPTER 23

Sam Pollard

Sam Pollard has been working as a feature film and television editor and documentary producer/director for nearly 30 years. He and I worked together on two documentary series for PBS, *I'll Make Me a World* and *Eyes on the Prize*. His other documentary credits include *Goin' Back to T-Town*, the series *The Rise and Fall of Jim Crow*, and *American Roots Music*.

Sam has edited several dramatic features directed by Spike Lee, including *Mo' Better Blues, Jungle Fever, Girl 6, Clockers*, and *Bamboozled*. For HBO, he and Lee produced and Sam edited the documentary *4 Little Girls*, an Academy Award–nominated film about the 1963 church bombing in Birmingham, Alabama, that claimed the lives of 11-year-old Denise McNair and 14-year-olds Addie Mae Collins, Carole Robertson, and Cynthia Wesley. They teamed up again to produce *When the Levees Broke: A Requiem in Four Acts*, a documentary about New Orleans during and after Hurricane Katrina that aired on HBO a year later, in August 2006. As this edition goes to press in 2010, he and Spike Lee are working on a sequel. *If God Is Willing and Da Creek Don't Rise*, scheduled to air on HBO in August 2010, on the five-year anniversary of the storm.

Sam is a professor at New York University's Tisch School of the Arts, where he teaches Fundamentals of Sight and Sound: Documentary, a sophomore course; Advanced Video Editing; and History of Editing. This interview was conducted in 2003 and 2006, while Sam was editing *Levees*.

As an editor, what's your role in structuring the film's narrative?

You get three types of documentary producers. The first type will say, "I went out, and I'm doing a film about these four girls who were killed in Birmingham, Alabama. Here's my script, here's my structure, we'll screen the dailies together, and I want you to follow that template."

Second type of producer says, "I went out, I shot this footage about four little girls who were killed in Birmingham in 1963. I filmed their parents, their nieces, their cousins, I talked to ministers in the community of Birmingham, I also talked to Andrew Young and other people involved in the civil rights movement, because Dr. King went there in 1963. I think the story is going to be not only about the girls, it's also going to be about the historical event of Dr. King trying to break down the walls of segregation in Birmingham. That's my story. I haven't written anything down, but that's the idea." That's the second approach.

Third approach, the producer comes in, says, "I shot all this footage about the four girls killed in Birmingham. I'll be back in eight weeks; you let me see what there is—create something." I've done all types of documentaries, all three types.

In the case of *4 Little Girls*, Spike was like the third producer. He basically said, "I've got to do this story about these four girls; it's been in me about 15 years. I need to do this story." And he went down and he shot. He never really figured out what the arc of the story was, but he'd been carrying this story around with him so long—and his aesthetic is so artistic. He just knew he didn't want to make an ordinary-type documentary. Just not his style.

He came up with a list of people he wanted to interview, and after he shot for a month with the family members and people involved in the movement, we went into the editing room. For about three weeks, from 7 to 11 in the morning, we would screen dailies and talk. I came up with the idea of trying to do the parallel story. On one track we have the girls' lives unfolding; on the other we see the movement as it moves into Birmingham, and then they collide with the bombing of the church. And that's how we basically approached it.

One of the strengths of the film is the stories and storytellers, particularly Denise McNair's father, Chris.

They were good stories. But you know, it was interesting. I was on that shoot when he did Chris. This was like a feature shoot. Spike had a truck, he had tracks, he had dollies, he had all these lights. I said, "Jeez, what's all this equipment?" And Spike had done a lot of research, but when we got to the interview that day, he didn't have any questions on paper. I was sitting behind him, and I had my own sheet of questions. And I swear, I thought he was so haphazard in how he was asking questions; his style is, to me, so indirect. I thought, "He's not going to get anything good out of this guy." But Chris really connected with Spike; he was able to convey emotion and was such a good storyteller. Mrs. Robertson [Alpha Robertson, mother of Carole] was also a good storyteller. They'd been living with their children's deaths for so many years, and they had stored so much, probably, things they wanted to say. And they all trusted Spike.

From your own experience, how do you think filmmakers establish that kind of trust? I'm thinking, for example, of Big Black (Frank Smith), a former Attica inmate you interviewed for Eyes on the Prize.

You know, it's a funny thing. Sometimes when I interview people, there's a kind of connection where I feel like I'm with family. I feel just very open myself. I don't feel couched; I don't have anything to hide. And I think people feel that and connect. Sometimes, I don't feel that comfortable with the person I'm interviewing, and it comes through. I interviewed Nell Painter for this Jim Crow show. I didn't feel I had done my homework in terms of what questions to ask, and I never connected with her. Everything was very stiff.

What if you're interviewing someone whose views you strongly oppose?

You still try to be as human as possible. For *The Rise and Fall of Jim Crow*, I interviewed this white gentleman in Florida who, when he was 10 years old in Georgia, saw four black people killed. At first I said [to the other series producers, Richard Wormser and Bill Jersey, both of whom are white], "You want me to do the interview?" Because this guy was 70 years old, he's still a redneck; you can see it, he still carries that baggage. But somehow, when I sat down and interviewed him and really touched on some areas that were so painful for him to remember, and really understanding his ambiguous relationships with black people—this guy opened up to me.

The only person that we knew I wasn't going to interview was in northern Georgia, this gentleman named Gordon Parks [no relation to the filmmaker]. He tells a story in Bill Jersey's show, in show three, about how when he was 15, his grandfather took him to a lynching of a black man. And even now he's unrepentant. I mean, he's surrounded by young white guys who are Klansmen, he's still a Klansman.

How do you feel about projects where the footage is handed off to an editing team and the initial connection is lost? Someone like the old man in Florida could be treated very badly.

Mutilated. I've been fortunate enough to not yet have someone else take the footage that I've shot. I feel it's my responsibility to be the one to help shape their story, and tell that story in the editing room. If somebody in *Jim Crow* says, "Well, I never said it like that," then I'm the one they're going to have to deal with. It's a delicate thing. You have to make editorial adjustments, sometimes, to try to get the story across clearly, concisely—because it's always about trying to be concise. The problem is that most times when people do their interviews, they don't quite understand that they're going to be edited. I've had it happen so many times. Someone will look at the interview and say, "What happened to what I said? I talked to you for two hours and you used two minutes?"

How much of a story do you work out before you film?

With *T-Town*, I did a treatment, and then when I got back, before I gave the footage to [the editor], I worked out a complete structure, a 20-page template. With *Jim Crow*, basically, I had a 40-page fundraising script. When we went into the editing room, I followed the script, and when we looked at it, it was slow. Meandered. And then we went back and restructured, and then we looked at it again; it looked a little better. It's a process.

But the thing is, it's always better to have a foundation, a template. So you know you have something there in front of you. Most documentary filmmakers, even the students, go out and shoot and they don't have a clue what the story is. I mean, I'll do it. I've been trying to shoot something about my father, and even though I know I'm not doing it the right way, I'm still just going out and shooting. But I don't have any money, no deadlines, I don't feel constricted. When someone's paying me, before I start editing I will always write down the structure.

Do you look for a story arc?

I usually do. A transformation of a state of being. Sometimes I don't have to have a character take me through. And sometimes I can feel there's a sense of artifice. Part of me with Ali [a story about fighter Muhammad Ali, in *Eyes on the Prize*] always felt that—even though Ali's a great character, even though it's his real story—it feels a little jerry-rigged. It doesn't feel like it quite unfolds; it feels like you see the hands of the filmmakers moving the pieces. And that always throws me.

4 Little Girls begins in a cemetery, with Joan Baez's "Ballad of Birmingham" on the soundtrack relating the tragedy that's about to unfold. How do you feel about the need for a "hook" at the start of a film?

I have two feelings about it. Sometimes you've got to give them a hook right up front, like the bombing. Years ago, I did a film about Langston Hughes. We basically kill Langston off at the beginning. "He's a wonderful poet, but then he died." Then we backtrack and tell you the story. I always kind of liked that, that old movie thing. But I thought it was a mistake in retrospect; it underwhelmed the whole film, dramatically. Sometimes if you give them the hook up front, then when you build up to it again, you say, "Oh, I already know that." Sometimes the hook can be detrimental. In *4 Little Girls*, it wasn't. The reason we started with Joan Baez was because the song was so great. And Spike had had Ellen Kuras [the director of photography] shoot the cemetery footage in that very weird style. He didn't know it was going to be at the beginning, but he shot it.

How do you approach issues of balance in your work?

Even when we were doing *Eyes*, I always questioned that, having to get the opposing point of view to give you the balanced perspective. I think the word shouldn't be "balance." I think that if you interview people that have contradiction, that to me gives it a more textured perspective. In *4 Little Girls*, people said we took a cheap shot at [former Alabama governor] George Wallace. Well, I don't think so. He was not in the greatest health, as we know. But it wasn't like he had just been thrown the questions and didn't know what to say. He knew. Before he even consented to do the interview, Spike had to send him all the questions. And when I look at the outtakes—I put the whole outtake of the interview on the DVD—I really didn't cut that much out. So I didn't think we did him a disservice. It's a funny thing about people. Part of the reason George Wallace did the interview, I think, is because Spike Lee wanted to interview him.

What are the biggest storytelling issues your students face?

The biggest pitfall is understanding what their film's about right from the beginning. Before they sit down to write a page of the narration or script, what's the theme? And then on the theme, what's the story that they're going to convey to get across the theme?

For me, the theme of *Jim Crow* is how a people of color, who were given their freedom in 1863 with the Emancipation Proclamation, had to struggle mightily against tremendous odds to be able to find that window of opportunity, and the things they had to do on all levels to move themselves forward. Richard and Bill may have a different approach, but that to me was what it was always about. So the next step was to find the stories that were going to help convey that. What I liked about *Jim Crow* is that there's an ambiguity in these real-life characters. Look at Booker T. Washington. On the one hand, he's this great man who starts this wonderful school [in 1881] to help black people. On the other hand, he basically says to black people, "Don't try to go but so far; take it to a certain level but don't rock the boat." None of this is simple. I always believe that nothing is black and white, that it's textured, shades of grey. To me, if that comes through, we did our job.

How do you evaluate story ideas?

What makes an idea great for a documentary is if you're introducing me to a world I've never heard about, and there's some story within that world that's going to be new and attention-grabbing. A student of mine who's Muslim came to me; she was down in Trinidad one summer and shot all this footage, so she wanted me to take a look at it When you say Trinidad, my assumption, the first thing I think of, is Carnival. People in costumes dancing, having a good time; everybody's trying to do a film about Trinidad and Carnival. So I figure this is what she's going to show me.

She puts the footage up on the TV, and it's about a Muslim sect in Trinidad that's been in conflict with the government about being able to have freedom of choice in their own mosque, their own communities. Their government feels that they're like a terrorist group and they've been clamping down on them. There's been violent struggle, shootouts. So all of a sudden I'm saying, "Wow, this is interesting. I never knew there was a Muslim sect in Trinidad. I didn't know there was all this tension that's been going on for about 12 years." It's very interesting material for a documentary. Her problem is, she just went out and shot. Her father's Muslim, he knew about this group, introduced her to some people. Now she has no clue how to put the film together. What I said to her is, it's like doing the homework in a backwards way. You have to sit down and write down on paper, "What am I trying to say? What's the arc of this film?"

As a filmmaker, do you work to ensure that your storytelling is inclusive, that it covers voices and experiences that might not be readily available in archival material or secondary research?

I met filmmaker St. Clair Bourne in 1980, when I did his film about the blues in Chicago, *Big City Blues*. He basically became my mentor, in making me understand, as an African American, that the voice of "the other" is an important voice that has to be conveyed because you rarely hear or see it. Since that time, I've always believed strongly that, be it films about African Americans or Native Americans or Asians, women, it's important to be involved in those films. And if you're involved in a film that doesn't have that, you try to find that in the material.

Bennett Singer came to me a few years ago, wanted to do a documentary that I'm now executive producer of, *Brother Outsider: The Life of Bayard Rustin*. That to me was important. Not only because Rustin was so active in civil rights, but because he was a gay man who wasn't afraid to say that, no matter what the consequences. That probably drew me more to it than the fact that he was the main cog for the [1963] March on Washington.

The aftermath of hurricane Katrina, from *When the Levees Broke: A Requiem in Four Acts*. Photo credit David Lee, *40 Acres & A Mule*, courtesy of HBO.

With any documentary, music is an important part of the storytelling. At what point do you start to think about it?

All the time. I love music. You have to be a little careful because sometimes music can overwhelm the storytelling and undercut the drama of just letting the images play. Years ago, when we were doing the *Eyes* show, you were opposed to a piece of music, "Keep on Pushing," that we put in at the end of the Ali story. You thought it was going to detract from just listening to Ali and the narration. And I argued with you, "No, no, Sheila, you're wrong." But in retrospect, you were right. I watched that show recently—the music was too specific, too on the nose. You've always got to be careful about how you use music. I like it to be a little more indirect now, as I get older.

Tell me about your most recent collaboration with Spike Lee, When the Levees Broke, *which premiered on HBO in August 2006, a year after Hurricane Katrina. How did this film come about?*

We were driving downtown [in September 2005], and Spike says, "You know, Sam, I've got a great title: *When the Levees Broke.* I want to do a documentary about New Orleans." So that night, I did some research on the Internet and wrote some notes. And the next day, I said, "We could do a doc that looks at the complications and the evolution of the hurricane and the personal stories of the people who were there." So Spike called Sheila Nevins at HBO and set up a meeting.

When was your first shoot in New Orleans?

Thanksgiving. We went down with this mammoth crew of 25 people. Normally when you shoot a doc, it's you as the producer, camera, an assistant (if you're shooting film), sound, and maybe a PA [production assistant]. But when we flew out of Newark the day after Thanksgiving, it was Spike, me, a line producer, three cameramen, four assistants, and six graduate students from NYU. Then, when we got to New Orleans, we got a location manager with his four location people, five vans, five drivers, a camera loader—I mean, it was like an army. And Spike gave us our assignments: This crew goes to this parish, this crew goes here.

Spike returned to New Orleans several times, and also filmed evacuees in New York. I've read that there were about 130 interviews in all, some 200 hours of footage. I'm curious about your role, not only as supervising editor but also as co-producer.

Basically, my charge is to figure out how to make this thing a film. As with *4 Little Girls*, I'm given a task of combing through all this material and trying to figure out a structure to make it come to life. Spike will come in and critique it and want changes, but I'm trying to build it, trying to tell a story and figure out how to make it exciting. And I've got about 18, 20 weeks to make it happen.

When did you start to edit?

I brought on three assistants in February 2006 to start logging and digitizing the interviews, and they were all transcribed, and the assistants went through the transcript books and wrote down the time code numbers. Then I figured out what I call subject bins, such as *The Days before the Hurricane; The Day Katrina Hit; They Thought They Had Dodged the Bullet.* If anybody talked about one of those particular subjects, the assistants put that bite into that bin. And then when I started, on March 6, I started going through each bin, putting together all the interview bites and whittling them down, shaping them. I don't go but so far, because I know that as soon as I start to put footage in, which is the next stage, it'll change.

Do you draft a script on paper before you cut?

I don't usually do a paper cut; I'm more instinctual now. But I will write out a structure—where I want to start, how I want to get to the end. I sketch out scenes and what the order should be. Then I start adding footage and stills, assembling edited sequences. What happens in this process of building is that I'll see things from my paper structure that aren't working, so I start to move things around. And I'll go back through the transcripts sometimes, like when I need a way to transition to certain footage. And then when I show Spike a cut, he'll ask, "How come you didn't put this in; how come you didn't add this sequence?" So I'll go back and look at the material and rebuild.

Do you find that your subject pulls—those bins—stay intact as sequences?

Not always. For example, initially I had a *Superdome* subject bin. But I've opened up: One sequence is about when people first got to the Superdome, another is about people dealing with it after they were there for four days, and another is about people evacuating the Superdome. So it's broken up into different sections.

With 130 storytellers, isn't there a risk that the film will be a long montage, and not a coherent story that carries viewers through an experience?

That's the challenge. Everybody's got different pieces of the story, and someone who might be good at the beginning is not so good when it comes to talking about the evacuation. Someone who doesn't say much in the beginning is great when it comes to talking about the flooding. So I'm trying to find the rhythms of these people, to create a journey, an arc. I've noticed in a lot of sequences where we've tried to intercut people telling the same story, I've gone back and I've taken out some voices, to allow one person tell the story. If you find the right characters, the right interviews, they can give you a visceral sense of immediacy, of being there, so you feel emotionally connected to it. When this man tells you about finding his mother's body under the refrigerator, because she hadn't gotten out. . . . Or this woman whose daughter went to stay with her father in the Ninth Ward, and she couldn't find her and was having dreams that she was falling, falling, falling, and then a few months later they found her daughter's body. . . . That's powerful. You try to get out of the way, not to condense too much, edit it too much.

You also have a unique challenge in that the four-hour film will be shown in various configurations—as a four-hour special, in two 120-minute blocks, and as individual hours. How do you make each of those presentations feel complete?

I have a beginning, middle, and end for each hour, and we're also doing it by acts—my first hour is Act One, the second hour is Act Two, and so on. The first hour begins pre-Katrina and ends on people who were in the Superdome, who do anything—songs, games—to keep their spirits up. Act Two looks at the city in tremendous chaos, and the evacuation of people, and ends with all of these dead bodies. Act Three picks up with where the people landed, and what happened when they arrived there, and builds to the question of staying or coming back. And also deals with the psychic and emotional toll of the hurricane. The fourth act gets into what happened when people did come back, and rebuilding.

If each of the hours is an act, what is the overarching story?

A people under siege. One and Two are chronologically driven; Three and Four [edited by Geeta Gandbhir and Nancy Novack, who started in April] are more thematically driven.

How do you think your experience editing dramatic features impacts your work in documentary, and vice versa?

What we're involved in, always, is trying to tell a story. Before I became a producer in documentaries [in 1988, on *Eyes on the Prize*], I had edited a lot of docs, but I wasn't always thinking about how to tell a story and have it escalate dramatically and emotionally. That's something I learned from the irascible Henry Hampton [executive producer of *Eyes*, a series that used a three-act structure to tell historical stories]. And then right after, Spike called me about cutting *Mo' Better Blues*, and I've worked with him since on a series of narrative fiction features. What I've learned from both is to always make the story dramatic. Get the characters up a tree, how're we going to get 'em down? I apply three-act structure to everything. I don't always adhere to it as closely as we did on *Eyes*, but it's always in the back of my mind.

Last question. Given their cost, which is money that might be spent elsewhere, why do documentaries matter?

Being documentary filmmakers, I think part of our responsibility is to be able to make people aware of history: social history, racial history, economic history. Nine times out of 10, people can only deal with that history when it's in the past, 30 years, 40 years. Sometimes you've got to jolt people a little. Because if you don't deal with what's happening now, you're just going to repeat the same problems, which we can see now in New Orleans. I think, because of Spike, that this film will have tremendous impact. It will reawaken people's outrage and frustration at what happened last year in New Orleans. It's present history that needs to be considered, needs to be evaluated.

CHAPTER 24

Deborah Scranton

Deborah Scranton's first feature-length documentary, *The War Tapes*, won the award for Best Documentary at the 2006 Tribeca Film Festival and Best International Documentary at the 2006 BritDoc Festival, among many other honors. *The War Tapes* follows three National Guardsmen—Sergeant Steve Pink, Sergeant Zack Bazzi, and Specialist Mike Moriarty—during a tour of duty in Iraq that began in March 2004 and ended a year later. Scranton broke new ground by putting cameras in the hands of the soldiers themselves, training them as cinematographers and communicating with them through instant messages and e-mail. She and cinematographer P.H. O'Brien filmed the soldiers before, during, and for several months after their deployment, and also followed the women and families they left behind.

A New Hampshire–based filmmaker, Scranton had previously directed *Stories from Silence: Witness to War* (2003), the World War II remembrances of 47 veterans, including one woman, from the small farming community of Goshen. After *The War Tapes*, she produced, directed, and wrote *Bad Voodoo's War*, a 60-minute film commissioned by WGBH and ITVS, which premiered on the PBS series *Frontline* in 2008.

This interview was conducted in February 2010, about a month before it was announced that Scranton's second theatrical documentary, *Earth Made of Glass*, would have its world premiere in competition at the 2010 Tribeca Film Festival. Scranton describes the film as: "One man's fight for his family; one president's fight for his country. Though they never meet, Jean Pierre Sagahutu, an ordinary man, and the President of Rwanda, Paul Kagame, battle to uncover and expose the truth, each ultimately coming face to face with the same choice: to enact vengeance or turn the other cheek. . . ."

To start from the beginning: In February 2004, you received a call from the public affairs officer of the New Hampshire National Guard, Major Greg Heilshorn, asking if you'd be interested in embedding, as a filmmaker, during a tour of Iraq. And you came up with a novel alternative.

My background was working in televisions sports, like the Olympics, the Tour de France, big sports events, as well as doing a lot of adventure or extreme sports. And literally, the night I got the call, I woke up in the middle of the night with the idea: What if I could virtually embed? And what if I could cover a war as if you covered a sporting event? That sounds distasteful, but in the sense of: When you're covering a big event, one camera [isn't enough]. You can't film a football game with just one angle; you're going to have a very limited view. What if you could have a multicamera filming platform, which was the background I came from, and through that, try to tell the story of war?

And they agreed.

They gave me my pick of units, and I picked Charlie Company, 3rd of the 172nd, which is a mountain infantry unit, because infantry typically is like the "tip of the spear," as they say. And I knew that they were going to be based in Balad, in Anaconda [Camp Anaconda is a large U.S. military base near the Balad Airbase, about 40 miles north of Baghdad, located in the Sunni Triangle], and they would have Internet access. Because in order for this to work, I needed for them to be able to communicate with me. And don't forget, that was in '04, so cell phone use wasn't as common for communicating data. I wanted to be where their home base would have Internet access.

So I went down to Fort Dix [New Jersey], where they were training, getting ready for their deployment, and my caveat for the access was that I had to get the soldiers to volunteer. So I hopped out in front of the unit, like 130 guys, and told them what I wanted to do. And the commanding officer said, "Well, whoever is interested. . . ." They gave me a day room; I went in and had a further conversation for a few hours with the guys. Because by nature, I think, people in the military are skeptical of the media. They figure you've got an agenda. And I needed to make my case that I really wanted to know what it was through their eyes.

I mean, look: The war is often highly politicized, but soldiers rarely take part in that discussion. And my intent was to try to capture the experience of combat and everything that goes along with that: the fear, the boredom, the humor. What does it mean to be a soldier on the ground in Iraq, through the eyes of the soldiers themselves? I felt that was a voice that was really missing. Their experiences are important to understand, regardless of one's political beliefs. And I think often beliefs can be a way of avoiding looking at reality. People can stand behind their beliefs, and they disconnect. One of my major reasons for making the film was to try to help bridge that disconnect between those who know a soldier and those who don't. They're there (in Iraq and Afghanistan) in our name. Soldiers swear to uphold the Constitution of the United States. They don't swear fealty to an administration's policy.

I read in your press materials that 10 soldiers volunteered; five stayed with it for the entire year, and overall, 21 soldiers contributed. Each of those 10 was given a one-chip Sony MiniDV camera along with some microphones, lenses, and lots of blank tape. How did you prepare them to document their lives, to shoot in a way that would convey stories?

I think that's where the Internet really came in handy. Before they left, my cinematographer—P.H. O'Brien, a technical whiz—and I went down to Ft. Dix, and we talked them through different things, as far as framing, and you don't want to be backlit, and everything. And we came up with all these innovative things [for] mounting cameras on the dashboard, mounting them on the gun turrets, to have steady shots. So we did chest mounts and things that would have that stability. And they understood the basics—everybody, by and large in our society, has picked up a video camera. It was important not to inundate the guys too much; it was just basically to get them filming, and then we refined it as the process went on. Tapes on average took two weeks to get from Iraq to me, so it wasn't that long. We could see what they were doing, and send e-mails, and talk and make suggestions.

Dust was a real factor. We had some underwater housing that we used. It was always a fight against the sand. And the cameras would get blown off sometimes, so we had to have a steady supply of cameras. We'd cycle them from Iraq back here to New Hampshire; I'd get them serviced and send them back to them. We sort of had this round-robin of cameras going in and out at all times.

In 2007, you gave a presentation at the TED Conference in which you described this process, and the more than 3,200 e-mails, IMs, and text messages that went back and forth (and that's after you started keeping count). You talked about how you'd captured the scene in the film that follows the explosions at Al Taji, an airfield about 17 miles northwest of Baghdad. You wanted to be sure to get an immediate response—what the military calls "hot wash." Can you explain?

Yes. There's an incident in the film where there was a double VBIED, which stands for Vehicle-Borne Improvised Explosive Device (IED)—a word for a car bomb, basically. And there was a double VBIED outside the gates of Taji as Steve Pink's crew was getting ready to go out on a mission, and they responded to the call.

So how it worked was, Steve Pink had sent me an e-mail at the end of the day, and attached still photos of the burned body that was outside the car. And in the e-mail, Pink said that it had been a really bad day, and he told me a little bit about what had happened. I saw in one of my IM windows that Mike Moriarty was online. So I pinged Mike and I said, "Hey, Mike, I heard Pink's squad had a bad day today, and I wondered if you could go over and do an interview with him," because I wanted to get that interview within 24 hours. So what you see in the film is the actual film of the event as it unfolds, which is from Pink's camera; you see an interview done with Pink, that Mike Moriarty did within 24 hours; then you have audio from an interview that I did when Pink was home; combined with him reading his journal. (Several months after he came home, he felt comfortable enough to read his journal for me.) So it's all layered in there, this multifaceted perception of that event.

And that's what I talk about in the TED talk, [in part] because it illustrates what the process was for making the film, but also for the fact that we sometimes hear that soldiers are disappointed with the media, and that's a perfect example [of why]. Because you see the scene; it made the news; it made CNN; it was an event covered in the traditional media, but they didn't add one more line, which was: "And U.S. soldiers spent the entire day, at great risk to themselves, trying to save Iraqi lives." There were no U.S. soldiers outside the gate. Those were all Iraqis.

You've said that for you, "truth resides in contrasting ground level narratives—and amplifying the voices of the people truly involved."

Yes. I don't like narration-driven pieces. I think when you write and you have a narration in it, you're framing it. And it's true, what I chose to edit and include, that's also a framing device. But I feel that when you write and have a narrator, you have a point of view and you get sound bites to support that point of view, versus looking for different points of view and trying to put them together to share with the viewer this multifaceted perspective, which I think is much more representational of what reality is.

When you look at Rotten Tomatoes, for *The War Tapes* we have like a 98% rating, which very few films do, as far as people responding to it. That was very . . . gratifying is not the right word, but it felt good because it felt like we had done what we set out to do, which was share their voices. And people listened and responded.

This also means that you, as the filmmaker, are letting the contrasting narratives speak for themselves, and trusting audience members to make up their own minds.

Right. I think you have to have more faith in people. We grow up surrounded by stories; it's how we share meaning and create meaning and share experiences and build meaning. And I think that if you communicate different visceral experiences, then, in a way, you're opening a window so other people get to meet those people, versus having an agenda. I understand auteur-driven pieces. Somebody has a point of view and they have something to say. I just think that we need to hear more voices.

In all my interviews and in all my appearances, inevitably somebody would ask what my position on the war was. And I said I would never answer it in the context of Deborah Scranton, director of *The War Tapes*. If we were having dinner and we were having a conversation, of course I'm happy to have a conversation. But for me to go on the record and to say what my views were, it would diminish everything that the guys and I had done in making that film. The whole point was to try to share what their experiences were, and to amplify their voices.

You've said in other interviews that you were impressed as a student by works such as Let Us Now Praise Famous Men, *and the idea of living journalism.*

Those photos and that type of journalism just struck me as very honest and very true, and it didn't have an agenda. It was bearing witness to what people were experiencing at a very difficult time. And those were stories and pictures that the rest of society needed to see, to hopefully empathize and better understand and be aware of what reality is. It goes back to that whole thing of: Beliefs can be a way to avoid looking at reality. This is reality.

I'm curious about the logistics of it. This is a 94-minute film, made up of about 800 hours of footage that came back from the soldiers, plus about 200 more hours that you and your crew filmed with the men and their families here in the United States. I noticed, for example, that there were a lot of people credited as "loggers."

They were college students nearby. Basically, the guys [soldiers] had to roll a lot of tape, and there was a lot of empty tape with nothing happening. But if you're not rolling—they're not going to press "record" when they get into a firefight or an IED explodes. You have to hope the camera's rolling when that incident occurs. Right? The guys would tell me, "We got this firefight. It's on these tapes." So I knew which tapes had material that I definitely needed to go through with a fine tooth comb. But I wanted to make sure that we saw everything. So we watched everything and made sure that we noted [anything] that maybe would come in handy—it could have been a funny one-liner that they had just said. So the logs didn't necessarily have a lot, but even if one tape had one one-liner, I wanted it. Some logs were just like "driving in the desert..." and you'd know there was nothing on it. But I didn't want the guys to risk injuring the tape or recording over something. They would often ask me, "Should I just rewind and take the tape out again?" And I said, "No, send them to me."

Your film is only as good as your database of footage that you have. Because when you make a film, you have to think of it—or I think of it—as one giant puzzle. And you have to know all the pieces that you have. It's like painting a painting. You don't just paint with primary colors. You want all of your shades. You have to know where everything is. I use a database called Filemaker Pro, which is a searchable database. So something that comes in, that at first maybe you don't think could be important, later—because of something that happened—all of a sudden becomes very important. And you want to be able to find it. So logging is crucial.

I'm curious about the various collaborators involved. You got the initial call from the National Guard in February 2004, and by March the unit was headed to Iraq. At that point, you were only working with executive producer Chuck Lacy, is that right?

I had met Chuck, [who] is a former president of Ben & Jerry's. So he helped us get started financially, to be able to buy the cameras and to do this, and was instrumental in us getting started. So, we had been working on the project for eight months before I met Robert May.

So the guys were still over in Iraq at that point?

Yes. And we had cut a little trailer. Very often, when you produce a film, you've got to raise the money to do it. And typically, when you start out, you don't have anything to show. The big question is: "Are you going to get it? Are you going to be able to do it?" People aren't necessarily willing to take that risk; they want to see that you're already succeeding and that there's something there. So we had cut a 15-minute trailer and applied to go to the Sundance Producers Conference, and [there we] met a few different producers. Robert May, one of the executive producers of *The Fog of War*, watched it and decided that he was interested and wanted to help us produce it, help us raise the additional money.

And I read that Robert May connected you to Steve James, who came on board as a producer and editor, with Leslie Simmer. Can you talk about what you look for from an editor?

An editor has to have a very good background in story structure, in finding story and coming up with how scenes will come together. Any film is a collaboration; film by nature is a collaboration. You have to find people who are willing to go on the journey with you and to bring their eyes and ears to the project.

Before I agreed to bring Robert or Steve onto the project, I vetted them quite rigorously, because I didn't want anybody involved in the project that was going to try to insert a political bias into it. That was very important to me, because I had given my word to the soldiers that we would tell the story through their eyes, and the footage wouldn't be taken and made into something that had a bias.

You edited for about a year, and as part of that, chose to focus on just three of the original 10 soldiers: Pink, Bazzi, and Moriarty. Why?

We ended up picking the three most divergent stories, in the sense of what they represented. We had done some test screenings with more soldiers [in the film], and we got audience comments that they couldn't tell the soldiers apart. It was quite disconcerting. But on the other hand, I can understand what they're saying. And I prefer to go very personal, character-driven: people really do get into their lives. So in the end, I think it served the film best. And that informed [my decision], when I made the *Frontline, Bad Voodoo's War*, to just work with one platoon [30–35 soldiers, rather than a whole unit] and one main character, the Platoon Leader SGT Toby Nunn. We had 12 cameras filming in that one platoon. I felt there would be more of a chance for these different intersections because they were all out on the same missions together. We could gang more cameras together and get an even more intimate view.

As you approach the editing, do you work at all on paper, like with an outline?

I do colored index cards. So I have different colored index cards by character, and I put it out on a wall, and I move them around.

So you've mapped out when, for example, you want to come back to the firefight that you opened the film with, at Fallujah.

Right. I knew it had to come in later, because it happened in November 2004; it was the second siege of Fallujah. The actual timeline of events definitely informs it. You just don't know how fast— the second act can be pretty big. And then you have to pick what your climax is, what is *the* moment of the movie. Which in the case of *The War Tapes* was the tragic scene of Moriarty's squad hitting and killing the civilian woman by accident.

Did you screen The War Tapes *for the soldiers and their families before it was released?*

We did a screening, and they could comment on their section. It's really important for me to say if you feel that you've been represented accurately. I think it's always hard for people to see themselves distilled on film; I don't think it's easy for anybody to do that. And I think it takes a lot of courage to be willing to share your story. For *Bad Voodoo's War*, for instance, the whole reason that Toby Nunn, the main character, agreed to work with me on the film was because on his prior tour, one of the guys on his squad, Jake Demand, had been killed, and no one had told his story.

Let's move on to Bad Voodoo's War, *a one-hour film that you made for the PBS series* Frontline. *The film is similar in that it is also a "virtual embed," but as you noted, it follows a single platoon; also, you're present in the film, both as narrator and as your process of directing is seen.*

The whole reason to do *Bad Voodoo's War*—the war had changed, it was around the time of the surge, and the whole reason for it was [to] see what that meant for those guys. *Frontline* was adamant that my process and what I do be part of the story. I think they were interested in the step beyond, the "2.0" of *The War Tapes*—to make it even tighter and more intimate, and to show the process more. And I came to see what their point was, because it added a layer to the story that wouldn't have been there otherwise. So in the end, I was grateful that they pushed for that inclusion, but it was not my idea.

Were there any technology changes that made a difference in how you worked?

With *Bad Voodoo's War*, we could do stuff over iChat, so that I could listen, which you see in the film. I could be listening while Toby was doing an interview of one of the guys. So it was as if I was in their tent with them, listening to the interview. I would say both of these films aren't *about* the Internet, but neither of them could have been made without it. The Internet allowed the soldiers (in *The War Tapes*) and Toby (in *Bad Voodoo's War*) and me to talk about what happened, and to examine how to best tell the story as it unfolds.

Which is remarkable when you consider, as you've noted, that the first live reporting from battlefields didn't occur until the first Gulf War (1990–1991).

Right, on CNN. Now, if you look at the London bombings (in 2005), that's the Nokia effect. That's on cell phones. The Green Party in Iran, with the death of Neda [Agha-Soltan, in 2009], that was all [reported] by cell phone and cameras. And I think that speaks again to the ground truth, again away from some of that narrator-driven information. It's irrefutable. This is what's unfolding on the ground right here. It's not necessarily a summation of everything, but it's like "This is true right here. You can't deny this."

Do we need to be concerned about a lack of training in ethical journalism? There are things one can do with visual images and sounds that are not honest.

Right. But I think some journalists have been doing that for years too.

So how do you impart the guidelines of what's good citizen journalism?

You have to stick to the truth. You have to decide what truth you're telling, whose truth, whose voice, what stories you want to share, and then you have to be true to it. I don't believe in objectivity. I think that we're all shaped by the experiences of our lives, and we bring all of that to it, and anybody who says they're objective, I just flat out don't believe. My personal belief is, you have to decide whose story you're going to tell.

Very often in Q&A's I'd get asked, for *The War Tapes*, why didn't I tell the other side of the story. That wasn't the story I said I could tell. I could recommend other films that told the Iraqi perspective, and they're wonderful films. But you can't tell the entire story in a 90-minute film—any story.

And it's very transparent what story you're telling, whose story, and how.

I think a film can be really illuminating when you construct it in this multifaceted framework. You see these things unfold in real time; you hear their reflections and their perceptions of what the experiences were like for them within 24 hours; and then you hear the words after they've had a few months to process it out, and time has kind of weathered the edges around it. For me, that as a style is a really, really important way to see the world through someone else's eyes.

Sound plays a big role in these films. I'm thinking of The War Tapes, *especially. Before you even see the opening image of the battle in Fallujah, you hear a man breathing heavily. There's a heartbeat to the way sound and music are used in the film.*

There was a lot of audio work done on the film. Those small cameras don't have the best audio function. We re-layed every single bullet under that film, to make sure that it [was heard]. We wanted a visceral experience; we wanted it to sound like you were there. We didn't add anything artificial, putting stuff in that wasn't there. It was just making sure that when you're in the theater, [you get] the feeling of what it was like to be there. For instance, when you see the shots of the guys up in the turret, what they kept talking about to me was the wind;

they kept feeling the wind. So I wanted to make sure that when you see the film, you'll [hear] the different wind tones when the guys are up in the turret, because that's what they said they heard. And it was certainly windy up there.

Can you talk about your relationship with the military, in terms of access? Don't most audiences assume you were carefully watched, if not censored?

The access that I got [for *The War Tapes*] was from the New Hampshire National Guard, and they were very committed that the story be told, so they didn't hold back. People are stunned, but that was a fact. Look, it's all based on trust and relationships. If you're not good at establishing trust and building relationships, you're never going to be a good filmmaker. You earn your trust day after day. In order for [the soldiers] to film that much, they had to trust me and not self-edit. They had to be able to be vulnerable, and know that I wasn't going to take advantage of that vulnerability and make them look stupid. We could all be filmed and somebody could cut it and make us look like bad people. So it all comes down to trust and relationships and being a person of your word. And I think it may have been helpful that I'm not, at this point in time—nothing against being New York- or LA-based, but it's not like I was some slick producer coming in who didn't know anybody. These guys are my neighbors. I live here. I'm not going to take them out of context. I understand their world, and I'm not going to make them, on purpose, look bad. On the other hand, they were very clear that I wasn't going to make them look good either. They just wanted a fair shot. They just wanted somebody to say the truth.

Production on The War Tapes *began with a basic narrative arc: the year of deployment. Beyond that, how did the shape of this film, its story, emerge from all of those hours of footage? Steve James is quoted as saying, "If the story we ended up with works, it should seem obvious and self-evident. But, believe me, it wasn't."*

The story emerges from within, and it sort of becomes obvious. You know when you look at it—as it's unfolding, when a monumental moment happens—you know for sure that that's one of your main story points. You may not know what act it's going to be in, but you know. That's where the puzzle part comes in. And the art is in how you link those, and what you butt up against each other for whatever effect you want. I enjoy that process.

Do you consciously work with act structure?

Yes. I work in scenes. You know when you have a scene: For instance, when [the convoy] hit and killed the civilian woman, that was a scene that was going to be in the movie, so we could cut that scene. The double car bombing outside of Taji, I knew that was a scene. Mike Moriarty had told me endlessly about that vehicle graveyard and how he found it so haunting. When I got that in and looked at it and heard the commentary, I knew that was a scene. So you sort of fill it out. And then you start seeing who your character is, and how you've come to know them, and make sure that you have on film the different aspects of a person that they are, that you can share with the audience their strengths, their vulnerabilities, their fears, their hope. So it's all a big hero's journey: Set up the premise, the characters, situations and relationships, the confrontation. They've got to encounter the obstacles, the dramatic need, and the resolution, which doesn't necessarily mean the end. It's got to have a beginning, middle, end. Was it Godard who said, not necessarily in that order?

For me with *The War Tapes*, probably one of my most influential films—well, there's two of them. One was a movie called *Before the Rain* by a Macedonian director called Milcho Manchevski. It won at Venice. And it tells the story in a circle, which is why I wanted to open the film up with the firefight in Fallujah and go back to it again. Because sometimes you think you see one thing, but then when you come back around, you have a different understanding and a greater context for what world you're actually in. And then the other one was *Black Hawk Down*, where I think Ridley Scott did an amazing job at showing the two different worlds: the world on the ground and the world of the U.S. soldiers, and how isolated they were from each other. As well as the *Iliad* and the *Odyssey*, the two greatest books ever written. I think all stories, no matter what, it's a hero's journey. You take a flawed hero; they're on their path, and you want to go with them on the journey and see where they end up.

I film my docs like dramatic [films]; one of my favorite books is *The Screenwriter's Bible*, by David Trottier. Without a strong story structure, you don't have a movie. For me, making a film is kind of like a diamond shape. You start out, you think, "Okay, this is where we're going," and then you'll reach a point in production (and almost every filmmaker I've talked to has this experience) where you feel, "Uh oh, I have something here but it's not what I thought I was going to have." At that moment, you have to trust in the story itself, that it *will* become clear and come back down again to the other end. You can't force it, and you shouldn't try to superimpose something on it. You just have to listen. Just simply listen.

The story is a living, breathing thing. You have to be informed by what you're finding; it's a constant refining process. But in that process, you have to be aware, you have to have a structure to hang it on. So you have to be thinking: "What are the inciting incidents? What am I going to use for that? And then if I use this one, what am I going to need to follow up? If I use that one, what am I going to need to follow up?" Because what you don't want is to end up in the editing room with not enough of the needed material to tell the story you've chosen to tell. That's the other reason why I always start editing my films two-thirds of the way into my shooting, so that if I find that I need something, I'm still shooting.

So it's flexible but not spontaneous. Before you go out, you have a suggestion of a narrative—

Or a question you're trying to answer, and you don't know who's going to give you the answer. So for Rwanda it was: "What happens after war ends?" That was my question. We still have all these areas of conflict around the world that are locked in cycles of violence and retribution. Rwanda charted a different path, different from South Africa, different from anywhere in the world. And they're having success at it. So what does that mean? What does forgiveness mean? What I found so interesting was that it's a different definition of forgiveness than I've ever seen articulated, which was basically a decision made to stop the cycle of violence in this generation, and at great sacrifice to themselves. That they will not teach or perpetuate hatred to their children, regardless of the incalculable brutal losses that they suffered. Fascinating.

But if I had gone in there saying, "Oh, I want to find someone who has said, 'I totally forgive and love who did this. . . .'" I didn't go in with an agenda. I really wanted to find out, "What is really going on here?" I don't want them to tell me what they *think* I want to hear. What *really* is going on there?

Jean Pierre Sagahutu (l) and Gaspard Bavuriki (r), in *Earth Made of Glass,* © 2010 Sparks Rising LLC.

So we set out to make this film about what happens after war ends, and forgiveness. And as we're about to touch down, France arrested Rwanda's chief of protocol, Rose Kabuye, on terrorism charges. Three months earlier, on August 6th, 2008—against the backdrop of the world's deadliest war in neighboring Eastern Congo—Rwandan President Paul Kagame had released a report detailing the French government's hidden role in planning the 1994 Rwandan genocide. Rose Kabuye was his closest aide. So all of a sudden we end up in a whole different world. And it basically was Rwanda taking on France to expose the truth about what really happened in Rwanda, which was France's active complicity in the genocide. A million people died in three months. The world was told one story, and the truth was buried.

So it's a president's search for truth for his country. And then it's a genocide survivor's search for his father's killer, a very personal story, and the choice of what he does and what he teaches his children. And we find one of his father's killers. So you see it unfold. That's what I mean when I say it's a documentary, but it's filmed as if it was a narrative, because it has those scenes. Instead of a talking head telling you what happened, it's built in scenes.

For *Bad Voodoo's War*, the story was about the dread of being attacked. It was the tension of wondering if today was the day. And the decision for *Bad Voodoo's War* was: end it with them going back [returning to Iraq after a mid-tour break]. That was really important to me, that the film end with them going back, because we're still there. I didn't want to make another film that brought the guys home, because those guys may be home but others are sent in their place. The viewer response to *Bad Voodoo* was off the charts. It crashed the server twice, as far as viewers writing in. There are some amazing comments, people's reactions. And that was really important to me, because I didn't want to let the audience off the hook. Guys are still there.

PART IV

Additional Material

Sources and Notes

In most cases, quotations in this book are drawn from interviews conducted by the author during preparation for the first, second, and third editions. These include conversations with Michael Ambrosino, Paula Apsell, Steven Ascher, Ronald Blumer, Liane Brandon, Victoria Bruce, Ric Burns, Gail Dolgin, Jon Else, Boyd Estus, Nick Fraser, Susan Froemke, Alex Gibney, Jim Gilmore, Karin Hayes, Susan Kim, James Marsh, Muffie Meyer, Hans Otto Nicolayssen, Sam Pollard, Kenn Rabin, Per Saari, Deborah Scranton, Susanne Simpson, Bennett Singer, Holly Stadtler, Tracy Heather Strain, Melanie Wallace, and Onyekachi Wambu. Additional information about films and filmmakers was taken as noted from a range of sources, including information provided by the filmmakers themselves through their official websites and press material and in material included on their DVDs.

Throughout this book (and all previous editions), attention has been paid to not only effective but also ethical uses of storytelling to enhance the power and appeal of documentary films. In September 2009, the Center for Social Media—the group responsible for *The Filmmakers' Statement of Best Practices in Fair Use*—published *Honest Truths: Documentary Filmmakers on Ethical Challenges in Their Work*. The report is the beginning of an important conversation that is only now getting under way, in which filmmakers share their experiences and thoughts on their ethical responsibilities to their audiences and their subjects. Written by Patricia Aufderheide, Peter Jaszi, and Mridu Chandra, the report, which was funded by The Ford Foundation, is based on interviews with 41 directors or producer-directors. Jon Else, Bill Nichols, and I served as advisors. The report is available online at www.centerforsocialmedia.org/ethics.

Chapter 1, Introduction: For additional information on current trends in documentary, see for example Paul Arthur, "Extreme Makeover: The Changing Face of Documentary" and Pat Aufderheide's "The Changing Documentary Marketplace," both in *Cineaste*, Summer 2005. Definition of documentary, in Erik Barnouw, *Documentary: A History of the Non-fiction Film* (New York: Oxford University Press, 1974). Information about creative nonfiction from Philip Gerard's *Creative Nonfiction: Researching and Crafting Stories of Real Life* (Cincinnati: Writer's Digest Books, 1996). Information about

DOI: 10.1016/B978-0-240-81241-0.00032-0

the WGA documentary screenwriting awards can be found at www
.wga.org/awards/awardssub.aspx?id=2946#doc. Films must have
been shown theatrically in New York or Los Angeles for at least a
week during the nomination year, but scripts do not need to be
written under WGA jurisdiction. Credited writers submitted for
consideration "must be or apply to become members of the WGAW
Nonfiction Writers Caucus or the WGAE Nonfiction Writers
Committee."

Chapter 2, Story Basics: Story elements from David Howard and
Edward Mabley, *The Tools of Screenwriting* (New York: St. Martin's
Press, 1993).

Chapter 3, Finding the Story: Gerald Peary's interview with Frederick
Wiseman (*Boston Phoenix*, March 1998) can be found at www
.geraldpeary.com/interviews/wxyz/wiseman.html. Additional information on Frederick Wiseman and his films can be found at his
website, www.zipporah.com. Information on *Sound and Fury* available at www.nextwavefilms.com/sf/joshnotes.html. Information
on *Capturing the Friedmans* is available at www.hbo.com/docs/
programs/friedmans/interview.html.

Chapter 4, Story Structure: Reference to Robert McKee, *Story* (New
York: HarperCollins, 1997). George M. Cohan reference in Wells
Root, *Writing the Script* (New York: Holt, Rinehart and Winston,
1987). Reference to Madison Smart Bell, *Narrative Design* (New
York: W.W. Norton & Co., 1997). David Mamet, *On Directing Film*,
pages xiv, xv (New York: Penguin Books, 1991). *Lalee's Kin* is available
through Films Media Group, http://ffh.films.com/search.aspx?
q=Lalee. The interview with Michael Glawogger was conducted at
the Venice Film Festival on September 4, 2005 by Ginu Kamani, and
is reproduced in the film's online press materials at www
.workingmansdeath.at/main_interview_en.html. To watch *City of
Cranes*, which is included by Channel 4 in "16 short docs to watch
before you make one," see www.4docs.org.uk/films/view/17/
City+of+Cranes. The film can also be viewed online at the website
for the PBS independent series *POV*, www.pbs.org/pov/cityofcranes/.
The film's official website is www.cityofcranes.com/. More information
about *Betty Tells Her Story* can be found at www.newday.com/films/
Betty_Tells_Her_Story.html.

Chapter 5, Time on Screen: Harlan Jacobson, "Michael & Me," *Film
Comment*, Nov/Dec 1989.

Chapter 6, Creative Approach: Aufderheide, Patricia. *Documentary
Film: A Very Short Introduction*. New York: Oxford University

Press, 2007. Information on *The Sweetest Sound* can be found at www
.alanberliner.com. Information about *The Fog of War* is available at
www.sonyclassics.com/fogofwar/_media/pdf/pressReleaseFOG.pdf.
Discussion of *Eyes on the Prize* comes in part from my own involvement
as a producer/director/writer. Ken Burns' comments on *The Civil War* in
Sean B. Dolan, ed. *Telling the Story: The Media, The Public and American
History* (Boston: New England Foundation for the Humanities, 1994).
Information about Maysles Films is available at www.mayslesfilms
.com/company_pages/maysles_productions/history.html.

Chapter 7, Case Studies: Prose, Francine. *Reading Like a Writer*
(New York: Harper Perennial, 2007). Transcripts and additional information about *Daughter from Danang* can be found at the *American
Experience* website, www.pbs.org/wgbh/amex/daughter/filmmore/
pt.html; also see the film website, www.daughterfromdanang.
com. Press material and general information about *Murderball* can
be found at www.murderballmovie.com; see also information on
Participant Production's "Get into the Game" outreach campaign,
http://participate.net/getintothegame. The official website for *Super
Size Me* is www.supersizeme.com. Information about documentary
box office can be found at http://documentaries.about.com/od/
basics/tp/top10gross.htm, which as of July 2006 put *Super Size Me*
in seventh place; a second source, www.documentaryfilms.net/
index.php/documentary-box-office/, also as of July 2006, listed
the film in sixth place.

Chapter 8, Research: Jason Silverman's interview with Alan Berliner
can be read at www.pbs.org/pov2001/thesweetestsound/thefilm
.html; see also www.alanberliner.com. The Jay Rosenblatt press
material and other information about the filmmaker can be found
at www.jayrosenblattfilms.com. The discussion of *Miss America*
comes from my own involvement with the film's development.
The U.C. Berkeley Library offers some guidelines for evaluating
web pages; see www.lib.berkeley.edu/TeachingLib/Guides/Internet/
Evaluate.html.

Chapter 10, Selling: Note that these *American Experience* guidelines
refer to "films in production or at rough cut." It was never our intent
to actually submit program ideas to that series. For a discussion of
artistic license with fictionalized drama based on real events, see for
example Linda Seger, *The Art of Adaptation: Turning Fact and Fiction
into Film* (New York: Henry Holt and Co., 1992). If you are planning
to submit a proposal for funding consideration, it's sometimes possible to ask the funder for examples of successful submissions.

Chapter 11, Shooting: Information about *Winged Migration* is available at www.sonyclassics.com/wingedmigration/_media/_presskit/presskit/pdf. Information about *My Architect* is available at www.myarchitectfilm.com and at www.hbo.com/docs/programs/myarchitect/index.html. Additional information for *Betty Tells Her Story* is available through its distributor, New Day Films, www.newday.com. For more information on Errol Morris's *Interrotron*™, see Morris's website, www.errolmorris.com.

Chapter 14, Storytelling: A Checklist: Credit and thanks are due to Steve Fayer and Jon Else, who created earlier versions of this list for the producers at Blackside, Inc., in Boston.

Chapter 15, Steven Ascher and Jeanne Jordan: The filmmakers' website is www.westcityfilms.com. Goldy Moldavsky reviewed *The Filmmaker's Handbook* in "30 Quintessential Books for Independent Filmmakers," *The Independent*, October 6, 2009; see www.independent-magazine.org/magazine/2009/10/bestbooks.

Chapter 16, Victoria Bruce and Karin Hayes: The filmmakers' websites are www.urcuninafilms.com and www.pipandzastrow.com. For additional information on *The Kidnapping of Ingrid Betancourt*, see also www.wmm.com/filmcatalog/pages/c625.shtml, and www.cinemax.com/reel/ingrid_betancourt/interview.html.

Chapter 17, Ric Burns: Ric Burns' website is http://www.ricburns.com. Information about *New York* can be found at www.pbs.org/wnet/newyork/ (episodes 1–7), and www.pbs.org/wgbh/amex/newyork/ (episode 8). Information and transcripts for many of his films (search by title) can also be found at the *American Experience* website.

Chapter 18, Brett Culp: Examples of Brett Culp's work can be found at his website, www.brettculp.com.

Chapter 19, Nick Fraser: D.H. Lawrence, "Never trust the artist. Trust the tale." In Lawrence's *Studies in Classic American Literature* (1923), available online. Information about *Storyville* and many of the films discussed can be found at www.bbc.co.uk/bbcfour/documentaries/storyville.

Chapter 20, Alex Gibney: The website for Gibney's company is www.jigsawprods.com. The official website for *Gonzo: The Life and Work of Dr. Hunter S. Thompson* is www.huntersthompsonmovie.com. The website for *Taxi to the Dark Side* is www.taxitothedarkside.com; information can also be found at www.pbs.org/independentlens/enron/film.html. Information on *Casino Jack and the United States of Money* can be found at www.participantmedia.com/films/

coming_soon/casino_jack_the_united_states.php. For more information on *Taxi to the Dark Side*, see also Tim Golden, "In U.S. Report, Brutal Details of 2 Afghan Inmates' Deaths," *The New York Times*, May 20, 2005, online at www.nytimes.com/2005/05/20/international/asia/20abuse.html. Interview with Alex Gibney on Gonzo by Alex Leo, "The Gonzo World of Alex Gibney," *The Huffington Post*, posted July 3, 2008, www.huffingtonpost.com/alex-leo/the-gonzo-world-of-alex-g_b_110695.html.

Chapter 21, Susan Kim: Information about *Imaginary Witness: Hollywood and the Holocaust* can be found at http://www.ankerproductions.com/imaginary/. Susan Kim's Amazon.com author page is at www.amazon.com/Susan-Kim/e/B002MA0V78. The segment of Hanna Bloch Kohner on *This Is Your Life* (aired May 27, 1953) can be viewed online at the Internet Archive (a terrific resource for documentary filmmakers to know about), www.archive.org; the segment is at www.archive.org/details/this_is_your_life_hanna_bloch_kohner.

Chapter 22, James Marsh: The website for *Man on Wire* is www.manonwire.com. A.O. Scott's movie review, *Walking on Air Between the Towers*, was published in *The New York Times* on July 25, 2008, and can be viewed online at http://movies.nytimes.com/2008/07/25/movies/25wire.html. Information about the BBC *Red Riding* trilogy can be found at http://news.bbc.co.uk/newsbeat/hi/entertainment/newsid_7923000/7923556.stm.

Chapter 23, Sam Pollard: Information on *When the Levees Broke* is available at www.hbo.com/docs/programs/whentheleveesbroke/index.html. Information on *The Rise and Fall of Jim Crow* is available at www.pbs.org/wnet/jimcrow/. Information on the classes offered at NYU can be found at http://filmtv.tisch.nyu.edu. *Fundamentals of Sight and Sound: Documentary* "teaches students to look at their world and to develop the ability to create compelling and dramatic stories in which real people are the characters and real life is the plot. Through close study and analysis of feature length and short documentaries, and hands-on directing, shooting, sound-recording, editing and re-editing, students will rigorously explore the possibilities and the power of non-fiction story telling for film and video. The course is a dynamic combination of individual and group production work, in which each student will be expected to complete five projects."

Chapter 24, Deborah Scranton: TED is a nonprofit that brings people from technology, entertainment, and design together to share ideas. The conference is held annually in Long Beach, California. Scranton's talk, filmed in March 2007, can be viewed online at www.ted.com/talks/lang/eng/deborah_scranton_on_her_war_tapes.html. Scranton quote from an online discussion with her, conducted April 2, 2008, following the PBS broadcast of *Bad Voodoo's War*. Published online at www.washingtonpost.com. Rotten Tomatoes (<www.rottentomatoes.com>) gathers reviews from a selected pool of sources, including some media outlets and online film societies, and merges ratings and other data into a single measurement, the "Tomatometer." With 64 reviews counted, *The War Tapes* scored a 98% on this meter. The Sundance Institute's Independent Producers Conference evolved in 2009 into the Sundance Creative Producing Summit. Held annually, the gathering is now an invitation-only event. For more information, go to www.sundance.org/press_subgen.html?articleID=12&colorCode=. *Bad Voodoo's War* premiered on *Frontline* on April 1, 2008, and as of this writing can be viewed online at www.pbs.org/wgbh/pages/frontline/badvoodoo/. See Milcho Mancevski's website for information, www.manchevski.com. *Before the Rain* is a dramatic feature that won numerous awards at the 1994 Venice International Film Festival. The film was released on DVD in 2008; the screenplay is available at the website. For information on *Black Hawk Down*, a dramatic feature released in 2001, see www.sonypictures.com/homevideo/blackhawkdown/.

Films

Many documentaries, including not only recent releases but also classics from previous decades, are now available through online vendors such as Amazon, Netflix, Intelliflix, and such, and/or through the channels on which they aired (such as PBS or National Geographic). Some of this work is also legitimately made available for free viewing online, either through commercial sites such as Hulu.com or through public broadcasting venues, such as the BBC or PBS. Please do not use or condone the use of pirate sites.

Through the web, readers may be able to find information about specific films, including official press kits, teachers' guides, and outreach plans. This is especially true for theatrically released documentaries. Otherwise, be careful of web-based information about films and filmmakers. IMDB, for example, is a user-generated site, and as such the information it contains may not be accurate, complete, or up to date. Wikipedia, for the same reasons, is not a reliable source.

Transcripts and other useful materials are available online for many documentaries that have been shown on U.S. public television, including *American Experience* (a historical series, www.pbs.org/wgbh/amex/), *Nova* (science, www.pbs.org/wgbh/nova/), and *Frontline* (current affairs, www.pbs.org/wgbh/frontline/). These can be very useful as a reference while watching and analyzing story and structure.

Alexander Hamilton: Produced and directed by Muffie Meyer; co-produced and written by Ronald Blumer; co-produced and edited by Sharon Sachs and Eric Seuel Davies.

Bad Voodoo's War: Produced, directed, and written by Deborah Scranton. Co-produced by P.H. O'Brien and Seth Bomse; edited by Seth Bomse.

Balseros: Produced by Loris Omedes; directed by Josep Ma Doménech and Carles Bosch; scripts by David Trueba and Carles Bosch; edited by Ernest Blasi.

Betty Tells Her Story: Produced, directed, and edited by Liane Brandon. This film is distributed by New Day Films, www.newday.com/films/Betty_Tells_Her_Story.html.

Blue Vinyl: Produced by Daniel B. Gold, Judith Helfand, and Julia D. Parker; directed by Judith Helfand and Daniel B. Gold; edited by Sari Gilman.

Born into Brothels: Produced and directed by Ross Kauffman and Zana Briski; edited by Nancy Baker and Ross Kauffman.

Bowling for Columbine: Produced, directed, and written by Michael Moore; additional producers, Kathleen Glynn, Jim Czarnecki, Charles Bishop, and Michael Donovan; edited by Kurt Engfehr.

The Boys of Baraka: Produced and directed by Heidi Ewing and Rachel Grady; edited by Enat Sidi.

A Brief History of Time: Produced by David Hickman, Gordon Freedman, and Kory Johnston; directed by Errol Morris; edited by Brad Fuller.

Brother Outsider: The Life of Bayard Rustin: Produced and directed by Bennett Singer and Nancy Kates; edited by Veronica Selver and Rhonda Collins.

Building the Alaska Highway. Produced and directed by Tracy Heather Strain; co-produced, written, and edited by Randall MacLowry.

Cadillac Desert: Hours 1–3 produced, directed, and written by Jon Else; based on Marc Reisner's book, *Cadillac Desert*; Hour 4 produced and directed by Linda Harrar; based on Sandra Postel's book, *Last Oasis*.

Capturing the Friedmans. Produced by Andrew Jarecki and Marc Smerling; directed by Andrew Jarecki; edited by Richard Hankin.

Casino Jack and the United States of Money: Produced by Alex Gibney, Alison Ellwood, and Zena Barakat; directed and written by Alex Gibney; edited by Alison Ellwood.

City of Cranes: Produced by Samantha Zarzosa; directed by Eva Weber; edited by Emiliano Battista and Ariadna Fatjó-Vilas.

The Civil War: Produced by Ken Burns and Ric Burns; directed by Ken Burns; written by Geoffrey C. Ward and Ric Burns, with Ken Burns; edited by Paul Barnes, Bruce Shaw, and Tricia Reidy.

Control Room: Produced by Hani Salama and Rosadel Varela; directed by Jehane Nounaim; edited by Julia Bacha, Lilah Bankier, and Charles Marquardt.

The Cove: Produced by Fisher Stevens and Paula DuPré Pesmen; directed by Louie Psihoyos; written by Mark Monroe; edited by Geoffrey Richman.

Culloden: Produced, written, and directed by Peter Watkins; edited by Michael Bradsell.

Darwin's Nightmare: Produced by Edouard Maruiat, Antonin Svoboda, Martin Gschlacht, Barbara Albert, Hubert Toint, and Hubert Sauper; directed and written by Hubert Sauper; edited by Denise Vindevogel.

Daughter from Danang: Produced by Gail Dolgin; directed by Gail Dolgin and Vicente Franco; edited by Kim Roberts.

The Day After Trinity: J. Robert Oppenheimer & The Atomic Bomb: Produced and directed by Jon Else; written by David Peoples, Janet Peoples, and Jon Else; edited by David Peoples and Ralph Wikk.

A Decent Factory: Produced by Thomas Balmès and Kaarle Aho. Directed and written by Thomas Balmès.

Deliver Us from Evil: Produced by Amy Berg, Hermas Lassalle, and Frank Donner; directed and written by Amy Berg; edited by Matthew Cooke.

The Donner Party: Produced by Lisa Ades and Ric Burns; directed and written by Ric Burns; edited by Bruce Shaw.

Earth Made of Glass: Produced and written by Reid Carolin and Deborah Scranton; directed by Deborah Scranton; edited by Seth Bomse.

Enron: The Smartest Guys in the Room: Produced by Alex Gibney, Jason Kliot, and Susan Motamed; directed and written by Alex Gibney; edited and co-produced by Alison Ellwood.

Eugene O'Neill: Produced by Marilyn Ness and Steve Rivo, with Robin Espinola and Mary Recine; directed by Ric Burns; written by Arthur Gelb, Barbara Gelb, and Ric Burns; edited by Li-Shin Yu.

The Execution of Wanda Jean: Produced by Liz Garbus and Rory Kennedy; directed by Liz Garbus.

Eyes on the Prize: America's Civil Rights Years (hours 1–6): Produced by Orlando Bagwell, Callie Crossley, James A. DeVinney, and Judith Vecchione; edited by Daniel Eisenberg, Jeanne Jordan, and Charles Scott; series writer, Steve Fayer; executive producer, Henry Hampton.

Eyes on the Prize: America at the Racial Crossroads (hours 7–14): Produced by Sheila Bernard, Carroll Blue, James A. DeVinney, Madison Davis Lacy, Jr., Louis J. Massiah, Thomas Ott, Samuel Pollard, Terry Kay Rockefeller, Jacqueline Shearer, and Paul Stekler; edited by Lillian Benson, Betty Ciccarelli, Thomas Ott, and Charles Scott; series writer, Steve Fayer; executive producer, Henry Hampton.

Fahrenheit 911: Produced by Jim Czarnecki, Kathleen Glynn, and Michael Moore; directed and written by Michael Moore; edited by Kurt Engfehr, Christopher Seward, and T. Woody Richman.

The Fog of War: Produced by Errol Morris, Michael Williams, and Julie Ahlberg; directed by Errol Morris; edited by Karen Schmeer, Doug Abel, and Chyld King.

4 Little Girls: Produced by Spike Lee and Sam Pollard; directed by Spike Lee; edited by Sam Pollard.

Gimme Shelter: Directed by Albert Maysles, David Maysles, and Charlotte Zwerin; edited by Ellen Giffard, Robert Farren, Joanne Burke, and Kent McKinney.

Gonzo: The Life and Work of Dr. Hunter S. Thompson: Produced by Alex Gibney and Graydon Carter, with Jason Kliot, Joana Vicente, Alison Ellwood, and Eva Orner; directed by Alex Gibney; screenplay by Alex Gibney, from the words of Hunter S. Thompson; edited by Alison Ellwood.

Grey Gardens: Produced by Albert Maysles and David Maysles; directed by David Maysles, Albert Maysles, Ellen Hovde, and Muffie Meyer; edited by Ellen Hovde, Muffie Meyer, and Susan Froemke.

Grizzly Man: Produced by Erik Nelson; directed and narrated by Werner Herzog; edited by Joe Bini.

Guerilla: The Taking of Patty Hearst: Produced and directed by Robert Stone; edited by Don Kleszy.

Harlan County, U.S.A.: Produced and directed by Barbara Kopple; edited by Nancy Baker, Mirra Bank, Lora Hays, and Mary Lampson.

Hoop Dreams: Produced by Frederick Marx, Steve James, and Peter Gilbert; directed by Steve James; edited by Frederick Marx, Steve James, and Bill Haugse.

Human Remains: Produced, directed, written, and edited by Jay Rosenblatt.

I'll Make Me a World (series): Produced by Betty Ciccarelli, Denise Greene, Sam Pollard, and Tracy Heather Strain; edited by Betty Ciccarelli, David Carnochan, and Eric Handley; series writer, Sheila Curran Bernard; series producer, Terry Kay Rockefeller; co-executive producer Sam Pollard; executive producer, Henry Hampton.

Imaginary Witness: Hollywood and the Holocaust. Produced by Daniel Anker and Ellin Baumel; co-produced by Susan Kim; directed by Daniel Anker; edited by Bruce Shaw.

An Inconvenient Truth: Produced by Lawrence Bender, Scott A. Burns, and Laurie David; directed by Davis Guggenheim; edited by Jay Lash Cassidy and Dan Swietlik.

Iraq for Sale: Produced by Sarah Feeley, Jim Gilliam, Robert Greenwald, and Devin Smith; directed by Robert Greenwald; edited by Carla Gutierrez and Sally Rubin.

Jonestown: The Life and Death of Peoples Temple: Produced and directed by Stanley Nelson; co-produced by Noland Walker; teleplay by Marcia Smith and Noland Walker; story by Marcia Smith; edited by Lewis Erskine.

The Kidnapping of Ingrid Betancourt: Produced and directed by Victoria Bruce and Karin Hayes; edited by Geof Bartz, Karin Hayes, and Victoria Bruce.

Kurt & Courtney: Produced by Nick Broomfield, Michele d'Acosta, and Tine van den Brande; directed by Nick Broomfield; edited by Mark Atkins.

Lalee's Kin: The Legacy of Cotton: Produced by Susan Froemke; directed by Susan Froemke and Deborah Dickson, with Albert Maysles; edited by Deborah Dickson.

The Liberace of Baghdad: Produced and directed by Sean McAllister; edited by Ollie Huddleston.

Man on Wire: Produced by Simon Chinn; directed by James Marsh; based on the book *To Reach the Clouds* by Philippe Petit; edited by Jinx Godfrey.

March of the Penguins: Produced by Yves Darondeau, Christophe Lioud, and Emmanuel Priou; directed by Luc Jacquet; narration written by Jordan Roberts; based upon the story by Luc Jacquet; based upon the screenplay by Luq Jacquet and Michel Fessler; edited by Sabine Emiliani.

A Midwife's Tale: Produced and written by Laurie Kahn-Leavitt; based on a book by Laurel Thatcher Ulrich; directed by Richard P. Rogers; edited by William A. Anderson and Susan Korda.

Miss America: Produced by Lisa Ades and Lesli Klainberg; directed by Lisa Ades; written by Michelle Ferrari; edited by Toby Shimin.

The Multiple Personality Puzzle: Produced by Holly Barden Stadtler and Eleanor Grant; directed by Holly Barden Stadtler; written by Eleanor Grant; edited by Barr Weissman.

The Murder of Emmett Till: Produced and directed by Stanley Nelson; written by Marcia A. Smith; edited by Lewis Erskine.

Murderball: Produced by Jeffrey Mandel and Dana Adam Shapiro; directed by Henry Alex Rubin and Dana Adam Shapiro; edited by Geoffrey Richman.

My Architect: Produced by Susan Rose Behr and Nathaniel Kahn; directed, written, and narrated by Nathaniel Kahn; edited by Sabine Krayenbühl.

New York: A Documentary Film: Produced by Lisa Ades and Ric Burns; directed by Ric Burns; co-directed by Lisa Ades; written by Ric Burns and James Sanders; edited by Li-Shin Yu, Edward Barteski, David Hanswer, and Nina Schulman.

Nobody's Business: Produced, directed, and edited by Alan Berliner.

Recording The Producers: *A Musical Romp with Mel Brooks*: Produced by Susan Froemke and Peter Gelb; directed by Susan Froemke; co-directed and edited by Kathy Dougherty.

Roger & Me: Produced, directed, and written by Michael Moore; edited by Wendy Stanzler and Jennifer Beman.

Shelter Dogs: Produced by Heidi Reinberg and Cynthia Wade; directed by Cynthia Wade; edited by Geof Bartz.

Sing Faster: The Stagehands' Ring Cycle: Produced, directed, and written by Jon Else; edited by Deborah Hoffman and Jay Boekelheide.

So Much So Fast: Produced, written, and directed by Steven Ascher and Jeanne Jordan; edited by Jeanne Jordan.

Sound and Fury: Produced by Roger Weisberg; directed by Josh Aronson; edited by Ann Collins.

Southern Comfort: Produced, directed, written, and edited by Kate Davis.

Spellbound: Produced by Sean Welch and Jeffrey Blitz; directed by Jeffrey Blitz; edited by Yana Gorskaya.

Srebrenica: A Cry from the Grave: Produced, directed, and written by Leslie Woodhead; edited by Ian Meller.

Standard Operating Procedure: Produced by Errol Morris and Julie Bilson Ahlberg; directed by Errol Morris; edited by Andy Grieve, Steven Hathaway, and Dan Mooney.

Super Size Me: Produced by Morgan Spurlock and The Con; directed and written by Morgan Spurlock; edited by Stela Georgieva and Julie "Bob" Lombardi.

The Sweetest Sound: Produced, directed, and edited by Alan Berliner.

Taxi to the Dark Side: Produced by Alex Gibney, Eva Orner, and Susannah Shipman; directed and written by Alex Gibney; edited by Sloane Klevin.

The Thin Blue Line: Produced by Mark Lipson; directed and written by Errol Morris; edited by Paul Barnes.

Troublesome Creek: A Midwestern: Produced, written, and directed by Jeanne Jordan and Steven Ascher; edited by Jeanne Jordan.

Waltz with Bashir: Produced by Ari Folman, Serge Lalou, Yael Nahlieli, Gerhard Geixner, and Roman Paul; directed and written by Ari Folman; edited by Nili Feller.

The War Tapes: Produced by Robert May and Steve James; directed by Deborah Scranton; edited by Steve James and Leslie Simmer.

The Way We Get By: Produced by Gita Pullapilly; directed, written, and edited by Aron Gaudet.

When the Levees Broke: Produced by Spike Lee and Sam Pollard; directed by Spike Lee; supervising editor, Sam Pollard; edited by Sam Pollard, Geeta Gandbhir, and Nancy Novack.

Why We Fight: Produced by Eugene Jarecki and Susannah Shipman; directed and written by Eugene Jarecki; edited by Nancy Kennedy.

Winged Migration: Produced by Christophe Barratier and Jacques Perrin; directed by Jacques Perrin; Written by Stéphane Durand and Jacques Perrin; edited by Marie-Josèphe Yoyotte.

Wisconsin Death Trip: Produced by Maureen A. Ryan and James Marsh; directed and written by James Marsh; edited by Jinx Godfrey; adapted from the book *Wisconsin Death Trip* by Michael Lesy.

Workingman's Death: Produced by Erich Lackner, Mirjam Quinte, and Pepe Danquart; directed and written by Michael Glawogger; edited by Monica Willi and Ilse Buchelt.

Vietnam: A Television History: Produced by Judith Vecchione, Elizabeth Deane, Andrew Pearson, Austin Hoyt, Martin Smith, and Bruce Palling; edited by Eric W. Handley, Carol Hayward, Ruth Schell, Eric Neudel, Glen Cardno, Paul Cleary, Mavis Lyons Smull, and Daniel Eisenberg; chief correspondent, Stanley Karnow; executive producer, Richard Ellison.

Yosemite: The Fate of Heaven: Produced and directed by Jon Else; written by Michael Chandler and Jon Else; edited by Michael Chandler; executive produced and narrated by Robert Redford.

Index

Note: Page numbers followed by *f* indicate figures and *t* indicate tables.

E

Earth Made of Glass, 331, 342f
Editing
  act structure, 61–63
  to anticipate audience confusion, 193–194
  assembly script, 191
  from audience's viewpoint, 203
  basics, 187–188
  collapsing interviews, 74–77
  considering, while shooting, 176–178
  creative techniques, 203
  entering/exiting scenes, 192–193
  fact checking, 197–198
  film length, 44, 198
  film structure, 61–63
  filmmakers on, 245, 246, 255, 260, 268,
    317–318, 321–322, 323–324, 328,
    335–336, 337
  fine cut to picture lock, 197–198
  interviews, 191–194
  juxtaposition, 192
  narration script, 200
  opening sequence, 198–200
  paper edit, 189, 191
  problem solving, 200–202
  rough cut, getting to, 188–194
  rough cut script, 191
  rough cut to fine cut, 194–197
  screening tips, 195–197
  sequences, 193
  speech, 75–76
  transcripts, 190–191
Elkind, Peter, 82
Else, Jon, 3, 21, 33, 141
  on advisors, 122
  on budgets, 44, 45
  on crew size, 174
  on fallback plans, 36
  on narration, 205
  on shooting, 177–178
  on themes, 18
  on time treatment, 67
  on two unfolding stories, 43
Emotional storytelling
  basics, 27–30
  raising stakes, 29–30
Endings, 30–31, 201–202
Enron: The Smartest Guys in the Room, 1–2, 8,
  28, 34, 83–84, 209f
  archival filmmaking, 87–88
  narration, 205, 207–208
  omniscient narration, 82
Entering/exiting scenes, 192–193
Estus, Boyd
  on interviewing, 184–185
  on shooting, 175–176
Ethics
  filmmakers on, 258–259, 271, 272,
    293–294, 339
  guidelines, 6
Evaluating films, 93–95
Evergreen film, 39
Ewing, Heidi, 25
Execution of Wanda Jean, The, 23
Expanding/collapsing time, 72–73
Experiencing film, 97
Experts, casting, 142
Exposition, 15–20

Eyes on the Prize series, 17, 26, 34, 73, 122–123,
  227, 323, 324
  approach, 84–85
  archival filmmaking, 88–89
  sequences, 140
  telling details, 218

F

Fact checking, 123–124, 197–198
Fahrenheit 9/11, 21
Fair approach, 85–86, 294–295
Fair use issues, 90
Falsifying time, 68
Fear and Loathing in Las Vegas, 290, 293
Feasibility and story ideas, 36–37
Feedback on screenings, 195–196
Film format, 241
Film length, 44, 198, 329–330
Film structure
  applying story structure, 61–63
  finding, in edit room, 61–63
  revising, in edit room, 63
Filming over time, 73–74
Filmmakers. *See also* interviews with filmmakers
  approach to documentary, 7
  observations/tips, 10–11
Filmmaker's Handbook, The (Ascher and
  Pincus), 176, 227
"Finding" story during production, 34–35
Fine cut, 187, 194–198
First-person narration, 206
Fog of War, The, 83–84, 85, 336
Folman, Ari, 8, 20, 303
Footage. *See* shooting
Foreshadowing, 216
4 Little Girls, 40, 321–330
Frame, narrative, 49
Franco, Vicente, 34–35, 95–96
Fraser, Nick, interview on filmmaking,
  275–284
Froemke, Susan, 53, 61–63, 119, 174,
  178–179
Frontline, 93, 227, 275, 293–294, 331, 337, 338
Fundraising, scripts for, 155
Fundraising proposals
  basics, 158–161
  elements of, 158–160, 161
  planning and writing, 157–158
  tips for writing, 161–163

G

Garbus, Liz, 23
Gaudet, Aron, 21, 79
Gender-neutral wording, 214–215
Gerard, Philip, 3–4
Getting Over, sample treatment, 163
Gibney, Alex, 3, 4, 8, 49, 79, 91, 136–137
  interview on filmmaking, 285–296
Gimme Shelter, 3
Glawogger, Michael, 64–65, 67
Goals
  active vs. passive, 24
  difficulties/obstacles, 25–27
  proposal description of, 159
  story basics, 24
  tangible, 27
  worthy opponents, 26–27

M

Mabley, Edward, 22–31
MacLowry, Randall, 142–143
Made in China, 281
Mamet, David, 47
"Man on the street" interviews, 144
Man on Wire, 49, 198–199, 304, 305
  interview with filmmaker, 307–320
Manchevski, Milcho, 341
March of the Penguins, 174, 180
Marker, Chris, 67
Marketplace, 6–7
Marsh, James, interview on filmmaking,
  307–320
May, Robert, 336
Maysles, Albert, 179, 280, 282–283
McKee, Robert, 53
McLean, Bethany, 82
Midwife's Tale, A, 34
Milltail Pack, The, 151, 163
Miss America: A Documentary Film, 127
Missing Peace, 56
Mo' Better Blues, 321, 330
Monroe, Mark, 8
Moore, Michael, 21, 36, 37, 68–72, 82,
  277–278
Morris, Errol, 19–20, 30–31, 34, 72–73, 79,
  83–84, 85, 90, 184, 185
Mostoller, Katy, 142–143
Multiple story lines, 59
Murder of Emmett Till, The, 50–51
Murderball, 19, 59–60, 82, 176–177
  act one/title sequence, 101–104
  act three, 106–107
  act two, 104–106
  case study, 100–107
  epilogue, 107
Music, 327, 339–340
My Architect, 17–18, 21, 29, 174, 283–284

N

Narration
  active voice for, 220
  anachronisms, 215
  anticipation used in, 214
  avoiding stereotypes, 214–215
  basics, 205
  creative approaches, 81–83
  fact checking, 197–198
  filmmakers on, 242–243, 246, 305
  foreshadowing important information,
    216
  hype, avoiding, 217, 221
  identifying names/unfamiliar words, 219
  nonspoken, 207–209
  point of view, 206–207
  telling detail, 218
  time treatment, 70–71
  using words sparingly/specifically, 217–218
  writing to picture, 210–213
Narration script, 200
Narrative, story as, 15
Narrative frame, 49
Narrative spine. *See* train (narrative spine)
Narrators, casting, 146–147
National Geographic Explorer, 181
Nelson, Stanley, 50–51
Nevins, Sheila, 56

New York: A Documentary Film, 23, 56, 251
  interview with filmmakers, 251–260
Nicolayssen, Hans Otto, 38
Night and Fog, 67
Nobody's Business, 33, 87–88
Nolan, Christopher, 67
Nolan, Jonathan, 67
Nonexperts, casting, 142–143
Nonfiction film/video
  creative, characteristics of, 3–5
  documentaries as subset of, 3
Not a Rhyme Time, 215–216
Noujaim, Jehane, 79, 281
Nova series, 83

O

Objectives. *See* goals
Objectivity, filmmakers on, 245
Obstacles, 25–27
Omniscient narration, 82, 206
O'Neill, Connor, 102–103
On-the-fly casting, 144
Opening sequence, 198–200, 228, 229
Open-minded approach, 84–87
Opponents, 25–27
Opposing voices, casting, 144
Organic editorial approach, 10
Outlines
  basics, 135–141
  historical stories, 139–140
  present-day stories, 140–141
  purpose of, 136
  sample of, 163
  sequences in, 136–141

P

Paper edit, 189, 191
Passion and story ideas, 37–38
Passive goals, 24
PBS, 83, 93, 125, 155–156, 251
Peary, Gerald, 35
Petit, Philippe
  collaboration for *Man on Wire*, 307–320
  photograph, 310f
Picture lock, 187, 197–198
Pip & Zastrow: An American Friendship, 239
Pitch, defined, 133
Pitching
  basics, 133–135
  effective vs. weak, 133–135
  out load, 135
Plan of work (proposal), 161
Planning, filmmakers on, 281–282, 291, 324
Plots, 19–20
Point of attack, 55–56
Point of view
  filmmakers on, 243, 244, 282
  narration, 206–207
  story, 21–22
Pollard, Sam, 20–21, 57, 77, 173, 188
  interview on filmmaking, 321–330
Present-day films
  chronologies for, 127–129
  story outline, 140–141
Print research, 129–131
Privacy of subjects, 242
Production, "finding" story during, 34–35
Project Nim, 310, 311, 315